Second Ch...

...infantry, the OSS,
...during the Liberation of

STEPHEN J. WEISS

Si vis pacem, para bellum

("If you seek peace, prepare for war")

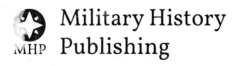

**Military History
MHP Publishing**

Military History Publishing
4 Dencora Park
Shire Hill
Saffron Walden
Essex, CB11 3GB
United Kingdom

First published in 2011

ISBN-13: 978-1-78039-232-5   paperback

ISBN-13: 978-1-78039-466-4   hardback

Front cover image

Stephen J. Weiss, with other members of his infantry company, board an amphibious landing craft from Pozzuoli, Italy to make the allied invasion of Southern France, Operation Dragoon, D-Day, August 15, 1944.

Rear cover image

36th 'Texas' Infantry Division soldiers practice landing on an 'enemy-held' beach in July 1944, during amphibious exercises near Gaeta, Italy, in preparation for Operation Dragoon, the invasion of Southern France, August 15.

Dedication

To those young combat soldiers who, as boys, fought and died at the Sharp End.

The servant of a Middle Eastern Lord was sent to shop in the local market place and saw Death standing near a merchant's cart, staring at him. In panic, the servant fled to Samarra, a nearby town. The next day, the Lord met Death in the market place and said, 'You frightened my servant, and he ran away.' 'I'm sorry,' Death replied. 'I didn't mean to frighten him. I was simply surprised to see him here, because we had an appointment in Samarra.'

(NOT PRINTED AT GOVERNMENT EXPENSE)

Congressional Record

United States
of America · PROCEEDINGS AND DEBATES OF THE 93ᵈ CONGRESS, FIRST SESSION

| Vol. 119 | WASHINGTON, TUESDAY, APRIL 3, 1973 | No. 51 |

House of Representatives

COMMENDATION TO A GROUP OF COURAGEOUS FRENCHMEN

HON. THOMAS M. REES
OF CALIFORNIA

IN THE HOUSE OF REPRESENTATIVES

Tuesday, April 3, 1973

Mr. REES. Mr. Speaker, despite international tensions, there is often harmony among nations and cooperation between peoples. This is brought to mind by a constituent of mine, Stephen Weiss. Mr. Weiss recently vacationed in France and was able to locate two members of a group of Frenchmen who saved his life in an incident during World War II. It is fitting that we pay tribute here to these men whose courage and intelligence were exemplary in a time of war, exhibiting a spirit which transcends national boundaries.

At this time, Mr. Speaker, I would like to briefly recount the story behind that incident.

During the summer of 1944, in the fight for Southern France, the 36th Texas Division met retreating elements of the 19th German Army.

This meeting produced a battle which lasted the better part of the evening of August 24. The American forces sustained a sizable loss in men and materiel. Eight soldiers of C Company, 143d Infantry, 36th Division emerged to find that the remaining U.S. forces had advanced without them.

The eight sought refuge at the farm of M. and Mme. Gaston Reynaud. Despite the proximity of the Germans, M. Reynaud promised he would aid the American infantrymen. His commitment exposed his family to great risk in the event of a search by German patrols.

Reynaud held a conference with members of the local resistance—Police Commissioner Gerard, Marcel Volle, M. Guillon, Agent Salmon, M. Crespy, Captain Ferdinand, Lieutenant Maurice—regarding the Americans in his custody. The means of escape to be followed called for the Americans to don French police uniforms and reach safety in a police car.

The Germans were engaged in a farm-to-farm search for the infantrymen when the police car arrived to the Reynaud's home. Communication between the two allies was difficult, but the imperatives of the situation produced the greatest sort of cooperation, transcending the bounds of culture and language.

Through the entire course of the operation, the eight Americans were neither stopped nor questioned. On three separate occasions, however, members of the Reynaud family were queried as to the whereabouts of the American soldiers. Throughout, the incident was kept in confidence.

As the Germans widened their search to the outskirts south of Valence, the eight members of the 36th were rowing across the Rhone River, with the assistance of Robert Debreuil and Augustin Bouvier, the mayor of St. Perey.

In late September of 1944, after aiding an OSS Special Forces Company, the infantrymen rejoined the 36th far to the north. The attempt had been entirely successful.

Its success can be traced, in part, to the bond of friendship between the United States and France. The willingness to cooperate, evidenced on both sides, should serve as an example to us all.

U.S. Congressional Record, April 3, 1973. An official tribute paid to the group of gallant Frenchmen involved in the evasion and escape story.

Table of Contents

List of Figures

List of Maps

Acknowledgments

I wish to thank Professors Michael Dockrill, Arthur Layton Funk (d), and Richard Overy for their encouragement. My thanks to Major General François Binoche (d), General Bill Jackson (d), Royal Marine Major General and author Julian Thompson, Brigadier and QC Ralph Kilner-Brown (d), Colonel Roy Rickerson (d), Staff Sergeant Bob Reigle (d), and Ted Berlin (d), PT boat commander, who shared their war experiences withme. My appreciation to Dr. J. Victor Monke, my former psychiatric colleague, regarding the psychological dimensions of war. To Bertrand Cochery, French Consul General, Colonel Laurent Kolodziej, French military attaché, Guy Audibert, President of the AMAC French Veterans association, Keith Taylor and Dick Kirby, formerly of the Metropolitan Police, Brigadier Tony Hunter-Choat, Peter Green, Frank Ledwidge, Alexander Donnelly, and SAS veterans Ray Windmill and Nigel Keegan, for their views on men in battle. For my increased understanding of the art of war, thanks to Hugo Basinger and Victor Meyer for clarifying a number of issues. To Marie-Pierre Belliere and Valerie Delage, whose assistance in researching parts of Paris on foot was incalculable, and to Nadine Crouzet for a similar exploration along the Rhone River, my gratitude.

My appreciation encompasses authors Charles Glass and Martin Windrow, editor Kate Moore, and Claudia Walker, my public relations advisor, who offered sound advice, which I followed. Thanks to Alex Bowlby (d), Robin Kilpatrick, Molly and Jim Cameron for editing and indexing, Bogdan Dumitru for final formatting, John Richards for maps, and John and Duncan Evans at Books Express for leading the production team and publishing 'Second Chance,' all of whom accepted the gruelling task of correcting and designing the manuscript, and doing so without complaint. Many thanks to Justin Stead, CEO of Aurun Holdings and Mappin and Webb for his impressive post-production ideas, to Peter Joanes and his IT brilliance in resolving some difficult electronic problems, and, for improving my sense of timing, thanks to Bart Roe, Jack Cash, Holly Kamen, and Dick Schacht, formerly of Hollywood film and network television.

To Claudia Reynaud, Jean-Claude Haas, and Gerri Dahan, French wartime friends, and to all my comrades associated with the French Resistance, The OSS Society, The 36th 'Texas' Division Association, The

American Society of the French Legion of Honor, Special Forces Club, Stephen Ambrose Historical Tours, the Kings College War Studies Department faculty, the Kings College War Studies Society, and to those Open University and Kings College students who attended my Experience of War lectures who, much like Paul Tanner and the late Johnny Desmond (d) (formerly musicians with the great Glenn Miller orchestra), said time and time again, in their own inimitable ways, in French and English, 'Write that story, Steve. Write that story!' My indebtedness. All of you are memorable!

To Stephen and Ami Abou-Bakr, Leo and Carmel Anazemi, Michael and Carla Berlin, Dom and Laura Biddick, Gerard Binoche, Kevin and Jane Bly, Chester and Mary Brown, Angelo and Sue Bruzzeze, Ronnie Bregman, Roger Cavill and m Square neighbors and the Finzborough Wine Cafe, Giles and Emma Clayton-Jones, Herve and Sylvie Claudon, Erika and Nick Cohen, Rhoda Cohen, Michael and Marcella Collins, James and Geraldine Conroy, Valerie and David Crabbe, Maria deRossi, Judith Flanders, Christina Fogarasi, Martin and Jackie Fortis, Julia Linzee Gordon, Lindsay and Candice Hooper, Matt and Amir Jones, Jackie Jordan, Yakir and Edie Katz, Stan and Mary Lelewer, Fiona Leslie, Sissy Liu and Emily, Joe and Juliet Mankowitz, Larry and Helen Merken, Michael and Sharon Moore, Mike and Gordana Moriarity, Fred and Lil O'Rourke, Dennis and Thomas Mui, Louise Oliver, Ike Ong, Mo and Andi Ortiz, Ingvar Petursson (son in-law), Charles T. Pinck, John and Nuala Rawnsley, Linda Rose, Robert Smith, Harry and Julia Sullivan, Hildi Santo Thomas, Kaye Thompson, Mark Tunney (son in-law), Phil and Hanie Weitzman, Guy Wildenstein, Paolo and Wilma Wrobel, and my American, British, French, and Hungarian friends, thanks for all their expertise and enthusiasm.

Finally, to my children, Claudia Petursson, Alison Tunney, and Andrew Weiss, with growing families of their own, who listened to portions of my tale more than once, offered here in its entirety for the first time, hugs and thanks again.

Introduction

Military history is a harsh science. Whole armies are moved hither and thither across the narrative of battle; commanders order, men obey. The individual soldier becomes anonymous, an ant in the military anthill. The language of combat, casualties, and losses is amorphous and impersonal. Yet, for those who have to fight, war is an intensely personal experience. It is about survival or death; it is about finding an extraordinary courage and commitment distinct from any demands that might be made in civilian life. War is not fought by armies, but by men and women pushed to the very limits of physical and psychological endurance.

Stephen Weiss was just such a man when he found himself in 1943, at the age of 18, sucked in by the United States' vast military machine and disgorged onto the Italian front five months later. After surviving Anzio, he was sent in the force that seized southern France in August 1944. Here, he became a scout behind enemy lines, cooperating with the French Resistance.

His recollections of Army life have about them a vividness and candor that set them apart from much memoir literature. He was a spirited and committed youngster who found himself at the sharpest end of war, face to face with a tough and fatalistic enemy, backed by an insensitive and tough Army regime. He survived the first encounter but not the second. Finally worn down by months of danger, squalor, and Army bull, Weiss gave up. He was court-martialed and sentenced to military imprisonment. Only the efforts of a prison psychiatrist — who realized that Weiss was not a deserter but a psychological casualty — won his freedom and cleared his name.

This is a refreshingly honest account of how men react under fire. It is also an indictment of how armies treat the raw material on which they thrive. Weiss came to terms with his ordeals and rebuilt a successful life after the war. The cost was very great, however: 'I've become my own battlefield,' Weiss once confessed.

This striking metaphor might surely be applied to thousands of veterans left to make what peace they can with the demons provoked by combat. We are slowly coming to terms with what war does to people,

1

both winners and losers. Weiss gives us a remarkable account of that process of endurance and overcoming.

His memoir is not just a challenge to conventional military history; it is a richly human story.

Richard Overy
Professor of History
University of Exeter
October 2010

Prologue

In 1996, I gave a talk for the Open University at York entitled 'Behind the Lines in World War Two.' It went well. During the lunch that followed three students who'd missed the talk asked me if I could give it again. They'd heard it was something they shouldn't have missed. I asked the head tutor if I could repeat the talk and he agreed, arranging it for the next day. The talk drew even more applause than before. And it set me thinking. If a group of students who had no first-hand knowledge of the war were so enthusiastic about my experiences, why shouldn't I seek a wider audience? Why not write a book, so that I could share a story of my generation with the next one, which had no direct experience of the magnitude and trauma of total war, the consequences of defeat, and the price of victory. I wished also to close the gap between an older generation that had failed to answer the question, 'And what did you do in the war, Daddy?' posed by a younger generation eagerly seeking an answer.

What follows, therefore, is a story dependent on memory alone. I kept no diary or written accounts, relying instead on an ability to remember names, dates, places, and events, as if it were yesterday. For example, on June 12, 1944, I was fighting eight miles below Siena, Italy; my division was relieved later that day by the 34th 'Red Bull' Infantry Division, an Army National Guard infantry division from Iowa.

There was another reason for the lack of written evidence. If I were captured, a diary would have brought aid and comfort to the enemy, adding to his knowledge of an American soldier otherwise unknown to him. Common within the Army was the use of the last name as a direct and clear form of address. In most cases, I have chosen to use last names for a different reason, even though I knew the men in this story by their first names, too. Simply, I've used it as a personal protective device, however unsuccessful, to keep emotional intimacy and potential loss at a distance! As one officer put it, 'So many men passed through the company, I can't remember who you were.'

When placing my division within the 'greater strategy of the war,' I have applied my doctoral 'War Studies' research skills to fulfill this purpose for the benefit of the reader. Told in its entirety for the first time, my story is a study of a young soldier's apprenticeship in living, a rite of passage, a lifelong journey that, thus far, continues, and what the author Eric Maria Remarque, a German World War I veteran and author, called 'The Road Back.'

London,
June 2011

1
My Journey into War

'I regret to say that I learned too late that it was not what a person did, but what he got the credit of doing that gave him a reputation.'

Major General George Crook, 1864

The Invalides, Paris, Friday, November 5, 1999: in a large salon of the Chancellery of the Order of Liberation, the military life of Charles de Gaulle was portrayed by a group of paintings adorning the walls between two majestic floor-to-ceiling windows that overlooked the tree-lined boulevard. A crisp November morning light brightened the deep blue of the carpet on which stood, side by side, the American and French flags. In the middle of this historic room, I stood at attention a few feet away from Jean Simon, a legendary five-star French Army general. The ceremony was about to begin. He stood ramrod straight, an aged warrior, who had lost an eye at the Battle of Bir Hakim during the North African Campaign 57 years before. Entering the room, my friends and relatives, glad to have escaped from the cold, shed their wraps and overcoats and greeted each other with affection. Many had journeyed to Paris from their homes in America, the British Isles, and France, and both the French and American governments had sent military representatives for the occasion.

The ceremony, arranged in my honor, epitomizing a lifetime of alarums and excursions, was an emotive, exquisite, and long-awaited moment. The general's aide, a young officer and veteran of the Indochina War, asked the 50-odd guests to move closer as General Simon, Chancellor of the Order of the Liberation, immaculately dressed in uniform, nodded in affirmation and began reading aloud in French from a paper held in his frail hands. News photographers and a Los Angeles Times reporter, like the others in attendance, moved toward the two principal actors to hear the general's words. General Simon intoned, 'On this occasion, I am glad to welcome an American citizen whose attachment and devotion to France has been recognized by Mr. Jacques Chirac, President de

5

la Republic Française. He has decreed and I have the honor of making you, Monsieur Stephen Weiss, a Chevalier de la Legion d'Honneur. I am proud to give you this medal, rarely given to foreign soldiers.'

There was a spontaneous burst of applause, camera bulbs flashed, and tears filled my eyes. My chin trembled with emotion. Within, I felt proud and humble, enveloped by a kaleidoscope of feeling and ever-present memories. The memory of one episode, more persistent than the rest, almost ended in my premature and violent death. Men, with whom I served in the Army and the Resistance, French and American alike, crossed my mind. Because of them, I would never accept any military decoration as mine alone. The general approached, holding the medal designed by Napoleon, his hand poised. I mentally pinched myself. The present and the past merged in my mind, my heart pounded with excitement, as General Simon bestowed upon me France's highest honor — and my journey into war began once again.

German machine gun and rifle fire have pinned my rifle company down. It's early June 1944, and the Italian summer day is hot and bright. The enemy is holed up in a farmhouse 80 yards away to our company front. We're stuck in the farm's fruit orchard, the enemy hidden within his natural camouflage, a combination of deep shadows and blotches of color. It's hard to see clearly.

The German Mg. 42s, firing at 1,300 rounds per minute, generating immense fire-power and noise, momentarily stop our attack. Bullets ricochet off peach trees, clipping leaves, shredding fruit. On our stomachs, behind the trees or in the grass between, we fire at the farmhouse's apertures with little effect, except windows are shattered, doors perforated. No orders are given and no plan is executed. Firing yes, maneuver no!

To our rear, through the tumult, an officer calls off a series of numbers, aiming at the farmhouse, to his two-man 60-mm mortar crew. Seconds tick by. Just as he is about to give the order to fire, he shouts, 'No! No!' Correcting himself, he increases the range and shouts, 'Fire!' The three-pound mortar shells hit the farmhouse roof, which bursts into flames and implodes with a roar. Firing is sporadic and stops. Leaves stir in the breeze. Germans are shouting. Some leap from the hayloft, others rush out from the animal stalls below with their hands up. Some are mere boys, others look Asian, and all seem bewildered, scruffy, wearing worn, ill-fitting uniforms.

While taking them prisoner, stacking their rifles, and piling their ammo and grenades in front of the farmhouse, I mused, while taking a swig of water from my canteen, 'If the mortar crew, following orders, had used the original numbers and fired, the mortar shells would have fallen short and landed among us with disastrous results, as an example of 'Friendly Fire.' If the original numbers were obeyed, as expressed in a New York Times editorial comment regarding another subject, 'it could have been just the mundane blend of bad luck and error from which neither fame nor wealth nor lineage nor youth nor beauty could protect any one of us.' A lottery? Sigmund Freud stated that luck did not exist, but whatever the reasons, I found surviving this experience most welcome. I'd been given a chance to fight another day! I looked at the other men and thought, as a matter of fact, that all of us have an appointment with death, some sooner than later. But until that moment arrives, the time and place are hidden, even if infantry combat speeds up the inexorable and guaranteed result.

Spring 1944. I returned to Naples on a train of dilapidated, narrow-gauge, wood boxcars, of questionable reliability, half full of hay and smelling of horses. On the exterior of each car 'quarante hommes et huit chevaux' was stenciled in fading black ink. The Army's Replacement Command had assigned all 90 of us to the 36th Texas Infantry Division, a former Lone Star State National Guard infantry division. To complete our journey, a U.S. Navy ocean-going, flat-bottomed Landing Ship Tank (LST) was placed at our disposal. Once onboard, final preparations complete, the ship weighed anchor, left the safety of the harbor, and ploughed through the Tyrrhenian Sea. It followed the Italian coast 84 miles north to Anzio, a former seaside resort now a part of Operation Shingle, an Allied beachhead under siege. I had followed the story in the Army newspaper *the Stars and Stripes* and talked to soldiers who had been there.

The battered town had survived four months of enemy bombardment and air attacks. From January to May, the Germans had done everything possible to drive the Allies into the sea — and failed, although it was a close run thing. Allied soldiers lived and fought within shattered buildings and caves, illuminated by candlelight and the marshlands beyond — even General Lucien Truscott, the Allied commander, had his headquarters in a wine cellar. Winston Churchill, the British Prime Minister, fumed, to no avail, as the stalemate continued, 'Instead of hurling a wildcat on to the shore, all we got was a stranded whale…'

Now, in May, Allied forces had increased to seven divisions from an original two; a new plan, 'Operation Buffalo,' evolved. Set for the latter part of the month, Rome was its objective. We were part of that plan.

Soon after disembarking, we unexpectedly came face to face with a group of 50 American soldiers penned within a small makeshift stockade of logs and barbed wire. Under armed military police guard, some of the prisoners seemed weary and disorientated, like vagrants down on their heels and luck. Others, more aggressive than the others, threatened and hurled obscenities at us, warning, with pointed finger or clenched fist, we'd end up like them, misunderstood and deserted by the Army. They were charged with desertion, a capital military offense potentially punishable by death. There was no escape from their abuse while we waited for 6x6 trucks to arrive.

We amateurs were jarred by the encounter, even though ignorant of the reasons for their imprisonment. Joined by three 36th divisional guides who escorted our group through the ruins of Anzio, we bivouacked on a hillock overlooking the harbor for the night. The following morning it rained, and feeling anxious after my encounter with the deserters, I attended a Catholic mass conducted by an Army chaplain in an open field. I knelt in the mud and prayed, 'The Lord is my shepherd, I shall not want.' And I wasn't even Catholic! Our guides waited for further orders, and I was allowed time to look for Hal Sedloff, a soldier friend. We had met at Fort Meade, Maryland, just before I shipped overseas. He left the States on another ship and arrived at the beachhead days before I arrived. Hal was hospitalized.

Following directions, I stopped at a large pyramidal tent hospital sprawled across a field a few miles away, where I asked an Army nurse on desk duty if Hal Sedloff were a patient. I introduced myself and told her my reasons for inquiring. 'We met at Fort Meade and became good friends,' I said. 'I'm trying to find out if he's OK' She checked his name against the ward numbers and scanned through a pile of folders, found his, and after quickly reading the report to herself, summarized the following events to me: He had left Newport News, Virginia on a ship as part of a large convoy bound for Italy. The German Air Force (GAF) attacked the convoy in the Western Mediterranean for a couple of days running, but it arrived in Naples without loss. Sedloff joined the 45th Infantry Division on the beachhead. He complained of 'night blindness' and failed to function properly in his first attack. He malfunctioned during a second attack.

According to the platoon medic, Sedloff's behavior was a liability not only to himself but also to the GIs around him. Unable to overcome the stress of battle, he was relieved and sent to the rear, reporting to his unit's aid station. The 45th sent him here for treatment. Word had it that he was overly concerned about his wife and new baby.

'I'd like to see him.'

'No.,' she said, 'Off the record, he's suffering from bouts of depression and is sedated.'

'What's wrong?' I asked.

She replied, 'In layman's terms, it's called combat fatigue.' The nurse stared at me, dropped her voice, and warned, 'No one is immune.'

'Thanks for taking the time,' I said.

Standing there, as she turned to enter one of the tents, I was transfixed, saddened, and shocked at this unexpected turn of events. I thought Hal, at 28, was someone to depend on, because of his age and experience. I was chilled by the prospect of carrying on alone, without the support of and belief in some kind of father figure. If it could happen to Hal … hmm. My thoughts trailed off as I walked away.

Below our temporary encampment, while our guides awaited further orders, disregarding the danger from enemy shellfire, I went swimming in a temperate, stunning azure sea nearby and splashed in its surf on a warm and sunny day; it was and remains an incomparable, momentarily carefree, and refreshing experience.

That night the GAF succeeded in breaching our air defenses ringing the harbor and achieved complete surprise. Silhouetted against the dark sky, an enemy squadron of five HE 111 medium bombers, each carrying 800-pound bombs, flew over our heads, at about 500 feet. They headed out to sea, dropped flares that turned the sky from deep blue to sickly green, and wheeled about. Streaking over our heads on their bomb run, I felt more like an observer than a participant, held hostage to outrageous fortune. In an instant, I had no choice but to await the outcome of whether I lived or died. Our ship and shore "ack ack" were erratic, no spirited defense here, as white tracers filled the night sky and reflected on the waters below. Whether by design or accident, the twin-engine raiders hit a large ammunition dump about a quarter of a mile away.

There was a tremendous earth-colored explosion and the slamming of shock waves, followed by other explosions of varying intensity. As far as I know, all of the raiding enemy planes got away, but they left fires of exploding ammunition in their wake that burned throughout the night. Black smoke drifted skyward. There were no casualties among us. We were informed by our guides that Rome, just 30 miles up the road, a half hour's Jeep drive away, had fallen to our forces, attacking out of the beachhead. There was other momentous news and cause for celebration. Allied armies based in Southern England, mounting a major amphibious operation, had successfully invaded Normandy in Northern France. We cheered. Maybe the war will end soon, after all! The exultant mood was contagious! With the road to Rome open, we broke camp, were herded on to the trucks, and departed. Waving to Roman citizens enjoying their newfound freedom, we drove north in the early June heat. Eventually, we found the 36th thrusting 80 miles beyond Rome. The retreating enemy was heading north too, but just out of reach.

We stopped that night beside a remote field strewn with dead bodies wrapped in canvas shelter-halves. My skin crawled. I felt angry and physically ill from this bizarre introduction to combat! Where was the 'Joker' who played 'trick or treat' with my feelings, as if it were Halloween in June? Rather than a Jack O' Lantern in the window, dead bodies were put on display instead. Here, they were bartered for live ones. We dismounted and formed up beside a waiting sergeant who took a head count; none of us was missing. We staggered into the field and dropped onto the ground to get some rest among the wrapped shelter-halves.

At first light, after a short and uneasy night, speculating when my turn for wrapping would come, I noticed the canvas shelter-halves stirring; the *dead bodies* of the previous night wakened and emerged. They weren't frightening gothic goblins, but ordinary GIs! I was assigned to a 12-man rifle squad in Charlie Company, 1st battalion, 143rd Regimental Combat Team (RCT) of the 36th 'Texas' Division by a sergeant not much older than I. My former traveling companions were assigned elsewhere within the division's rifle companies. As for me, there were openings for a First Scout and one of three Browning Automatic Rifle (BAR) positions to replace those men lost in combat; I didn't like the BAR, a World War I slow-firing, .30 caliber (550 rpm) automatic assault weapon. The choice was mine; the options limited. I chose the First Scout position. Although it was the most dangerous position in a rifle squad, I thought it offered better flexibility of movement than the cumbersome inter-linked three-man BAR team in combat.

In addition to the positions mentioned, the squad, in single file, consisted of a Second Scout, the Squad Leader, a two-man bazooka rocket team known as Ike and Mike (regardless of their real names), three riflemen and, bringing up the rear, an Assistant Squad Leader, the 'Get Away Man.' Like most of my squad, I carried a nine and a-half pound semi-automatic M-1 .30 caliber Garand rifle, two cloth bandoliers filled with clips of rifle ammunition, and two fragmentation hand grenades in preparation for the next firefight. I nearly forgot that I also carried a bayonet.

The field's short brown grass glistened in the morning sun, as the squad, one among many, lay in some furrows, overlooked by an unseen enemy dug in on a string of low-lying brown hills a mile away. Captain Allan Simmons of Belfast, Maine, our Company Commander (CO), approaches from the rear. I was neither introduced to nor acknowledged by him — then or later. Of an indeterminate age, he drifts across my line of sight, hunched over, his green fatigues powdered with dust, matching the grime on his face and his three days' growth of beard. None of the soldiers shout, 'Hey, 'Capt'n, how's it going' or wave in greeting; he stares into space, locked within himself, his own emotional executioner, so it seems, a missionary shuffling by, lacking conviction. I soon learned that camaraderie was non-existent between Simmons and us. He lacked the ability to create a clear sense of purpose and raise morale — vital ingredients in combat. He never visited the front again during my time with the outfit.

'Weiss,' the platoon sergeant, a tall fellow from Beaumont, Texas, shouts, 'I need a two-man patrol to find Able Company. Corporal Reigle has the details. Go!' I grab my gear. Reigle thinks Able Company is about a mile to our left front, and we need to make contact. Of medium height and from Pennsylvania, he's a survivor of earlier battles — Salerno, Cassino, and the Rapido River — fiascos all. This is my first patrol, and I hope to learn much and return alive under Corporal Reigle's lead and tutelage. The two of us head out, hacking our way noisily through a jungle of heavy underbrush. Skirting the side of a hill toward a canal, we walk in single file. Closing on the canal, preparing to leave our forest cover, he signals to stop and lifts his finger to his lips in warning. I move slowly across the intervening space to his side and crouch beside him.

Walking swiftly towards us, with one arm in the air, shouting 'Kamerad,' was a German soldier wearing a canvas camouflage sniper's cape and carrying a Mauser rifle.

'He must have heard us coming,' I whispered.

Reigle spoke quietly, 'Damn! We're exposed as hell, and it could be a trap. Might be more Krauts around.' He put his hand on my arm and said, 'Let him come to us.'

As soon as he did, we shoved him deeper into the woods, pushed him up against a tree, and searched for weapons. 'He's clean,' Reigle said. The German smelled of the rations he ate — black bread and sausage. 'Check his pay book.' I found it in a pocket of his tunic and flipped through the few pages, stopping to look at his photo and then at him, a small, dumpy man, looking more like a ticket taker at an amusement park than a soldier. There was little resemblance between the man in the photo and the man before us. He kept prattling away in German, seemingly glad that for him the war was over.

'Are you a Nazi?'

'Nix.'

'Look at this, Reigle.' Referring to the pay book once more, I pointed to a line, asking Reigle, 'Doesn't this mean he joined the Party in 1940?'

'Looks like it. What's his job?'

I read further and then stopped. 'Reigle, this guy's a sniper with the Hermann Goering Parachute Panzer Division.'

'Steve, that's the outfit that wiped out two Ranger Battalions in battle six months ago at Cisterna, a town on the Anzio beachhead.'

'How do ya mean?'

'Seven hundred Rangers were either killed or captured. This guy and his pals ambushed the Rangers.'

The three of us huddled there, but only two deliberated. 'Let's shoot the sonovabitch,' Reigle whispered.

'Is that legal?!'

He looked at me disapprovingly. The German, perplexed, turned pale. Reigle said, 'I'd do it, but his pals are bound to hear the shot. They'd finish us off. Let's turn him over to Intelligence, instead. If they don't want him, I can shoot him later.'

We turned around and headed back, one behind the other, with the sniper loosely sandwiched between us. At 1st Battalion Headquarters, the S-2 Intelligence corporal, a naturalized American of German-Jewish parentage, was pleased we brought the sniper back alive. 'I've lots of questions to ask him before I throw him in the cage.' We never found Able Company.

Somewhere north of Rome, we're crouching in the woods on the edge of a field, when the squad leader, a staff sergeant, orders me to 'Move across it until you're forced to stop. The Germans are out there somewhere.' It's raining, the green field slopes away for 100 yards, joining a wood beyond; all woods are dark. The damned slanting rain makes the only sound, hitting and falling off the surrounding leaves. I'm soaked through, my light clothing no defense against the inclement weather.

'We'll cover you from here.'

I think, 'I've gotta go out there by myself.'

Alone. I'm a clay pigeon, a fall guy, but it's not deliberate, just stupid. My turn to be set up! I feel a thousand hostile unseen eyes are watching my every move. Will the Germans take the bait?' Gathering together my limited inner resources, I move into the unknown, adrift. My teeth hurt and I feel cold. I walk crouched over, rifle ready, the grass squishes under my boots; I look back. The men wait, and the sergeant signals impatiently to keep going.

Approaching the opposite wood, tensely peering into the soggy blackness, anticipating violence, I feel the rain dripping down my neck. I turn and wave for the squad to come on; the men emerge from their hiding places at the edge of the woods and move toward me in single file. The sergeant is satisfied. I discover that the battlefield is a lonely place, increasing fear to a higher, unexpected level, and alienating soldiers rather than bringing them together. For the moment, I'm off the hook and still wriggling.

Later that afternoon, the rain increases in volume and tempo. Dug in on the side of a hill, we're deluged with water rushing down from above, filling our fox holes to overflowing. The squad is soaked through. Hunching over, I realize I know very little about life and myself. Feeling wet, cold, and depressed, my eyes fill with tears; cradling my head in my arms, I cry. My tears merge with the rain. I think of my mother;

I call out to her, in need of her comfort and protection. This longing for the past is juxtaposed with new considerations of life and death, stirred up by the current extenuating circumstances and potentially danger-ous, unpredictable outcomes. This unexpected emotional outburst is frightening, painful, and beyond my grasp.

The whole division was thrusting toward the town of Grosetto, and we marched 24 hours over furrowed ground. Trying to go forward was like walking on the crest of a wave or the top turret of a child's sand castle, as the raised earth collapsed under the weight of our boots. Within this furrowed landscape, streams or small rivers slowed our advance. During the night, sliding down an unknown riverbank, I lost my footing and fell into the mud at the bottom; in desperation, I lashed out and grabbed something that felt like the smooth branch of a tree.

My second scout, following behind, who had witnessed my fall and helped me up, said later, 'You know what you grabbed when you slipped?'

'No, what?'

'The arm of a dead German!'

Although in excellent physical shape, I could not ward off a sense of weariness brought on by the cumulative stress and nightly exertions. It had been reported that the German infantry soldier in Russia could march 42 miles a day, day after day. I didn't believe it. We halted our pursuit after crossing the road on the outskirts of Grosseto. The platoon sergeant shouted, 'Take a break! Piss call! Smoke if you've got 'em!' I calculated that about 170 heavily armed men sought momentary rest in the middle of and alongside the road. Whenever the opportunity arose to 'take ten,' I had a way using my combat pack and helmet as a pillow, while reclining. Most of the other guys did the same.

Lying on the pavement, I lit a Camel, took a drag, tossed the cigarette away, and closed my eyes. In what seemed like an instant, I opened them. Much to my surprise, the street was empty. I was completely alone and realized, with increasing speed, that every man, ordered about by shouting non-coms, had risen, adjusted his pack and weap-ons that clanked and banged, and marched off. In this eerie silence, not only was I alone, I didn't know where the hell I was or where the company had gone.

Fleeing through the deserted streets, the silence shattered by the firing of a German machine gun, I ran toward a clump of houses, dove into one of the cellars to avoid being hit and found a battalion command post (CP).

An officer looked up from his map table and demanded, 'Who the hell are you?'

'I'm Weiss from Charlie Company. I'm lost.'

'Lost?' he snarled. 'Cut the crap. You probably took off like a jackrabbit.'

'No, sir,' I insisted. 'I was left behind.'

He turned to one of the other officers and said, 'Hey, Larry, you ever hear such bullshit? I ought to have you court-martialed for desertion.'

As the enemy fire increased, he lost interest in my story, so I scrambled out of the cellar and, crouching low, ran toward the sounds of battle. Charlie Company was dug in amidst some houses at the other end of town. I never discovered, nor did anyone volunteer to explain, why I was left behind. Reigle said, 'You're lucky; I thought you were either killed or captured.'

If we pushed the Germans out of a town like Grosseto, there were momentary displays of Texas country music. The few Texans left in the division emerged wearing Stetsons, sporting guitars, and carrying a Lone Star Texas flag. They hung it on a nearby battered house, strummed their guitars and sang: '*Deep in my heart lies a melody, The Rose of Ol' San Antone ...*' We'd gather around and join in, singing songs such as *The Wabash Cannonball*. The opening words were, 'Listen to the jingle, the rumble and the roar...' Or *Blood on the Highway*, a musical tale of death and destruction. If I didn't know the words, I pretended. When Noel Coward wrote that men from Texas were stalwart and men from Brooklyn were not, he was sadly mistaken. We all succeeded and failed, so that most divisions took on the same coloration, regardless of attempted mythology. Why? Because bullets and shell fragments stop men in their tracks, indifferent to their region of origin, and the weather and terrain are impartial and dynamic.

Somewhere between Grosseto and Siena, dug in on the crest of a hill, our regiment trapped a German horse-drawn artillery battalion. Our own artillery opened up. German tanks responded and fired at our position from the other side of the hill in relative safety because our

105 mm howitzers could not achieve the proper angle to destroy them. Keeping a low silhouette, I went from my foxhole to another. When the 105 barrages increased, their shells skimmed inches above ground or skip-bounced on their casings. Although invisible, the shells caused the air to tremble on their passage. So far, none had exploded.

The voice of an unseen soldier spoke from his foxhole, his camouflaged helmet protruding inches above ground and lost in shadow, 'If you want to stay alive, get back in your hole and stay there. Otherwise, you'll get your head blown off. Got the picture?' I stopped tempting fate and returned to my foxhole. Late in the afternoon, the Germans retreated and headed north. We followed, edging our way down the other side of the hill. Leading the way, I reached its base and turned a corner in the woods. I jumped. Sitting on a tree stump, no more that five feet away, a German soldier, in full uniform, sat staring at me. Beneath his helmet, his lips showed bright red against his white face. Some flies buzzed lazily around his head. Recoiling, I raised my rifle and aimed, but he made no move. Approaching, I realized that he was dead. There were no visible wounds, a trickle of blood on his green tunic. I whispered to him, 'Who would ever play a joke like this?' Maybe his comrades had set him up as an emotional booby trap simply for shock value. They had succeeded.

As we moved further into the woods and underbrush, I bore witness to the amount of carnage wrought by our artillery bombardment once it zeroed in on the trapped enemy formation. Caught unaware, its draft horses died chained to the surrounding trees. Terrorized, unable to stampede, their torn and ripped bodies remaining upright, held by the tensile strength of the chains that bound them, there was no exit. These once bold and powerful brutes, similar to those who spent the best years of their lives pulling Sheffield Farms and Borden's milk wagons peacefully through the quiet streets of Brooklyn, had been inducted to serve the Germans, pulling artillery wagons north of Rome. They were like the horses I fell in love with as a kid, whose smooth, glistening backs were big enough to lay a picnic lunch and support a rider. Artillery pieces and equipment had been tossed sky-high and wrecked in a deluge of exploding shells. German bodies, like dismantled puppets, were strewn across the uneven ground, and bits of clothing and personal effects were festooned on the branches of surrounding trees. Surprised, the enemy had died without any chance of taking up arms against us. The stench of decomposition pervaded the air.

Holed up in a devastated village as the enemy continued to retreat, we dug in against an enemy night attack. Earlier, the company clerk delivered mail from home. I received a letter from a former New York Office of War Information (OWI) colleague who, since my enlistment, had been trying to facilitate a transfer for me from the Infantry to the Psychological Warfare Branch. I read it by the light of a flickering candle, as rain poured through the roof of the broken house. The firing of our 155 mm 'Long Tom' field guns, dug in close by, jolted me. It felt as if their shells were hurtling through one window and out the other of my temporary shelter. Between the noise of the storm and the guns, the end of the world seemed imminent. Noting that my request for transfer to Psychological Warfare had failed, I sat there bereft and trapped, awaiting the signal to move out on patrol, into the unrelenting rain. She wished me luck. I felt that this outcome was the result of my dithering between three possibilities prior to enlistment: the Air Corps, the Engineers, or the Signal Corps. Being indecisive, allowing time to slip by, I contributed to my present situation. I was nothing more than a dogface — a slogging infantry soldier.

The previous enemy night's attack petered out inconclusively, it being nothing more than a spoiler operation, used as a means to slow our advance. Around mid-day, a seemingly deserted two-story stucco farmhouse, standing alone, drew our attention. 'Check it out,' said the sergeant, nodding to me and jerking his thumb at the same time. I approached the house cautiously while the squad waited.

All was quiet until I kicked the front door in, only to find it inhabited by an Italian family of four, parents and a teenage boy and girl cowering in a corner of the living room. The daughter took my fancy.

'Tedeschi?' (Germans) I inquired.

They answered immediately, shaking their heads and sounding like a chorus from *Aida*. 'No, no,' they shouted.

I moved cautiously from room to room, breaking into some, searching closets and opening cupboards. I thrust my rifle within, imagining an enemy a rifle bolt away. The father followed, hat in hand, trying to explain in Italian, as if I understood. For a brief moment, I felt all powerful and in command. I, a stranger, an unwanted teenager, controlled this family's destiny, and I, not he, for this brief moment, was the head of the household. The son had displaced the father. Ludicrous! There were no Germans. I tried to apologize for the intrusion and shrugged my shoulders. They stood there smiling in unison, nodding their heads in relief. When I left, the family had regained its composure and signaled me to return at the end of the war.

We attacked uphill. Leading, I forced my way through some heavy undergrowth. Suddenly, two of the enemy, not four feet away, came out with their hands up. I jumped back, at the same time pointing my M-1 at them. They jabbered in a foreign language, small Turcoman tribesmen from Central Asia with a fierce reputation for rape and pillage, indentured into the German Army. North African Ghoums fighting for the French had at times behaved similarly. Waving them aside, I looked deeper within to discover five more of the enemy waiting to surrender, armed with a German Mg.34 light machine gun aimed directly at my head and a cache of small arms and grenades. 'Come out,' I shouted, adrenalin pumping through me, my heart pounding. Why they didn't kill me first and then wipe out the rest of the squad, rather than giving themselves up, I'll never know. That would have conformed to the rules of war!

While this was going on, Able Company had gotten into trouble attacking another hill to our left front. Simmons ordered us to attack the same hill with fixed bayonets to stabilize the situation. Lying in a fold in the ground, I fixed my bayonet and noticed my hands were shaking. None of the 'old-timers' in Charlie Company had ever attacked with bayonets before, a rare occurrence for Allied infantry in Europe. Able Company fought its way out of trouble and Simmons canceled the order.

'Get your squad into those woods and find out what's going on,' the platoon sergeant ordered.

'Scouts out,' our sergeant yelled.

I led the way, based on his directions. There was no banter, no 'horsing around.' How unlike the Hollywood war films I saw as a kid! Spread out, 15 feet apart, in single file, we were ready to fire at the slightest provocation. We were jumpy. One of our pilots, flying a Piper Cub, a small unarmed aircraft used for artillery spotting, observed us from the low height of 300 feet as we climbed to the summit of another hill. He flew a line across us and circled about three times, watching our every move. I saw his face, and he seemed irritated by our presence.

'Maybe he thinks we're Germans,' Gualandi, a veteran rifleman, remarked.

'Hope not,' said Shanklin, our squad leader. 'I'll call Simmons on the walkie-talkie. He can contact regimental artillery to get that fly-boy off our tail. Charlie One, Charlie One, come in, Charlie One.'

There was no response as the plane circled overhead as we edged along the ridge. The sergeant tried again with the same negative results. 'This damn walkie-talkie radio must be broken. Of all the lousy fuckin' luck. All right,' he said, 'we gotta get off this hill right now, and fast. We'll take cover, down below. That pilot must be radioing map co-ordinates to our artillery.' He spat, 'Killed by friendly fire? Shit!' We immediately rushed off the hill. Within seconds, we heard the close crump of our 105s, followed by a stream of shells ripping through the air and exploding on the knoll we had just left.

Combat has its ironic moments. Consider the time Sheldon Wohlwerth, another rifleman and my 'foxhole-buddy' from Cleveland Heights, Ohio and I were dug in on a flat open space near a crossroads. At 28, ungainly, artistic, and bright, Wohlwerth was on the older side for dealing with the rigors of infantry combat but, having known him since basic training, I knew his common sense was invaluable. The Germans were dug in on the ridgeline a few miles away overlooking our position on the valley floor. Every time one of us reached for some gear or canned rations strewn beside our hole or tried to climb out of it to relieve ourselves, an enemy shell would tear through the air and explode no more than 35 yards away, spraying us with bits of earth and metal fragments. At first we thought, 'They're going for the crossroad traffic,' which was pretty desultory. Finally, we got the message, putting two and two together.

'Sheldon, they're after us; maybe they think we're artillery spotters.'

'How the hell would I know,' he shot back.

It got so that we were afraid to blink, feeling that our every move was being observed.

'Some Kraut up there is watching us through binoculars and having fun at our expense,' Wohlwerth said. 'The only consolation is that his firing program isn't cost-effective, and the Krauts are going into the red. If they keep this up, there will be an earlier end to the war.'

'Quit the jokes, Wohlwerth,' I replied. 'Our next move could be our last.'

Soon after, attacking along a flat, straight, shattered, tree-lined road littered with debris, pot holes, and busted and drooping telephone wires, we were shelled by high-powered, rapid-firing enemy 88 mm artillery. The flat trajectory shells screamed through the air. Leaping off the road to an adjacent field, I ran toward a stand of trees, only to have the shells follow, some bursting close behind. I skidded and made a quick U-turn, reacting like a character in a *Tom and Jerry* cartoon, and headed back toward the road, only to have the shells follow once more. 'Damn, that Kraut observer is out to get me,' I said in panic. Exasperated and frightened, I bounced into some of the other men lying on the grass verge as the shelling slowed. Shanklin signaled to move forward.

One day, an intrepid artillery forward observer — seemingly more pirate than soldier — and his radioman joined our company on one of Italy's interminable hills. His was a highly dangerous occupation. I lay beside him in the brush, out of sight, overlooking a valley and the foothills beyond. He closely followed enemy activity around a building, surrounded by trees, with a red cross painted on its roof. Through his binoculars, he observed the enemy, finally concluding that the Germans were not using the building for peaceful, humanitarian purposes. Believing that the enemy stretcher-bearers were carrying ammunition and not the wounded under the blankets, he ordered his radioman to instruct regimental artillery to fire a number of 105 mm rounds on the building. The order was followed immediately by the distant crumps of artillery firing and then our shells whizzing through the air. No skimming this time; within seconds, shells exploded on and around the target, turning it into a smoking ruin, and abolishing uncertainty. I learned that uncertainty in combat is to be eliminated quickly.

In the skies above, I followed the vapor trails of Allied heavy bombers heading for targets in northern Italy, Austria, and southern Germany. At one point, when our front line was close to Siena, three U.S. Army Air Corps P-51 fighters, returning from a mission, flew toward us at great height. Lying in a ditch, I noticed that one was trailing smoke, losing altitude and speed, while the other two acted as shepherds. As they crossed over our lines at about 5,000 feet, the pilot of the damaged fighter flipped the plane over on its back, releasing himself, a black object falling through space. The pilot's chute opened, as the plane nose-dived, gathered speed, crashed, and burst into flames immediately behind our lines, all in a matter of seconds. The pilots of the two other planes formed a protective circle around him, as he floated down and landed safely. Assured that he was OK, they waggled their wings and headed for base. That afternoon, a B-24 four-engine Liberator bomber arrived above the crash site and circled at about 1,500 feet for 10 or 15 minutes before flying away. I'll never know how the fighter pilots knew they were over our lines before one of them jumped free of his crippled aircraft.

By the middle of June, having advanced almost to Siena, we were relieved by the men of the 34th Red Bull Iowa National Guard, another hard luck division, which had seen action in North Africa on Hill 609 and in Italy on Monte Cassino and, like other American infantry divisions in the Mediterranean, had paid dearly for its accrued combat experience. In the mountains around Cassino, those survivors of that battle were so frozen when relieved that they had to be lifted out of their holes by the men who had come to relieve them. Our relief was infinitely easier.

I grinned from ear to ear. Hot dog! I was alive and eager to leave the front as quickly as possible. We drove south to Rome by truck, bivouacking on its outskirts. Standing in line before the entrance to a huge portable de-lousing machine the size of a car wash, I eagerly bathed in the spray of a hot shower but could not avoid the disinfectant spray of powdered DDT that followed. Dressed in newly issued olive drab (OD) uniforms, we were issued one-day passes to visit Rome.

Wohlwerth and I sallied forth, knowing intuitively that restaurants, not the Coliseum or St. Peter's, were high on our agenda. As two young GIs, starved of real food, having lived off concentrated D-ration Army chocolate bars made from cocoa, oat flour, and milk powder, or unimaginative canned beans with stringy meat fillers and weak gravy (that the Army called 'C rations,' better identified as 'dog food') for a month, we were ravenous, our teeth fangs. 'Meat and Spaghetti,' identifiable by name only, was another canned product, better known as 'Army noodles in gravy.' We suffered from weight loss. Not for the first time in my life, I dreamed of food.

Referring to my pocket-sized Army glossary and guidebook for Italy, I inquired phonetically of any inhabitant passing by, *Dovez andaday un bona restaurante pour mangarez la farine?* Pasta was on our minds. One old grizzled character, looking more like a buccaneer than an urban dweller or boulevardier, intrigued and puzzled by my accent, finally shrugged his shoulders in amazement, threw a few words at me, and shuffled off.

We were on a mission: to find at least one restaurant open for business so soon after Rome's liberation. 'Hey, kid.' I addressed some gamin about eight years old with '*Mangarez*,' followed by an impromptu pantomime performance of eating, moving my mouth and licking my lips. Other kids gathered around and joined in the merriment. Like a roving band of troubadours, we wandered off in search of sustenance, the oldest boy, Alessandro, leading the way through the narrow winding streets. All we needed were a few fifes and drums, garlands of flowers, and petals strewn before us to mark our passage. My thoughts drifted to those halcyon days on Manhattan's Lower East Side, where Italian delicatessens thrived, their interiors filled with the pungent smell of numerous imported and regional cheeses, Gorgonzola and Parmesan, gnarled foot-length salamis, and pasta, cut to every size and shape. A king's ransom!

Saint Martin of Tours and Saint Maurice, patron saints of innkeepers and infantry soldiers, smiled down upon us and, as if by a miracle, five previously shuttered restaurants opened their doors. Drifting from one to the other, we refueled ourselves by devouring five three-course meals in six hours — or was it six meals in five hours? With our strength returning with each mouthful, our hosts hovered about. The children waited patiently outside and watched our every disappearing mouthful through the windows.

Our patrons apologized for the lunch set before us, saying that it failed to compare with the meals served before the war. Ah, be not concerned, because we were raised on Army chow, a cuisine unfit for the Mediterranean palate. Liter carafes of ordinary vino from the nearby slopes, although red and raw, trickled down our throats and entertained. A song crossed my lips, one from the Greenpoint, pronounced 'Greenpernt,' section of Brooklyn that was full of Italian immigrants; I sang about a guy in love with a girl, early in the century. '*Oh Marie, Oh Marie; in your arms, I'm longing to be; Um, baby, tell me you love me; kiss me once while the stars shine above me.*' The kids started dancing and sang the same tune with Italian lyrics. The chef came out of the kitchen, joined the party, grabbed the owner's wife, and together they danced a tarantella. Wohlwerth and I kept time with our knives and forks.

I mentioned to more than one patron, 'Make sure the kids have a good round of pasta too, if you please. 'Buono appetito!' Wohlwerth and I were surprised that the people willingly shared their meager resources with us, particularly after nearly starving under the recently terminated German occupation. Italians are kind, festive, and generous and, like their relatives in Brooklyn, these 'old country' folk demonstrated the same affection for two hungry soldiers who had expended all their youthful energy at the front. At one restaurant, a customer accompanied himself on the mandolin, singing one romantic Italian ballad after another, like *Take Me Back to Old Sorrento*. His timing was excellent because, by now, feeling one with the world and experiencing little pain, Wohlwerth and I became Italian in spirit and gesture. How we loved to touch! Our tastes were basic; we roamed about on full stomachs and waved at the local girls, who only smiled and playfully thwarted our seductive advances with Roman sophistication, knowing we were as harmless as butterflies.

In late June, Charlie Company boarded a small U.S. Navy amphibious landing craft at Civitavecchia, a seaport 42 miles north of Rome, and set sail south on the Tyrrhenian Sea. The night was filled with stars. More like a cruise in peacetime, the voyage had great appeal to those romantics among us. I stood guard over an Oerlikon Swiss-designed 20 mm rapid-fire gun. Within the craft's small wheelhouse sat an American sailor, a member of the crew, eating a bowl of hot beef stew. He looked up and our eyes met, neither of us saying a word. He lowered his gaze, glanced at the beef stew, looked at me, and stopped eating. I watched him in anticipation like Pavlov's dog, salivating. The next moment, the sailor thrust his bowl of stew at me with an outstretched arm; grabbing the bowl, I attacked the stew without pause, nodding my head in appreciation. His gesture not only contained an unspoken statement of, 'Here, you need it more than I,' but also expressed a kindness rare in one so young. A stranger, he knew intuitively what I needed, which was to consume all the food in the world.

On the following day at twilight, with the clouds still tinged with the setting sun's riotous colors, after a sea voyage of 180 miles, we moored at Amalfi, a yacht anchorage and village on the southern side of the mountainous and picturesque Sorrento peninsula. Army trucks waited on the quay to take us down the coast another 30 miles to our bivouac and training area near Paestum. Chosen for its wide sandy beach, this small seaside resort on the Bay of Salerno was the home of two magnificent pre-Christian Greek temples, those of Neptune and Ceres, the scene of heavily contested battles only 10 months before. For some GIs, it was a homecoming, because during the invasion of Italy in September 1943, 10 months earlier, the 36th was nearly driven back into the sea by the German defenders, the 16th Panzer Division of General Vietinghoff's 10th German Army, which bitterly opposed the landing. With their Panzer IV medium tanks — armed with a 75 mm gun that could penetrate 99 mm of armor at a hundred yards and reinforced by parachute battalions and armored infantry — the 16th attacked in full force, intending to reach the sea at Paestum and cut the beachhead in half. Infantrymen, paratroopers, and more than one overwhelming barrage by Allied destroyers and cruisers, firing their five-inch and eight-inch guns, stopped them.

Individually established in our pup tents, consisting of two 7.5' x 5'-feet shelter-halves fastened together, each soldier got a candy ration of 24 peanut-filled, chocolate-coated Clark bars. Sitting in front of my small tent, I opened my box of Clark bars, chose one, undid its wrapper, looked hungrily at the bar, took a bite, and relished the taste. I continued with another bite and another, until the bar disappeared. I moved on to the second, then the third, and the forth, one after another, savoring and devouring each one, until, after 45 minutes, all that remained was a batch of discarded cellophane wrappers and an empty 8' x 10' cardboard box. Still hungry, I scouted the neighborhood of our company area and found a local farmer's peach orchard. I disregarded the 'off limits' sign, climbed over the four-foot wire fence, and chose one of the many trees ripe with fruit. I filled my helmet with three or four specimens, sat and leaned against the tree. Firm, yet full of juice and flavor, with an attractive reddish-yellow color, the peaches were delicious. When my helmet was empty, I added another batch and repeated the process. Assured, ennobled by the moment, knowing that I would pay the physical consequences for such gluttony, I felt that it was the human thing to do, a prize for surviving combat.

In my new-found 'land of plenty,' trouble was brewing. When we returned from the front, looking more like rabble than a combat division, piled on the back of 6x6 trucks and proceeding to our bivouac area, we exchanged jeers, boos, and catcalls with smartly dressed rear echelon troops, who rarely heard a shot fired in anger, or whose lives were ever in jeopardy. The Allied 5th Army, of which the 36th was a part, was segregated not only by color, but also by uniform. In summer, when light-weight khaki uniforms would have been the appropriate dress code for all units, only rear echelon Peninsula Base Section (PBS) supply personnel ('pencil pushers') had the right to do so. By contrast, we wore heavy olive drab uniforms — as personified by Bill Mauldin's uncouth cartoon characters 'Willie' and 'Joe' — on and off the front, regardless of weather. This visual distinction benefited rear echelon soldiers, who were our competitors for girls. PBS men warned them of our fearsome, irrational behavior. Dressed in coarse, ill-fitting uniforms, we behaved, according to them, like beetle-browed savages who raped unsuspecting Italian females. We could do little to dispel such fears of the girls our own age who gathered at the local Red Cross Club, some of whom sought the continuity of a long-term relationship. The khaki-clad soldiers were the odds-on favorite.

Nevertheless, all of us overflowed with testosterone and were highly competitive for the limited female resources available, and tensions persisted. However, if our sole purpose was getting laid, these 'desk-jockeys,' in their lightweight garb, had little impact upon us, because nine out of ten widowed women, prowling as prostitutes in Naples, were available. They inquired of a potential customer, 'Zig, zig, Joe?' In 1944, out of 150,000 women living in the city, 42,000 were engaged in selling themselves, either on a regular or occasional basis. In 1943, due to a water shortage, three or four young girls out of a family of seven or eight could be had for a canteen cup of water. In many cases, social standing had nothing to do with it, because most families were impoverished.

I noticed that team spirit and competition between members of different combat units on leave in Naples or Rome were a fact of life, but the majority of front-line soldiers quickly closed ranks against the arrogance of the common enemy, the soldiers of the PBS. Out of harm's way, after two or three days, I began to relax and my sexual interest increased, although I couldn't be greener behind my ears. If I briefly 'lived it up,' got drunk, and raised hell at some roadside mom and pop cafe, both as a release and as a form of denial, it could be for the last time. Combat loomed with its awful statistics. Thus, rotation to the rear was brief because of a shortage of infantry. An acquaintance at divisional headquarters told me that the division had been replaced twice already. I learned that rifle companies, such as Charlie Company, as well as formations of combat engineers and medics, suffered 100 percent to 120 percent casualties during a month of intense fighting, regardless of scale. From my own brief experience, death lurked and struck at random, and my chances of surviving the war were much lower compared to a PBS Army clerk working a 9-to-5 office job in Naples, for example,. How I envied the 'pencil pushers!' Wouldn't it be more fair if everyone took a turn at the front and the Army eliminated sinecures? By that I mean, as things were, once a clerk or first scout, always a clerk or a first scout; the position was yours for as long as you lived.

Not far from our bivouac overlooking the Gulf of Salerno, squad members Reigle, Gualandi, Wohlwerth, and I discovered a small, primitive stone farmhouse situated on a dirt road, whose aged, toothless owner sold his wine by the glass, poured from a large five-gallon jug. Even with the little Italian money we had, we could easily afford to drink his produce. Standing on the earth floor within, before a wood counter, we ordered a round of an olive-colored white wine. It tasted vile and raw. After each of the others had bought a round of drinks, when my turn arrived, I nodded in approval but declined another refill. But my buddies, feeling relaxed and merry, insisted I join them. That fourth round was the turning point and my undoing. Even though other rounds followed, from that moment on, I was a very happy drunk.

Filled with merriment, the four of us staggered outside. Exiting, Wohlwerth spied the farmer's decrepit white horse standing in an open field opposite; he unhesitatingly jumped on its back, facing its tail, and encouraged it to move. We laughed, staggered about, and I fell into a ditch along the side of the road. However hard I tried, I could not climb out on my own, relying on Reigle and Gualandi for assistance. By this time, Wohlwerth let go of the horse's tail, fell off, and tumbled into the ditch unhurt, laughing. When it was time to leave, I was pulled from the ditch and staggered into the arms of my companions, who manhandled and dragged me along the road. I was no more than a cardboard cutout. Rapidly, as if on cue, my eyes filled with tears, and I wept for all the fellows who had been killed. My alcoholic memory didn't square with reality because the company's losses were light, given our recent battles. Tossed like cordwood onto the back of a passing truck, which stopped long enough to take on a mendicant drunk spewing drivel, it was the last thing I remembered before passing out.

The following morning, having slept most of the day away, I awoke with a terrible hangover, but none the worse for wear. I wondered about the sense of loss I experienced the night before, concluding that its deep sadness had more to do with separation from home than my present predicament, even though its reality was fraught with anxiety and tension.

Something else slowly dawned on me. I sensed that friendship was going to be limited to a few people and short lived. Friendship needs not only time but also continuity, the kind found in units in which men trained together for at least one, or possibly two years, before entering combat. The 36th was like that originally because it began as a National Guard division, in which men assigned to units like Charlie Company came from the same town in Texas and were much like an extended family. That ended with the introduction of the Replacement System, when many of the original Texans were lost during the first nine months of the Italian campaign, September 1943 to May 1944.

I had made three friends, limited by the above definition, all from the same squad: Reigle, Gualandi, and Wohlwerth, my foxhole buddy. Both Reigle, from Philadelphia, and Gualandi, from Peoria, Illinois, had sunny and unflappable dispositions. Their smiles were infectious. Small men, I could imagine them working as clerks or light-factory workers. Wohlwerth, from Cleveland, Ohio, was mercurial, artistic, and somewhat ungainly. His rifle and pack always seemed too heavy for him. None of us had attended college, although I graduated from high school more than a year early. As for some of the others in the company, Weidaw, from rural Pennsylvania, was big and rawboned, quiet but with a killer instinct. We were at Fort Blanding, Florida together. Dickson, from upper New York State, had a reputation of disappearing from the line when the fighting started. Although not accused of any military crime thus far, his behavior was common knowledge throughout the company. The following two men were not in my squad but were well known throughout the company. Bocarsky was a street-smart New Yorker, light-hearted and quick-witted; he entertained. Staff Sergeant Jerstad was unavailable to the outside world. He had been badly wounded, recently released from the hospital, and returned to duty. That didn't make him a thruster. I remember asking him what it was like on the front. He looked beyond me and didn't respond. I sensed that he already knew what I was to learn later in France, that time was running out.

After the morning's British battle drill exercises, introduced to improve fitness, we had time either to go swimming or visit the Greek temples at Paestum. Before deciding, a group of Italians, two men and three women, arrived in the field adjacent to our bivouac, reminiscent of Shakespeare's strolling band of itinerant players in *Hamlet* or Waugh's roving Welsh singers in *Decline and Fall*. They were neither actors nor singers, but a motley group of travelling pimps and prostitutes. The women were willing to sell themselves for a can of meat and beans, the staple Army diet, recently referred to. I chose a small dark-haired woman, who told me in pantomime that she was having her period. We decided to go ahead just the same. I'd just taken my trousers down when someone yelled at us. It was the battalion medical officer (MO). 'Stop that,' he shouted, on the run. 'Stay where you are.' We both ran, but I had to stop to pull my pants up. The MO bore down, I jumped and bounced, my trousers a potato sack. Plunging into a nearby thicket, I avoided capture and stayed out of sight until the coast was clear.

I berated myself for my stupidity. From the time of my enlistment, the Army discouraged such high-risk encounters. Venereal disease (VD) was considered a self-inflicted wound, and in U.S. and British military VD hospitals, patients were treated like dirt. Our platoon lieutenant informed me that the German Army used mobile brothels under supervision of MOs and their VD rate was lower than the Allied armies. The German system was fit for purpose; their men were served properly.

My stupidity and ignorance continued. It's hard to erase the memory of joining a long, meandering line of humanity in uniform that seemed to include everyone serving in the Mediterranean. Awaiting my two-dollar turn with an unseen prostitute sequestered in a room at the top of a tall flight of stairs in the slums of Naples, I asked the GI standing in front of me, 'What's the babe like?'

'Never seen her! S'posed to be a beaut, though,' he replied.

'Has to be another Joan Crawford,' I added.

When my turn finally came, a pimp tossed me into a bare room where a skinny urchin, as Mediterranean as a flannel cake, wearing a faded cotton dress, remained standing. 'What am I supposed to do? Wrestle you to the ground?' I shouted. Passion? I threw my money down and walked out in disgust.

For the moment, the war seemed to favor the Allies. Thus, I was issued a 24-hour pass to Naples, 48 miles away. With another soldier, I hired a horse, carriage, and driver soon after arriving. As the horse slowly plodded along Naples narrow streets, we picked up two aging prostitutes and spent the night at a local third-rate hotel. It was a forgettable encounter and I felt underwhelmed. The next morning, having separated from my Army friend, I walked around the harbor and entered a café before thumbing a ride back to Paestum. Standing behind the counter was a young dark-haired barmaid with even darker eyes set in a finely featured face. We looked at each other and lightning flashed between us. Over coffee, we chatted and then she said, 'Would you like to go upstairs?' In love, I replied, 'Oh, yes, please!' She moved effortlessly and gracefully up the narrow stairs, as I followed her to an upstairs bedroom. She raised her dress over her head, revealing a well-proportioned body. Further intimacy revealed that we were well suited, and she was imaginative, forthright, and endearing. She led. I followed. Long after we parted, the memory of her Mediterranean beauty and demeanor remained, and I was filled with regret that we hadn't met the night before. Who knows what might have followed; although our encounter was brief and uncomplicated, she had cast a spell over me!

Returning to the company area, a rumor circulated that both the Army and Corps commanders, General Mark Clark and Major-General Geoffrey Keyes, were displeased with the division's overall performance and, in particular, the leadership of its commander, Major-General Fred Walker. Failure at the Rapido was mentioned. Walker was relieved, never to lead troops in combat again and, pending transfer to the States, was reassigned as Commandant of the Infantry School at Fort Benning, Georgia. Clark and Keyes should have been fired for their incompetence, not Walker, who took the heat as the fall guy.

The men requested a farewell divisional parade in review near Paestum on July 7, before Walker relinquished command. His face was furrowed, his expression, grim, sad. He loved the 36th. Fifteen thousand men stood in the bright sunshine and listened to the general's closing remarks, quoting from a letter he had received from the widow of a captain killed on the Rapido River, he read, 'The next time you meet the Germans, give it to them.' He knew about river crossings, having been on the opposite side of the Marne River during the action that stopped the Germans from crossing and taking Paris in 1918. Based on that experience, he had pleaded with Clark and Keyes for more time, equipment, and preparation prior to the Rapido River attempt, but to no avail.

We snapped to attention, reacting to the numerous barks of command that mixed with the sounds of the divisional band; division and regimental flags snapped in the incoming sea breeze. Saluting as one formation after another marched past, executing the command, 'Eyes right,' the general stood ramrod-straight on the makeshift grandstand, to the fore of his three regimental colonels and Aide-de-Camp (ADC). After we passed in review, he was gone. Some of the veterans thought Walker had done a good job under difficult circumstances, particularly at Velletri during the Anzio breakout. But, for the average GI, unqualified to judge a senior officer's plans and performance, generals were a rare species and hardly seen.

One day, a company of blacks arrived and bivouacked on the beach near us. They had been given little specialized training and were assigned as laborers in service units, performing dockside and railroad cargo-handling tasks. I remembered the lyrics from the song *Show Boat*, 'Lift that bale, and tote that barge.' Sometimes I'd bump into clusters of them on my way to the beach, even stopping for some light-hearted banter. Words bounced between us like ping-pong balls. I liked chatting with their first sergeant, a big, muscular, pot-bellied guy from Hoboken, New Jersey, across the river from Brooklyn, whose joviality reminded me of Fats Waller, the jazz piano player. His rich bass-baritone voice was perfect, either for singing or shouting commands. The blacks were a good bunch of guys, but we were warned by our officers to stay away from them, 'Don't fraternize; they're contaminated with venereal disease and they smoke dope.'

I wasn't surprised by this caveat, because some of Charlie Company's officers were from the South. Although a northerner from Brooklyn, with black Harlem a part of Manhattan close by, I didn't attend high school with black students. They were out of my school district. My prior arm's-length association came either through jazz or film. When I got to know the first sergeant better, he spoke of what the blacks were up against. The Army was segregated, and its bureaucracy considered the black soldier inferior because of his low scores on the General Classification Test (GCT). He spoke guardedly. As a means of assessing 'usable intelligence,' it concluded that blacks were only adequate soldiers, nothing more, when led by white officers. General George C. Marshall, the Army's chief of staff, lamented their 'relatively low intelligence average,' and General George 'Blood and Guts' Patton held that they could not think fast enough for armored warfare. Although the Army did not sanction discrimination against men of any color or race, its policy of equal but separate conditions produced racial tensions and waste. 'We're here to do our job, however restricted,' Patton said. Soon after the U.S. declared war, many blacks sought to enlist but encountered quotas and discouragement, although those already in uniform had an 80-percent re-enlistment rate, compared to 40 percent for whites, according to company records. The significance of what 'the land of the free and the home of the brave' meant to blacks took on a different connotation.

One particular afternoon, free from duties, I walked to the beach and went swimming. It was a perfect Italian summer's day. Lying on the soft brown sand and basking in the bright Mediterranean sun, I gazed out to sea and thought of an experience I had with my father, and later with Jeanie, my girlfriend.

Approaching my 18th birthday in the summer of 1943, I returned home one evening with the Army's enlistment papers. I had graduated from high school a year-and-a half before and was working as a photo- lithographer in the Manhattan branch of the Office of War Information (OWI). I was living at home and paying my share of expenses. It was the 'Swing Era.' Eager to enlist in the Army's psychological warfare branch, after enjoying the benefits of a major city since graduating, I needed my father's signature and approval.

'You'll sign them, Dad, won't you?' I implored.

He looked at me with a combination of shock and regret, inquiring, 'Do you know what you're doing?'

I replied, 'Yes. I don't like waiting around to be drafted; I want to go.'

'Real war isn't like the movies. It's dangerous and could be fatal.' His face mirrored a deep sadness. 'You know how the war's affected me.'

'Yes, Dad.'

He looked beyond me and stared into an earlier time. 'Seems like yesterday, but in the spring of 1918, I was wounded and gassed near Fismes, and those experiences still tick over in my head. I've spent most of my life trying to recover, starting with four months in a French hospital in Tours and at least two years recuperating out West, at a remount station in Oklahoma, oil fields in Texas, the wheat fields of Kansas. Worked as a wrangler, farm hand, and roustabout. I accidentally shot and killed a man on the streets of El Paso working as a Federal Narcotics Agent. Did you know that? Since then, I've never had any energy left for ambition. Too scared to try.'

'Dad, I…'

'Wait,' he pleaded, 'I wish you'd reconsider.'

'Are you trying to frighten me?'

'No. I'm just asking you not to make any sudden moves. If the Army needs you, it will find you soon enough.'

Instinctively, my mother didn't want me to go. Romantically, my girlfriend didn't either, but between my father and me, it was different — generational. I was unmoved.

He paused to catch his breath, and I quietly implored, 'Dad, you enlisted, why can't I?' He had no comeback. I had him, but he said nothing. We stood there in the silence and then I said:

'Dad, if you don't sign the enlistment papers, I'll forge your name and run away.' I threatened blackmail. He signed without further protest, and I mailed the completed papers that evening. Even now, I don't think either one of us fought fairly, but I remained troubled and riddled with guilt for years.

It was during my tenure at the OWI that I became friends with a neighborly teenage girl not much older than myself. Jeanie was tall and slender, with brown hair that cascaded to her shoulders, small but developed breasts, and long shapely legs.

One evening before curfew, we strolled into Prospect Park. There, we could get lost in the shadows or find seclusion in a secret bower of our own making. When the air-raid practice sirens suddenly wailed and the city went dark, its lights seemingly extinguished by the throw of a master switch, the tracery of searchlight beams quickly illuminating the night sky, I held her close. We heard the drone of planes overhead. A waning moon was our only witness. Neither of us knew anything about making love; that required a level of knowledge and experience beyond our years, but we were eager to touch and explore. Her graceful sapling-like body configured with mine, and time was suspended.

A few days before reporting for military service, having passed my Army physical exam with ease, armed with a condom, I tried to make love to Jeanie one afternoon in her mother's apartment. I groped and fumbled, my cavalry-charge eagerness overshadowing her apprehension. She succumbed; Jeanie wanted me, but fumbled as well. High school coursework in Home Economics excluded sexual instruction and cast us adrift. The liberating factors of the 'pill' were yet to be discovered. Feeling foolish and defensive, I left on a discordant note, promising to write. I lacked the wherewithal to retreat gracefully and still express loving feelings to match her own.

The author with General Jean Simon after being awarded the French Legion Honor in Paris in November 1999

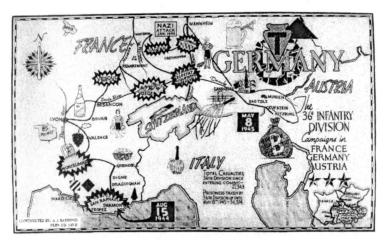

Division commemorative calendar depicting battles from Italy to Austria via France and Germany

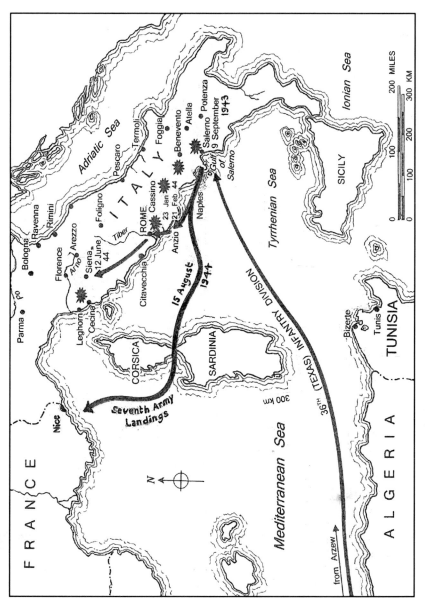

36th Division, Mediterranean Operations, 1943-1944

2
Ducks in a Shooting Gallery

In early December 1943, I was sworn in at the Army's induction center on Church Street in lower Manhattan with 50 other civilians of assorted ages. I turned to my father and said, 'Well, Dad, I'm in the Army now.'

Walking over to a mainline railroad station nearby and standing beside the train, he looked at me and said, 'If you need me, just say the word.'

We embraced and he walked away, looking back once through the crowd. No military band, unfurled flags, or pretty girls punctuated our separation and my departure. I left soon after with a batch of recruits on a train destined for Fort Dix, New Jersey, a permanent Army post. No soldiers waved goodbye from open coach windows to tearful mothers, wives, and girlfriends tossing flowers. I felt apprehensive and sad to say goodbye and yet eager to begin a new life.

Two hours later, as recruits, we sat in a makeshift Fort Dix auditorium. Sergeant Jack Leonard, formerly a singer with the Tommy Dorsey swing band, officially greeted us. He sang *Marie*, a song he and the band made famous prior to his enlistment and, from what I gathered, singing that song was his only major contribution to the war effort. Frank Sinatra, who had failed his Army physical and was rejected for military service because of a perforated eardrum, took Leonard's place with the Dorsey band. More than once I had seen Sinatra entertain in Manhattan with Dorsey during the height of the Swing Era, and he did more as a singer for the war effort than if he had been a soldier. Sinatra's interpretation of the romantic ballad 'I'll Be Seeing You' is a case in point.

I sailed through another medical exam, coughing when required, while the doctor fondled my testicles, tilted my torso over a metal table, and probed my prostate with a finger protected by a rubber glove. We were issued Army olive drab wool clothing, a cotton green fatigue uniform, khaki leggings, brown leather boots, an olive wool 'beanie' cap, and a light cotton field jacket, the equivalent of a civilian windbreaker, by a bored supply sergeant. That evening, lying in an upper bunk in an almost empty and unfamiliar barrack and in need of someone to talk to, I listened to the distant sound of rushing steam engines, their whistles wailing and moaning in the empty night, underscoring my loneliness. Like a five-year-old beginning school, I suffered pangs of homesickness and finally fell asleep just when it was time to rise.

Fort Dix served, in part, as a transit camp for men recently introduced to Army life. At this stage of my service, I awaited shipment to some unknown destination to begin basic training. While waiting, I spent 14 hours of the following day working in the kitchen, scrubbing and mopping floors, peeling potatoes, washing dishes, and serving food. I jumped to the tune of a demanding, indifferent, and impatient mess sergeant who, from my lowly position of indentured servant, seemed to have absolute power. 'Your soul belongs to God, but your ass belongs to me,' he chanted. With little chance to 'take ten,' I felt that this was a piss-poor introduction to Army life, it being too severe and abusive. The mess sergeant and his staff should have lessened the pace of acclimatization, particularly since it was Thanksgiving, the most familial of national holidays, the loss of which increased my pangs of homesickness. I felt intimidated and in awe of the sergeant's power. Feeling unsure, having no way to judge, I wondered if I were overreacting to contemporary Army life.

Four backbreaking days passed. I was naïve and too frightened to revolt. Having seen nothing of Fort Dix except mess halls and garbage cans, a number of similarly victimized recruits and I, seemingly harvested together like bunches of drooping celery, boarded a southbound train. We were destined for Camp Blanding, an Infantry Replacement Training Center in northern Florida constructed for New England and southern troops, covering 170,000 acres of Florida scrubland and swamps 40 miles west of Jacksonville.

Arriving two days later, we had journeyed 800 miles between the Eastern Seaboard and the Appalachian mountains of Virginia, the Carolinas, and Georgia, replete with, farmlands, cities, and American Civil War historic battlegrounds where Union and Confederate generals such as Lee, Grant, Sherman, and Johnston fought each other from 1861 to 1865. Previous high school history classes came to life.

We were subjected to a battery of exams and the GCT at Blanding, on which an assigned military specialty would be based. I scored high enough to qualify for Officer's Candidate School (OCS), but in late 1943 the Army needed infantry replacements, not junior officers. I was questioned by a second lieutenant, who derided my use of OWI photographic copy cameras and offset printing machines. Jokingly, he wanted to know if I could make counterfeit American dollar notes, and I said 'yes' to avoid a straight infantry assignment. Full of the power invested in him, he decided instead to send me to a Combat Intelligence (CI) 17-week Basic Training Course. He described 'combat intelligence' as the gathering of tactical enemy information, obtained by specialized CI infantry probing beyond the front line, patrolling and observing, either on foot or by jeep. To qualify, map reading, aerial photographic interpretation, enemy identification, prisoner interrogation, infantry tactics, use of weapons, and small group cohesion were high on the agenda. Although seemingly glamorous, I felt that CI missions would be more dangerous than those assigned to the regular infantry.

We were housed in 15-man Nissen huts, half-cylinder pre-fabricated structures of corrugated iron. Ours was a polyglot group drawn from different states, some from farms, others from cities. A fellow from Philadelphia and I were the only Jews. He was devout and drew attention to himself because of his sincerity, praying every morning beside his bunk. Many of the soldiers, who had not seen a Jew before, thought him strange. He became the butt of their jokes, teasing, and latent hostility. When this went on for a few weeks, I challenged one Southerner who seemed to be the most vocal and belligerent, stating that if he continued tossing jibes at 'Philly,' I would 'stomp his ass.' The guy shut up, but there was more to come.

It came suddenly, when both men were working in the mess hall's kitchen. I was standing nearby 'shooting the breeze' with a bunch of other recruits, standing on the duck board sidewalks surrounded by sand, when the mess hall's rear door opened with explosive force and banged against the clinker-built wooden wall. Down the steps the Southerner and the Jew rushed, one a step behind the other. At the bottom of the stairs, they faced each other in anger. The first sergeant, hearing the noise, rushed from his office, separated the two, listened to their protests and decided to settle the dispute the Army way, by putting on the gloves. The square of sand between the duckboards would serve as the prize ring. A group formed; two soldiers, serving as seconds, laced up their gloves. 'OK,' yelled the first sergeant, 'Go to it.' The Southerner rushed from his corner and attacked Philly, fists flailing. The Jewish kid didn't look strong; because of his retiring and introspective nature, I assumed that the battle would soon be over.

The sturdy Southerner hit his opponent with left jabs and rights to the body. Red welts rose on the Jew's stomach. They squared off again in round two and moved cat-like around each other, searching for an opening. The sand slowed their footwork. Philly moved in and pounded away, not as one trained to fight, but instinctively, aggressively. He took a few more punches to the body, but in the process countered with a hard right to the jaw that knocked the Southerner down. And, to everyone's surprise, he stayed down, squirming on the sand. Jeered by the first sergeant and the loser's fellow trainees, he refused to rise. 'Get up! Get up, you bastard,' some yelled. Shouts, exhortations, and threats would not budge him. He whimpered, shaking his head, as Philly hovered above him, his chest heaving, ready to hit him again. As the first sergeant stepped between both men and proclaimed the Philadelphian the winner, he warned the Southerner that, 'If you don't change your attitude, I'll have you court-martialed.' The men turned their backs and left the loser sitting between the duckboards. I felt exultant, as did the other spectators, sensing that this was an object lesson in human rights connected to the war itself. Justice had triumphed after all, and the Jew proved he was no slouch.

In the rush to create a gigantic army in the shortest possible time, newly created officers and inexperienced non-commissioned officers (NCOs) were bound to make mistakes during our training, from which we suffered, but I never felt that as recruits we were deliberately mistreated. We were mass-produced soldiers, unseen individuals. Blanding was like a boomtown, ill prepared to handle the military population explosion and the increased need for training facilities, goods, and services.

Magazine stories described Florida as a paradise and winter playground that included swaying palm trees, blue seas, white sand, and 80-degree weather down around Miami. That's true, but Blanding, further north, on the same line as Jacksonville, is really 'Southern Georgia,' a land of poor soil, scrubland, and stunted pine. The winter of 1943 was so cold that my fingers froze within my gloves and I could not pull the trigger of my rifle during early morning target practice on the firing range. For more than three hot and humid months, we trained, route-marched, and lived in the neighboring swamps. We killed poisonous snakes and were threatened by wild pigs. Attacking, they even tore up my tent and partially devoured a gift box of chocolates, bits of which stuck to my sleeping bag for days and attracted long columns of ants. Cloudbursts trapped us on the march or converted our foxholes into cesspools crawling with insects, known as 'critters' in Floridian.

One of the instructors, a strong rawboned Southern country boy called Howe, was at home in the scrub and swamps. Howe knew how to kill coral snakes with his bare hands, a deadly gamble. Smaller and more colorful than cobras, they were just as venomous. In one blurred, split-second continuous movement, I watched him seize one from a swamp and slam it against a tree, killing it instantaneously.

Many recruits like me, living in this monstrous environment, ended up on sick call with a variety of complaints. Treated by medics who knew little about simple first aid and proper medication, they often dispensed the wrong prescription to the unsuspecting sufferer.

'Here, take two tablets per day for your stomach trouble,' one of them said, pushing the packets toward me.

'But I don't have stomach trouble — I've got 'athlete's foot.'

'Oh! It must be that other guy,' he replied, somewhat abashed.

A little later, these same medics zeroed in and jabbed me with a series of shots, including typhus and tetanus, which combined to raise my temperature to fever pitch. I passed out and ended up spending the next five days in the camp hospital, not caring whether I lived or died. Because the swamps waited, there was little incentive to leave and return to duty once I recovered.

During my 17 weeks at Blanding, I viewed a series of eight Army documentary films titled *Why We Fight*, compiled and directed by former Academy Award-winning Hollywood director Major Frank Capra. Actual newsreel footage with added English narration described Hitler's rise to power and Japanese aggression in Asia; however, by staging scenes of trench warfare and men in battle, he gave a false impression of modern war, which added little to our preparations. In retrospect, the series had little influence on my feelings about the war in general and added little to my reasons for enlisting.

If I were lucky enough to get a one-day pass, there was a bus service to Jacksonville, one of Florida's major cities. It was part of the South, faintly charming, but strong on prejudice. Overwhelmed by the thousands of sailors, soldiers, and Marines that flocked to it on weekends from the various bases ringing its perimeter, Jacksonville offered nothing more than a minor-step change from the dreariness of Blanding. Pilots from the Jacksonville Naval Air Station, wearing a pilot's gold wings on their spotless white tunics, representing the romantic best of American manhood, easily attracted the prettiest women. I, by comparison, was easily identified as a raw recruit because of my crew cut and ill-fitting olive drab uniform; I failed in my quest for female companionship. Out of my depth and with limited resources, all that remained was an over-priced meal and a walk along the oceanfront. On one my forays, I met a young woman at a concert where Don Redman and his swing band were playing. During intermission, with the steps of the music hall crowded with people, for some unknown reason, I called her 'white trash,' an expression I had learned recently and, in this instance, most inappropriate. She burst into tears, and I beat a hasty retreat, ashamed to return for the second half of the concert.

Army chow played a prominent part in our expanding lives, and at our mess hall in Blanding, we were served family style. The men on KP duty, servings as waiters, placed large bowls and platters, piled high with vegetables and slices of undercooked, 'rubberized' pork in the middle of each table. Even recruits were expected to behave in a civilized manner, described in this case as passing the bowls and plat-ters from man to man, each helping himself to a reasonable amount. An additional serving would follow if there were anything left over. One fellow, less gracious than the rest, always grabbed the steaming bowl of mashed potatoes first, taking an oversized double portion for himself, with complete disregard for those sitting beside him.

This ritual looked as if it would go on forever but, a couple of weeks lat-er, another soldier, named Shearer, more disgusted than the rest, asked the glutton as we took our places around the table, 'You like mashed potatoes, don't you?'

'Hell, yes,' the glutton replied.

Shearer's words and actions merged into one gymnastic movement. 'Well, have some!'

Shearer lifted the full bowl, rose, and dumped its contents over the soldier's head. His brown hair turned a curdled white, and his eyes merged with potato lumps.

So much for the vegetables, now for the meat! At least twice a week, we were served chipped beef on toast for breakfast; we called it 'shit on a shingle,' black pebbles half submerged in a sea of white gravy, as tempting as a South Sea island holiday during a monsoon. Dinner frequently included fried pork chops, dumped onto our plates, undercooked and tasteless. One afternoon, another soldier and I were returned early from swamp maneuvers, ahead of the main body of troops, to work in the kitchen. Upon completion of our chores, we asked the mess sergeant if we could prepare our own dinner. He replied, 'Sure, why not. It's less work for mother that way, if you see what I mean.'

I took six pork chops from the refrigerator, set the deep fry oil gauge to high and waited. When the oil reached the proper temperature and began to gurgle, I tossed the meat in, watched, and waited. Retrieved from the hot oil, soon after, were six glowing, crisp, brown pork chops. Were they the best ever cooked at Blanding? The Mess Sergeant, duly impressed, asked for a serving of his own; we gladly complied. His mastery of the culinary art was so limited, I wondered if he had served his apprenticeship in a penal institution. His top priority seemed to be stealing bags of sugar and coffee, commodities subject to wartime rationing, for his girlfriend who lived off the base.

Even if the classroom training was good — and it wasn't — I found the subject matter uninteresting and repetitive. Blanding housed German prisoners of war (POWs), and I stood guard over some of them, a mean and arrogant bunch of Afrika Korps professionals captured in Tunisia during 1943. I felt inadequate and intimidated in their presence. To increase my frustration, I got into trouble with the local battalion commander, a former Federal government Works Progress Administration (WPA) bureaucrat who, as a major, took a dim view of my attempts to transfer out of the infantry. He expressed his displeasure publicly, without mentioning my name. I expected to, but hadn't applied through proper channels for a transfer to the Psychological Warfare Branch (PWB). From then on, I was expected to cease and desist or face the consequences. Because of him, my letters to my former OWI colleague, who supported the change, may have been intercepted and 'lost' within the camp's gates.

Near the close of our training period, we speculated about the theater of war to which we'd be assigned. One of our junior officers, a former Marine who had served in China and the Pacific before the war, was forbidden to reveal our destination. However, he hinted obliquely that, if he could choose, Europe was his first choice every time. 'Why?' we asked, gathering around him like a gaggle of geese, eagerly awaiting an answer. Because Europe had cellars where bottles of wine could always be found! In the Pacific, there was nothing but ocean, jungle, and swamp. Another Blanding! He sure had a point!

At the end of the 17 weeks, I graduated as a CI Observer and was given 10 days' leave, known as a 'Delay on Route,' before reporting to a final stateside post. This short break from the military provided an opportunity for soldiers to say farewell before shipping overseas. We marched to the railhead singing, *the doughnuts that they serve us, they say are mighty fine; one fell off the table and killed a pal of mine. I don't want no more of Army life; gee Ma, I wanna go home.* Camp Blanding no longer exists, but in its place, close to the small town of Starke, stands the Florida State penal institution, a fitting memorial.

Gladly, we departed from Blanding for New York, travelling by passenger train on the Southern Seaboard Railway. What seemed like an escape became an ordeal, because any other train, whether it was freight or passenger, whether it was loaded with cattle or iron ore, took priority. I conjured up the idea that even any enemy train had the right of way over ours. Repeatedly shunted to the side, sitting idly and silently beyond the pale, with only the wind rustling through the adjacent knee-high grass for company, we waited. Reluctantly our 'Flying Dutchman,' a 'phantom' train, hours behind schedule, began to move, seemingly toward some mysterious destination. No longer were steam engines, their whistles moaning during the day or night, objects of gratifying speculation. Sweating for lack of air conditioning, soot filling our eyes, sitting on rock-hard wooden seats nailed to old rolling stock, ours was a nightmare, not a journey. Frustrated, insisting inwardly that we weren't forgotten or destined to travel along the tracks of the Southern Seaboard for an eternity, I'd mumble derisively to myself, 'Be patient, don't you know there's a war on?' Finally, the South released its hold.

The old neighborhood looked much like the way I had left it, busy with trolley cars moving like insects along Flatbush Avenue and subway trains like caterpillars carrying passengers to and from Manhattan. There were fewer automobiles on the streets than before, due to gas rationing. The newspaperman selling papers in front of the local subway station greeted me like a long lost friend. I shoved my overseas cap to the back of my head and shifted my heavy green barracks bag from one shoulder to another. I walked up Ocean Avenue, with its six-story apartment houses on one side and Prospect Park, greening itself with the coming of spring, on the other.

I put my bag down, waiting, beads of perspiration gathering on my forehead. I carried the bag across the apartment house lobby, manhandled it up the three flights of stairs and onto the landing, where my mother Jean, father William, sister Helen Ruth, and grandfather Joe (Gramps), waited. Our initial awkwardness retreated before a genuine sense of belonging; joy and excitement remained. It was good to be home. And for the next 10 days, I reveled in my family's hospitality. Only my father knew what I was heading for; toward the end of my visit, he looked at me deeply and shook my hand, but said nothing.

When my leave ended without having seen Jeanie, who was working in Miami, I reported to Fort Meade, Maryland, a permanent Army base situated between Baltimore and Washington, D.C., for overseas assignment. After Blanding, Fort Meade was reassuring, expressing an air of permanence; one-day passes were available for either city, but I chose Washington, because some of my mother's relatives lived there. I knew them from the time I was four, when my family and I moved to Washington for a brief period during the Great Depression, a prolonged economic disaster that affected the whole nation. Of intense proportions, I carried the memory of that experience into the Army.

My Uncle Jack, who owned a Southern-style restaurant in the downtown district, treated me as 'one of the family' and refused payment for all of the delicious fried chicken dinners I ate there. There was no comparison between the food Uncle Jack and the Army served, but the steaks at Fort Meade were excellent and far ahead of anything served in Blanding. Uniformed women were in abundance, and I thought 'If you can't find beautiful service women in our nation's capital, where can you find them?' During my short stay at Fort Meade, feeling intimidated by Washington's corridors of military power, so close at hand, I didn't pursue my transfer to the PWB.

At the Fort Meade Rifle Range, I was able to set a personal best. Using a newly issued M-1, which was infinitely better than my original issue, I qualified with ease, hitting the bull's eye time and time again in whatever body position required. As a mass-produced weapon, my original M-1 might have been flawed, as I struggled to qualify as Marksman. With the second, I qualified for Sharpshooter, hitting the bull's eye repeatedly from all required positions at 500 yards. Without putting too fine a point on it, my new weapon seemed to have a positive sense of self.

I met Hal Sedloff, a New Yorker, at Fort Meade and realized soon after that he was ill-suited for the rigors of active military service. In the short time allotted, we became good friends. He was at least 8 years older than I, had poor eyesight, and was depressed and preoccupied about his young wife and new-born baby girl, left on their own in Manhattan. Thus, I was surprised that the Army not only had inducted him into the infantry but also planned to send him into action.

In early April, the equivalent of two companies of infantry, a total of 400 men, replacements all, wearing helmets, carrying rifles, and lugging long olive drab canvas barracks bags stuffed with Army gear, depart from Fort Meade's parade ground at first light on a freezing late winter's morning. Like so many other soldiers shipping out, I am an anonymous replacement, in transit, going to war. The men around me are strangers wearing the same uniform, a disciplined mob; each soldier is in search of a unit. I'm nothing more than the end product of an assembly line that, instead of stamping steel into cars, is trying to stamp civilians into soldiers by introducing them to a few basic concepts of military doctrine and a preliminary use of arms. In a race against time, quantity, not quality, prevails!

We traveled by train to Newport News, Virginia, our port of embarkation. No bands played when we left Fort Meade, boarded ship, or set sail. Our arrival and departure added little to the usual activity of a seaport at war. Amidst the dockside cranes, sailors in dungarees, oil slicks moving with the tide, ships — from tugboats to cruisers — and squawking seagulls, we boarded the *General Mann*, a large two-stack Army transport. Doused in grey paint, she was armed with two five-inch guns and smaller weaponry. We left, not as a band of brothers, but as a disparate group with no sense of belonging. To minimize my sense of loneliness and rising anxiety, I began to smoke, something I'd never planned to do.

The *General Mann*, because of her speed, could outrun German submarines lying in wait. Relying on high speed, like the Cunard Line's *Queen Mary* and *Queen Elizabeth*, the *General Mann* didn't require the protection of a naval escort. Loaded to the gunwales, the ship carried 5,000 soldiers who lounged topside or lined up everywhere, for everything — waiting to eat, to urinate, to sleep — usually measured in hours to complete. After a few days at sea, a U.S. Navy PBY *Catalina* twin-engine flying boat, like the aircraft that spotted the German battleship *Bismarck* in the North Atlantic, flew alongside us off the coast of Bermuda, circled, and left, confident that we were friendly and still afloat.

Our ship's gunners practiced daily; once they hammered at a derelict lifeboat drifting 200 yards off to starboard with their 20 mm and 40 mm cannons but failed to sink it. With everything going for them, a smooth sea, clear skies, close range, no counterfire, and unlimited visibility, their attempts left something to be desired. I thought. 'With shooting like this, we might have to take to the lifeboats just to save ourselves.' Skirting the Azores, the *General Mann* headed for the Straits of Gibraltar. As we approached the Straits, two American destroyers came tearing at us — at first only a smudge on the horizon, traveling at high speed, looming larger by the minute, tossing bow waves over their decks. Lining up abreast, they slowed, turned around, and took up stations to our front, on guard against lurking U-boats.

On a beautiful afternoon, escorted through the Straits, with the blue hills of Africa on one side and the Rock of Gibraltar dominating southern Spain on the other, a quartet from an artillery battalion travelling with us gathered 'round, and sang, among other songs, one filled with nostalgia, *I'll Be With You in Apple Blossom Time*, made famous by the Andrews Sisters, a singing group of three. It was one of the few times during my military career that it was I who should have paid the Army, and not the other way around, for such a memorable interlude. The transatlantic journey had turned into a Mediterranean cruise.

With so many men aboard ship, 'scuttlebutt' and its thematic variations concerning our destination reached endemic proportions. Some fellows broke away from their ceaseless crap games to place a bet on our going to Iran in the Persian Gulf.

The conversation went something like this, 'Where's that?' one GI paused momentarily, looking up from his crap game, clutching a wad of one dollar bills between the fingers of his left hand.

'In the Persian Gulf.'

'The what?' another GI nearby asked, throwing down his poker hand. 'I'm out.'

One of the onlookers, a known Lower New York Eastside kibitzer, volunteered, 'You know, Arabia, on the road to Zanzibar.'

'Naw, it's closer to India.'

'Five will get ya ten, you're wrong.'

Another street-smart GI chimed in, 'Done,' and dug into his pocket for more cash. Others placed money on Oran, Algeria, believing an 'O' was a better bet than an 'I'.

Ten days after leaving Virginia, we dropped anchor in Oran's harbor and a lot of money changed hands. With a pre-war population of 200,000, Oran was situated in a group of jagged mountains, 2,000 feet high. Above the harbor sat a medieval fort. The overall scene was Moorish, alien, and mysterious, and light-years away from the skyscrapers of Manhattan. Below, a moored battle-damaged French warship, listing to port, was being repaired, a possible casualty of the 1940 Anglo-French fleet battle of Mers-el-Kébir, a neighboring naval base.

Once ashore, we traveled by coach along a mountain road high above Oran to our destination, an Army transit camp adjoining the village of Canestel, 20 miles away. Both overlooked the Mediterranean from on high. Rumor had it that Canestel was one of the places where the Duke of Windsor, before he ascended to the throne of England, had pursued his love affair with the American heiress Wally Simpson before the war. He would abdicate his position as Edward VIII 'for the woman he loved' in December of 1936.

The views of the Mediterranean in one direction and the mountain landscape in the other were both spectacular in their immensity and color. The war seemed far away. One day, writing a letter to my father, I sat on a rock overlooking the sea. I tried to put the view into perspective. What seemed to be an ordinary-sized boulder was located in the middle distance, much like the one I sat on. Scanning the boulder from top to bottom, I made a startling discovery. A house nestled at its base! Immediately, I was struck by the sheer size of the African continent.

Oran was not a safe place for a soldier to enter on his own. Of the few who did, defying Army regulations, some were killed and wounded by marauding street Arabs brandishing knives. I did see the outcome of one knife attack, when a GI in need of immediate attention was delivered into the camp by Army ambulance. With blood dripping out the rear door, the wounded soldier lay unconscious.

Our interregnum ended two weeks later when we received shipping orders. A robust, red-nosed British sergeant and his British Army band lined up at one corner of the uneven pebbled parade ground. As we climbed on board the waiting trucks, the sergeant waved his band to life. Finding the right cadence on this sunny day, with the sergeant in the lead, the marching bandsmen played a stirring version of *The Colonel Bogie March*. It was 'enlistment entrapment' music, but I was already a soldier. Our two 6x6 trucks kicked up parade-ground dust as we rolled down to Oran's harbor and boarded a British ship, the *S.S. Strathnaver.*

The voyage from North Africa to Naples took four days, a journey in primitive conditions, outdoing the usual wartime privation. On board the *Strathnaver* — a former passenger ship that plied the South Seas in peacetime and later, in 1953 carried British Field Marshal Sir William Slim, late General Officer Commanding (GOC) 14th Army to his post as Governor-General of Australia — there were swaying hammocks instead of anchored bunks and most of the food was inedible. Standing in line for breakfast, I was served an unlikely mixture of fish, porridge, and sugar dumped into my open mess kit. I couldn't eat the slop or stand the smell, and I didn't. Aboard the *General Mann*, although we had to eat in shifts, there was some semblance of edible ingredients. Sugar wasn't mixed with butter or fish with porridge. Other meals suffered as well. The cold Argentine canned corned beef was barely edible and a poor replacement for those hot corned beef sandwiches served at Katz's Deli on Manhattan's Lower East Side. I avoided sleeping in the hammocks, dimly lit by red electric lamps set in black bulkhead fixtures around the sultry, smoky hold, not even fit for pirates. After one night below on this '18th-century prison hulk,' I moved topside and slept on deck from then on. I had to scrounge for something to eat.

We chugged past Sicily and the 10,000-foot snow-capped Mount Etna gleaming in the Mediterranean sunlight, the ship rocking from side to side like some punch-drunk boxer. On the fourth day, the *Strathnaver* trundled across smooth azure seas, sailed between the islands of Capri and Ischia, and cleared the Sorrento Peninsula, the roofs of its villas covered in a splash of red tiles and blossoming bougainvillea, before entering the bombed and battered port of Naples. A plume of dark smoke emanated from and drifted above Mount Vesuvius, which had recently erupted. Encircled by devastation at sea level, we disembarked on to one of a number of makeshift floating piers surrounded by half-sunken ships lying on their sides; shattered masts and superstructures protruded from the water, victims of German air raids. Indifferent to our passing, dark-eyed women, their thick black hair parted in the middle, sat on makeshift stools, openly breastfeeding their babies and begging for food.

Naples was under siege; the Luftwaffe attacked at night. At a dilapidated railway siding, its buildings destroyed from the air, we climbed onto shop-worn railway goods wagons reminiscent of the previous war's 40-men and 8-horses variety. Our destination was a cobbled replacement depot near the Royal Palace of Caserta, north of Naples. Although I didn't know it at the time, the palace, a huge Italian 'Versailles' built in 1762, housed the headquarters of the 15th Army Group, commanded by British Field Marshal Harold Alexander.

Unlike the field marshal, we, at the 'repple depot' were herded together like cattle, waiting for assignment to any one of a number of infantry divisions fighting across the Italian peninsula. I was adrift, alone and friendless as usual, in a sea of olive drab, feeling more like a living spare part. We lolled about, day after day, while rear echelon NCOs dashed from the compound's clapboard huts to call out names from a list of candidates. The procedure seemed more like a lottery than an administrative procedure. Our 'repple depple' at Caserta and the British World War I replacement center at Abbeville, France, known as the 'Bullring,' had much in common.

Without permission, I exited through the repple depple's barbed wire and explored the nearby countryside one afternoon and found a farm nearby. Its silo was surrounded by a high iron-mesh fence to which a sign was stapled. Below its painted black skull and crossbones were words in Italian I interpreted to mean that anyone caught climbing over the fence would be shot. I was disturbed by its severity because trespassing on someone else's property back home was a misdemeanor and subject to a fine, not death. Was the message a legacy of Mussolini's Fascist Italy, where real estate was more important than people? On further deliberation, had I stumbled upon the fenced edge of a minefield? I was wrong on both counts, I discovered later. An Italian-American soldier told me that it was nothing more than a warning regarding electric shock.

I don't remember being at Caserta for more than two weeks in May. Rumor had it that a big battle had begun; we witnessed the gun flashes lighting up the night sky in an incessant crackling and pounding artillery barrage on the Cassino front, midway between Naples and Rome and less than an hour's drive from our location. The noise and gun flashes reminded me of some of the barrages on the Western front I had seen on film. Called *Operation Diadem*, the action was a two-pronged Allied attack against those Germans defending Cassino and the Anzio beachhead, although I didn't know that at the time. Waiting ended when a sergeant yelled my name, along with 93 others. Feeling like ducks in a shooting gallery, we were assigned as replacements to the 36th Texas Division, one of the major infantry formations breaking out from Anzio, 84 miles northwest of Naples.

Two young recruits, Steve Weiss and Martin Wax, with M-1 rifles at
Camp Blanding, Florida. November 1943

3
Desolation and Betrayal

The 36th Infantry Division was a Texas National Guard division mobilized and federalized to serve as part of the U.S. Army in late November 1940. Soon after, it trained at Camp Bowie, Texas, participated in the Louisiana Maneuvers of 1941, and continued training in 1943 at Camp Blanding, Florida and Camp Edwards, Massachusetts. After landing at Oran, Algeria in April 1943, the 36th began amphibious training in preparation for Operation Avalanche, the invasion of Italy at Salerno on September 7, 1943. It was designated to be the first American combat division to land on the continent of Europe. Commanded by Major-General Fred L. Walker, its insignia consisted of an olive drab 'T' on a blue flint arrowhead and represented the Indian Territory of Oklahoma before it became a state; the 'T' stood for Texas.

Prior to its first series of battles, the original Texan cadre had great pride in the 36th, but hard luck dogged the division throughout the Italian Campaign of 1943–44, and morale suffered. Losses at Salerno, the Rapido River, and Cassino thinned their ranks. Most Texans disappeared from the rifle companies, their places filled by replacements from all over America.

The 143rd Infantry Regiment of the 36th, to which I was now assigned, literally was wiped out twice, the first time at the battle of San Pietro in December 1943 and at the Rapido River, one month later. Quoting in part from the divisional history, 'The bleakest chapter in the history of the 36th Division was their failed attempt to cross the Rapido River on 20 January, 1944; after trying to maintain a foot-hold on the north side of the river, the assault was called off on the 22nd.'

Having fought in bad weather against a well-prepared enemy, in which mined high ground and a swollen, overflowing river were part of the enemy defense, 143 men were killed, 663 were wounded, and 500 were captured by the 15th Panzer Grenadier Division. Eight hundred and seventy-five men were reported missing. Only in the relative safety of the division's rear did some of the original Texas cadre remain. Later, I learned that most infantry divisions suffered from 'hard luck,' simply because of their combat role. Now, in the summer of 1944, the 36th was preparing to enter battle again.

Without a hint or rumor, 24-hour furlough passes were canceled, as was British Battle Drill training, a system that taught men how to react under enemy fire at the platoon level. Commands of 'under fire,' 'down,' 'crawl,' 'observe,' 'fire,' and shouts of 'bullets, bullets, bullets,' 'charge,' and 'fix bayonets' were to evoke aggressive responses automatically, even if we were cold, tired, scared, and disoriented. I thought it was a waste of time. The black unit was transferred elsewhere. At mail call, I received a letter from home. My folks and I shared what news there was by V-Mail, a simple and expeditious way of communicating, with the use of microfilm as part of the process. We tried to keep each other's morale up, they by sharing home town news, and I by letting them know I was OK. Having read the letter, I felt homesick and idealized the life I had recently exchanged for my current one — a predictable response.

For one month, commencing on July 6, we began a series of amphibious training exercises that included attacking from landing craft on to 'enemy-held' beaches. Two combat engineers demonstrated the use of plastic explosive against barbed wire entanglements and reinforced steel and concrete pillboxes. After a day of practical exercises with Bangalore torpedoes, one soldier who witnessed the display held a dynamite cap filled with fulminate of mercury in his hand while taking a shower. Sensitive to body heat, the cap exploded and blew his hand off. The next day, the two engineers, lacking teaching skills and arrogant in manner, were killed demonstrating the use of plastic explosives to another group of soldiers. 'I'm not surprised,' Wohlwerth said. 'The job's too dangerous.'

Coupled with specialized amphibious training, our schedule included 25-mile hikes, the usual close-order drill and calisthenics, bayonet and rifle practice, and map reading. I never figured out why we had to continue the physical fitness side of training once we achieved tip-top shape. Our time could have been better spent. Rumor had it that we would participate in an invasion somewhere in the Mediterranean. For the next four weeks, during night and day exercises — some lasting up to 48 hours — we trained in every type of landing craft imaginable. Sizes varied, speed was essential. Sea smells mixed with diesel fumes. Below decks on the larger craft, the air was humid and still, and the drone of generators merged with the sounds of pounding turbines; blue engine exhaust dissipated on the breeze. LSTs (Landing Ship Tanks) loomed as large as Channel ferries and LCVPs (Landing Craft Vehicle and Personnel) looked as small as inner-harbor powerboats. Streams of armed men went over the sides of large LSTs and, facing inward, feeling their way down hemp cargo nets, they searched tentatively for footing on the designated small LCVPs below. Even in a smooth sea, the boats rocked, creaked, and bumped against each other, widening and lessening the gap between. Men that easily misjudged the heights and distances, particularly at night, were locked in a wet, dangerous, and shifting world. The possibility of breaking a leg or being crushed between boats was a major concern, but once we were aboard, the navy coxswain and his full complement of human cargo joined a circle of similar craft milling about. From eight miles out, signals were exchanged amidst shouted commands. The little boats peeled off, formed a line abreast, and then drove at full speed through the water to the far shore. Fifteen or more landing craft were timed to hit the beach together. They never did.

Our training destinations and times aboard ship varied; sometimes we practiced out in the Gulf of Salerno or sailed north of Naples into the Gulf of Gaeta, each time attacking an 'enemy-held' beach strewn with barbed wire and interlaced with concrete gun emplacements. Only enemy mine fields were missing. All units of the division participated in these realistic dry-run exercises, which included naval and air support, simulating the actual conditions to be met later. Live ammunition, white phosphorous shells, and naval gunfire, the laying of smoke screens, and the firing of rockets at the beach from landing craft all contributed to wartime reality. Bangalore torpedo and Bee Hive dynamite teams from each craft were responsible for the neutralization or destruction of the beach obstacles and pillboxes. Excluded, much to my surprise, were lectures giving specific details of our mission at the company level as well as teaching tools, such as maps and a diorama. Any Hollywood war film worth its salt always included them, but in reality, they were missing.

Although some of the landing craft hit the beach according to schedule during rehearsals, others, because of poor boat handling or problems at sea, did not, thereby jeopardizing the mission's success. This was one time when *timing was everything*. As a consequence of the non-synchronous landings, those companies that arrived late were exposed to the full force of an adjacent unit's explosions. Bangalore torpedoes, long slender metal pipes filled with dynamite, and bursting Bee Hives, satchel charges containing 30 pounds of explosive, blew up with resounding force. Jagged bits of barbed wire, bits of reinforced steel spikes, and concrete zinged through the air with invisible speed, adding to the confusion building up at the water's edge. As we lay bunched up on the wet sand, our legs half in and half out of the surf, a colonel, serving as monitor and observing our poorly timed efforts, kept shouting, 'You're prime targets. You'll never get off the beach alive! This is an absolute disaster!' We knew we needed more training, but time was running out as the assault-landing deadline loomed. It was the unforgiving moment all over again. I thought: 'In war, time is blood.' Exiting from the beach behind schedule, we'd work our way inland. Climbing forever upward on the hills overlooking the sea, we paused briefly to catch our breath or to take a swig of water. Our mission was to find a railroad line beyond the coastal range and secure it. Like beasts of burden, we found the work exhausting and unrewarding, but we were tough and in excellent physical shape.

Unlike the GI who threw up just from inhaling a boat's diesel fumes, I was never sick throughout my time at sea, regardless of the hour, weather, and type of craft. Eventually, Charlie Company was assigned to an ocean-going American-built LCI (Landing Craft Infantry), displacing 380 tons. It carried 200 troops or 75 tons of cargo, was 158 feet long, and fitted with catwalks on both sides of the bow; these could be lowered into the surf and used for unloading. Defensive armament was composed of 20 and 40 mm cannon. I don't recall its ship number, but an experienced British naval crew who had participated in the North African, Sicily, Salerno, and Anzio landings manned it. However, every time the skipper tried to run his boat onto the beach, we were dropped from the catwalks into water above our waists. We complained after each exercise, only to be told by one of the crew, 'Don't worry, mate, when we do this for real, you won't even get your feet wet.' The other crew members nodded in agreement, but we'd shout in disbelief.

Captain Simmons told us in early August that we were going to invade Southern France as part of an operation called 'Anvil-Dragoon.' The 36th would join two other veteran infantry divisions, the 3rd and 45th, who had fought alongside each other in Italy. They would constitute the American 7th Army under the leadership of Lt. General Alexander Patch, who had served successfully in the Guadalcanal campaign of

1942–43. French Army B would follow under French General Jean de Lattre de Tassigny. Later, in September 1944, it would be renamed the 1st French Army, swelling to eight combat divisions. Our immediate objective was to liberate that part of France under enemy control. We would attempt to crush the defending German 19th Army in the process. The French beach was supposed to be physically similar to the Italian one we trained on. Staff Sergeant Harry Shanklin, our squad leader from New Jersey, being fed up with straight infantry combat, had volunteered for the paratroopers and was accepted. He trained with us while awaiting his airborne reassignment orders.

British paratroopers came to visit. These men from the 2nd Independent Parachute Brigade, wearing their distinctive red berets and battle smocks and temporarily assigned to the American 517th parachute regiment and the 509th parachute battalion, were to drop inland beyond the invasion beaches on D-1. Through the introduction, we hoped to limit any casualties from friendly fire (later known as 'blue on blue') during the planned link-up between airborne and ground forces once the beachhead was established. These men impressed me because they represented the highest degree of fighting spirit and cooperation. Volunteers all, they were exceptionally well trained and organized, an effective and specialized fighting force. We familiarized ourselves with their uniforms, their equipment, and weaponry — the Lee Enfield No. 4 rifle, the Enfield No. 2 Mkl revolver, the Sten MkII submachine gun, the Sten Mk5 submachine gun, the No. 36 Mills grenade, the PIAT Anti-Tank weapon, the Bren light machine gun, and the 2-inch mortar. They demonstrated the rapid-fire effectiveness of their weaponry on a rifle range nearby.

I recognized that ever since our meeting with the British paratroopers, I had felt uneasy. The only weapon with which I was familiar was my M-1 rifle, admitting that my ability to use an array of weapons, similar to those just displayed and fired, was non-existent. As in Italy, preparation for an introduction to combat, Blanding's basic training, and the 36th together had let me down. How in hell was I going to survive the cut and thrust of combat so poorly prepared? With my confidence hitting a low ebb, I felt depressed. To make matters worse, separate from the chaos experienced during the amphibious exercises, I felt distracted by the lack of teamwork within the squad. The required minimum of squad cohesion, a mutually supportive and protective factor, was not achieved for a variety of reasons; one was the infusion of replacements, another was Simmons's lack of leadership, and a third was Shanklin's wish to transfer. We were adrift, and it seemed to me that our squad was a reflection of a conscripted, entrepreneurial American wartime army, with every man for himself. Amateurs, whatever our attempts!

Before we left Italy, I went over to find a friend in B Company, bivouacked nearby. I immediately sensed a change in morale and mood between Charlie and Baker's officers and men. One small group was sitting on the sand with the CO, reminiscing about former comrades. My friend and I joined the group and sat down to listen. The conversation was easy-going; the CO aware, accessible, and friendly; the men relaxed, appreciative, and respectful. Part of their talk was about their former CO, Captain Henry T. Waskow, a beloved and legendary leader, killed at age 25 by a sniper at Cassino a few months before. Ernie Pyle, a well-known newspaperman, had written about Captain Waskow in a recent article. (Ernie Pyle was killed in the Pacific the following year). When I left, I told my friend that this was the kind of team spirit lacking in Charlie Company.

Pozzuoli, a small, poor fishing village west of Naples, noisy and self-absorbed, was selected as our port of embarkation. The village, until now overlooked by raiding planes or attacking armies, was transformed. Thousands of soldiers, beasts of burden carrying their accoutrements of war, filed into its port area, where a score of landing craft (LCIs), rode at anchor rather than local fishing boats. One popular photograph of the embarkation, taken from a tall building overlooking the port, reveals a circle of men gathered around a soldier lying on the ground. What is not revealed in the photo, taken from that height, is that the soldier was suffering from a grand mal epileptic fit. I was part of that circle, by sheer accident.

On August 12, our British LCI weighed anchor with Charlie Company on board and slowly motored out of the harbor to take up station with other ships steaming away from the Italian coast. Everywhere, LSTs and LCIs bobbed and weaved, diminutive armored metal strands cutting through the gentle swells. The blue-green summer sea sparkled. Navigating through the Straits of Bonifacio, between the mountainous headlands of Sardinia and Corsica, our convoy anchored off on Corsica's west coast. Two hundred miles beyond lay our destination, the coast of Southern France. From two miles off shore, on a bright summer's morning that accentuated the red-tiled roofs of Ajaccio, our landing craft rolled gently on the swell. Founded by the Genoese in 1492 and remembered as the birthplace of Napoleon, Ajaccio is nestled against the broom-covered hills leading to its mountainous interior. Some of us stripped on deck and leaped into the clear blue water 20 feet below. Swimming and cavorting in the bay as playful as dolphins, it was hard to believe that over the horizon a war was raging. We emerged from the sea, climbing hand over hand to the deck above, our wet bodies glistening in the sun, the interlude over. It was great to be alive!

Relaxation gave way to a persistent ache in my stomach, evoking thoughts of the invasion to come. I turned to Dickson and Reigle, two of the old hands in my squad. The conversation went something like this:

'Will we survive?'

'Who knows?'

'What will the opposition be like?'

'Could be severe, if the fighting in Italy is any guide.'

'Will we get off the beach on time?'

'Not likely, if our rehearsals mean anything.'

The answers to these questions were only hours away, but the waiting seemed interminable; while pacing the deck, the tightness in my stomach increased. It never dawned on me to write a last letter home in case I were killed, nor did I carry a lucky charm like a rabbit's foot to ward off personal destruction, admitting that survival could not be guaranteed. Plans end when the battle is joined, and the Montgomerys and Eisenhowers of this world must wait until the decisive battle is won or lost by the combat soldier at the 'sharp end.' We were motivated to win the war and go home as quickly as possible. Strange that helpful information regarding the preceding Normandy landings was not shared with the lower echelons of our invasion force, although a number of the warships steaming with us had engaged the enemy off Omaha and Utah beaches.

Instead, we received American flag brassards, a booklet entitled *A Pocket Guide to France*, boxed rations for the first five days, and two packs of cigarettes. I had endless conversations with Dickson concerning the landing, which only increased a sense of mutual foreboding and of being held hostage to our fears. Harry Shanklin sailed with us as squad leader, disappointed that his transfer to the airborne had not been expedited. Rumor had it from one of the sailors on board that the initial stages of the Normandy invasion had not gone well and a prominent naval officer had committed suicide. Off Omaha, the boats and tanks were launched too far from shore in heavy and stormy seas, and many of the men landed on the wrong beaches, seasick and confused; casualties were high, men drowned on the incoming tide or died at the water's edge, caught in enfilade and cross-fire. Having recently assessed our own amphibious attempts as doubtful at best, I wasn't at all surprised at this news, if true.

Weighing anchor off Corsica on August 14, we took up station with the other units of the invasion fleet. It was one of the few times in which I experienced the magnitude of American power. It was awesome. I say one of the few times, because I had seen this kind of raw, overwhelming power in Italy. Hundreds of bomber and fighter aircraft, B-17s, B-24s, P-38s, and P-51s of the 12th and 15th Air Forces, taking off from the airfields around Foggia, east of Naples, filled the air with crashing noise and nearly blotted out the sun on their way north to attack enemy installations. From the deck of my LCI, turning in any direction I saw warships of every description, from battleships to attack transports to PT boats. Having come from various Mediterranean ports, more than 800 ships sailed toward the invasion beaches on the French coast. Deck-loaded on this fleet were more than 1,200 landing craft.

Early the next morning, August 15, all was grey: the ships, the sea, and the sky. Visibility was four miles, hazy and improving, with a gentle shifting wind and negligible sea. We raced through a swarm of cargo ships standing five miles from, and at right angles to, the French coast, noting our passage and waiting for us to secure the beaches before they moved closer in shore to unload. We weaved between cruisers and destroyers, charging like greyhounds, firing their 8- and 5-inch guns in support of the landings. The American battleship *Texas* hammered the shore with its bevy of ten 14-inch guns. Each time the guns fired, a massive yellow-red muzzle flash and shattering explosion followed. The *Texas*, displacing a massive 27,000 tons, reacted as if it were stung, wallowing and rocking from the combined recoil, and slapping the sea before righting itself. I actually watched its black 2,000-pound projectiles, tossed pieces of luggage, flying through the air. Against this merging canvas of sea and sky, other Allied warships, the *Arkansas*, the *Tuscaloosa*, the *Brooklyn*, and the *Emile Bertin*, fired their powerful guns at the enemy fortifications on the beach and at unseen targets deeper inland, the crack of their explosions adding to the existing dissonance.

Large formations of Allied fighters, part of their wings painted in the black-and-white striped invasion insignia, patrolled above the beaches, protecting us from enemy air attack, while twin and four-engine bombers droned inland to attack enemy targets of opportunity. Just before we hit the beach, specially equipped landing craft (LCRs) streaked in front of our flotilla and blasted enemy shore emplacements with thousands of rockets, creating a high-pitched swooshing sound on take-off. The sound was deafening, a cacophony of banging frying pans, the neutral sky a mixture of yellow-red explosions and black spiraling smoke trails. Cordite stung our nostrils. Exploding German shells from 88s and 105s sent geysers of seawater skyward. Hidden enemy machine gunners on the bluffs above the shore fired across the beach, their Mg 42s firing at the rate of 1,300 rounds per minute and generating immense defensive firepower.

Our landing craft jolted across the Gulf of Frejus, toward the invasion beach east of Saint Raphaël, as part of the tenth wave. Off to starboard, a small volcanic island, the Isle d'Or, loomed a short distance away; on it was perched a fortified crenellated medieval tower of questionable origin, fortuitously unmanned by the enemy. Beyond, past Cape Dramont and its semaphore tower, as the coast curved away, rising steeply in height to the east, were the sea-girded, red porphyry cliffs of the Esterel Mountains. They were thickly covered in pine and cork forests, and we had been told that a scenic road, the Corniche d'Or, ran through them to the seaside playground of Cannes.

The LCI's hull grated on the rocky beach between St. Raphaël and Agay at 09:45. As soon as the craft's two parallel ramps tilted toward the surf, we moved along their length and onto the beach. The Brits delivered; my shoes were dry. The axiom that experienced invasion troops follow is: 'get off the beach fast,' but it's tough enough trying to move at all when you're loaded down with 90 pounds of equipment. Enemy machine gun fire slowed momentarily. Our beach was in a small cove, surrounded by rust-colored hills covered with pine. A coast road and a railroad line ran parallel to each other about 200 yards above us. There were few houses. Tracers from well-placed German machine guns zipped outward from the beach. Enemy shells exploded at the water's edge and into the sea. After the opening stages of the battle, German opposition ebbed and became sporadic and isolated.

My personal infantry baggage consisted of webbing and leather straps supporting bandoleers of 30-caliber ammunition, a canteen, medical kit, and two hand grenades, all of which clinked, rocked, and bumped against me in the increasing sunlight. Although a First Scout, I had landed carrying a 78-pound fully loaded two-tank flame-thrower, a weapon that sprayed a long stream of burning napalm at a temperature of 2,000° F. I volunteered to haul it off the beach for another GI whose newly discovered back pain had stopped him from further action. The closer we got to the French coast, the worse his back problem became.

I was given no instruction whatsoever, so as a weapon it was useless in my hands. Both he and I knew the potential danger inherent in flame throwers: if a bullet or shell fragment penetrated either of the tanks and ignited the napalm (the highly flammable petroleum jelly made from naphthalene and coconut oil) within, I would have been converted into an unrecognizable fragmented part of the French coast rather than re-maining an active participant of Camel Force (our code name for the landing). Although I didn't qualify, the most hated man in an outfit was usually assigned the flamethrower. Bad Back's guilty smile and in-formative shrug confirmed my suspicions soon after, but before I could square the account, Simmons sent him home for being underage.

German JU-88 twin-engine light bombers hit LST 282 with radio-con-trolled bombs in a daylight raid soon after we landed. I witnessed the ship's superstructure disappear in a tremendous explosive flash that killed and wounded 40 sailors. LST 282 burned for hours. A pall of smoke hovered above and, from its interior, ammunition popped and cracked for hours. Later, above the beach, standing beside the open turret of a Sherman medium tank, we listened to fragments of a Bing Crosby-Bob Hope Armed Forces radio show on its receiver. The tank-ers were arrogant, having little time or patience for the 'dog-faced' guys like us. Revving their engines, they sped away, leaving us choking in a cloud of dust beside the road and crashed seconds later, 70 yards further along. We raced to help. The driver had lost control, causing the tank to tip over at an extreme angle, with one track slowly rotating in the air; there were casualties — the tank driver broke his arm, the gunner, his ankle; we administered first aid but felt the tankers had it coming.

On the coast road, an overzealous artillery truck driver had overturned his 105 mm howitzer, causing a 3-mile traffic jam that stretched all the way back to the beach and delayed the movement of heavily laden motorized transport, tanks, and guns coming off the beachhead in increasing numbers. The division's rifle companies' advance slowed. As if rising from the ground, a black North African soldier with flashing white teeth, wearing a French helmet, his legs wrapped in puttees, joined our troupe. With a warm and friendly personality, a born hunter of small animals and men, carrying a long curved dagger, he offered his services. We accepted, he joined us on patrol, but disappeared as mysteriously as he had appeared a few days later.

We took comfort in knowing that two other veteran divisions, the 3rd and the 45th, had landed to our left, followed by units of the First French Army. On D-1, French Commandos, the 1st Special Service Force of Americans and Canadians, the British 2nd Independent Parachute Brigade, and the 1st Airborne Task Force had landed during the night, seeking a variety of objectives. Finding them and linking up was another matter.

Our regiment traveled west and captured sun-drenched St. Raphaël, a town and seaside resort on the Côte d'Azure favored by British and American tourists before the war. The early morning haze gave way to afternoon blue, and moderate sea breezes softened the sun's intensity. An attractive homeowner observed our armored passage as she watered her garden. The birds sang. During a momentary lull in the fighting, my squad relaxed next to a pillbox defending a small iron bridge, minutes away from the town's famous beach-lined tourist hotels visible in the middle distance. Even the architecture of the town's cathedral, Notre Dame de la Victoire, seemed lighthearted, less Catholic. At the same moment that I drank from my canteen, a lone enemy shell roared through our air space and exploded against the pill box 20 feet away. The explosion destroyed the concrete, ripped away the interior metal rods, and shattered Private Truman Ropos's right leg. For him, as for all of us, the difference between heaven and hell was measured in inches. The dust hadn't settled before he disappeared on a canvas stretcher under a pile of olive drab blankets, carried by two medics. The third medic performed a balancing act by holding a bottle of plasma above the pile, its hollow line attached to one exposed arm. At 18, Truman's war ended abruptly, and shaken by the loss, with one man short, we gathered our gear and moved out. Truman's shattered leg was amputated later that day.

Skirting the beach, on the western suburbs of St. Raphaël, we captured the local airfield in a brief firefight and cut the east-west railroad line that ran through a viaduct. Enemy planes caught on the ground were set alight and destroyed by rifle fire. We ran into sporadic resistance and took some prisoners who knew that 'For you the war is over.' They seemed dispirited and confused as they shuffled to the rear, some without tunics or insignia, their suspenders and underwear showing, some with their arms in the air, others with their hands clasped behind their heads, submissive, compliant. One young soldier smiled at me in relief. How different were they from the Afrika Korps prisoners I had guarded in late '43 as a raw recruit at Blanding, an arrogant lot believing that Nazi world domination was only months away.

Ordered north, we attacked through Fréjus, causing little damage to that Roman town or its ancient amphitheater and bull ring. We trekked into the dry hills beyond. There were some small firefights in which we surprised the Germans, but in one mêlée we received word that our squad's two-man rocket launcher 'bazooka' team' was trapped in a gully. I volunteered to help, but others were chosen. The attempt failed, and we never saw the bazooka team again. As a defense against their loss, I downplayed the episode. The rumor was that they had either been captured or killed.

According to Simmons, Anvil-Dragoon, a well-executed amphibious operation, was thus far considered a success. Our invasion forced General Wiese's German 19th Army, defending the region, to retreat or risk encirclement and destruction.

I led the climb to the top of the hill, the rest of the squad strung out behind. Where the canvas straps of my combat pack crossed my shoulders, my shirt was drenched in sweat. Everyone was tense and hypervigilant. Equipment jiggled, boots scraped, but no undue chatter or horseplay prevailed within the squad. Appropriate intervals were kept because bunching up created hazards and offered easy targets to snipers. We took a 10-minute break but didn't smoke, feeling the enemy was watching.

It was a glorious Provençal morning of intense shadows and shimmering highlights reflecting off the damp rocks and scrub. We were like farm hands 'shooting the breeze,' taking a well-deserved break, distinguished only by our uniforms and the rifles we carried. Taylor and Reigle sat a few feet across from Wohlwerth and me on a rocky outcrop near some trees. Trying to get comfortable, Wohlwerth accidentally banged the butt of his rifle on the ground. The rifle grenade loaded at the end of the rifle barrel hurled across the short intervening space and slammed into Taylor's mouth with great force-without exploding. The blow drove him backwards, the front of his mouth distorted from the head-on collision, while teeth fragments and bits of flesh flipped through the air. Simultaneously, we rushed across the short intervening space to Taylor's side, appalled at the sight and his bad luck. A writhing Taylor, treated by the medics, was carried down the hill and evacuated, never to return. The war was chipping away at us in an insidious manner. It remains a mystery why the grenade didn't explode, killing all of us.

On August 17, as the Germans retreated to the northeast, we liberated Draguignan, a dusty market town and regional capital, whose 20,000 newly liberated citizens rejoiced. French women who had recently consorted with the enemy had their heads shaved publicly. Even so, it was more like a Broadway musical than an act in war. Nevertheless, the gaiety had a darker side. A local farmer showed me a two-pound, jagged, razor-sharp, 5x7x2 inch piece of shrapnel. USA was engraved on one side. It was part of a U.S. Navy ship's artillery barrage, the shells of which had exploded on his farm two days before. I offered to buy the piece of steel with cigarettes, but he declined. It was too good a souvenir to part with. I agreed.

With enemy defenses crumbling, the war became one of movement, and early the next morning we mounted trucks, traveling northeast in a powerful armored convoy on Highway N-85, the same mountain road Napoleon traveled in 1815, to seize the Castellane road above Grasse. There was an aroma of roses and lavender in the clear, bright air; perfume was manufactured in the region. On August 18, with Task Force Butler — consisting of mobile infantry, tanks, and artillery — probing for the enemy ahead, we continued our pursuit toward Gap. As we mounted our big 6x6 trucks on August 20, I thought that we were taking the land portion of a Mediterranean cruise through the lower Alps.

Compared to the coastal mountains and plateaus of Inner Provence, we traveled through a land more mountainous and barren at its higher elevations. I felt small among the rows of huge stone needles outlined against the intense blue sky. Armed Frenchmen of the Resistance, dressed in baggy trousers and ill-fitting mismatched suit jackets, some with home-made cigarettes dangling from their lips and holding obsolete rifles in their hands, protected our route and the heights above the Route Napoleon. During our mountain advance, serving as an early warning system, they minimized the threat of German counterattacks, ambushes, and blocking tactics. Traveling on, doing 144 kilometers in 14 hours, our column wound its way through the majestic beauty of the lower Alps and searched for an enemy that continued to retreat.

Instead, villagers and townspeople clustered beside the road and waved, shouted words of encouragement, and tossed flowers in one kaleidoscopic blur as we sped by. If we paused for a moment's respite, our shirts bathed in sweat and covered with dust, our mouths parched with thirst, they would run to greet us, arms outstretched, with tears of joy streaming down their cheeks. Four years of emotional depriva-tion expressed itself in a volcanic surge of feeling, which engulfed us all. I was hugged and kissed by people of all ages until my face and ribs ached. When I shared my rations with them or made small talk with pretty girls of my own age, the melancholy of war seemed very far away. Amidst their wine and our cigarettes, against a backdrop of olive-green tanks and trucks, we struggled for the appropriate words in either language that somehow never expressed or matched the mo-ment. It was ineffable. When all of the towns along the highway — Cas-tellane, Digne, Sisteron, and Gap — were set free in four days, the spirit of Libération was sublime.

We came as liberators, not as emperors, but the acclaim we received was comparable. When our motorized column rumbled into Grenoble on August 22, thousands of people filled the streets to greet us, a huge exuberant crowd shouting its welcome, rejoicing in its freedom. French flags waved triumphantly above the throng. The citizens of this old university city, surrounded by snow-covered mountains and hemmed in by two bustling rivers, invited us to join with it in joyous celebration. It was a day like no other. But the Army had other ideas and billeted us in a caserne, containing a series of two-story stucco barracks sur-rounded by a high stone wall. I resented the decision; disliking the idea of being isolated from the townspeople, I searched for a way to escape. Dickson and I found an old, possibly forgotten, rusty iron door, falling off its hinges, embedded in the stone wall. It gave way to our touch, opening easily but noisily as we stepped into the street.

Walking along, we approached a baker's shop on the opposite side. Housewives were lined up, waiting for their turn to enter. They watched us advance in awe, fell silent; as we came closer, the women, of all ages, broke into spontaneous applause. On cue and in the spot-light, we smiled and waved back, enshrined in the glory of the moment; they, in turn, shouted greetings in French, mingled with a few words of fractured English. We were conquering heroes keeping step with the sound of their applause that followed us on our journey. An insistent tapping sound intruded. From a second-story window an attractive young woman tapped and beckoned. Believing French women were amorous, we concluded we were going to be rewarded for our heroism, an opportunity not to be missed. With an eye for romance, we took the narrow stairs two at a time. A simply dressed, slender, dark-haired woman in her late 20s opened the door in greeting. The room was empty of furniture except for a standing corner cupboard, with a mullioned glass upper front, tilting ominously on the rough-hewn floor. A closer look revealed a scarecrow of a man standing silently next to the cupboard in the half-light; six or seven wrinkled potatoes were cast about its base. The woman spoke in simple, halting English, choosing her words carefully, shy in our presence. Although my French was extremely limited, I understood her to say that the silent man standing next to her, in his ill-fitting trousers and threadbare wool jacket, was her husband. This wasn't what I expected. Damn! 'Ever since the German Occupation,' she continued, 'he longed for the day when the Americans would come.' With his four-year ordeal over, Dickson and I stood there at the beginning of his freedom. The husband's thin face reflected a subdued excitement, and he nodded imperceptibly in agreement, as if the slightest movement sapped his energy.

The young woman went to the cabinet, disclosing a large bottle of cognac, hoarded for this liberating moment, empty except for a thimbleful of the amber liquid at its bottom. She found four small glasses, gave each of us one, and then poured a molecular amount until the bottle was empty, except for the liquor's oil, a residue that clung to the inside of the bottle in long descending streaks. She lifted her glass and proposed a toast in French. As we lifted our glasses in response, the man burst into tears and began sobbing. The woman reached out to comfort him, pressing her cheek against his, taking his hand and muttering words of compassion; his silence now ended, the slow 'drum-beat' ritual over, she explained that he had saved the cognac for four years, awaiting this moment, never doubting we would come. We licked rather than sipped the liquid from our glasses. Overcome by their humanity and the solemnity of the occasion, Dickson and I said little. Embracing the man and woman, we slowly retreated down the stairs, and after regaining the sunlight, soon reverted to our self-absorbed adolescent behavior.

Yes, in all of this emotion and jubilation, I was a young and willing participant, and the war seemed to end in this momentary triumph.

Grenoble was in the midst of celebrating its liberation publicly. Hordes of men and women strode arm in arm singing and drinking champagne. Strangers, citizens all, embraced each other; they stood at in café and bar and toasted each other's health and liberty. As for Dickson and I, we agreed that cycling was needed to serve as an antidote to war and Army discipline. We found a shop owner who willingly put two bikes at our disposal and said, 'The Germans took my bicycles without paying; take them without charge, just return them when you're finished. It's the least I can do.' Off we rode, into the center of Grenoble, chasing a day that was like a Mardi Gras carnival and July 4th holiday combined.

For those French willing to translate, it was a fun fair moment, a fête folle. We cycled from one café to another, revelers barring the way, plying us with thirst-quenching red wine from the nearby slopes. A mixture of French and English, combined with an impromptu pantomime, added to the conversations between the liberators and the liberated. When the light began to fade, we returned the bicycles and rejoined the crowds on streets illuminated by the flames of numerous bonfires. Fantastic shadows were cast on the glowing buildings, adding a mysterious medieval quality to the joyous spectacle, an unending Saturnalia. I never knew — nor was it ever mentioned in basic training — that, in the midst of war jubilation of this magnitude could be one of war's outcomes. In the early hours of the morning, after a night of revelry, we lay on the concrete forecourt, protected from above by a gas station's overhead extension. Liberation required further understanding. Before falling asleep, I couldn't help feeling that, to survive, an infantry soldier either must be fighting or training, not reveling.

The following morning, August 23, Dickson and I hitched a ride on a jeep into the center of Grenoble. Driving along the Boulevard Gambetta, as the jeep slowed in traffic, I noticed Reigle and two other soldiers drinking coffee with three attractive French girls on the terrace of an elegant sidewalk café. Relieved that Dickson and I weren't the only ones who had taken off, we abandoned the jeep to join -them in their banter and 'devil-may-care' attitude. Our lighthearted repartee turned serious when one of the men said that the outfit had pulled out earlier that morning, destination unknown. One soldier reacted to the information lightheartedly but was met by a chorus of: 'C'mon! Get serious!' The majority concluded that we ought to head out immediately and find them. No one made a move.

This was unknown territory for me, and I remember saying 'Sure, but let's finish our coffee and pastry first. It might be a helluva long time before we eat this well again and in such company.' Dickson winked at the girls and had them write down their names and addresses. Concern arose. What might Simmons's reaction be to our going absent without leave (AWOL)? Were we in serious trouble? Teenagers all, French and American, it was hard breaking away. Leisurely, but with growing concern, we ambled out of town in twos and threes, a tribe of ragtag chimpanzees moving in a northerly direction. Having walked out of the caserne the day before, leaving our equipment behind, we were unarmed, with nothing more than the clothes on our backs. The terrain ahead was uncharted territory.

Flagging down a White M-3 half-track armored personnel carrier with a crew of three at a suburban crossroad, we convinced the driver, a corporal from Alabama, to take us on board. Impatient, in one synchronous move, he gunned the engine, released the brakes, shifted into gear, stepped on the gas, and charged down the winding, narrow mountain road at high speed. 'Fire away, buckeroo,' one of us yelled.

When the half-track leaped forward, I grabbed the barrel of the .50 caliber Browning machine gun, locked to its stanchion behind the cab, and held on. With siren blaring and headlights flashing, we left Grenoble, breaking the speed limit within the first 60 seconds. Farewell to the brake pedal; it didn't exist for the driver.

Chickens beat the air with their wings as they leapt out of the way of the oncoming iron monster; mothers frantically grabbed their children in fear, pressing them to their breasts or shoving them against the nearest village wall, shouting defiantly, '*Scorpion de la route!*' Clenched female fists rose up against him. In the rear of the half-track, we tossed from side to side with every curve of the road, holding on as best we could, shouting, 'Steady as she goes,' while the vehicle raced on like an amusement park roller coaster, the wind whistling through the canvas. Two hours and 45 miles later, 'Wild Bill Cody,' our driver, slowed at a T-junction, allowing us no more than a split second to abandon ship. Jumping over the side, I was sure I heard him yell, 'Hi Ho, Silver,' as he sped away in a cloud of dust. So what if this were the Rhône River Valley? Charlie Company was nowhere in sight.

The dirt track cut through flat empty scrubland; halfway to the horizon, two young women raced toward us on their bicycles, skirts billowing over sun-drenched thighs. Standing in the middle of the road with legs apart and arms outstretched, I signaled them to stop as the others gathered around. They skidded to a halt, smiled, and greeted us in French. The 'Beautiful One' of the two said that the night before, many Americans had marched through her town, Romans. She heard them while lying in bed. 'I ran down stairs, opened the front door, and kissed every soldier who went by.'

'Well,' I said, 'I'm a day late, but I'm here to collect my kiss.' She reached across the handlebars, placed her hand behind my neck, and kissed me on both cheeks. That did it! For me the war was over; I wanted this woman.

I turned toward her and said, 'Hey! I've got an idea. Let's have a picnic.' The others agreed and moved closer; the girls giggled, nodding their heads in affirmation.

The Beautiful One spoke. 'Romans is only five kilometers from here. Before we return, we shall buy baguettes, sausage, cheese, and fruit.' She looked at me and asked, 'What is your name?'

'Stephen,' I answered, feeling somewhat out of breath.

As they cycled away, Reigle called, 'Don't forget the wine.'

We were lounging on the grass when Colonel Paul Adams, commanding officer of the 143rd, of which Charlie Company was a part, and an entourage of six jeeps drove by. We started to rise. 'There goes our afternoon rendezvous,' Dickson whispered. But the colonel and his driver ignored us; however, just as I thought we had escaped, a junior second lieutenant riding in the last jeep ordered his driver to stop, stood up, and asked, 'Who's in charge here?'

Reigle stood up, trying to smooth out his trousers before approaching the lieutenant. 'Hell, soldier! Move when I say so.' Reigle saluted and stood at attention. We gathered around.

'What outfit?' the lieutenant inquired.

'Charlie Company. We're lost, Sir.'

The officer fumed. 'Where the hell are your rifles and helmets?'

'Don't know, Sir; we got separated.'

'Oh yeah?' he eyed us suspiciously. 'I'll find your outfit. Charlie Company, you say? Hop on the jeep.'

'Where to, Sir?' Reigle asked.

'Smart'n up soldier, or I'll have you charged with insubordination and court-martialed,' the lieutenant warned. 'Your CO and I are gonna have a little chat once we get to the RCP (Regimental Command Post) to find out what the hell's going on,' he replied sardonically. 'As far as I'm concerned, you guys are in deep shit.'

'God! Where did the Army ever find a lieutenant like this?' I mused, shaking my head behind his back.

From the CP, an isolated stone farmhouse on the scrubland, the junior officer rang Simmons. 'Hold them there for pick up,' Simmons shouted over the phone.

We lounged around for about 20 minutes when the company driver arrived in his jeep and trailer. After we loaded up, he headed for the company CP with all of us piled on board.

'How's the Capt'n, today?' one of the others asked.

'Hard to know, really. He holds his cards pretty close to his vest, if you get my drift.'

Simmons emerged from a farm building buttoning his shirt and walked toward us in silence as we dismounted. He raised one hand in greeting as the jeep driver shifted gears and drove off. We stood at attention and saluted. He shook the salutes off with an indifferent shrug of his shoulders, like a duck flicking water, and in a rather matter-of-fact, non-threatening voice, said, 'Gather around, guys.'

I thought, 'Hey, he's not sore!' I relaxed and thought of the woman I'd just met.

Then his voice rose, his tone strident; he exploded, and his words ripped across us like a cat o'nine tails. 'If one of my men had been killed while you were playing heroes to all those French babes, I'd have you up before a general court-martial and charged with *Article of War 107, Desertion Before the Enemy*. He threatened, 'Get it right and get it straight; desertion is punishable by death by firing squad.'

He waited for the penalty to sink in. 'No half measures, see! A dishonorable discharge and a long prison sentence would be too good for screw-ups like you. You're in contempt; you've lowered the morale of my company, failed the other men, and in your absence put them under additional pressure against the enemy.' Finally, he said, 'Your squad leaders will set the punishment, but remember this, if you ever step out of line again, I'll have your ass in such a sling you won't know what hit you. The equipment you left behind, I'm charging against you. See supply sergeant for equipment!' He shouted, 'Dismissed,' turned, re-entered the farmhouse, and slammed the door. We stood there waiting for orders. Although he gave us an 'ass-chewing,' Simmons made his point and 'saved face.' He also let us off the hook.

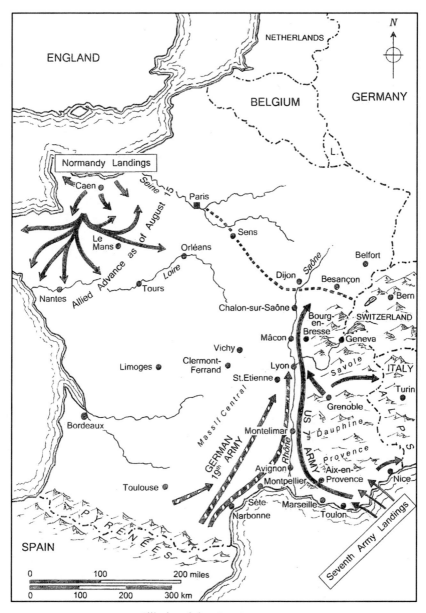

Allied activity, Summer 1944

4

Night Attack

Staff Sergeant Shanklin and the rest of the squad were lounging in a ditch on one side of a straight secondary road surrounded by farmland, their conversation interrupted by the sound of distant explosions. From the same westerly direction, at the horizon, a pall of black smoke rose in the air and drifted above the town of Valence, as indicated on our Michelin map. Some of the men believed that the Germans were attempting to destroy the town and whatever supplies they couldn't move before they pulled out. Shanklin, not to be deterred by the noise and smoke, looked at Dickson, Reigle, and me, and shook his head in a mixture of disgust, anger, and pity.

Derisively, he addressed us as 'The Lover Boys.' He wasted no time chewing us out and reprimanded us for taking off, leaving him high and dry without a word of warning. Shanklin mocked us: only amateurs leave their rifles and equipment behind! Simmons had accused him of poor leadership by allowing three of his men to disappear and was warned to get a grip, take charge, or else. Reigle, Dickson, and I remained silent. Now Shanklin sounded more hurt than angry by our betrayal. He demanded we check with him before attempting to do anything so stupid again. The three of us apologized. I felt foolish and contrite, as did the others. Shanklin was a 'right' guy, doing a job he didn't want, waiting to transfer to the airborne, and we 'nut-cases' added to his burdens. He said, 'You'll have to be punished,' but I knew that this 'reaming out' was as far as he would go. The matter was closed.

Valence had to be taken because it was an important rail and road net of tactical importance. During the late morning of August 24, Charlie Company was ordered to attack. The men mounted three open-turret M-10 tank destroyers (TD) armed with a 76 mm cannon and a 50-caliber machine gun, pointing west on D-68, the Chabeuil-Valence two-lane departmental road. Light and fast, better in defense, the TDs lacked armor protection. Whenever possible, I sat on a TD's left front side; the rest of the squad followed, finding their own places on the armored chassis. Three or four minutes later, the company runner rushed over, shouting above the noise of the idling twin diesel engines, 'Change of orders!' he thumbed his finger at me. 'Move your squad on to the second TD.' Irritated by an order that didn't make any sense, I jumped off the first TD and relocated on the second.

While we were waiting, one of the TD's three-man crew offered me a cigarette. I noticed there was a large gouge on the top of his turret. 'Thazright!' He told me that his tank commander, a lieutenant, was standing with his head above the turret when a 'Jerry' shell skipped across the top of it. The unseen shell gouged the turret, severed the lieutenant's head, and kept on going. The rest of him fell into the tank. His head was never found. He thought an 88 mm killed the lieutenant and caused the damage, because of its flat trajectory. I pondered this. There's a saying in Brooklyn that seemed appropriate, 'Don't ask!'

We moved out in bright sunshine. Two thick five-foot high concrete posts, one on each side of the road, left little room for the TDs to pass. The first one edged its way between them, but in the process a GI whose foot was dangling over the side had it crushed. There were shouts of 'Medic.' After evacuating the injured man and clearing the obstruction, our TDs traveled at 20 mph in single file for 25 minutes. We were approaching a crossroads. To our right front, there was an airfield and some large buildings; to our left front, a string of small one-story wood dwellings.

Rolling into the junction, we were hit by rifle and machine gun fire from either side of the road. Werdmann, the GI with whom I had changed places on the first TD was hit immediately in the chest, toppled off the TD, and fell into a growing pool of his own blood. He was dead before he hit the ground. I leaped off the TD, adrenaline pumping at a rapid rate, and like the others, jumped into a shallow ditch by the side of the road. There was little protection from the firing that was coming from the small houses and the airfield. At the same time, a German truck had ground to a halt on the side road, its driver severely wounded. He was swaying, more in death than in life, behind the wheel. I straddled a GI in front of me whose left leg couldn't stop nervously twitching under my stomach. Finally, overcome by stress, the GI rose on one knee, muttering, 'Aw, fuck,' aimed his M-1 at the German driver slumped over the wheel, and fired two rounds in rapid succession through the windshield. The windshield shattered on impact, the driver's head jerked upward, collapsed against the steering wheel, and stopped moving.

The TDs were firing three-inch cannon shells from their main arma-ment over our heads into the fields beyond. We rose out of the ditch and ran toward the houses, firing at point blank range. Some of the houses were already burning; others burst into flame. Eighty yards away, three Germans were racing across a field under a hail of rifle fire but they didn't go down. I ran back to the TD, jumped aboard, grabbed the .50 caliber machine gun anchored to the open 'pulpit' turret, and began firing short bursts at the retreating Germans 500 yards away. I didn't hit them either, and they got away. As abruptly as the firefight began, it ended. We took some prisoners.

After the crossroads ambush, Simmons changed his tactics. From now on, one 12-man squad would follow the TDs on the road, the second squad would advance in the field to its left, and the third in the field to its right. The rest of Charlie would follow our spearhead. The road stood higher than the surrounding fields and was lined on either side with poplar trees. The scene before me looked like one found in the New York Times travel section, with photos and text inviting the tour-ist to 'Spend Your Next Holiday in France.' We moved out, our boots scraping across the landscape in unison with the TD's pounding rub-ber tracks and whirring gas engines, all of which added to the noise.

Wary of mine fields, I take the lead as First Scout in the adjacent field to the right. Just as the sun is setting, shots ring out across the road, fol-lowed immediately by an agonized yell and gagging. The squad to our left has bumped into the enemy in the receding light. Men shout and the firing increases. We stop in our tracks, prepared to leap across the road. One soldier is dead. Alarums and excursions are wearying.

Fifteen minutes later, the same squad bumps into another enemy out-post, and two GIs are killed. Taylor, Longo, and I took Basic Training together in Blanding. At 19, before he left, the Army dentists pulled out all of his teeth. Now he's dead, seven months later! How ironic! Longo, unable to fire a shot in anger, stumbles onto a waiting enemy, who suddenly open fire, killing him instantly at close range. Stress reactions increase. Night falls.

Charlie Company pauses momentarily, then follows the TDs as they resume their advance. In the darkness, I trip and fall across a barbed wire fence into a thicket. Thorns cut my hands and some embed them-selves. I'm sure the Germans have heard my clatter, but there is only silence. I move into the black space ahead.

Suddenly, out of the inky blackness, someone shouts in German, '*Halte Meichter*' (sic) and fires two shots at point blank range. Bang! Bang! The gun flashes are yellow colored and close enough to touch. The hidden and disembodied voice seems an arm's length away. I hit the ground waiting for my Second Scout and the rest of the squad to come up from behind, fan out beside me, and form a skirmish line. From that position, we'll break through the enemy's defenses and take our objective. Seconds tick by. It sinks in! No one is coming. The squad, to a man, has run away! I'm on my own, 'hung out to dry.' One thing's sure, I've got to get the hell out of here — or else I'm dead. I'm too involved to panic.

My dance begins. I retreat. I rise and run 10 yards before hitting the ground. As I do, a potato masher, a German hand grenade, explodes next to my waist, sending pods of earth and bits of metal skyward. Gulping air, I get up again, rush another 10 yards, and slam into the ground. Wham! The second potato masher explodes by my right hip, tossing dirt and metal everywhere. I repeat the maneuver for the third time; the grenade explodes almost on top of me. My unknown and dedicated assailant tosses one more, but by now I'm out of range and close enough to leap into the ditch beside the road. I'm shook up but unhurt. Some squad members and Simmons have already taken cover. I'm tired and pissed off but glad to be alive.

If the timing between my unseen assailant and me had been different, I would have taken the full force of any of the three explosions while running. The rhythm between the German and me was exquisite and, like experienced ballroom dancers, we were in step not once but on three different occasions. A war dance!

Simmons climbs out of the ditch and is squatting against the nearest tree. He's about 30, but tonight he looks 60. Enemy gunfire is sporadic. Dazed, lacking will power and self-confidence, Simmons seems to be seeking a solution to the present problem as if relying on an OCS (Officer Candidate School) card file in his head and is flipping through it to find the answer. I've never felt confident in his leadership, and I sure as hell don't tonight.

As if thinking out loud, he sees me, nods his head, and orders, 'Take your squad back out to that field. Keep moving toward Valence.'

I noticed that Simmons is taking cover and leaning behind a tree trunk with his back to the enemy. I thought, 'What can you do that way, except get hit in the ass first?'

Reigle, Gualandi, Wohlwerth, Caesar, Fawcett, Garland, and Scruby are left and have gathered around. I know the first three men, the other four are shadowy figures, and four others are missing, including Shanklin. Reluctantly, eight of us return to the open field, as ordered. There's no time to berate the men who left me in the lurch. I'm leading — again.

Walking in single file toward the enemy, I hear the clanking of tank treads and the revving of gas engines; the TDs are moving down the road. I think, 'We've lost all surprise. Christ!' Reacting instantly, the Germans open fire with their self-propelled guns, 88s, and 57 mm anti-tank weapons at point blank range; their artillery is zeroed in, not only on the TDs, but on the trees bordering the road. The three TDs are hit immediately and are set on fire. Illuminating the landscape, they reveal an eerie scene, in which they burn fiercely and then explode. Enemy shells detonate in the trees, showering those taking cover below with wood shards and steel fragments. Within seconds, men die; piercing the night, the wounded scream and shout for medics.

Like guests at a spectacle, we view the battle on the road at close range; from the field, we stalk an elusive enemy, diminishing the distance between us. German artillery men, silhouetted against the muzzle flashes of their weapons at a distance of 90 yards, fire repeatedly along the road and into the trees. They seem close enough to touch. We're being hammered by the rear guard of the German 19th Army trying to escape from southeastern France to the Franco-German frontier. Suddenly, German flares explode above us, turning the blackness into a sickly yellowish-green twilight. Seemingly in slow motion, the colors drip and fall casually to earth. Following their cue, we sink slowly to the ground, lying on our stomachs, trying to be invisible and one with the earth. The enemy gunners spray the field with their MG-42s, firing at 30 inches above the ground. If, for whatever reason, I rose above that height, I would be killed instantly. The flare dies, the black returns, and no one is hit.

The Germans outgun us. The idea that eight men, armed only with rifles and grenades, could defeat the rearguard of a German army is idiotic. However, with the benefit of darkness and stealth, we might have changed the outcome of the battle by attacking, even if we were killed in the process. Instead, we decide to pull back. But, pull back to where? Other than the crackling of the burning TDs and their intermittent explosions, no human sounds are heard; the surviving men of

Charlie Company have disappeared. The air is full of smoke, cordite, and ashes. Breathing is difficult. We stumble across an L-shaped irrigation ditch a little further back and fall into it. Our refuge!

What Charlie Company didn't know as it engaged the enemy on D-68 was that indigenous armed Resistance units of the French Forces of the Interior (FFI) in the Drôme Department, which included Valence, were also engaged as part of an overall Franco-American plan. Prior to the attack, on August 23, a Colonel Steele, attached to 36th Divisional Headquarters, visited the command post of Colonel J. P. de Lassus Saint-Genies, the regional head of the FFI. Steele's role was more political than military. Both officers agreed that Valence must be taken as quickly as possible because the Germans held many Allied prisoners within its precincts and its citizens were suffering unduly. Steele returned to his headquarters and convinced his superiors that an immediate attack was necessary, even though the enemy was threatening elements of the 36th further south, near the Rhône river town of Montélimar. Colonel Paul D. Adams, commander of the 143rd Infantry Regiment of the 36th, was placed in charge of the attack on Valence. At 18:00 hours of August 24, Colonel Adams told de Lassus at dinner that he wanted to begin the attack at 20:00 that night. De Lassus declined because he could not communicate with and prepare his Resistance forces on such short notice. Adams decided to attack at 22:00 hours instead, to which de Lassus agreed.

Dispositions for the attack were as follows:

a) One column on the route Alixan-National Route 92, Saint-Marcel-lès Valence; this column will be protected by two TDs. Four French infantry companies will be involved.

b) One column will be in the center on the Cabeuil-Valence D-68, composed of the main force — primarily American (Charlie), consisting of one battalion of infantry, two battalions of tank destroyers, and two French infantry companies.

c) One column to the south, on the axis Beaumont-Valence, protected by three TDs and including seven French infantry companies.

Toward 2200 hours, de Lassus, accompanied by Colonel Saint-Sauveur, found Colonel Adams's command post situated in a barrack on the Chabeuil airfield, which had just fallen to Charlie Company. Several German prisoners had been taken. Two groups of American 105 mm guns near Chabeuil were hammering the enemy defenses in and around Valence. Toward 23:00 hours, while the attack was in progress, some enemy 88 mm artillery pieces situated at the outskirts of Valence went into action and set three TDs on fire. The American reaction was unexpected and immediate.

Colonel Adams abandoned his part in the attack without even trying to chase the enemy down because he found his losses (Charlie's) too heavy. At the same time, the battle at Montélimar flared up, and that action diverted Adams from driving the enemy out of Valence. According to de Lassus, these forces were not employed because Adams had already called off the attack. Adams had been ordered to pull out of the melee at Valence by his superiors before that battle had been decided. He was ordered to disengage and move his regiment, of which Charlie was a part, south to Montélimar, where a larger battle with much more at stake was raging. The 36th was assigned to destroy the entire German 19th Army. The two other U.S. divisions would help after the battle was joined.

According to what de Lassus told me later, although his forces had been increased in fighting power by one battery of artillery and one battalion of TDs while moving on Chabeuil, he was ordered by General Patch — American 7th Army commander — by radio link that the attack was not to be continued. This information was news to me because I had always thought that we had acted alone and not in conjunction with the French.

Years before my meeting with de Lassus, I learned that TDs, although wholly satisfactory in fire power, suffered from the disadvantages of thin armor and an open turret, having been designed for a defensive role only. It was far more dangerous for a TD to move forward or withdraw than to fight from a fixed position, particularly against enemy armor. Why then were the three TDs sent down a two-lane departmental road, in defiance of standard tactics, nose to tail, at night in unfamiliar territory, against a strong German defense line? In addition, the table of organization of a tank destroyer battalion totaled 36 TDs and, according to the attack order, two battalions had been assigned to the 143rd. Where were the remaining 66 TDs? Why were they not deployed?

On the night of the 24th, as we sought shelter in the irrigation ditch, American 105s bombard but never succeed in destroying the enemy positions. The air is polluted. Outgoing shells whine through the air and explode around us. I'm hyper-vigilant, attuned to the slightest noise or movement. No human sounds reach us from the road, or cries of the wounded. Charlie, a ghost company, disappears as if it never existed. Simmons, along with what's left of the company, has vanished. I'm outraged. By bugging out, by taking off (retreating), he has thrown us to the wolves and lost the battle. I'm overcome by a sense of desolation and feel betrayed.

Like the TDs burning on the road, we in the irrigation ditch are sitting ducks — there for the taking! At first light, I realize that we're surrounded. Sitting on a stone wall, not more than 50 feet away, a German soldier is watching our every move. We stare in disbelief but don't fire; he climbs off the wall and walks away without comment or raising an alarm. A truce? Contrary to the final scene of a John Wayne Hollywood film, in which he fights it out with the 'bad guys' and wins, the Germans need only to stand out of range and lob in a few mortar shells, a surgical and cost-effective solution. We creep and crawl up and down the length of our 20-foot ditch until our shirts and trousers are bloody and worn through at the elbows and knees. Blood mixes with the earth at the bottom of the ditch and quickly disappears. Our movements are those of caged animals. It's as if expending physical energy will reveal the answer to the question, 'How can we escape safely from this ditch?' It's 11:30 and getting warm.

Sergeant Scruby is a stranger to me, a fellow of about 23, a bit stockier than me, with closely cropped straw-colored hair. Shanklin, our squad leader, who disappeared in the previous night's battle, never mentioned him. Crouching in the irrigation ditch, Scruby gives voice to what we're thinking; time is running out. We move nearer to each other and talk in low tones; it's almost noon; the day is bright. If we remain where we are, we'll either be killed or captured. At the other end of the field is a peach orchard; beyond it a farmhouse, whose upstairs windows are barely visible. Scruby insists that we leave the ditch and make for the farmhouse. He decides to go first. If he makes it, he'll signal from that second-story window. Each man is to follow at two-minute intervals from the same place in the ditch. We all agree, because Scruby's plan is our only chance.

He crawls to the take-off point of the ditch, pauses, leaps up, and rushes across the open field. I'm watching a horse race, a combination of the Kentucky Derby and the Grand National, not from the forecourt but from the edge of a ditch, betting everything I have. Winner takes all! I keep rocking back and forth, the jockey urging my horse on, murmuring, 'Come on Scruby. Come on Scruby,' as our long shot reaches the peach orchard and disappears. While he's lost from view, we're left hanging, waiting. Five minutes later the shutters of the upstairs window slowly open a fraction, as if jostled by the breeze. He's made it; he gives the signal.

We follow suit, exiting from the ditch. When my turn comes, I dash across the field and gain the peach orchard; running between the trees, dodging roots, and stepping over the bumpy, uneven ground littered with leaves. My rifle, helmet, and pack try to impede my forward motion. I exit from the orchard, dash across a road, and into a farmyard, where Scruby and those preceding me are waiting.

The others follow in quick succession. We're greeted by a family of three: a farmer, his wife, and their 10-year-old daughter. Believing we've come as liberators, they are excited and friendly. Trying to set the record straight in a foreign language, I discover that my high school French is not good enough; I'm better at conjugating irregular French verbs than at creating a string of meaningful sentences. The farmer tries to make sense of my agonizing and desperate attempts. I race against the clock. My gesticulations and damaged French, his intelligence and perseverance, pay off. The farmer nods his head in understanding and leads us up some stone steps, through a wooden door, and into a hayloft, a momentary sanctuary. I volunteer to stay below, as a lookout with easy access to the men above.

A cyclist dressed in a blue uniform approaches the farm. Hiding behind the bushes near the stone staircase, I decide to kill him, but suddenly realize that the sound of a rifle shot would alert the Germans. There's something else. I can't kill a man in cold blood. However, if he threatens the farmer and then attempts to leave, I'll kill him. He rolls into the farmyard, shouting a greeting to which the farmer responds in kind. *'Bonjour, Louis.' 'Comment* ça *va, Gaston.'* He dismounts, they shake hands, and both seem out of breath, their voices dropping. The conversation ends abruptly; the mysterious man in blue remounts and pedals off, increasing his speed with every rotation of the crank.

Louis Salomon, the police officer I held in the cross hairs of my rifle, is also a member of the local Resistance. Earlier that morning, at the police headquarters in Valence, Chief of Police Gerard asks for a volunteer to visit Les Martins, that part of Valence where the previous night's battle had taken place. Since Louis knows the area and some of the farmers very well, he steps forward. The Chief needs a current assessment of the damage.

Cycling from Valence, carrying authorized German and French police passes of transit, he is stopped at the western edge of the field attacked the night before. The German officer commanding the barrier demands to see his papers and, while looking at them, says, 'Those American swine, we really taught them a lesson last night. We knocked out three of their tank destroyers and killed and wounded 68 men within 10 minutes!' Stamping the papers, the officer laughs and waves Louis on. Beyond the burned out TDs on D-68, Louis turns left, and approaches the farm of his friend, Gaston Reynaud.

Having entered the farmyard, Louis greets Gaston and dismounts, saying intuitively, 'Gaston, I think there's something you want to tell me.'

Gaston replies in a whisper, 'I've got a terrible problem that needs to be solved.'

'What problem?'

'I have eight Americans hiding in my hayloft!'

Louis Salomon returns to Valence in haste and immediately reports to his Chief, who urgently calls a meeting with some of his key Resistant activists. These policemen, disguised as civilians, gather in the cellar beneath the Crystal Bar in downtown Valence to decide on the best plan for launching our escape.

Louis later poses three questions to himself: what would have happened if Chief of Police Gerard had not asked for a volunteer that August morning? Secondly, what if I, who knew the region so well, had not volunteered? And finally, what if I had not picked my friend Reynaud to call upon first? It is not difficult to imagine what would have happened.'

The farmer insists that I join my comrades up above, feeling that the less movement around the farmyard the better. The hayloft, partially full of hay, is about 20x40 feet square. Scruby is in shadow, keeping watch near the window, looking through a crack in the shutters onto the field we have just left; the others are resting on the hay, their weapons beside them; the farmer insists that we move as little as possible and remain silent. The loft is old and the floorboards creak. We break into our small boxes of concentrated D-rations, a highly concentrated emergency 'iron ration' chocolate bar; the farmer's helper, a small, kindly peasant wearing a soft peaked cap and ill-fitting clothes, nods as he ladles drinking water from a bucket. I look at my watch. We've been in the hayloft for two hours. Suddenly, the silence is broken by the bleating, cackling, and braying of the farm animals below. The sound of their agitated and indiscriminate movements fills the hayloft. We've no idea what has provoked this outburst. Now, an enemy machine gun opens up, firing short bursts. The animal sounds increase. We grab our weapons, alert to a German break in. Tension reaches an excruciating level, not comparable to anything heretofore experienced. It is alive and dangerous; it snaps and stings and fills every available space.

Automobile tires grate on the gravel below. Strangers race up the stairs, taking the steps two at a time, shouting in French, 'Allons, allons.' Standing, we point our rifles at the entrance. The hayloft door bursts open; a man in civilian clothes rushes in, followed by two men wearing the same blue uniform as the man on the bicycle. He shouts, 'Hurry! You must leave the hayloft! The Germans are coming; they've killed many of the wounded and are setting fire to farmhouses nearby. You'll be trapped, then killed!'

The civilian carries a large brown paper parcel tied with brown string. He breaks the string and rips the paper open. The package contains four French police uniforms; mixing French and English together, he insists that we leave the farm in the waiting unmarked black Citroën police car disguised as French policemen. With only four uniforms, two journeys are necessary, consisting of the civilian, 'Ferdinand' of the Deuxieme Bureau (French Secret Service), one uniformed driver, an assistant, and four of us. No other option exists. I am one of four who volunteers to stay behind, a rear guard for those trying to escape, and my contribution to mankind. If all doesn't go according to plan, there won't be a second journey. The worst that can happen is that the first four are killed on the journey and we're killed in the hayloft. I've no time to ponder whether the lives of those leaving are more valuable than mine, but my decision feels right. The first four force themselves into the uniforms, discovering that the trousers are too short, the caps and tunics too tight, exposing the shirt cuffs and trousers bottoms of their American uniforms. 'This isn't going to work. We're too big,' Reigle complains. Gualandi pipes up, 'Got a better idea?' Dressed in their ragtag outfits, they are hustled through the door, following the Frenchmen down the stairs to the waiting car. Time is unforgiving and relentless! 'Good luck!' we whisper.

The other three and I are suffocating from the heat and tension that saturate the hayloft. Reclining, we nod to each other, mute. The wait weighs heavily and is interminable. The silence crashes between us. I sweat. Soft light filters in from the crack in the shutters and up through the decaying, ill-fitting floorboards, but all else is in shadow. About 45 minutes later, the car returns. Ferdinand is carrying the police uniforms, a good sign. Now it's our turn. We hide all our equipment and personal effects deep in the hay. I leave my rifle behind for the second time, as if I'm not destined to have one. Only our names, ranks, and serial numbers remain. We don our makeshift disguises, knowing that they do not sustain the mark of authenticity.

Like those before us, we rush the exit and hustle down the stairs with the French team leading. The car, a black mid-30s, four-door, mid-size Citroen 'traction avant,' an innovative front-wheel drive automobile, enjoyed by both the Gestapo and the Resistance, is waiting, its motor ticking over. The interior is not large enough to hold all seven of us comfortably, so I sit on Wohlwerth's lap on the rear seat. As we drive out of the farmyard, nodding goodbye to the farmer, I realize I don't even know his name.

Rather than returning to the safety of our assembly point near Chabeuil, where our abortive attack first began, the driver turns right and drives directly into German-held Valence. I'm stunned! The car rolls on and slows only to enter the same enemy lines we tried to penetrate the night before, and we are scrutinized by the same soldiers we fought the night before. Armed sentries and machine gunners in armored cars, manning an in-depth series of roadblocks constructed of trenches, barbed wire, and pillboxes, wave us on reluctantly. They're close enough to touch. We drive deeper into an urban mass of windowless, dun-colored buildings and cobbled streets, leaving D-68 behind. Germans are everywhere; a two-man foot patrol, carrying Schmeisser 9 mm submachine guns, suddenly appears next to the Citroen. The driver ignores them, and I quickly look away. The patrol continues on, their metal weapons glistening in the sun, turns a corner, and disappears. Valence is a dusty old town.

The black Citroën is moving so slowly that we're on the edge of stalling. No quick getaway or high- speed car chase here! Off to the left,

German officers, dressed in the usual Wehrmacht slate-gray uniforms, binoculars hanging from their shoulders, holstered Walther P-38 pistols strapped around their waists and carrying map cases, are engaged in animated conversation. They point first to their maps and then to some nearby buildings. American prisoners are herded together beside a 10-foot high concrete wall. Some stand with hands clasped behind their heads, others sit dejectedly on the ground. One prisoner looks familiar. All are unkempt and weary, and so are their captors. I'm very thirsty, and my throat is parched. Wohlwerth moves, I squirm on his lap.

At a busy thoroughfare, our driver pulls over to the curb and stops with the engine running. Ferdinand, our man in plain clothes, leaves the car and steps onto the pavement, seeking anonymity in the shifting crowd. Before he disappears, I reach into one of my pockets, roll down the window halfway, and press a small packet of Camel cigarettes into his hand, with the logo clearly visible and easily identifiable. Pedestrians, trapped in their own world, seem indifferent or unaware of my expression of thanks, but my comrades are furious, apprehensive. They consider my behavior the height of stupidity and an act of folly. By a show of appreciation—appropriate in other times—I have jeopardized their lives and those of our French helpers. If our cover were blown by either a French collaborationist or German passer-by, we would have been shot where we stood, because categorically, if not specifically, as stipulated in Hitler's Commando Order of October, 1942, '....*all commandos operating against German forces are to be <u>annihilated to the last man,</u> whether they be soldiers in uniform, or saboteurs, <u>with or without arms, and</u> <u>whether fighting or seeking to escape... Even if these individuals on discovery</u> <u>make obvious their intention of giving themselves up as prisoners, no pardon</u> <u>is on any account to be given.</u>'*

We sweat out the moment, unarmed, expecting the worst, but no passer-by raises the alarm; our man in civilian clothes has gone as the driver shifts gears, unobtrusively steps on the gas, and leaves the scene. I feel like an amateur with no sense of proportion. Snared in this high-stakes drama over which I have no control, it seems I am not one of its major participants but an observer, more a part of the audience than a lead actor. If caught, I might say to my deadly serious, trigger-happy, Schmeisser-toting opponents—more so, if they've fought in Russia—'What's all the fuss about?'

We leave the town behind as it reluctantly gives way to isolated farms that dot the low-lying alluvial landscape on our drive south along the Rhône River. As the car approaches one of the farms situated near the river's east bank, our driver slows before a herd of sheep grazing 15 yards away. He twice blasts the car's horn, startling the animals, and an aged shepherd standing beside his flock replies. As if in slow motion, he takes out a large, crumpled, red-checkered handkerchief from his worn, ill-fitting jacket pocket and blows his nose, evidently the all-clear signal for us to proceed.

Once inside the farmhouse, controlled by members of the Resistance, we quietly reunite with the first group. After quickly discarding our police uniforms, exposing our true identity, each of us gets a small 7.65 mm Italian Beretta automatic pistol.

Comparing our two journeys, I discover that the first group's experiences were more harrowing. Twice, suspicious German officers stopped the first four at enemy roadblocks, but the policemen were able to talk their way out of both interrogations. However, if either of the German officers demanded to search the car and question its occupants, none would have survived. The first four, the two policemen, and our man Ferdinand would have been killed beside the car and we, waiting in vain, would have died in the hayloft. Not trusting to luck, the French driver decided to change the route for the second journey, believing it less perilous, but one of the policemen, overwhelmed by the high risks, refused, deciding one journey was enough. With their part of the escape accomplished, the two policemen in their black Citroen left to report to Gerard, their mission accomplished. To reach momentary safety, we had entered a world of signs and counter-signs, of cover stories and cover names, of agents and stratagems.

I had no way of knowing that while we were trying to remain alive, according to Army policy, each of our families received a telegram similar in every respect except for the soldier's name: THE SECRETARY OF WAR DESIRES ME TO EXPRESS HIS DEEP REGRET THAT YOUR SON STEPHEN J. WEISS HAS BEEN REPORTED MISSING IN ACTION SINCE TWENTY-FIFTH AUGUST IN FRANCE. IF FURTHER DETAILS OR FURTHER INFORMATION IS RECEIVED, YOU WILL BE PROMPTLY NOTIFIED.

SIGNED: J. A. ULIO, THE ADJUTANT GENERAL

Preoccupied with my own survival, I could not imagine the agony my family went through. Sometimes, being listed as 'Missing' was a transitory condition in which the Army shuffled its paper work and waited. For the most part, the soldier had been killed, but his remains had not been found and might never be. If so, the name on the list became eternal while his family waited forever.

Systematically, the Germans widened their search. Fifteen minutes after our arrival, one of the Résistant lookouts burst in shouting, 'Gestapo!' Their black Citroens were coming down the track! With only minutes to spare, we ducked out of the rear door behind a French guide, raced headlong down the steep riverbank, and jumped into two waiting rough-hewn wooden boats bobbing on the water. Two anonymous Frenchmen, one of whom, wearing a black beret, tan duffel jacket, and drooping grizzled moustache, offered doubtful protection with an age-encrusted, round magazine submachine gun. They knew that for every Allied soldier helped to escape, a French, Belgian, or Dutch Résistant died. There were eight of us. Mountain climbing on the Eiger in peacetime is one thing, attempting to row across the Rhône under attack in wartime another.

In 1944, the Rhône was the fastest flowing river in Europe; originating from a Swiss alpine glacier, it moved swiftly toward the Mediterranean. Three local bridges that spanned the Rhône at Valence had been destroyed by hordes of 12th Tactical U. S. Army Air Force (AAF) P-47 Thunderbolt fighter-bombers, their attacks visible to the naked eye. The pilot would line up on his target, go into a steep dive, drop his 500-pound bomb, and pull out just before crashing. He'd then go scooting away at full speed, inches above the surrounding hills. During July of '44, Lieutenant Roy Rickerson and his Office of Strategic Services (OSS) Operational Group, code name 'Louise,' destroyed another.

The metal structure of one bridge lay nearby, twisted and broken in the water, starkly framed by its concrete pillars standing in mute testimony on either shore. The strong current pulled us diagonally downstream; the far shore, three-quarters of a mile away, seemed as remote as ever, in spite of how hard the Frenchmen rowed. The Germans were nibbling at our heels, ready to pounce, gathering on the recently vacated shore. Images of sitting ducks — then roast ducks, and finally, a cooked goose — filtered through my mind at breakneck speed, unlike the largo movement of our craft. Jumping overboard was not an option, regardless of the river's current. Due to the combined weight of our boots and clothes, and the icy water, we would have drowned in any case.

The Germans opened fire, but their firing was sporadic and desultory. For whatever reason, the Germans chose not to follow us across. Finally, the boats bumped against the gravel and, with our French guide in the lead, we scrambled up and over the bank and crossed a narrow road running parallel to the river. I crouched low, broke through the metal gate of a small garden punctuated by black, sinister trees, raced up a short flight of tiled stairs to a covered entrance, and entered a stucco, three-story, Belle Époque shuttered house. The last man slammed the front door behind him.

Gaining entry to a bedroom off a narrow corridor, I fell across a bed, still in my dirty clothes and muddy boots, soiling the heavy red brocade bedspread that matched the closed floor-to-ceiling window drapes. It was the middle of the afternoon, the room dark, and I had been awake for more than 48 hours. Although yearning for sleep, I was too keyed up even to try.

I dozed fitfully. My comrades were somewhere in the house, but until nightfall, I was alone in the room. I don't remember receiving any food or drink. When night fell, with our guide at the head of our ragtag group, we walked north along the river road through Soyons, a small village. Somewhere a dog barked, irritated by our momentary passage. Vineyards and houses blurred in the night landscape. There was no horse cart or auto traffic. The route seemed endless. Three miles later, we trudged into St. Péray, leaving its 2,000 inhabitants undisturbed, and halted below the dimly lit sign of the *Hôtel du Nord*, a three-story stucco building situated on the west side of a poorly illuminated square, although the monument honoring the fallen of the 1914–1918 war was faintly visible. There was no foot traffic. Besides offering the obvious to the weary traveler, the hotel doubled as the local Resistance headquarters. Mort pour la France!

Jostled through the café entrance, we were hustled unceremoniously into a back room, containing a few bentwood chairs, a marble-topped table, and a wall map stretched across a blackboard. Security was non-existent. About five Résistance men entered and began speaking in French, asking questions concerning our attack, deception, and escape. Two of them were carrying British Lee Enfield bolt-action rifles. I replied as best I could, but my French hadn't improved in the last two days. Expecting a show of Allied solidarity, I was caught off balance by the persistence and impatience of my interrogators. They rarely seemed satisfied with my short, hesitant answers, shrugging them off with an air of disbelief. I hoped they were hiding their Gallic charm under a bushel because none of it was forthcoming. Using my index finger to make up for any foreign language deficiency, I repeatedly pointed to the map, indicating the positions of the airfield, the cross roads, D-68 and where the TDs had been destroyed, the farmhouse and the surrounding fields. The French were surly. I despaired. They were not shocked into recognition. Suddenly, defying comprehension, their demeanor changed for the better, and the atmosphere brightened. My answers were good enough! Smiling, slapping us on our backs, gripping and shaking our hands, they passed tulip-shaped wine glasses all round and filled them with the local red *Côtes du Rhône*. We stood there, wine glasses in hand, perplexed by the sudden turnabout, glad that the 45-minute inquisition was over.

Who could blame them? The preliminary doubts of our French comrades were not surprising because, with all bridges blown across the Rhône, with most communication facilities destroyed, in a country divided ideologically, collaborators and double agents not only were common, but a threat. To protect a Resistance network from being infiltrated or destroyed either by the Germans or French traitors, counter-measures were taken, such as the determined questioning I experienced. 1944 was the year of rough frontier justice, similar to that of the American Wild West almost 200 years ago when old scores were settled between Frenchmen with guns and grenades, and proof of who you were and what you had done were a matter of life and death. At the *Hôtel du Nord*, in a town known for its sparkling wines, I assumed that from now on, the local Resistance and we were brothers in arms.

Thoughts of a hot meal, accompanied by an excellent wine and a comfortable bed, were suddenly interrupted. Elements of the German 19th Army, moving north along the west bank of the Rhône, were threatening the southern approaches of the town on the same road we had recently traveled. To avoid capture, we joined a makeshift convoy leaving St. Péray, whose cars and trucks were fueled by charcoal-burning combustion 'gazogènes,' due to a severe gasoline shortage in France.

Leaving a series of concrete and barbed wire roadblocks behind, we traveled west on D-533, a steep, twisting, and narrow road that rose steadily above the nearby hills, hoping that the gazogène wouldn't break down. Producing less power than a gas-driven vehicle, our gazogène struggled, groaned, and coughed for over an hour as it laboriously beat its way for 16 kilometers to the small remote mountain village of Alboussière, perched on a windswept plateau 600 meters high. Most of the village straddled a departmental road that continued on to Le Puy, 75 kilometers distant.

A solitary figure awaits our arrival. He stands near the side entrance of a two-story country hotel, weakly illuminated by a raw electric bulb. The man is dressed in jodhpurs and black riding boots, wearing an open cotton shirt. He tosses the remains of a lighted cigarette into the shadows. The right sleeve of his shirt is empty, its cuff loosely tucked between his belt and waist. Extending his left hand to those who dismount, he says, 'I am Auger; welcome to Alboussière.' He is in fact, François Binoche.

He leads us through the narrow hotel corridor into the Fin de Siècle lobby and assigns each of us a room. This time, I undress, place my boots at the side of the bed, and fall deeply asleep for the first time in three days. Because I'm homeless, everywhere is my home; because I'm without identification, I'm attached to no one, possibly not even to myself. Sensing that I'm nothing more than a cork bobbing on a tumultuous sea, I feel disturbed by these intimate and troubling revelations.

The next morning, devouring a continental breakfast of bread, jam, butter, and large bowls of hot coffee, I sit alongside my comrades in a large rustic dining room overlooking a patio and walled garden. Auger is in reality French Army Captain (later General) François Binoche, an officer commanding a Resistance formation in the Ardèche Department. Situated across the Rhône from Valence, the Ardèche is a hilly agricultural region whose inhabitants are Huguenot Protestant, not Catholic. Binoche has adopted 'Auger' as his *nom de guerre*, a cover name in an attempt to deny his true identity from the enemy, whether French informers or Germans. His cover is questionable, possibly of little value, because once seen, he is easily marked by the loss of his right arm. Unfortunately, it was shattered during a firefight with the enemy on July 5, two months ago, at Desaignes, a medieval village further west on D-533. He is a career officer, considered an excellent leader, and uses the Hotel Serre as his headquarters.

We are not the only guests of Maurice and Odette Serre, the owners of the three-story country hotel. Many are refugees from Paris, some of whom are Jewish, like M. Haas, a small man in his 40s, imbued with an intelligent and whimsical personality, a former international merchant banker and a veteran of the First World War. Subsequently, I am introduced to his two sisters, tall and slender figures, who speak, no, *sing* French with an unerring musicality, and his nephew, Jean-Claude, a boy of my own age who resembles his uncle. Fortunately, they were able to escape from German occupied Paris. Unfortunately, by a concatenation of mishaps, they were not able to leave Occupied France and gain safety. Wanted by the French militia and the Gestapo, thus far they have avoided capture and certain death. The Hotel Serre is their sanctuary.

By following the daily BBC radio news reports, M. Haas marks the Allied advance across France with string and pins, stuck on a Michelin touring map of Western Europe affixed to his bedroom wall. Sometimes he invites me to his room to view the map and talk about the current military situation, of which I know little. Sitting on his bed, I'm told that Valence still remains in German hands, and that a much bigger battle is raging 60 kilometers to the southeast. Near Montélimar, a town made famous for its nougats, the 36th and two other American divisions of the American 7th Army are attempting to destroy the German 19th Army.

I'm getting to know the guests by sight. Another refugee, a woman in her late 30s, sits in the garden, knitting constantly. The ball of yarn turns, the needles click, conjuring up a scene of peasant women knitting in tune to the fall of the guillotine during the French Revolution. The garden overlooks a valley undulating toward a group of mountains of volcanic origin to the southwest, their blue shapes shimmering in the mid-day heat, at least a day's march away. Two plane trees frame the mountain landscape and offer what little shade there is. An attractive theatrical-looking woman in her early 20s walks onto the terrace; she is slim, with dyed red hair, and rarely speaks.

The Serres are protective and considerate of their charges, who thus far have been fortunate enough to avoid the collective wrath of the French Milice (militia) and the Gestapo. Madame Serre provides food and shelter without conditions; if their guests are impoverished, payment can be deferred until after the long-awaited liberation or written off entirely. Maurice Serre scours the surrounding area for produce, a difficult task in these mountains, which are partly wilderness. Elise and Simone, the two teenage chambermaids, keep the hotel scrubbed and clean for Madame Serre. They also help in the dining room. The meals are simple, ample, and well prepared but, however large and satisfying the portions, I cannot get enough to eat.

Wine is a different matter. Binoche and his second-in-command, Lieutenant Paul Goichot, a former civil engineer, are relaxing in the dining room one evening after dinner and both are in a playful mood. Their eyes twinkling, they ask if I would join them for a glass of wine and then give an opinion of its quality. Although I know nothing about wine, Goichot insists and pours some into my glass; the wine is deep crimson. Both identify it as a Chateauneuf du Pape, whose red grapes are grown in vineyards near Avignon, on the other side of the Rhône and southeast of here. I drain the glass in three or four sips and decide the Chateauneuf, although full-bodied and aromatic, tastes like onions. Reacting to my opinion, Binoche and Goichot roar with laughter. 'Onions,' they shouted in unison. 'Surely, not onions!'

Embarrassed at the moment, I discovered two years later that the Chateauneuf wine growers plant onions in the furrows between their vines; thus the wine's mild oniony flavor. 'Ah, where are the two great wine connoisseurs today?' I chuckled.

Some of Binoche's men, returning from a patrol, reported that scouting units of the German 19th Army were probing our part of the St. Péray-Le Puy road as an alternate escape route in their retreat northward. To deny them access, Binoche then decided to blow up the bridge on route 533, three kilometers below Aboussière. A number of men and I, armed with Lee Enfield rifles, the result of Allied parachute drops, were to seal off the southern approaches to the bridge, while the demolition team, guarded by Reigle and Scruby, carried out their responsibilities. Twenty of us left Aboussière for the bridge in an open truck that night and arrived soon after. The demolition team clambered beneath the bridge and set their explosive charges, while the guard detail surveyed the ghostly scene from the hill above. Twenty minutes later, we retreated further up the road beside the truck and waited. Binoche depressed the plunger. The explosion shattered the still August night and reverberated against the steeply sloped mountains and across the valley; pieces of the concrete bridge, ripped from its moorings, rose then fell into the chasm below with a whooshing sound. The German 19th Army's retreat was now canalized to both sides of the Rhône, its elements strafed and bombed by P-47 Thunderbolt and F6F Hellcat fighter-bombers and B-25 Mitchell medium bombers. We had deprived the enemy of a detour.

The afternoon was warm, the shadows deep, and dust swirled about the roadside of the hotel when two of Binoche's men escorted a man into the village under guard. Of medium height and build, he wore a short-sleeved khaki shirt, open at the throat, khaki shorts with large military pockets, a black belt, white socks, and black shoes. He hands and legs were bound in chains. None of the three uttered a sound as they marched past the hotel and down the road. Sensing my curiosity, a wrinkled and cigarette-stained Résistant, whom I knew by sight, hissed to me that the man was a traitor and sentenced to be shot the next day. On the following morning, I was standing outside the small café across from the hotel when I met the old Frenchman again. He was carrying a rifle and seemed mildly drunk.

'Bonjour, mon Américain. Come, my friend,' he insisted, taking me by the arm, we have work to do today and you can help. *'Mais, oui!* Join the others and me on the firing squad detail, as an act of Allied solidarity! *Eh, bien!'*

'Hold on,' I replied. 'What's the fella done?'

The old codger said, 'He is a traitor. A collaborator, an informer.'

If I understood him, the condemned man had joined the Vichy-controlled Milice of French President Marshal Henri Pétain's 'puppet' government and informed against innocent people, killing some, and sending others to their deaths.

'What more do you need?' the old man questioned.

Out of my depth, the memory of a fading high school civics course to which I had paid scant attention came drifting back. Some ideas were more accessible than others, such as trial by jury, justice for all, due process, and equality before the law. I thought: If my conversational French is on the verge of extinction, to express myself philosophically to this old guy is impossible! Secretly, I wanted to refuse his offer as diplomatically as I could. I was not ready to shoot an unarmed, defenseless man from three feet away for reasons unclear to me. Not at 18 and having just left home!

Nevertheless, feigning interest, my French buckling under the strain, I asked, 'Was he tried in a court of law; did he have the benefit of counsel, and the right to appeal?' I gave up on the civics course and predicated my decision on the film *The Oxbow Incident*, produced in 1943 by Fox Studios, in which a town's inhabitants, in their self-righteousness and rush to judgment, sentenced a man to die without sufficient evidence — and are prepared to live with the consequences.

Grasping at straws, I stammered, feeling decidedly uncomfortable, mumbling something in half French and half English that this was a French affair, so without sufficient evidence, my answer was

'No! 'If Binoche wants me on the firing squad, he can ask me himself.' I shrugged and walked away.

The old guy seemed genuinely disappointed. And why didn't I go to Binoche and talk it over with him? Because it never entered my mind! I realized — no, I rationalized — that as an American, the man's fate was none of my affair. As a human being, it certainly was, but I hadn't the time or was too young to bridge the gap.

My comrades, the villagers, and I milled around on a large plot of ground between the café and the side wall of the village church around 2:00 on this sultry afternoon. Members of the firing squad, wine glasses in one hand, rifles in the other, mingled among us, awaiting the principals' arrival before the pageant began, and I was reminded of the English balls filled with gaiety in Brussels on the eve of Waterloo. Someone pointed out Gendarme-Lieutenant Ferdinand Mathey, the officer in charge of the firing squad, who had just arrived. Stocky, with square features, a Belgian 45-caliber pistol strapped to the side of his blue gendarme uniform, he reminded me of Jean Gabin, the French movie idol. Standing before the throng, he called the firing squad to order. At his command, they disengaged from the crowd and shuffled into line, but not before placing their wine glasses, some half filled, into the hands of some gathered for the event. Most of the firing detail had drunk one glass too many, with wine supplied by the café owner. Or was it my imagination? Certainly my brown-stained aged friend and his cohort had been lively drinking companions before Mathey's arrival. Binoche was not to be seen.

Desultory conversation subsided when the condemned man arrived walking between his two guards. His was a military cadence, if not a funeral march; only the roll of drums was missing. They walked to within a few feet in front of the stone wall, turned, and stopped, facing the crowd. The accused stood erect (without benefit of a wooden post) and waved off the blindfold Mathey offered, with a flick of his wrist. Given the opportunity to say a few parting words, he refused with a Gallic shrug of his shoulders and toss of his head. Only a deep inhale from a half-burned cigarette was missing! Mathey shouted one order after another, the firing squad tried pulling itself together; little sounds persisted, the buzzing of an insect, the rustling of leaves, as I sucked in my breath like the others, watching, waiting. We stood behind the line of armed men, pointing their Lee Enfields at the accused, taking aim. Mathey shouted, 'Fire!'; the crack of musketry ricocheted off the wall. At a distance of not much more than an arm's reach, most bullets found their mark. Hit, the accused slumped, knees hitting the ground, toppled over, and fell sideways, his body twitching on the ground.

Mathey rushed forward, waving his pistol. He stood above the man at point blank range, aimed at his head and pulled the trigger. No bang followed, only a click. He aimed again and pulled the trigger. Another click, one surely heard for miles around. The moribund man writhed at his feet. Shocked, the spectators looked on in disbelief, transfixed. As Mathey aimed again, his hand trembling, my brown-stained curmudgeon took matters into his own hands. Rushing to Mathey's side, he pointed his rifle not more than three inches from the man's head and fired. The bullet nicked part of the man's ear before entering his skull. The accused stopped twitching. The crowd that a few moments before had stood enthralled by the unfolding drama now slowly dispersed, muttering words of outrage under their breath, shocked by the bungled and repugnant affair, not a few shaking their heads at the dead figure sprawled on the blood-stained ground. This was no way to die! That afternoon, as I took a turn through the village, the traitor's body lay crumpled atop a full hay cart, awaiting disposal. Somebody had stolen his shoes.

The next morning, after breakfast, Binoche asked for our help. His men needed instruction in the use of newly acquired Allied weapons dropped by planes of the Royal Air Force (RAF). We nodded in agreement. He chose a deserted farmhouse in the vicinity for our training center and introduced one of his men as translator. The eight of us and 10 of his men gathered before the farmhouse. Sheep grazed nearby, guarded by a shepherd and his dog. We chose the bazooka (rocket launcher) as our first subject. Scruby described it as a simple, if inefficient, anti-tank weapon, bordering on the useless. A two-man crew fired a 3-½-pound projectile with a maximum range of 300 feet. The bazooka, shaped like a stovepipe with a small electrical fitting, was a simple weapon to dismantle. With practice, the trainees reached proficiency quickly and were now ready for a firing demonstration. Gualandi balanced the weapon's tube on his right shoulder, gripped the handle with his left hand, and placed the index finger of his right hand against the trigger. Meanwhile, Reigle, serving as loader, removed a rocket from its carton, shoved it into the rear of the tube; when ready, he tapped Gualandi on the shoulder. Peering over the gun sight at a stationary target 60 feet away, Gualandi, standing upright, took aim and fired.

Instead of hitting the front of the stone farmhouse, the rocket sailed over its roof and disappeared. Instantaneously, we heard the sound of an explosion in the fields beyond. As if on cue, a distraught shepherd ran out from behind the farm house, waving his arms in the air and shouting, 'Stop, stop; you're killing my sheep.' Embarrassment was written all over Gualandi's face, and I chuckled inwardly. We were supposed to be the professionals, trained to defeat the Germans! Enough of my earlier concerns! Now one of the Frenchmen took a turn. He held his breath, took aim, and fired. The rocket sailed through the farmhouse window and exploded within. We all applauded. No shepherd arrived to plead his case.

We moved to the American Heavy M2 Browning .50-caliber machine gun that fired 450 rounds per minute, with a range of 1.3 miles. It was mounted on the bed of a small truck that was parked about 300 yards from a bale of hay set in front of the farm house. After some preliminary instructions, I readied the machine gun for firing, gripped the handles, and pulled the trigger. Pointing the muzzle at the bale, I fired in its general direction without taking aim, as if I were a tail gunner on a B-17 Flying Fortress four-engine bomber, filling a space with lead. The target remained untouched. I fired another short burst to no avail. Perplexed, I gave way to one of the Frenchmen in waiting. He crouched low, took proper aim, fired, and hit the target each time in three short, successive bursts. Not only had I missed the target completely but I also had been outdone by a wily Frenchman. Our 'trainees' had done very well, but Gualandi and I concluded that we weren't as professional as we had thought. Our six compatriots smiled and shook their heads, and Binoche's men took it in stride, knowing more about fighting than we did.

One day after lunch, the slender redhead accepted my invitation to go for a walk. With the village at our backs, we found a small natural sanctuary screened from the road next to a stone wall. Lying there, enjoying the sun's warmth, we moved closer to each other and embraced. Grappling rather than holding on to each other, we tried to escape from the war's chaos and uncertainty that surrounded us. Both lonely and far from home, relying on touch for intimacy, we faltered. Suffering from mutual language deprivation, my French and her English collapsed after we spoke those few simple words. Regrettably, we would remain a mystery to each other. Seizing the day was beyond me and she could not take the lead beyond her first opening salvos. We were saved from further embarrassment by the arrival of Allied fighter-bombers, strafing and attacking an unseen enemy in the Rhône valley. The clatter and rattle of airborne .50-caliber machine gun fire and the whine of R-2800 air-cooled Pratt & Whitney aircraft engines ended any further amorous intentions. Reverberating from the tumult, troubled by the interruption, we crouched against the wall until the planes disappeared from sight and, moments later walked back to the hotel in silence.

Binoche asked me at dinner one evening, 'Monsieur Weiss, do you enjoy hunting rabbits?'

Coming from the big city, reared on a diet of baseball and other seasonal sports, I knew nothing of hunting. When I replied, 'I've never hunted a rabbit in my life,' he waved my excuse aside by saying good-naturedly, 'It's of little consequence.'

He scheduled a hunting expedition for 8:00 a.m. the next morning. His eyes twinkled. 'OK,' I replied reluctantly, admitting to myself that it would be bad form to refuse.

'Why had he selected me?' I mused, when country-boys like Garland, Fawcett, and Scruby were excellent candidates, having hunted from childhood.

Mathey stood alone in his blue uniform, cavalry boots, and kepi, cradling a British 9 mm Mark II Sten submachine gun, a rugged reliable weapon for close combat. A smoldering Gauloise cigarette balanced between his lips in the bright morning sunshine. Interpreting the questioning look on my face, he said, 'Binoche is not coming.'

I nodded my head in acceptance but thought, 'Not coming? Hunting was his idea, not mine. Let's do it some other time.'

I hadn't seen Mathey since the execution, but remembered him as a man in motion, a solitary motorcycle dispatch rider covered in dust, a worn leather musette bag full of secret military documents strapped to his shoulders, driving at high speed to and from our village. His conversations with Binoche were short, followed by action. He slowed down once, to command the firing squad. Until now, we had little to do with each other. When other armed Frenchmen began arriving, Mathey shoved a Lee Enfield .30 caliber rifle into my hands.

I look dubiously at the rifle and then at Mathey, inquiring, 'What's this for? Why do we need all this 'heavy artillery' for hunting rabbits?'

He bursts out laughing, saying, 'Rabbits, rabbits? Cher Stéphane, the only rabbits we're hunting today are Germans.'

Binoche has set this up, and the joke is on me. I'm angry. 'If you don't mind my asking,' I say sarcastically, looking at Mathey, 'What's our first objective?'

'Nothing of great importance.' He grins, pointing to the horizon, and says, 'A stone farm house sheltered in the valley below.'

Like a scene out of the Spanish Civil War, Mathey and the others fire their weapons into the air at the edge of the ravine, the sound reverberating across the boulder-strewn, dun-colored hills. My shoulders slump, I shake my head in disbelief. All surprise is lost. 'Christ,' I think, 'what a fuck up!' We've just fired a lead calling card to anyone hiding in that farm house. Whoever's in there will see us first, staring out from the shadows of the barricaded dark interior. The tables are turned; we're the long-eared stupid-ass rabbits. It smacks of a Simmons-planned operation. The morning is hot, and I could use a drink. Dislodged stones mark our passage and fall away. Having first moved down the valley for an hour in single file, on stage for all the world to see, we gather, crouching low near the farm house looming 30 yards away. The intervening ground is devoid of cover and strewn with rocks and dry manure that rises and dissipates in the slightest breeze. Mathey signals and we rush forward in small spurts of twos and threes, each group covering the other. Hand grenades would help, but we don't have any. The front door is kicked in and three men storm into the interior, firing blind. Above the noise of the melee, someone is shouting in French, followed by a group of four Frenchmen of questionable loyalty emerging from within with their hands held high. I offer a cigarette to the man standing beside me. 'Where are the Germans?' Mathey asks, physically prodding one of the prisoners. 'They took it on the lam, just before you rushed the house,' or so the prisoners say. The farmhouse is secured and I search for water.

Mathey, a French driver, and I requisition a small gaz-engine car for scouting purposes. We drive from village to village, slowly descending into the valley of the Rhône, asking the same question of persons en route, 'Where are les Boches?' It all seems hit or miss, and throughout the August day the enemy stays just beyond our grasp. At twilight, by some circuitous route, we arrive at the northern outskirts of Soyons, with the river to our left. We pull over. Mathey and the driver go forward to reconnoiter the village, but not before he asks me to pump some air into a weakened left front tire. As the tire pressure increases, I'm slammed against the left side of the car by a cyclonic rush of air. I hear a loud thud, followed by people shouting and screaming about 75 yards to my left front.

I drop the pump and race into the village. It is almost dark, leaves are falling; I try to avoid bits of debris strewn over the road and bodies lying on the ground. A shattered, uprooted tree tilts at a 45-degree angle. The scene is eerie and surreal. A wide-eyed old woman, dressed in peasant black, grabs my hand and pulls me into a small cottage with an earthen floor. In the flickering candlelight, a young man, his buttocks bare, is kneeling. He had a deep four-inch gash in the back of his thigh. Blood is seeping from the wound; the skin is red, blue, and puffy around the edges. She implores, 'Help him! Help him!' I have nothing, no bandages, no morphine, nothing. I leave her and the wounded man and rush into the street, seeking help. People gather. Mathey is running toward me, his upper right side bloody from a shoulder wound. He stops. The bloodstain on his shirt increases in size.

I ask, 'Are you OK?'

'For the time being,' he answers. I help him toward the car.

'What happened?' I shout.

He yells, 'Germans booby-trapped a tree with explosives; placed it across the road before retreating. A bunch of us — German prisoners and French locals — were moving the tree when the damned thing exploded. Twenty-five French and Germans killed and wounded.'

'Christ!'

Where's the driver?' Mathey asks. 'I thought he was with you,' I answer.

Some of the survivors are in need of immediate medical treatment. Mathey is one. A local Frenchman and I work as a team, the car becomes an ambulance, and we drive the wounded to a nearby cottage hospital. I stand guard without a weapon over a wounded German, a soldier in his 30s waiting for treatment. We try speaking in French, because my German is nonexistent and his English is severely limited. Sitting in the small car, we are traumatized and uprooted by the day's events. He shows me a few photographs of his wife and child. I have none to offer; my photographs are hidden deep in the hayloft on the other side of the river. Called abruptly, he enters the hospital and disappears forever.

Jean-Claude Haas, teenage French civilian, at the hotel gates in Alboussiere guarding two German prisoners

Copies of photographs from privately published book detailing the occupation and liberation of St. Peray. Scruby and the author are holding
rifles at port arms. Reigle and Gualandi are standing at ease. September 1944

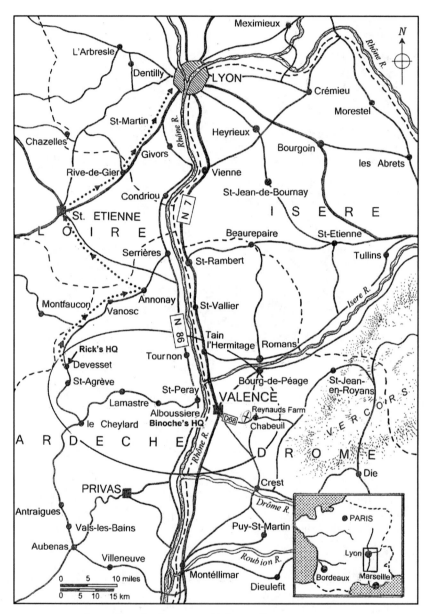

Operations in the Lower Rhône Valley, August 1944

Special Operations in Southeastern France

Presented by Lieutenant Roy Rickerson, co-leader of OSS Operation Louise, Grenoble, France, September 1944

The Missing In Action telegram sent to the Weiss family in September 1944

5
The French Resistance and The OSS

After being on the road for 14 hours, I arrived at Alboussière late that night, utterly exhausted; during my absence, Binoche had requisitioned a small private house for our living quarters. The village was dead quiet and most of my companions were already asleep when I stumbled upon the house, but Reigle, who was awake, wanted to know what had happened. He interrupted my summary and said, 'An American paratrooper captain from the OSS came to the village and requested we join him and his OG (Operational Group) 30 miles further west. They're operating around St. Agrève.' He could use the additional manpower we can supply. Some of his men have been hurt in earlier operations and we could make a difference.

My response was immediate. I wanted to stay with Binoche and his group. Unlike Simmons, I could depend on Binoche when serious matters like combat counted. No hard feelings; I felt that the rabbit trick was a side issue, and it wasn't his fault that it became deadly serious at Soyons. His judgment was sound, his experience extensive. To no avail, mine was the only dissenting vote.

Even in the light of day, with whatever time left to reflect on leaving, I wanted to stay. We left Alboussière early the next morning. Binoche, Madame and Monsieur Serre, the Haas family, Elise, and Simone came to see us off. Even the chef came out of his kitchen to exchange farewells. The driver, a former French Air Force pilot, whom we had never met, drove — no flew — the large four-door Buick-like sedan at seemingly aircraft speeds. I was sure, as he took the next turn without braking, that we'd never get out of this war alive. With battles to come, a chance to be brave, to die in a traffic accident was absolutely ludicrous!

Spinning out of the next curve on to the straightaway, 45 minutes into the journey, he slowed a little and then stopped abruptly to avoid hitting an armed Frenchman standing in the middle of the road, waving us down, while two others carrying rifles slowly emerged from some bushes on the right side. We cocked our weapons and opened the doors. They approached the driver and a brief conversation followed in French.

The driver turned to us and asked, 'Anyone here from Brooklyn?'

'Are you serious?' I shouted in disbelief.

'We are!'

The tallest of the three Frenchmen called to someone hidden in the underbrush. On cue, stepping onto the road as if she were a headliner on the Orpheum Theater Circuit in New York, an attractive young woman in her early 30s, unobtrusively dressed and wearing shoes that had seen better days, approached the car. She greeted us in an educated Brooklyn accent.

Climbing out of the car, followed by the others, I asked, 'What on earth are you doing here? This is the back of beyond.' Before speaking, her eyes filled with tears; she embraced me, then the others. I offered her and her three French friends American cigarettes. We all lit up and tried to relax.

Her story was simple enough: when Japan attacked Pearl Harbor on December 7, 1941, and Hitler followed suit by declaring war on the United States four days later, she was travelling through France on an art scholarship. Pursued by the Germans as an enemy alien, cut off from the States, she was forced into hiding and, incredibly, evaded capture thanks to a variety of sympathetic Frenchmen and outrageous good fortune. 'My French improved as the years rolled by,' she said. 'It was touch and go under extremely difficult conditions for a long time. In fact, about two and a-half years.' Up to now, she had been lucky, surviving on the kindness of strangers. Safe for the moment, overcome by our chance meeting, she asked for another cigarette. I lit one for her. She inhaled deeply and her hand trembled. With a shared sense of belonging, we spent a few more minutes reminiscing about Brooklyn and the Dodgers, its erratic baseball team. Putting on a brave face, we promised to meet in Brooklyn after the war, although it seemed like a long shot. Where we were standing was still enemy-held territory, and the war raged on. Our rendezvous ended as quickly as it began, but before we separated, I gave her two packets of K-ration Camels. There was little else I could offer. She and her three armed companions disappeared, as they had emerged, into the bush.

We found the OSS paratroopers of *Operation Louise,* heavily armed, and billeted in a secluded farm house on the outskirts of Devesset, a small village about four miles northwest of St. Agrève. *Louise* was one of six operational groups, most designated by a female code name, that had been dropped behind enemy lines into southern France between June 6, Overlord, and August 15, Anvil-Dragoon. Major Alfred T. Cox, a former Ivy League football player and a graduate of Lehigh University, was the battalion's commanding officer.

Louise, a section of the battalion, consisted of two officers, Lieutenants Roy Rickerson and W.H. McKensie, in joint command of 14 NCOs. Each section was staffed and equipped to operate independently but could call for mutual support when the success of a mission required it. The men were recruited from the Army for hazardous duty. Soon after our arrival, the 'pilot' filled his tank with petrol supplied by Rickerson, turned the car around, said a few words of farewell in French, waved, and drove off. We entered a large ground floor room. A big, superbly built uniformed paratrooper greeted us from his supine position on the floor. The trooper, Sergeant Adrian Biledeau, had his right leg immobilized and set in a primitive cast. After leaving a North African airfield hours before, he had jumped over southern France from an RAF Halifax bomber, fracturing his left leg between the hip and knee on exiting and breaking his ankle on landing. Most of the other men we met were from Louisiana, upper New York State, and Maine — wherever French was spoken, even if it were a New World patois. Lt. Rickerson, called 'Rick,' was framed like a middleweight boxer and, pound for pound, was every bit as tough.

Rick told me that a month before, he and McKensie had blown up both the Highway Bridge and Railroad Bridge at Viviers to block the Rhône River south of Valence. They placed 160 pounds of plastic explosive on the highway bridge and four charges of plastic at the railroad overpass. A 10-minute fuse was used and duplicated with a 20-minute time pencil. Twenty-five Résistants close to the bridge acted as security, even though the enemy was still using it. Leaving the scene, Rick and McKensie heard both explosions. A few days later, both men learned that the highway bridge had dropped flat across the river, making it impassable for barge traffic. All communication and power lines were broken, and a barge carrying a million gallons of enemy gasoline en route from Avignon to Valence could not reach its destination and had to turn back.

As part of Lt. Rick's OG, we were issued weapons and ammo. I was supplied with an M-1 and a Colt .45 and assigned to protect Frank Lauretta, the unit's radio operator. Lauretta hailed from Denver, Colorado, and whenever he transmitted to Algiers, the unit's headquarters, he used a coded signal plan called 'Strontium.' Like Frank, the other men were equally skilled, having trained together as airborne infantry in the States for a year before parachuting into enemy-controlled France in the summer of '44. Fighting consisted of tactical hit-and-run operations and smash-and-grab raids. This included deception and ambush, such as cutting telephone wires, sabotaging trains, and destroying bridges. Part of the mission was training, coordinating operations, and supplying the local Resistance. Although the big battalions are required to win, this kind of close encounter fighting, a throwback to the French and Indian Wars of the 18th century, kept the enemy off balance and offered great opportunities for killing Germans.

A few weeks before we teamed up with the *Louise*, Rick, Major Cox, and a small mixed band of OGs and Résistants bluffed the commanding officer of a large German field force at Privas, southeast of St. Agreve, into surrendering. Rick convinced the enemy officer that he and his formation, consisting of indentured Turkish, Armenian, and Indian nationalities, all of doubtful fighting efficiency and questionable loyalty, were surrounded by motorized elements of the American 7th Army. Rick warned the German colonel that unless he and his force surrendered, he would not take any prisoners. The ruse worked and more than 3,000 men, including two colonels, six majors, and ten captains, were disarmed and marched into captivity. By any standard, it was one of the single greatest achievements by an OG during the war. Moreover, unlike Simmons, Rick's feat of arms, for which he was never decorated, proved him to be an officer worthy of command. I needed that kind of leadership. Others were decorated for much less!

I was impressed with something else; the OGs had 'clout' — impact, influence, and respect. Moreover, within the military framework, unlike the straight infantry, a man had some control over his destiny. For example: before they jumped into enemy territory, all of the men were given 'escape money' consisting of French Louis d'Ors, 18th-century gold coins with the portrait of the king engraved on one side. Paper money was worthless if you had to negotiate your way out of a tight spot. Gold lessened the odds. The Army considered the OGs an important investment and was prepared to protect them wherever possible.

By comparison, I felt like a sacrificial lamb.

The farm house offered a commanding view of the high, rolling, well-forested country that became more tortuous further west. Because of its location, we were reasonably secure from ambush. Nevertheless, security was tight. Arrivals and departures were kept to a minimum. One afternoon, we gathered for a briefing in the large ground-floor room. Rick explained that our next mission was an attack on the 11th Panzer Division near Lyon, about 60 miles from here. 'It can't be done, we'll be wiped out,' I whispered under my breath to one of the paratroopers sitting beside me.

Rick described the firepower available to the 11th: one battalion of 50 heavy Panther tanks, one company of 12 Mark IV mediums, besides four motorized infantry battalions and an armored artillery regiment of 150 mm howitzers and 170 mm heavy guns. Its mission was to keep an escape route open for the German 19th Army to reach the Vosges Mountains. Once there, with the coming of winter, the 19th could fight defensively on forested, mountainous ground of its own choosing. Our job was to slow them down in the short term, until our 3rd, 36th, and 45th infantry divisions, in hot pursuit, could arrive on the scene to smash them. He glanced at me, looking somewhat amused at my constrained outburst. I felt that our effort would be like a flea attacking an elephant, mildly disconcerting, but nothing more. Having recently been on the receiving end of self-propelled enemy artillery, I was reluctant to meet them head-on again.

After deciding on an action plan with McKensie, Rick constructs a message requesting men, supplies, and money that Frank encodes; they are to be dropped by air. Frank and I walk up to a bedroom at the top of the house from where he will transmit. Frank retrieves the transmitter from its hiding place, switches on the power, opens the window, and clips the aerial to the edge of the roof. He aims the aerial in the right direction, tunes his set to the assigned frequency, puts on his headset, and starts transmitting his message in 'Strontium' code to OSS Headquarters in Algiers while I stand guard. After schedules, map grid coordinates, and supply lists are exchanged and settled, Frank shuts down.

'Frank, is Algiers going to send the stuff you requested — and on time?'

'Yeah, why not? They've never failed before. What's wrong?'

'Well, I'm not used to an army that operates on the belief that your wish is their command. Here we are in the middle of nowhere and you've got everybody jumping at headquarters on the other side of the Med. I'd be lucky to get a chalky D-ration chocolate bar if I asked my company supply sergeant for anything. You even have your own taxi service, courtesy of the Army Air Corps and the RAF.'

He jokes, 'Seeing is believing,' and walks out of the room to join the others below.

Three nights later, the American component of the Reception Committee (RC) leaves by truck for the DZ (Drop Zone), a large clearing surrounded by forest. Our French RC comrades arrive in horse-drawn carts. I am briefly introduced to Marcel who is a French Maquis (rural guerilla band) Captain, designated as an Operations Officer in charge of all parachute drops, and the choice of DZs and RCs in the Ardèche. He grunts and turns away. Markers are set out, visible from the air when illuminated, defining the clearing's perimeter. We check our watches and wait for the plane. The night is dark, the tops of the pine trees stand in silhouette against the sky; the air is cool with the coming of fall. Wohlwerth says to me, 'Did you hear something?' I strain my ears. Nothing! And then, slowly increasing in volume, there is the monotonous drone of aircraft engines.

Suddenly, we're overtaken by a whooshing sound above, as a big black four-engine B-24 bomber races overhead at an altitude of 800 or 900 feet. Action Stations! Recognition signals are exchanged. The B-24 circles above two or three times and then rushes toward us, diving lower, with the speed of an oncoming express train. Parachutes topple from its dark interior, linked to men and supply canisters. Canisters are either the C. or H. type. On this drop, some of the parachutes carrying them fail to open; some others are broken on impact. We run to meet the new arrivals and gather the supplies and their parachutes, a hundred yards away. The plane turns sharply, gathers height, its engines straining, its four propellers biting into the cold air, and retreats into the distance. Frank was right, and I'm dumbfounded. Even more so when I'm told by Rick that it wasn't one B-24, but two! Whoever wrote the song with the opening lyric, '*This is the Army, Mr. Jones, no private baths or telephones...*,' wasn't writing about the Army I had bumped into.

We get the new men and the supplies off the DZ as quickly as possible and into the waiting truck and carts. The landing ground is returned to its natural state, like sweeping an apartment clean after an evening of riotous living. Later at the farmhouse, over mugs of coffee and Spam and cheese sandwiches, we of the RC learn that the new team's flight plan, the journey, and the drop, recently executed, went off without a hitch. For the new arrivals, it is their first combat jump. Between mouthfuls, the new arrivals nod in approval. The operation was 'a piece of cake.' The new men are heavily laden with equipment and armed with United Defense 9 mm UD M42 Marlin 700 rpm submachine guns. It was a type I'd never seen before. I'm impressed. One of the new men argues that they're not as good as the Thompson because they lack hitting power and have a tendency to jam.

While the conversation continues, I think again, 'This is the kind of war I want to fight, with guys you can rely on. You hit the enemy, reach your objective, get relieved — that is, if you survive — to live well between missions. To hell with the foot slogging infantry, the unrealistic expectations, and its awesome casualties!'

Accompanying Rick early one afternoon, I ran into Marcel by accident, outside a farmhouse used as a Resistance headquarters. When I emerged from within and found him on the rear terrace, unseen from the air by an overhead trellis covered with grape vines, he whirled at the sound of my foot fall and aimed a Colt .45 at my head. I didn't make any sudden moves and spoke slowly, 'I'm Steve, Rick's friend. Remember?' Before returning his automatic to its holster, he gave me the once over and refused to acknowledge our first meeting. He was the toughest of men. Bigger than most Frenchmen, he had the same dark eyes and black straight hair. There was something unforgiving about him, a man who weighed each word before placing it, along with others, in short active sentences. He sat down on a wooden chair, hunched forward, and switched on a shortwave receiver sitting on a table before him. It hummed and squeaked. I was just about to say something when Marcel raised his hand, a sign to be quiet, and placed his .45 on the table. He checked his watch and slowly increased the receiver's volume. The first four notes of Beethoven's Fifth Symphony sounded twice and a voice said, 'This is the BBC.'

What followed were a series of coded action messages preceded by an introductory salutation in French beamed to various Resistance networks and individuals: 'The cat is on the ceiling; Jean-Claude wishes Marie well; Speak to me of love.' Hearing another message preceded by, 'The rabbits are more numerous in summer,' he jumped up, said 'That's it,' turned off the set, retrieved his .45, and disappeared from my life forever.

When Rick and I left the farmhouse, I asked, 'What gives with Marcel? The guy nearly killed me.'

'He's a good man,' Rick said, 'but always on edge, a loner and cunning like a fox. Makes trouble.'

Rick complained that, although dropped OG equipment was clearly marked in code, Marcel interfered with its distribution, thereby slowing the execution of planned OG operations. He and his men at times would keep or hide the newly dropped equipment, telling Rick nothing new had arrived at some remote site. 'We would find the containers later.' Rick argued, 'They were empty.'

Our operations were grinding down: the Germans were leaving the region. We cut the odd telephone wire, blew up the last remaining bridge, and avoided a persistent German radio detection van trying to discover our whereabouts. I watched it approach the farm one afternoon from an upstairs window. An unobtrusive gray pie wagon, it stopped at the perimeter fence, its circular antennae searching the air like some large insect; after a few minutes, it retreated and lumbered away. The whole exercise seemed like a half-hearted gesture.

One morning, I drove into St. Agrève with Rick and, while he conducted business, I sat in the shade of a tree-lined town square alongside the communal washing trough and watched the women scrub their clothes. Water poured into the trough from the open mouth of a concrete lion protruding from a large stone wall. The women scrubbed and pounded their piles of soiled clothes, piece by piece, with coarse bars of soap. Limited in oil content, the soap created few suds. The women's blouses were wet, outlining their breasts. The air was filled with talk and laughter, and they sensed my presence. We exchanged glances, and my basic French evoked an assortment of giggles and smiles. Regardless of age, the women were playful and seductive. In similar situations, as in this one, there was always one woman with whom I would have liked to explore further, but the opportunity never arose.

As the region returned to normal, that is, without Germans, and as the threat to my life diminished, I became increasingly ill. My stomach reacted with an unsuspected violence, to such an extent that I couldn't keep any food down, not even water. Dr. John Hamblet, the unit's Medical Officer (MO), prescribed bismuth pills for the condition, but that also failed. The doctor couldn't figure it out, nor could I, but I sure wasn't fit for any purpose.

My seven comrades fared somewhat better. Although not physically ill, they felt worn out; nevertheless, as part of the expanded OG, they prepared to attack the 11th Panzer Division covering the retreat of the German 19th Army before Lyon. Much like the charge of the Light Brigade in the Crimea, a hundred years before, the OG faced annihilation. Before the men left with Lieutenant McKensie, our farewells were no more than a laconic, 'See ya later.' War and train stations have something in common; they're full of arrivals and departures, and I wondered who felt the separation more, the person who leaves or the person who's left? My stomach contracted in response to this disturbing question, and I had no answer.

I stayed behind with Rick, Frank Lauretta, and 10 other men. We broke camp a few days later, loading our equipment onto the truck and command car, turned the farm over to its rightful owners, and headed northeast. I sat next to Rick as he drove the command car for 22 miles along secondary country roads to the small town of Annonay, where he planned to stop and visit some wounded OSS officers at a cottage hospital. One of the officers, Lieutenant Paul Boudreau, leader of *Operation Betsy*, had been hit in the thigh — friendly fire —by a .50-caliber shell fired from one of our P-47s on August 28. He looked to be a sturdy character and in good spirits, sitting in his shorts in the small ward, his legs dangling over the side of his bed. He didn't think this was the kind of war he planned to fight. The hole in his thigh refused to heal! Take a look at this,' he said, pointing to it. The hole was about the size of a quarter and deep but cleaner than some other wounds I'd seen. The skin was blue-green in color and puffy around the edges. I thought a skin graft would solve the problem. The local French doctor was limited in what he could do, not because of his lack of ability, but because of the lack of facilities and medical supplies.

Although thinking positively, Boudreau was worried, too. Nevertheless, I didn't think I'd be as matter of fact as he was. 'The last thing I need is gangrene and my leg amputated,' he said, and then asked, 'How are you doing?'

'Not too bad.' I played down my own complaints, unimportant compared to his.

'I'm a little tired, my stomach's funny, and I feel jittery. I don't know why.'

Rick told him that there was an Army hospital near Marseilles and, now that the highway was open to the south, plans were afoot to have him transferred there. It was time to leave. My hand trembled before we shook hands, then he slowly raised his legs and stretched out on the bed. We said 'So long,' and wished each other 'Good Luck!' Soon after, Lieutenant Boudreau was transferred to the 300th Gen. Hospital in Naples and shipped back to the States for further treatment.

Late that afternoon, after a short eight-mile drive, our small convoy arrived at the southern outskirts of St. Etienne, the major town of a large coal and steel region, surrounded by high dark hills. The Germans were destroying their ammunition dumps within the town rather than allowing them to fall to the approaching American and French forces; the heat, sudden flame, black smoke, and noise from the continuing explosions were inescapable. On one of the surrounding hills, I stood next to a man observing the destruction of the town spread out before us. He was nonchalantly smoking a cigarette and nodding with satisfaction. He seemed to have contributed to the unfolding scene. Mysterious, tall, with fine angular features, crisp dark moustache, and straight black hair, he wore a well-tailored two-piece suit and a black overcoat trimmed with a felt collar draped over his shoulders. He resembled the suave and intrepid British actor, David Niven. And like Binoche and Marcel, observing, controlling, and directing, the stranger stood at the center of events. One thing I did learn from my experience was 'never ask questions,' although I discovered later that he was a high-ranking Resistance officer.

The road was wide open beyond St. Etienne; no minefields barred the way, so we drove the remaining 30 miles to Lyon in about an hour. The Germans succeeded in withdrawing from the city in early September, with the 11th Panzer guarding against any Allied flanking attack from the east before retreating. The mixed group of paratroopers and infantrymen who had left with Lieutenant McKensie earlier had failed to make contact with the 11th, much to their good fortune.

The third largest city in France, after Paris and Marseilles, Lyon is situated at the confluence of two great rivers, the Saône and the Rhône, which are separated by an elongated island. Rick's team and a number of other OG sections took over the Grand Nouvel Hotel on the island's city center. To the dismay of the population who lived on either bank and worked in the commercial and financial institutions on the island, the retreating Germans had demolished almost all of the city's 15 bridges before it was liberated. Some people tried to cross using makeshift footbridges — more of them submerged than stayed afloat; they were unreliable. Without an available labor force, daily life had ground to a halt.

While the war raged further north, I was assigned by Dr. Hamblet and Rick to act as a guard and companion to a B-24 bomber pilot within one of the hotel's rooms, high above the city. The pilot had severely burned his hands in a crash after a bombing raid. His plane was hit by flak and fire broke out. The plane limped along and lost altitude. The heat and the smoke were intense and he was not sure if he ever gave the order to jump. Finally, the plane came in too fast, skimmed along the ground, and crashed into a stand of trees.

Regardless of the prescribed medication, he hardly slept because of the pain. The pilot usually sat in an easy chair, facing the window, wrapped in a bathrobe, his hands swathed in bandages. A dark-haired, reasonably good-looking fellow, he also suffered from survivor's guilt. We talked little during my four-hour shift, but he appreciated my presence. If he were hungry, I fed him as he sat in his chair. I never remember him lying down.

Part of our care was to prevent him from taking his own life. The pilot was usually deep in thought, his mind slowly ticking over. Who knew — and that included the pilot — if the combination of mental duress, physical pain, and survivor guilt would drive him to suicide. Unattended, he could have reached the window in three or four steps and taken his last flight. We couldn't take a chance and kept the window locked. It being summer, the room was uncomfortably warm. Whatever the holdup, the pilot awaited transfer to an Army hospital where he could be treated properly. The wait for all of us was interminable.

Binoche arrived in Lyon and invited Goichet, some of the surviving Ardèche Résistants, and me to a reception at a local restaurant to celebrate the Liberation. During the evening, I discovered that some of those present were Communists and complained to Binoche. 'Of course there are Communists among us,' he said, mocking me. 'There are also right-wing Army officers too. Why shouldn't there be? They were with me in the Ardèche. They're with me now.' But... 'Listen,' he interrupted, waving his finger at me, irritated at my naïveté, 'I didn't give a damn about a man's political persuasion during the struggle as long as he was willing to fight. I don't give a damn, now. Much of France is free! There's more to do!' Humbled, I retreated as the celebrating continued.

A group of our British counterparts called Jedburghs, three-man Allied special forces paratroop teams dropped into France soon after D-Day, invited the OGs and me to their party at another of Lyon's restaurants. When 20 of us took our assigned seats at the dinner table, I noticed that an additional setting and empty chair had been reserved for a Jedburgh comrade, recently killed. His ghostly presence was toasted and eulogized with a variety of local wines, appropriately supplied and drunk with each course. His pals talked to the empty chair as if he were sitting in it. I considered their performance somewhat bizarre until I found myself behaving the same way, a year later, before the newly dug grave of a school chum of mine who had been killed near Metz. Sure, I was denying reality again as a means of keeping death, impermanence personified, at arms length. What folly, because death always wins! With each glass drunk, our mood changed, shifting from somber to cheerful and back again; there was an edge to our bonhomie, jarred by those men with too much to drink, until it was time to go.

Milling about, we exchanged farewells in the darkened street outside. A beautiful woman, whom I had not seen before, standing within easy reach at the edge of the crowd, beckoned invitingly. Moving quickly through the throng toward this stranger, grabbing her in my arms, I pressed my lips hard against hers. In a flash, she became a man. Recoiling, as the others laughed, I was shaken by my incomprehensible public behavior. A grand illusion? A desperate need for closeness? The men, in riotous good humor, blamed the episode on drink and not on any sexual aberration. Unsure, lonely and depressed, returning to my hotel room, I felt like a ship without an anchor, drifting aimlessly on the tide! My dodgy stomach remained problematic and my jumpiness persisted.

Some of the Ardèche OGs had taken over a local brothel. Visiting, I found them lolling about in the large living room of a private house with their newly found, scantily clad, and willing girlfriends. Not to be outdone, I ended up with a woman in her early 30s, with whom I spent the day. She was kind and worldlier than I, both in and out of bed, but she revealed nothing about her life during the Occupation. The following day we met accidentally on the street, and she asked if I would walk with her in the autumn sunshine, a simple human request. Embarrassed to be seen in public with a prostitute, although who would have known, really, I stammered, found an excuse, and declined. She persisted but when refused a second time, turned and disappeared into the crowd, and from my life. An inconsequential meeting? I've never forgotten her.

A few days later, I was invited to another woman's apartment; she had difficulty in deciding whether she wanted me to stay. I wanted her. Finally, she reached a decision. Insisting that our lives were in danger from small marauding bands of former Vichy Milice terrorizing the neighborhood, she warned that if these enemies of Libération broke into her apartment, I was doomed. Unarmed, there was little point in proving her wrong. Without saying goodbye, I descended the back stairs two at a time, slipped out through the rear door and escaped onto the crowded street. Her ruse worked.

Orders came for the OG sections to move by convoy to Grenoble, 60 miles distant. To be seeing Grenoble again after my August escapade came as a complete surprise. I said goodbye to the burned pilot, left to be cared for by others, often wondering if his hands were saved. Major Cox found and requisitioned a three-storied former girls' school for our needs; overlooking a park about two miles from the city center, it consisted of a series of small private rooms, communal baths, and recreational and dining facilities. German prisoners would butcher our beef and young Frenchwomen would serve our meals. Soon after our arrival, we were assigned individual rooms and issued bathroom supplies.

With two other men from the section, I crossed the Isère River over an old stone bridge and followed the steep path up to the Fort de la Bastille. From its large terrace, the view of the city and surrounding snow-covered mountains was breathtaking. But there was a sinister side, for within the fort's cellars the Germans had tortured and murdered 'enemies of Hitler's Reich.' In the weak light of those damp underground caverns, we found the execution posts still standing in the uneven rocky soil. Hanging from some were the leather thongs used to tie the condemned man's wrists before the firing squad took aim. Chilled, I felt it was such a lonely way to die and, in many respects, a disappearance, address unknown.

At the school, we organized a ball, printed invitations, and invited the local girls, who eagerly responded. This was the second time in two months that Grenoble had entertained peace, not war, for me. Many of us attended church services and either mouthed or sang the usual hymns, while photographers from *Life* and *Yank* magazines snapped pictures of 'Warriors Relaxing.' Abe Rockman, an airborne radio man, and I attended the first post-war Jewish Yom Kippur service at a Grenoble synagogue, surprised that it had not been torched by the Germans. Just to be alive was revenge in itself for those surviving Jews — the few shattered survivors Hitler's henchmen had missed — and we liberators. Some of the small congregation greeted us in Yiddish or French, some shook our hands fervently, silently, others simply observed, their black-and-white striped prayer shawls draped over their shoulders. One aging Jew placed his head on my chest and cried with relief and sadness.

Suddenly I was gloating, my eyes full of tears: The Nazis had tried methodically to destroy a race and here was living proof of their failure. After the service, observing the Day of Atonement, the most solemn religious fast of the Jewish year, Abe and I spoke with two young women once we were outside; their shaven heads were concealed in bandanas. By their dress and demeanor, we were unsure if they were recently returned deportees, concentration camp survivors, or 'horizontal' collaborationists. Women living in France who fell in love or collaborated with the enemy, if denounced and caught, had their hair shorn and their heads shaved before their neighbors in a public ceremony.

Entering Harry's American Bar on a chilly fall night in Grenoble, I ordered a Brandy Alexander, a creamy cocktail, similar in taste to those chocolate milk shakes I used to drink at the candy store in Brooklyn. A piano player was playing *You Go to My Head* on a small studio upright. The bar was empty of guests except for a civilian sitting alone who, from time to time, spoke English with an American accent to the solitary bartender. Wearing a tastefully cut brown tweed suit, slowly sipping his Scotch on the rocks and smoking an American cigarette, the pack lying beside him on the bar top, he ignored my arrival, nor did the bartender improve the situation by failing to introduce us. I tried to engage the man in friendly conversation, both of us being thousands of miles from home, but he refused to participate, thwarting any attempt on my part with a disdainful wave of his hand or a look of mock surprise. I thought he was simply ill mannered. When I left for the evening after spending an hour in the bar's hushed funereal atmosphere, I no longer expected the man to reveal anything of himself, his purpose, or to explain why, when most Americans in France were in uniform, he wasn't.

Many of the paratroopers were protective and proud of the individual officers with whom they jumped into battle. Competition between sections sometimes ended in explosive hostility, with fists deciding the issue of who was the best officer. Usually the lead NCOs, representing the different operational groups, fought for dominance, much like male animals in the wild. Size meant nothing, testosterone everything. I witnessed one fight on the second-story stairwell of the girls' school. It all began when one of the troopers denigrated the reputation of the other man's CO, a captain. The early shoving and pushing and verbal slurs suddenly exploded into a hammering at each other with bare knuckles, the interior stonewalls and window glass as much a danger as the punches thrown. I was concerned that one or both of them would fall through the window to the pavement below as they belted, tossed, and chopped at each other. Fists and the edge of the hand did the damage. The cuts, bruises, and loss of blood meant nothing to these tough young men trained to kill. Five minutes later, they were both standing, glaring at each other, pronghorn antelopes, hands clenched, still trembling with anger, neither one having given ground. Gasping for breath, chests heaving, bathed in sweat and bloodstains, they had fought to a draw with their honor intact.

At Grenoble, I was determined to remain with the 'Ardèche' OG as a qualified member. The men were as eager for me to stay as I was. Our team spirit was high and we had served each other well in combat. I still have the silver plaque they gave me, which reads: 'to Stephen J. Weiss, in honor of the Third Section and missions accomplished in the Ardèche, July 17th to September 7th, 1944.'

I went to see Major Cox, volunteering my services. I, who had never made a combat jump, was willing to do so with a minimum of training. Cox was interested and, as the members of the 3rd Section had already spoken on my behalf, he was willing to explore the possibilities.

Cox arranged a meeting with a high-ranking officer at 7th Army Headquarters, requesting that I be transferred immediately. The transfer came under threat when the officer learned I was part of the 36th. Learning that I was straight Infantry and a First Scout, the officer told Cox that American divisions in combat needed all the experienced infantrymen they could lay their hands on, so why should I be an exception? Rifle companies in the ETO were undermanned, some had ceased to exist, and existing replacements were still in the States. The officer turned Cox down cold. 'No buts, that's an order!'

When we met, Cox briefly told me what happened and said, 'I tried, but it didn't work. You'll have to go.' I felt wretched.

How was I to know that the 7th Army officer's decision was based upon one made a year earlier by General George Marshall, Army Chief of Staff. He froze the Army at 7.7 million men and allocated 3.2 million of the 'best and the brightest' to the Air Force. By reducing the Army from 200 divisions to 80, he placed the responsibility for success on 750,000 front-line soldiers worldwide, and I was one of them, as part of a 'chain gang.'

I left Grenoble with regret, almost to the point of bitterness. Bidding farewell to Rick and the men of the 2671st Special Recon, 3rd Section, with encounters in the Ardèche still fresh in our collective memory, I left Grenoble for the third time and traveled by three-quarter- ton truck to Lyon with an unfamiliar OG sergeant, whose presence increased my sense of abandonment and separation. He sensed my mood, agreeing that I had been given a raw deal. Trying to lift my spirits, he mentioned a young couple he had met when we were billeted at the Grand Hotel in Lyon. 'I think the three of you'd get along. It would break your journey, even if it delayed hooking up with the 36th. That could wait. Whaddya say?' I was slow to answer, but in the end, I reluctantly agreed.

A young, animated Anglo-French couple, the woman pert and attractive, the man mildly dark with Semitic features, greeted us affectionately in French and English from the top of the stairs. Entering their apartment, I was introduced to Olga and Ronnie Dahan, whose lively personalities rekindled my spirits. After the second round of drinks, the sergeant rose, wished us luck, and departed.

I accepted Olga and Ronnie's invitation to stay, and after dinner slept in their nine-year-old son's bed. Gerri, their son, was at school in the country. Being out of Lyon served two purposes: receiving an education and avoiding the prying eyes of the Gestapo. For nine days, I stored up energy in squirrel-like fashion by sleeping and eating, in preparation for the ordeal ahead. I didn't realize how mentally unfit I was. Rarely did I leave the apartment. Olga and I listened to the BBC and the AFN (Armed Forces Radio) news broadcasts every morning after a simple breakfast of warm croissants and bowls of coffee while Ronnie left to find work. We heard that the Allied race across France had turned to into an attritional slogging match as German resistance along the Franco-German border stiffened. The Germans called this period 'The September miracle.' In October, bad weather, difficult terrain, and a drastic shortage of men and supplies were hampering military operations, in which the weary, under-strength Allied infantry divisions like the 36th suffered. Before the year ended, it would break the record for continuous days in combat without relief.

Before Lyon was liberated, the Dahans were enemies of Hitler's Reich; Ronnie for being Jewish, having left Algeria before the war to make his mark in Metropolitan France; Olga for being British. They had met at a Deauville gambling casino in 1934 where Ronnie had come to risk his money at the tables and Olga to entertain as part of an English dance troupe. They were married soon after. With Ronnie's piercing dark eyes, as mysterious as the Casbah, and Olga's beautifully proportioned dancer's body and light English coloring, they made a distinctive couple. When war came, they escaped from Paris with thousands of other refugees and settled in Lyon, until 1942 one of the major cities in the Unoccupied Zone.

The invasion of North Africa in November 1942 prompted the Germans to occupy all of France, a move that put enemies of the Third Reich, like Ronnie and Olga, in mortal danger. At one point in their saga, they sought immunity by purchasing a letter for an extraordinary sum from a Spanish consular official, which declared their Lyon apartment to be neutral Spanish territory and off limits to the Germans. However, this seemingly safe haven did not deter the Gestapo from raiding the apartment. During one of their random searches, they hoped to snare Ronnie.

Once, when Gerri was at home, a Gestapo agent, disregarding the consular notice on the door, forced his way in and tried to seduce the little boy into revealing when he last saw his father. The boy, forced to sit on the agent's lap, looked at Olga, turned to the German and replied, 'About a week ago.' The agent left in disgust. In actuality, Ronnie had had breakfast with Gerri only a few hours earlier before leaving the flat to go into hiding. Neither parent had prompted their son beforehand, much to their amazement. The little boy had saved his father's life.

During my short stay in Lyon, I met Laure, the woman who hid Ronnie. She was slender, dark-haired, and of medium height, with angular

Mediterranean features. While we walked to her apartment, 15 minutes away from his own, Ronnie took me into his confidence. What he was about to say must remain secret. Olga was not to be apprised of his clandestine relationship with the woman. 'You can't hide in a sewer 24 hours a day; if the dogs don't find you, the rats will. See what I mean? What's required is a safe house, unknown to your family, an ordinary place that you can enter and leave without raising a neighbor's suspicions. Laure offered that chance to me; desperate, I took it. During the time when the Gestapo was searching for me, Olga or Gerri never knew of my movements or location. Sometimes I'd be gone for days on end.' Ronnie insisted that the compartmentalization of his current relationships and the respect for security and protection must continue. I agreed.

The streets we walked through were crowded with pushcarts, itinerant peddlers, and shabbily dressed apartment dwellers. When we arrived at Laure's first-floor flat, it seemed jumbled and disorderly. I thought it longed for a clean sweep, much like the street below. Ronnie and Laure talked for about five minutes, and afterwards he pressed a wad of bank notes into her hand. Whatever their level of intimacy, stranger things than one woman hiding another woman's husband had happened during the Occupation.

The aftereffects of Klaus Barbie's brand of Gestapo barbarism penetrated and settled in Lyon during the early October chill. One of the Dahans' friends, a married woman in her mid-30s, had been severely traumatized and then hospitalized for a 'nervous breakdown,' having witnessed the following scene: one sunny afternoon, a few months before Lyon's liberation, on a quiet residential street, her father was attacked by one of Barbie's henchmen and beaten to death. The Dahans and the woman's relatives thought that if I stood beside her hospital bed dressed in my American Army uniform her condition would improve. I would represent 'safety.' Friends and relatives gathered around her. I stood there as if on parade. Voices swirled around us with words of reassurance.

'He's an American.'

'The Germans have gone.'

'Lyon is free.'

'You're safe and so are the children.'

'It's all right.'

Her husband moved to her side and wiped the beads of perspiration from her forehead while a girlfriend squeezed her hand affectionately. She looked straight through me without a flicker of recognition or understanding of what her friends were saying. My presence could not overcome her inner terror and accelerate her return to sanity. We left in despair, the attempt a failure. Ronnie told me later that the husband had already taken up with another woman. I felt aggrieved and out of my depth.

I hated to leave the safety and warmth of the Dahans' apartment. Trying to overcome a diminished desire to soldier on, I could find no further excuse to remain. Thanks to them, my physical health was restored; not so my emotional strength. We parted with every intention of meeting again once the war ended; little did we realize that it would continue for another nine long agonizing months. It was a painful separation for Olga and Ronnie. I was an older son going off to war.

The 36th was fighting somewhere in the Vosges mountains of Eastern France, northeast of Lyon, and I had to find it. It is early October 1944. The weather had turned cold, and my summer Army uniform offered scant protection. Somewhere in the Vosges, comparable in structure to the Black Forest across the Rhine plain, the 36th was anchored to the southern end of the Allied line. As part of the American 6th Army Group composed of the American 7th and French 1st Armies, it faced a resurgent adversary using every trick in the book to thwart our advance.

Working my way north from Lyon, standing beside the tree-lined highway in the pouring rain, trying to hitch rides on any vehicle that drove by — open 6x6 trucks, command cars, and jeeps — it became clear to me that the war I was expected to fight was not being fought by many others. Drifting through traffic from one town to another on narrow roads battered either by shellfire or motorized convoys, I discovered that GIs living in the rear fought the war as civilians in uniform. That is, they lived a civilized, predictable nine-to-five existence, surrounded by women of their own age who waited for them at the end of their paper-shuffling day. The sidewalk cafés and the quays along a river were filled with soldiers and their girlfriends, either joyfully conversing over drinks or walking arm in arm beside the moored boats. For these men of the rear echelon, physical and mental hardship as we knew them on the front were nonexistent, and the struggle to remain alive was never an issue. Their jobs kept them out of danger. For every man on the front, there were at least 11 others behind in a logistical-support capacity. How I envied those young lions and their sinecures! It was the Peninsular Base Section (PBS) all over again.

The next day, I reached Vittel, a spa on the western slope of the somber, brooding Vosges Mountains. The 6th Army Group was headquartered at the Hermitage Hotel, in whose art deco lobby two- and three-star generals lounged in small groups, while soldiers dressed in clean class-A uniforms strolled from one office to another across the parquet floors, carrying a variety of official documents; the shooting war seemed very far away. Standing knee-deep in glitter, I was surprised to run into a CI friend I had trained with at Blanding. Santorini was a small, bright fellow, working for a colonel in Intelligence. His colonel was in need of someone with my photolithographic qualifications and, after an interview, requested I be transferred to his office. While I waited for an answer, Santorini showed me around Vittel, particularly the recently liberated internment camp for British and American women. What I saw at Frontstalag 194 were small, ordinary apartment block flats built against the hillside, but Santorini said that some of the 1,300 women, interned since 1940, lived in hotels that were reasonably appointed. He had met a few of the women but by the time I arrived, they were already gone. The following day, I was notified that the 36th refused the colonel's request, reciting the same mantra as before.

Rebuffed and angry, I packed my meager belongings, thanked the colonel and Santorini for their efforts on my behalf, and left in search of the 36th. It took two days of hitching rides on military vehicles, sleeping rough, and depending on the kindness of strangers to eventually find divisional headquarters at Remiremont, a town on the edge of the Vosges. Located near a destroyed bridge that once spanned the Moselle in a house surrounded by others battered by enemy shell fire, I reported to a bored headquarters clerk. He told me that I'd been listed as Missing in Action since the 24th of August, and that my parents had been notified by telegram. I was sure they were overwhelmed with anxiety. I had to let them know I was OK. OK for what? At 19, I was a veteran and old before my time. I had to ask the clerk for a cup of coffee; nothing was on offer. What followed was a replay of the same charade when a divisional officer offered me a position at headquarters. The request was immediately denied. Regiment refused the transfer for the usual reasons. The divisional officer shook his head in resignation. I now knew that without my active participation on the front, similar to that of Eisenhower and Patton, the Allies would have to sue for peace. Time was running out.

Charlie Company was holed up in the woods about four miles beyond headquarters. To find it, I had to travel east from Remiremont on road D-159 to Docelles, the next village. The Germans consistently shelled D-159 with deadly accuracy, surprising those vehicles and personnel who risked traveling along its tree-lined road. Death along it was pointless, indiscriminate, and accidental. This being the case, during the many times I traveled on D-159, there was little I could do to ensure my survival. It was like taking a deep breath before plunging into an icy stream. Company headquarters was located in a forest near Docelles. Following a path in the woods, I reported to Simmons, snug in his forest Command Post (CP). He, Darkes, his executive officer, and Holecek, the first sergeant, were indifferent to my arrival, failing to express any signs of welcome. Having been told throughout my epic journey that that I was one of a group on the verge of extinction, I expected to be hailed as a conquering hero. It was more like, 'Who sent for you?'

Only Lawrence Kuhn, a responsible tall Texan, my platoon sergeant smiled in greeting. He said, 'Reigle told me you were alive.' I nodded in appreciation and stood about five feet across from Kuhn. I thought, 'Who in hell would live in a place like this?' Facing each other, it seemed that the distance between us was much too far. We stood as lifeless as this long-galleried empty room, devoid of any trace of previous human habitation. 'How's Shanklin?' I asked. He stiffened, took a deep breath, and said, 'Shanklin's dead.' 'Dead?' Kuhn's words jumped the distance between us and hit me in the chest with such force that I was physically stunned. My knees buckled. I loved Shanklin. I enjoyed seeing him grin and approved of his boyish good looks. He was wise beyond his years, easy-going, and protective. It dawned that for me leadership was synonymous with fatherliness. Kuhn was like him, but too remote as platoon sergeant. With Shanklin gone, my sense of defeat was immense. Something within me collapsed.

Shanklin was killed in his foxhole at the Moselle, downstream from Remiremont, in September. There was a mix up between Charlie Co. and the Germans at night. Because neither side could see anything, the firing was random and uncontrolled. He might have been taken by surprise. Suddenly, I felt cold, colder than this October day.

I waited for Reigle and the rest of the company to come off the line in the afternoon. They bivouacked in the woods to rest and refit. Reigle and Gualandi seemed pretty tired. We were glad to see each other, although they seemed troubled by my return. I asked after the others. They said that during the last two and a half weeks, Scruby lost a leg to mortar fire and Wohlwerth was hit in the chest by machine-gun fire. Now Shanklin's gone! Only Reigle and Gualandi remained, physically unscathed but showing the telltale signs of combat fatigue, slowness of speech and preoccupation. Reigle wasn't making new friends with any of the replacements and dug foxholes by himself. Gualandi was no longer his cheerful self, and quit smiling. As for Fawcett, Garland, and Caesar, I didn't remember seeing them.

Some of the men were surprised to see me, because Reigle had told them and Simmons that I was being treated for stomach trouble in hospital. Reigle said, 'I think Simmons wrote you off.' One by one, they asked repeatedly, 'Why did you come back?' 'Where was I to go?' I countered in irritation. I looked at them in the autumn light and knew that every one of us was trapped by the same MOS number (military occupation specialty) 745 Rifleman. Nothing else compares to it. I know. The 36th insisted I fight the war its way. Even when I volunteered to risk my life by parachuting into enemy territory, it refused to release me. Death was on its terms. Reigle and the others insisted that I should have figured something out. 'While you were away, sir,' they mocked, 'We've been tormented by S-mines, booby traps, mortars, machine guns, and heavy-duty artillery.' 'At least I'm loyal,' I shouted. They yelled in unison, 'Loyal? Are you kidding? You'll be dead in a month! Shanklin's gone, Wohlwerth's gone, Scruby's gone. What makes you so special?' The enforced togetherness of combat was diminished with each man's loss.

Then there was my friend from basic training, Clarence Weidaw; he was older than I by about seven years, a big, tough, raw-boned guy. After sitting on the damp ground, the weak sun failing to dissipate the cold, I walked over to greet him. 'Weidaw, it's me, Steve.' Not only didn't he answer, he didn't even look up. Balancing his mess kit on his lap, Weidaw kept 'scarfing' his tepid meat and beans slowly mixed with some watery tapioca pudding. 'Weidaw,' I repeated, 'It's me, Steve.' 'We were at Blanding together,' I implored. I looked around for help, for some explanation. 'You're wasting your time,' a GI, unknown to me, volunteered. 'Weidaw's gone mute on us'. 'What happened?' I asked. The same GI answered. 'The Krauts had him trapped in a hay-loft. He wouldn't surrender, so after they blasted the hayloft and set it on fire, Weidaw jumped and escaped under a hail of fire into a nearby wood. He wasn't hit, but he ain't talkin' neither.' I felt that if Weidaw couldn't stand up to this battering, how the hell could I? Change was the squad's main characteristic; all of us were transients, a replacement one day, a veteran the next, here today, gone tomorrow.

I was caught in my own petard. Thus far, our infantry squad had suffered one soldier killed (Shanklin), four wounded (Ropos, Taylor, Scruby, and Wohlwerth), two missing (Ike & Mike-Bazooka Team), and two incapacitated by Combat Exhaustion (Weiss & Dickson) since the Southern France D-Day landings. Men in other squads, like Weidaw, suffered from Combat Exhaustion. It was also known as Combat Fatigue. After approximately 35 days in combat, the symptoms of Combat Exhaustion would become manifest, rendering the combat soldier less efficient, less able to handle stress. Soon, he would be a danger to himself and to those around him. Men who were diagnosed for the condition represented 20% of all battlefield casualties. With one psychiatrist assigned to an infantry division of 15,000 men for the first time in 1943, front-line psychiatric treatment, in practical terms, offered little and was scarcely known to us. The danger signals, a surprise to many, were a slowness of thought, indecision and a lack of concentration, and a pessimistic fatalism. Emerging, as psychosomatic symptoms were dizziness, stomach cramps, hypersensitivity, headaches, the two thousand-yard stare, breaks with reality, and unrelated eruptions of anger. The protective factor offered by small group cohesion when a rifle squad functioned properly was disrupted and fractured by extended combat.

Offered to a selected few of psychiatric casualties was a sodium amytal drug-induced three-day sleep, hot food, and a clean uniform within the sound of the guns. Total treatment lasted between four and six days. After that, the soldier either returned to the front or was court-martialed. Eighty percent of those afflicted returned to duty, but having experienced front-line duty before, few were willing to live through it again. Similar reasons for his initial 'breakdown' remained and were all too apparent. Return is one thing, effectiveness is another. Front-line psychiatry for the fighting man didn't exist. Since no one in authority mentioned and discussed Shell Shock or Combat Fatigue, no personal preventive measures were recommended and pursued. The descriptive word 'trauma' was unheard of. Unwittingly, feeling scared and hope-less, the soldier could contribute to his own death. Who would know? Statistics were inconclusive. Under such deplorable circumstances, if the psychiatric casualty was seen on the front again, it was only for a short period, until he suffered a relapse or was killed.

Using an unauthorized 35 mm camera I had recently purchased in Lyon, 12 of my weary, and poorly clad comrades and I posed at the edge of a dark stand of trees, in which the men's tents were pitched. About 50 feet away a primitive two-story wood and stone farm-house stood alone in a hilltop clearing. That afternoon, in the weak fall sun-light, an enemy reconnaissance plane flew high above us, beyond the range of our rapid firing anti-aircraft guns. Behind my smiles for the camera, as the plane droned on and out of sight, I was at my wits' end.

Early that evening, the temperature dropped. I sauntered over to the farm house in my light clothing, seeking protection from the cold night air. Some soldiers and I were sitting quietly in a small room when the first German shells screamed overhead and exploded nearby. Many of them hit the tents across the way, taking the men by surprise. No fox-holes had been dug. The reconnaissance plane had accurately reported our position. Trapped in their small tents, the men, vulnerable and un-protected, were pulverized; tree and ground bursts combined and hit them from every direction. Shells exploded with an orange flash, light-ing up the woods at random, like fireflies darting between the trees. Screams and shouts mingled with the whine and crump of shells.

The enemy barrage crept out of the woods toward the farmhouse, rattling its stone foundations. Having left the farmhouse to help the wounded when the shelling began, I realized that the trapped men and I were cut off from each other while the barrage continued. In despera-tion, I retreated and rushed into the farm's small ground-floor stall, slid across some stinking muck, and came to rest looking up at the bellies of two agitated goats, standing in the eerie light and bleating. Shell frag-ments hammered the door and destroyed the roof. The barrage lifted within minutes, but yells and shouts continued for some time after.

I ran into the woods. Thirty men had been killed and wounded; their thin canvas tents had been torn to shreds. Tent poles were splintered; blood stained blankets and combat packs were strewn all over the tan-gled earth; all were stark reminders. More medics and stretcher bearers arrived from Docelles by ambulance to care for the wounded and to collect the dead. Without vials of morphine and bandages, I realized later that I had nothing to offer the wounded except compassion. In fact, I had little prior training in first aid.

The turnover and wastage of men continued. A few replacements arrived, far below our requirements. Retribution came when front-line losses overwhelmed the replacement system during the fall. Faced with an unacceptable shortage of infantry, generals 'drafted' five percent of the existing cadre of rear echelon troops for retraining as infantry. When infantry losses soared still further, they drafted an additional five percent. Front-line duty came as a shock to thousands of draftees who, considered the best and the brightest, had accepted a four-year stateside college education at Army expense. Known as the Army Specialized Training Program (ASTP), it collapsed for the same reasons. Suddenly, they were shouldering mortar tubes and firing BARs.

In the following morning's darkness, while in the relative safety and warmth of a neighborhood hayloft, members of my squad and I were issued the usual accoutrements of war, bandoliers of ammo and hand grenades, a clear indication of our return to combat. My heart dropped. Offered the rank of staff sergeant and squad leader, I refused, accepting that of sergeant and assistant squad leader instead. Having lost faith in the Army and feeling miserable, I wasn't prepared to take on the responsibility for 11 other men, particularly when my ability to function was impaired and continued to deteriorate. I got some proper clothes.

I had bad dreams of murky content, such as cleaning my M-1 or digging a hole, which cleared when I caught myself experiencing the same events in reality the following morning. Startled by this déjà vu experience, I interpreted the dream to mean that my death was imminent. At no time during my Army career was I told that every man had his breaking point. After-action psychological debriefing was nonexistent, so a review of the trauma that we experienced was never talked about or explained. Combat medics weren't trained to help diffuse these experiences soon after they occurred, nor was I warned of the tell-tale signs of looming breakdown, such as hyper-vigilance, irritability, intrusive memories, and psychosomatic reactions to combat.

It was pointless to go on 'sick call' and moan about psychic ailments beyond my understanding. Ill-defined symptoms and non-specific illnesses that everyone seemed to have didn't exist until they intruded and overwhelmed. Most everyone was scared; if not, then 'crazy.' I had no way to know that the experience of it, like that of grief, would re-main forever, part of our inner world. If not dealt with professionally, these damaging symptoms would break out again. All they needed was a 'trigger.'

We were not supposed to feel, but to perform. An added unwelcome ingredient was the tension between serving one's country and serving oneself — to follow orders, close with the enemy, and remain alive. In most cases, over time, this precarious balancing act could not be main-tained, even in the face of youthful omnipotence, insisting that death be deprived, regardless how grandiose a concept it was. How shocked are we when this defense, pierced by death's arrival, collapses! I was ill-prepared for what I likened to an 'emotional second law of thermo-dynamics,' being ground down to zero.

Compounding these issues was that since arriving in the Vosges, I could not get warm. The Vosges, higher and more extensive than the Ardennes, was a giant freezer compartment. Even if I wore two pairs of trousers, a tanker's jacket over a field jacket, woolen gloves and head-gear, this combination offered scant protection from the damp, per-sistent, and penetrating cold. Leather boots were inappropriate and unyielding in these sub-zero temperatures. Trench foot was a problem and men came down with bronchitis. Freezing was so preoccupying that it was impossible to think of anything else except finding shelter. Prompting an incipient case of trench foot into something more severe can result in a long hospital stay and a farewell to combat. Rather than shoot yourself in the foot, don't take your boots off for a week in foul weather.

I am ordered to lead a 12-man reconnaissance patrol the following night. We rendezvous in the drizzle with an unknown lieutenant who emerges from the warmth of his underground bunker, immaculately attired in winter clothing, to explain the mission. I take stock of the men nearest to me. My First Scout is trembling, my Second Scout is staring into space, and the knot in my stomach reaches strangulating propor-tions. No Man's Land is a brooding forest — no — an impenetrable jungle. It's pitch black, and the moon has waned. The sound of every advancing footfall, every falling leaf, is amplified. The wind, an enemy ghost army, rustles through the trees.

Hyper-vigilant, we are Shakespeare's Band of Brothers or Rodin's Burghers of Calais. There is a desire to cling together like Eric Kennington's statue of three soldiers in Battersea Park. We step into the void. As our patrol disappears from sight and the relative safety of our own front lines, we shall need all our resources, in this remote corner of France, to prolong our lives against the war's random nature. Our infantry training, such as it is, collides with our human inheritance, a combination of coiled aggression and fear.

To keep sane, one soldier told another, under similar circumstances, 'You have to treat death lightly.' While another offered the suggestion, 'Make believe you're dead already, the rest comes easy.'

We cross into enemy territory, failing to find the necessary landmarks on which we rely for completing our patrol. Was that a rifle bolt slamming into place? Or did someone step on a twig? If it's a rifle bolt, I'll pause, signal my squad to stop and remain silent, listening, assessing the situation further. If not, and no rifle shots follow, we'll carry on. Is that an enemy patrol filtering through the trees? I stiffen, more animal than human. Our mission is to reconnoiter, not to engage the enemy in a firefight.

We became lost in the Stygian darkness and trackless waste, and rather than risk stumbling across the Germans, we sink to the frozen ground, surrounded by wet, waist-high foliage, huddling together for protection. We spent our few remaining hours in front of our lines, just listening. Sometimes trees silhouetted against the skyline resembled the enemy, every bush sure to conceal a deadly device, and a sniper behind every rock.

Ward, my Second Scout, formerly young and fearless, was emotionally falling to bits, even though I tried to lessen his anxiety while battling with my own. I felt that Ward's reaction, like mine, was a failing attempt to create sanity where none existed. Nevertheless, this was not the time to reflect. Fortunately, the Germans were as passive as we. I checked my watch; it was time to return. We were debriefed — chewed out — by the same officer. He was furious at our lack of initiative and our failure to reach our objective. Easy for him to complain from his large protected dugout, wrapped around him like a full-length fur coat!

At the same time, a comrade from Davenport, Iowa lay wounded in the woods, trapped between the lines, close to where we had patrolled. He was too weak to crawl to safety and beyond our reach because of persistent enemy fire. He spent his last 12 hours alive crying for his mother and pleading for help. None was forthcoming. I never understood why

the Germans, by their intransigence, insisted that a GI of little consequence must die.

One afternoon, moving between foxholes constructed with roofs of
brush and branches, serving as protection from tree bursts, I heard a
voice emanating from one hole speaking to someone invisible as he
said, 'You never see any Jews up on the front; they're always behind the
lines working as doctors or dentists.' Quickly, I realized that the voice
belonged to a 'hillbilly' infantryman I liked very much. I felt the sting
of his prejudice.

I was running out of time. I could no longer use omnipotence as a defense: it can happen to the other guy, it can't happen to me. Sooner or
later, a bullet with my name on it would hit me. The thought of clearing
out entered my mind. With the old team gone, with no one to depend
on for guidance and direction, my bouts of anxiety and depression increased. One freezing night, on a wooded hill with the trees packed
tightly together, under a fierce enemy night barrage, its heavy-duty
shells sounding like torrents of water cascading into a bathtub before
exploding, I took whatever cover available by sprawling on the tilted
forest floor close to an older GI. I shouted across to him, 'Ed, what
keeps you going?'

'Blackmail! Married with a kid,' he shouted when the noise of the exploding shells momentarily subsided. 'I'd leave in a flash but for wife
and the kid. You know what I mean; No tickee, no washee.' The shelling
began again. He tried shouting over them; 'No government allotment
check means no support for the wife and no milk for the baby.' While
the landscape bounced with each explosion, I concluded that this guy,
looking disaster right in the face but accepting his family responsibilities, was caught between the devil and the deep blue sea. During another lull, we got up and ran.

Nothing in the civilian world replicates the hazards of combat or its
demands. Some law enforcement personnel may come close in terms
of the risks they run on duty. But 'on duty' means they work in shifts.
Infantry combat doesn't occur in shifts. Police officers may work exces-
sive hours, but their families know where they are and may even see
them on a regular basis. A night sleeping in bed in not considered a
privilege.

Frank Turek arrived as one of a few replacements in early October. A
slender blond kid of Polish descent, with sharp angular features and

wearing a brand new uniform, he took one look at the dead German ly-ing unburied between foxholes, his frozen arm used as a marker point-ing the way along an undulating path, and said, 'No way am I staying up here. This infantry work is for the misinformed.' I don't think he even soiled his uniform before he skipped.

One of the replacements, a fellow from Brooklyn, came looking for me, seeking my advice. He was a small man in his late 30s who had been drafted five months before, more at home in an office than the outdoors. Seemingly intelligent, I doubted if he had the guts and stamina to make it up here for long. I sensed his apprehension, his anxiety transmittable. His was a simple story: he had married within the last two years and recently became the father of a son. On the verge of being disquali-fied for service because of his age and marital status, his draft board disregarded his personal circumstances and appropriated him for the Army. To make matters worse, he was trained as an infantry rifleman, a demanding job even for those half his age.

Combat is for single, athletic, teenage boys and not for aging men of 38. 'What can I do to stay alive?' he implored.

'Watch me and do as I do,' I responded, cold as ice, 'and don't be too cautious or too aggressive; choose somewhere in between.'

I felt sick to my stomach, knowing there are no guarantees. Becom-ing combat-wise increases your chances of survival, but only up to a point. If luck exists at all, it soon runs out. What I couldn't tell him was that his days were numbered regardless of how he behaved, be-cause the accidentals of combat would overwhelm him like the rest of us. I believed that to come through physically unscathed, as some did, defied the odds and was a rarity. Maybe, I thought later, he ought to have talked to somebody else, someone upbeat, positive, encouraging. Between the two of us, I was the 'old man,' scared as hell and ready to bolt at the slightest provocation.

I don't know if he survived, but soon after, some older guy from Brook-lyn was killed. I think his name was Katz. Conflicted between the need to stay alive and the desire to serve my country, I walked off the hill the next day, October 16. Without any plan or destination in mind as both sides began shelling, poorly clad in the ever-present drizzle, walking down one hill and across the next, trekking through the wet brush, I followed a forester's trail for the next two-and-a-half hours. Emerging wet and cold from the dank foliage, I checked the landscape from the edge of the woods. I came upon four Sherman tanks manned by Arab tankers of the French 2nd Armored Division, bivouacked in a farmyard on the outskirts of a small village.

I approached, nodded, and, with their approval, climbed the wooden ladder up to the hayloft and dug in, placing my rifle beside me. I slept like a dead man for eight days. Outside my refuge, the temperature hovered near zero, but I remained warm, ensconced deep in the hay, having little need to leave. These men, cooking meals over a wood fire, offered chunks of roast lamb and thick brown bread, washed down by mugs of searing hot coffee. Their four American Sherman tanks, on which were stenciled the map of France, were close by. My French had not improved, but I did learn that these North Africans had served under General Alphonse Juin in Italy and fought at Cassino. None had been to France before! Feeling rested, I left the confines of the hayloft, thanked my adopted friends, and faded into the woods in search of Charlie Company.

Simmons and I stood facing each other within another cave-like CP in the woods. He wanted to know why I had taken off without saying anything to anyone. I said nothing but thought, 'What was the use? I'd been feeling increasingly exhausted and nervous ever since being surrounded.'

'You could have told me,' he continued. It seemed hopeless. From the quizzical expression on his face, he understood nothing. I heard him say, 'Don't you remember that when we first met in Italy, I offered to be your priest, rabbi, friend, and confidant rolled into one, that you could come to me with your troubles?' I didn't remember that. I held Simmons in contempt and made no request — not for hospitalization, not for rest camp. From my life experiences, I could not protest without destroying myself in the process — that would come soon enough. I simply was intimidated by the Army, the governing power, and Simmons, its representative.

Whipped, I didn't have the guts to say, 'But you were none of these, you bastard. You never gave a damn! When the shooting started, when the rest of us got knocked around, you played it safe and never led from the front. I know our casualty rate is consistently over a 100 percent a month, and you, your second in command Lieutenant Darkes, and the Company First Sergeant are still around? Not a scratch! How come?'

Before the conversation ended, I made one request. 'Let me work loading and unloading rations and supplies. I'd still be doing my duty while using the time to regain my health.' Other outfits sent men in need of rest on a three- to four-day fatigue detail to a service company, but not the leader of Charlie Company. He mumbled something about taking care of me and abruptly said, 'Dismissed.' I returned to my squad. Who knew what Simmons had in mind? My getting killed, in the meantime would solve his problem.

Fortunately for the remaining men, there were a few seasoned squad and platoon sergeants that tried to compensate for his lack of leadership. Learning from bitter experience, we old hands had to be self-reliant and decisive — that is, until fear and exhaustion set in. Young, inexperienced second lieutenant platoon leaders came and went with increasing rapidity because of their incompetence or inexperience. No court-martial for them if they failed, no accusations of misbehaving before the enemy, but instead an assignment to a safe billet behind the lines. We didn't want a so-called 'officer-apprentice' up here because of the trouble he'd cause. It was the responsibility of an officer to minimize the danger to the enlisted man. If his judgment were sound and his decision-making reasonable — under the circumstances — we'd protect him, regardless of his personality. According to a friend of mine who also served in the infantry, in his outfit, if an officer failed to qualify and placed his men in needless danger, minimizing their chances of survival, he was sometimes eliminated by one of the men in self-defense.

A newly assigned second lieutenant arrived one night and, bending low, entered a large dugout shared between me and two other sergeants. In the flickering candlelight, he looked no more than 20 in his spotless uniform. For the last few days, our front in the Vosges had been quiet. In spite of what seemed to be a tacit 'live and let live' arrangement between the Germans and us, he insisted on checking our defenses. 'Let's leave well enough alone,' one old hand implored, as the two of us nodded in agreement, but to no avail. The young 'shave tail' reconnoitered our perimeter, checked our supplies of ammo and rations, nodded his head in approval and, as he moved through the woods, tripped over a flare that whooshed and rocketed in flight high above the trees, turning night into day. That was enough for the Germans; they pounded our once quiet area with heavy-caliber shells for the next 15 minutes, sounding once more like tons of water exploding from broken water mains. It was enough for Simmons too; the young officer was gotten rid of immediately.

Night came early at this time of the year, and with it a sharp drop in temperature. Maintaining a poorly manned front line, I shared a hole with another soldier. GIs in holes on either side of us were far enough away to offer little mutual aid in an emergency. To offset our lack of manpower, I added a box of MK2 'pineapple' fragmentation hand grenades to my personal armament, placing it at the lip of the foxhole. I stood guard within the confines of my hole while my comrade tried to get some sleep hunched over at its bottom. Someone moved not 30 yards from me. I reached for a grenade and pulled the pin, pressing my right hand against its lever. Footfalls seemed to surround us in ever increasing numbers. Tense, I nudged my pal lying at my feet, whispering that the enemy had penetrated our positions. He stared into the darkness, poised, and listened intently for a few minutes, then said, 'Steve, I don't think so. The wind is bending the bushes into odd shapes and the footsteps are falling leaves.' I wasn't so sure and continued to peer into the blackness.

When nothing happened, still clutching the grenade, I tried to replace the cotter pin needed to disarm it. All was pitch black. One attempt after another failed, and it seemed that the only alternative was to toss it and risk an explosion that would incur an active German artillery response. Finally succeeding in replacing the pin, I realized my forehead was damp with sweat.

Foxholes without top cover were death traps because we were exposed to tree bursts, a mixture of steel fragments and wood splinters caused by exploding shells from high-velocity enemy 88s or deep-throated 170 mm cannon shells. It was suicide to be caught in the open.

The next day, Simmons issued the following order. I was notified by First Sergeant Holecek that for hightailing it (dereliction of duty) on October 16, I was ordered to dig a slit trench, six feet long, one foot deep, and one foot wide. I was to construct it for use as a latrine for the men of the first platoon.

On uneven ground, in a cold, driving rain, with the roots of the oak trees breaking through the earth's surface, I hacked away with my inadequate, primitive entrenching tool. Pelted by the rain, my uniform took on a darker color and rivulets of water ran down my cheeks and the back of my neck. The glutinous mud stuck to the tip of the entrenching tool and the roots refused to split under my hammering. Squad members hurried over in ones and twos, startled to learn of Simmons's punishment, watching in disbelief at the swinging and hammering of my entrenching tool that failed to penetrate the frozen roots. One of the men witnessing the scene said defiantly, 'Don't let him do this to you.' Feeling abandoned, weary of being under fire with no end in sight, I had reached my limit. Simmons never explained. I'm sure he considered my behavior dysfunctional and maladaptive; in some ways, I thought so myself. Even if my cause were just, I was self-destructive.

The hell with him; two days later, on October 28, as the battle for the small town of Bruyeres erupted, Privates Weidaw, Dickson, and I walked off a hill nearby and left the Vosges. Without recourse to any higher authority, we headed south, getting lifts on military vehicles from sympathetic truck drivers. We found shelter in wrecked or deserted farm buildings strewn along our way, but finding food was another matter. At rear echelon installations, mess sergeants' suspicions were aroused when they saw us hovering about begging for food. Our bedraggled olive drab (OD) uniforms and slovenly appearance clearly indicated we were on the run. Rear echelon soldiers looked, acted, and dressed differently. By comparison, they were well fed 'fat cats,' properly attired. Most mess sergeants rejected our pleas for food and instead gave us scraps that even a dog would reject. Was plying us with hot coffee and thick Spam sandwiches on white bread considered aiding and abetting three fugitives? If discovered, would a food-purveying mess sergeant be jailed as an accessory to our crime? As the days wore on, hunger and cold, food and shelter were major concerns. Even in civilian life, men died in less threatening surroundings.

We carried on for two more days and ended our trek at the military airfield on the outskirts of Lyon, where we found shelter in one of the huge hangers. Although there was broken glass everywhere and many of the buildings were damaged, squadrons of P-47 fighters and C-47 transports were the base's active participants. The air war added a whole new dimension to our understanding of combat. It seemed so modern and clean compared to our experience moored to the ground. We watched from the sidelines.

P-47s were used with increasing frequency as fighter-bombers as the war progressed; armed with eight .50 caliber machine guns and space for six rockets, they would take off with their one-ton bomb loads, form up in the sky above the field, and head northeast. We'd wait on the tarmac for their return, weather permitting. An hour or so later, first as dots on the horizon, then at close range, the P-47s would reclaim their full size at the same time their wheels hit the ground. As the planes rushed past us, their flaps were up, their 2,800-horsepower air-cooled engines exultant, their whirring propellers a blur.

Our venture was doomed from the start. Walking off a hillside does not constitute a plan and hope is not a method. If we had decided to walk into Switzerland or across the mountains to Spain or return to the Ardèche, either to seek asylum or simply to disappear, that would have sufficed. The three of us never sat down to discuss our future, possibly because we had none. Not being able to see beyond the next meal, we thought that the Army, in its infinite wisdom and benevolence, would sort out our immediate circumstances. We weren't rational and were bruised by the Army's callous disregard, its absolutism. Seeking redress but ignorant of how to achieve it, we were lost, disconsolate, and forgotten. We thought we had our youth, but even that was distorted by the fortunes of war. Feelings of anger and rejection were distorted by lassitude and isolation. Fair play was what I demanded, that each man do his duty and take a turn at the front. I didn't know how to protest, except through behavior, which was easily misinterpreted. It never dawned on me, for example, to have said to Major Cox in Grenoble, 'No, Major, I'm not going back. You might as well call the MPs.' I never confronted Simmons or disobeyed his order to dig, because I was too young, naïve, and intimidated by rank. Army power sided with him.

Rebuilding in Lyon continued apace. At its center, I mounted a crowded bus and was surprised to see Ronnie Dahan standing in its rear. I waved; intuitively, he knew what I'd done, or so I thought, and avoided my gaze. My rumpled uniform and disheveled appearance was out of place and decidedly suspect. He was not to blame for my transgression. Helping me now was risky; he would incur the wrath of the French and American authorities and jeopardize his family's future if discovered. At the next stop, he brushed by me and exited, disregarding my outstretched hand. At the very least, I could have used his advice.

Weidaw, Dickson, and I agreed to separate. They decided to turn themselves into an Army hospital near Lyon the next day, and asked if I'd join them. Both men hoped to receive medical treatment for their combat fatigue. I refused, believing the medics would turn them over to the military police first. They had nothing to lose, however, because we were at a dead end. Weidaw looked wearily at me. Neither one of us could have predicted that as recruits at Blanding, our future would go so grotesquely wrong. The next morning, they shuffled off, dispirited before their time. I was overcome by sadness and loneliness. Feeling unsure of my next move, as a last resort, I decided to return to the out-fit.

Traveling northeast, I was offered a lift by the driver of a command car. There was heavy military traffic on the tree-lined, two-lane road. The driver tried to pass a convoy of two-and-a-half ton trucks loaded with boxed 105 mm ammunition. Swinging wide and accelerating, we raced passed the first two trucks but coming abreast of the third, our right front wheel locked into the truck's left rear wheel. The truck driver tried to shake us off by swinging right; we tried to disengage by swinging left; oncoming traffic loomed a half a mile distant. We were running out of time and space. Finally, our joint maneuver to uncouple succeeded. Decelerating, we fell in behind, mindful that we either could have crashed into one of the roadside poplars or an oncoming vehicle, or blown ourselves to smithereens.

That night, I found refuge in a barn and remained hidden for two days. Leaving its protection, walking up the road on the outskirts of Vesoul, a road and rail hub at the base of the Vosges, recovering my composure, I surrendered to a rear echelon MP patrol commanded by a captain who never heard a shot fired in anger. After an initial inquiry, I was locked up in a dilapidated local French jail. The cells, looking more like clapboard outhouses, empty of furniture and open to the harsh winter weather. My state of mind stopped me from breaking out. A few hours later, the MP on duty told me that two 36th divisional MPs were arriving shortly by jeep. Who cared?

Late the same night, under armed escort, I was delivered to divisional headquarters, situated in a village on the western slopes of the Vosges. More like a mining camp or gulag, the village, drenched in black, stood outlined against the stark, glaring streetlights hanging from invisible wires. It seemed empty of life and surreal as the jeep's thick indented tires crunched against the snow. Simmons didn't claim me this time and he disappeared from my life forever, at least physically. I spent the rest of the night in an underground bunker guarded from above. I stamped my feet against the frozen earth and longed to wrap my hands around a hot mug of coffee. I lit a cigarette and exhaled, the smoke mixing with my frosted breath. Whether my immediate misery was self-inflicted or not, I was deeply depressed and felt that if I were taken out and shot, it would be a relief, not a tragedy.

The following morning, November 1, I am escorted under guard to a clinker-built single-story dwelling whose interior was converted into an office by divisional headquarters. A pot-bellied stove filled with burning wood warms the premises. I am charged by an officer for 'misbehaving before the enemy,' having abandoned my company twice, once at Laval on the 16th and again at Brechitosse on the 28th of October. He quotes from Article of War 75 that 'any conduct by an officer or soldier not conformable to the standard of behavior before the enemy set by the history of our arms is culpable,' and warns that the penalty for misbehaving could be death by firing squad. I shrug my shoulders, shaking off his threat the way a retriever flicks off water. When he says that the enemy is defined as any hostile body that our forces may be opposing, such as a rebellious mob, a band of renegades, or a tribe of Indians, I'm inwardly amused and filled with contempt. Accused of willful neglect, I will soon face a General Court-Martial.

Walking back to the bunker, I accidentally meet Sergeant Kuhn, recently awarded the Distinguished Service Cross (DSC) for gallantry, and another tech sergeant; they both were about to receive battlefield commissions, an outcome of the manpower shortage and their talent. Kuhn was combat tested and courageous and, compared to some of the other officers I had met, he was more efficient and practical than those from either West Point or OCS. I could have served under him, but the timing was off, and it was too late.

Learning of my predicament, they express feelings of concern and regret, recognizing my situation as one of the few choices facing an infantryman. As an alternative, I could have shot myself in the foot — a self-inflicted wound — as others had done under duress. Relieved, warming to their mutual regard, I know that the three of us have more in common than the types assigned to divisional headquarters who will survive. My route is tortuous and guilt-ridden; my survival in doubt.

Even as a prisoner, I discover that the Army, like a freight train shunting to and fro, hurries up and waits. What military justice there is grinds slowly, but I'm assigned a defense counsel, Major Benjamin F. Wilson, Jr., to whom I tell my story on demand — action in Italy and France, the D-Day landings, the night attack, evasion and escape, service with the French Resistance and the OSS, willingness to make a combat jump without training — that, it seemed to me, added up to a decent level of performance under hazardous conditions in such a short period of time. He seems disinterested and even stifles a yawn. Was he mirroring my own lassitude and ambivalence?

Then he says to me in hushed tones, 'We can make a deal.'

I stare at him in amazement. 'What do you mean?' I reply.

He answers, 'It's really simple; all you have to do is to go back to the front. The prosecution will drop all charges and forget everything.'

'Wait a second.' I say, 'You wanted to talk about extenuating circumstances relative to my case. I assumed we had a case and you wanted to help me. I'm not making any deals. What kind of a lawyer are you, anyway?'

I knew nothing of legal plea bargaining; either you have a defense or you don't. Until now, I had been taught and agreed that America was 'the land of the free and the home of the brave,' a democracy in which a man was judged by his peers. Innocent until proven guilty! I had taken high school civic courses that reinforced these fundamental principles. Now, at 19, talking with my lawyer, who wasn't one, my whole belief system unraveled. Betrayed, first by Simmons, now Wilson! Having been a Boy Scout and an athlete, I respected teamwork, appreciating such leaders as Al Cox, Roy Rickerson, Laurence Kuhn, and Harry Shanklin. What didn't exist was an equal opportunity exchange program between the front-line troops and the rear echelon. Under present conditions, Wilson had no front-line experience. If he had, he might have redefined the handling of my defense and appreciated my situation. I demanded equity!

It is pouring with rain on the morning of November 2. My MP guard and I drive along a wet farm track toward a cluster of olive drab pyramidal tents huddled against the first of a series of wooded hills, searching for the division's psychiatrist, a newly created position. Sounds of battle drift down from above. Because of my pending criminal charge, I am referred to Major Walter L. Ford, MD for psychiatric evaluation. Ford had joined the division in Italy in 1943 and was supposed to be an expert on the emotional disorders of soldiers. He was directed to testify at every court-martial in which the accused had allegedly committed a major offense, such as mine. In addition, Ford was instructed, after conducting his own psychiatric investigation of the soldier's life and background, to inform the court whether or not the accused was responsible for his behavior. If it were determined that the accused was not responsible, he would not be punished and go free.

Major-General Fred L. Walker, commander of the 36th in Italy, suggested to Ford that if a soldier had performed well at the front but now suffered from combat exhaustion, he was to be seconded to a rest area to recuperate for as long as necessary. Walker added that if some men lacked the physical courage or strength of will to withstand the exigencies of combat, they were to be transferred to less hazardous duties. Ford admitted that the general's suggestions were new to him. How he applied this additional information is unknown. Were Simmons and Major-General John E. Dahlquist, the new divisional commander, aware of Walker's views? Nothing is documented.

Ford must decide whether I am suffering from fear and raw discomfort or incipient breakdown. Some doctors already know that each moment of combat imposes a strain so great that men will break down in direct relation to the intensity and duration of their exposure; thus, psychiatric casualties are as inevitable as physical wounding. For example, 10 days in combat was worth 17 calendar days. Around 35 days on the line, most men display symptoms of combat fatigue. At 90 days, the soldier has reached his upper limit. Depending on the type of battle, the ratio of psychiatric casualties to battle casualties can range from 1:1 to 1:10. Finally, after calculating how many men in a 600-man infantry battalion suffered wounding after a battle, those remaining suffered psychiatric stress-related problems. Thus, who is left fit for the purpose?

Seeking protection from the bad weather in one of the large M-1934 pyramidal tents while waiting for the major, I help comfort the wounded of the Japanese-American 442nd RCT, lying on stretchers awaiting medical attention. Accreted to the 36th because of the division's manpower shortage, they are involved in an ongoing battle in the woods nearby, by orders of General Dahlquist. They are to relieve 275 trapped soldiers, led by Lt. Marty Higgins of the 1st battalion, 141st RCT, who are surrounded by the enemy. The rough terrain, first gradually rising and then falling away to a deteriorated escarpment, provides the Germans with every possible advantage. The chances of being overrun are high. The sounds of battle drift down through the heavy rain. Like other skilled special units appreciated by the high command, they perform as infantry.

Major Ford arrives, and after he and the MP have a word, the major signals me to join him at one end of the tent, where we can talk privately. A bland but harried man, he asks a few opening background questions and, in response, I list my combat experiences without any sense of reality. He seems indifferent and avoids asking me anything about death and dying, the loss of friends, and Simmons's invisible leadership. I make no attempt to convince him that my cluster of symptoms is real, that my bad dreams and déjà-vu episodes will contribute to my personal destruction. Nevertheless, I'm betraying my country and myself, but is my mood symptomatic of a deeper frustration? Disturbed or not, I am being held accountable. Isn't my anger directed against myself? Instead of a physical self-inflicted wound, is this mental? I'm bound to suffer, not the Army. He scribbles some notes and then nods to the MP that our half-hour meeting is over. No recommendations are forthcoming. I am returned to the bunker within the divisional stockade to await further developments.

A few days later, I discover that the 442nd has achieved its objective. Although 40 of the trapped men were killed, 214 men were saved, but at an appalling price; the 442nd lost 200 men killed and missing. Eight hundred are severely wounded. Under strength, as a result, the Japanese-American RCT — the most highly decorated unit of the U.S. Army — would never be as effective again.

Operation Louise OSS paratroopers in Grenoble, France, September 1944. 'Rick' Rickerson is standing on the far left, the author is in the middle.

Vosges diploma for contributing to its liberation in 1944

The author in Lyon soon after its liberation with an American
reporter in early September 1944

The author's rifle squad in the Vosges October 1944. Kneeling left is Fawcett, unknown; Standing second from left, Weiss, Dickson, Reigle, Gualandi, Ward

---

WAR DEPARTMENT

The following was submitted by the European Theater of Operations War Department Observers Board.

a) *The longer the 36th Division stayed in the line, the greater incidence of disciplinary problems and psychosis cases, as reflected in the increasing number of court-martials, stragglers, and hospital admissions for exhaustion. It was observed that sending a small group of men and officers on rotation and temporary duty to the U. S. during the latter part of this period caused a lift in the morale of the entire division out of all proportion to the number who actually benefited.*

(CSI Battlebook; Anvil/Dragoon, 62-67, edited quotes from AFG Board; Report 639; Combat & Staff Lessons, 7th Army, Invasion of So. France (WA. DC. 1945)

Extract from ETO Army Ground Forces after-action report related to the fighting quality of the 36th Division during Operation Dragoon.

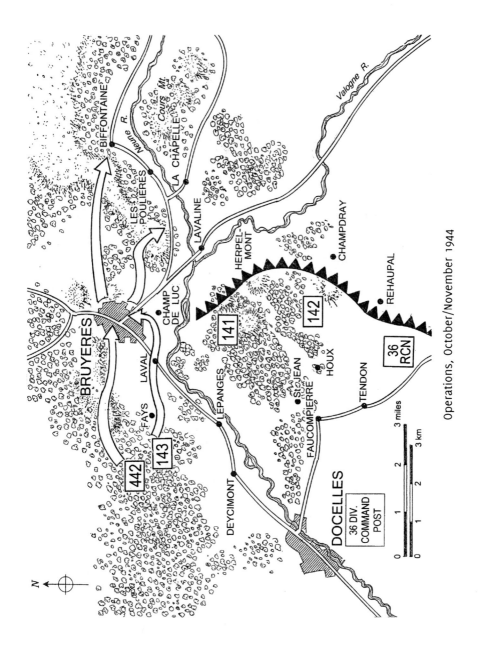

Operations, October/November 1944

6
Court-Martial

The winter of 1944 was one of the coldest on record. Some men leave the warmth of their billets in the village, above which curls the smoke from their pot-bellied stoves. Wearing olive drab parkas, mufflers, and combat boots over their uniforms, they trudge through the snow toward the church, slightly hunched over in the cold. At 09:30, November 7, 1944, facing the new arrivals, the Trial Judge Advocate, Captain John M. Stafford, calls the court to order to hear the case of Private Stephen J. Weiss, Army serial No. 12228033. Someone has forgotten to pre-heat the interior of the rough-hewn church, and it's cold. The court-martial detail of 15 officers take their seats behind a long makeshift table in front of the altar. A primitive effigy of Jesus, seemingly puzzled by the unfolding ritual, looks down from the wall behind. The members of the prosecution and the defense sit behind tables where once the congregation gathered. The court reporter, Corporal Russell C. Trunkfield, who charges 10 cents per 100 words, will transcribe. He prepares for the ensuing trial by moving his chair closer to his desk and opens his note pad. His bill will total $4.34.

The members of the court, trial judge advocate, assistant trial judge advocate, defense counsel, assistant defense counsel, personnel for the prosecution, and court reporter answer to their names and are sworn in. I am arraigned and charged with breaching *Article of War 75, Misbehavior*, to which I plead, 'Not Guilty.'

The prosecution calls its first witness, Major Robert O'Brian, Jr., Adjutant of the 143rd Infantry Regiment, who testifies that on the 16th of October, Co. C. was before the enemy in the vicinity of Laval, and that on the 28th October, Co. C. was before the enemy in the vicinity of Brechitosse, France. Co. C. Morning Reports, introduced as evidence, show that I was Absent Without Leave (AWOL) on both occasions. O'Brian testified that he spent half of his day at Regimental Headquarters. That's three headquarters behind the front, if you include the company CP. Inwardly, I refuse to continue as infantry to prop up the rear echelon at my expense.

Under cross-examination, O'Brian was asked if he were present at the 143rd Rgt. HQ.

'Yes,' he replied.

Defense: To your knowledge, was the entire regiment committed to the line on that date?

Witness: I can't answer that question [says O'Brian] because we were rotating battalions at that time.

Defense: Can you say for sure that Co. C. was before the enemy?

Witness: Yes I can.

Defense: How do you know?

Witness: Because, in addition to being Adjutant of the Rgt, I am its Historian and I spent four hours in the evening with the officers of the Rgt. getting the records in shape. I know they were.

Defense: And on the 28th of October can you say for sure that C. Co. was committed against the enemy?

Witness: I can. Yes.

Captain Jess W. Jones, redirects (examination) for the Prosecution: Sir, you mentioned that there were times when battalions were rotated. Are battalions taken from the actual fighting or are they in a reserve status?

Witness: They are generally in reserve status.

There being no further questions by the prosecution, the defense, or the Court, the witness is excused and withdraws.

The prosecution offers, as Government Exhibit 1, an extract copy of the Morning Report of Co. C. dated 3 Nov. 1944; the defense offers no objection, and it is received as prosecution's Exhibit 1 and becomes part of the record of trial.

At the request of the defense counsel, the court agrees to recess until 1300 hours because certain witnesses essential to the defense have not arrived. The court convened at that time, and the defense and prosecution were ready to proceed.

Defense: The accused has had his rights explained to him in connection with making a statement, sworn or unsworn, or remaining silent. He desires to take the stand and make a sworn statement.

Prosecution: Private Weiss, do you understand that you many remain silent or may make a sworn or unsworn statement before this court?

Accused: Yes, sir.

Prosecution: Do you fully understand your rights?

Accused: Yes, sir.

Prosecution: What do you desire to do?

Accused: I desire to make a sworn statement, sir.

I take the stand and present, upon direct examination, a chronological account of my Army career from the period prior to my enlistment to the present. My presentation lacks impact, directness, and focus. I relate my 'Missing in Action' experience in a jumbled and desultory fashion, a mirroring of the boredom that pervades the proceedings, although the episode and its implications are central to my case.

Under cross-examination, I testify that I went back into the lines with Charlie Company on October 15 and left the morning of October 16 because I could not stand the enemy artillery fire. I return eight days later and find the company in reserve. On October 28, I leave the company for the second time while it is tactically before the enemy because of intense enemy artillery fire. I have not convinced anyone, including me, that I suffer from combat fatigue, even though Major Ford's psychiatric report, introduced as evidence, indicates a mild psychoneurosis.

My actual defense that I served my country well and now seek parity with non-combatant soldiers working within the safety of the rear will never see daylight. Discouraged, I seek fair play, but this will remain buried under the notion that I suffer from combat fatigue. Obdurate, the detail will insist that I must return to the front, regardless of any extenuating circumstances. Feeling confused, I'm not capable of formulating ideas or dealing with reality. How conscious I am is questionable. Somehow, I sense that my shattered adolescent omnipotence, the realization that I too can die, has collided with fulfilling my oath of allegiance. I cannot find the inner resolve to carry on, because deep within me I'm angry, which emerges as indifference.

I am haunted by the fact that all the foot soldier can look forward to is an untimely death, being wounded, or being listed as missing, the latter a euphemism for death. Nothing exists in the infantry comparable to the Air Corp's 25- or 50-mission limit; when air crews reach these limits, they are relieved from further combat duties. Newly trained combat replacements arrive from the training centers or dissolved Army college programs. They are green and will be thrown into combat among strangers to learn painfully, as I had, and with high losses of their own, how to fight as individuals in old war-weary units. Most are ill-equipped to face the rigors of combat as the cadre of experienced infantrymen dwindles. As one combat veteran remarked, 'Don't send us any more replacements, we haven't time to bury them.'

I aided and abetted the prosecution lawyer's disinterest in my 'Missing' experience. He chose instead to dig right into the events during October.

Pros.: Did you leave your outfit on the October 16th, 1944?

Acc.: Yes, sir.

Pros.: Were you fighting when you left? Was the outfit fighting when you left?

Acc.: We were up on the line, sir.

Pros.: Why did you say you left on the 16th?

Acc.: Because I broke down inside; the artillery shells were coming in and I shook all over and just went to pieces.

Pros.: Then you turned yourself back in. How many days later?

Acc.: Approximately eight days later.

Pros.: Now, did you leave your outfit again on the 28th?

Acc.: Yes, sir.

Pros.: Why did you leave then?

Acc.: Intensified artillery barrage. I went to pieces again.

Pros.: Do you know what the 75th Article of War is?

Acc.: Yes, sir.

Pros.: On October 16th, 1944, did you understand what that was?

Acc.: Yes, sir.

Pros.: On October 28th, 1944, did you understand what the 75th Article of War was?

Acc.: Yes, sir.

Pros.: Tell the court just how you left on October 16th. When did you leave? At what time of day?

Acc.: It was in the early morning, about seven-thirty.

Pros.: How did you leave without anyone detecting you?

Acc.: I don't know if anyone detected me or not.

Pros.: Did you walk away?

Acc.: I got up and walked down the hill.

Pros.: Was there shelling at the time?

Acc.: Yes, sir.

Pros.: You ran down the hill?

Acc.: Yes, sir.

Pros.: Did anybody else run with you?

Acc.: No, sir.

Pros.: Were you in proper position in relation to your squad?

Acc.: Yes, sir.

Pros.: When you got down to the bottom of the hill, what did you do?

Acc.: I climbed another hill and walked along a narrow path and came to a village.

Pros.: How long did you have to walk to this village?

Acc.: I should say approximately two-and-a-half hours.

Pros.: When you left this first time, did you know you were leaving your outfit?

Acc.: Do you mean did I realize it?

Pros.: Yes.

Acc.: Yes, I realized it.

Pros.: Did you definitely make up your mind? Had you been thinking about it the night before?

Acc.: No, sir.

Pros.: When did you make up your mind to leave your outfit?

Acc.: When the enemy artillery opened up, and the shells began to fall.

Pros.: When you got away from the artillery fire, say down to the foot of the hill, what did you think about down there?

Acc.: I could hear it and was shaking.

Pros.: On the next day, did you feel it was your duty to return to your company?

Acc.: I still was nervous, sir.

Pros.: Were you trembling the next day?

Acc.: Yes, sir.

Pros.: Did you feel a duty to return to your company?

Acc.: Yes, sir.

Pros.: Did you make an attempt to go back the next day?

Acc.: I thought it over, sir.

Pros.: What conclusions did you come to?

Acc.: I wasn't fit; I would be a detriment to my unit.

Pros.: On the day after that had your nervousness subsided?

Acc.: To a degree, sir.

Pros.: Did you make an attempt to go back the next day?

Acc.: I was still nervous.

Pros.: Did you still tremble?

Acc.: Not as much as the first day.

Pros.: When you finally did decide to go back to your organization, what made you pick that particular day to go back?

Acc.: My mind was clearer and I realized in the full sense of the word that I had a duty to fulfill to my unit.

Pros.: And what did you do then?

Acc.: I returned to my unit, sir.

Pros.: When did you return to your duty?

Acc.: About October 24th.

Pros.: On October 24th, did you go up to the line?

Acc.: No, sir.

Pros.: What was the company doing on the 24th?

Acc.: The company was bivouacked in buildings.

Pros.: Were they within shell fire?

Acc.: You could hear our guns going off, but not the enemy's.

Pros.: When did you go back into the line proper after the 24th?

Acc.: The 25th, I believe, sir.

Pros.: On the 25th, was there any shooting up there?

Acc.: No, sir. I would say occasional machine gun bursts or rifle fire, but no heavy stuff by the 'Jerries'.

Pros.: On October 28th, 1944 when did you leave the company?

Acc.: I left very early in the morning.

Pros.: About what time?

Acc.: Around four o'clock.

Pros.: What made up your mind to leave at that time?

Acc.: The artillery barrage, sir.

Pros.: How did you get away? Did anybody see you when you left?

Acc.: I imagine the other soldiers saw me.

Pros.: Where did you go when you left?

Acc.: I walked down the road for a while. I got a 'hitch' on a truck and went through a few villages; I can't remember their names. I stayed in a barn and cried.

Pros.: What were you crying about?

Acc.: I was all shaken up inside.

Pros.: How long did you stay away?

Acc.: Two days, sir.

Pros.: Until the 30th?

Acc.: Yes, sir.

Pros.: What happened then?

Acc.: I turned myself in to the MPs.

Pros.: Where?

Acc.: At Vesoul.

Pros.: How did you get to Vesoul?

Acc.: By truck.

Pros.: What made you go to Vesoul?

Acc.: It was just as good a place as any. It was a town and I wanted to get away from the artillery.

Pros.: I ask you on both of these times when this artillery barrage started coming in, did you really try to stay there?

Acc.: Yes, sir.

Pros.: What went through your mind at that time?

Acc.: My mind was cloudy. I couldn't think straight.

The following three questions were from the court.

Court: When you were cut off from your company close to Valence, what did the tank destroyer open up with?

Acc.: Three-inch guns, sir.

Court: How close were they?

Acc.: Some hundred yards.

Court: During this period you were with the Maquis, did you have any combat with the Germans? Did you engage in any fighting against the Germans during that time?

Acc.: No, sir.

The first two questions astound me. Here I am, however disconnected internally, fighting for my life, and this officer wants to know the caliber of a weapon. I've no idea what he's thinking or what his priorities are, but his question is totally irrelevant to me. My eyes wander heavenward in disbelief. Regarding the third question, Mathey and I spent 14 hours hunting Germans, but recalling that episode, in which many people were killed and maimed completely escaped me.

Although my court-martial is my protest, I see through the flimsiness of my one-dimensional defense. But I'm sure, even though I don't give a damn, that the prosecution and the court see through it too. Moreover, I feel that I'm poorly advised by an amateur and have little faith in the judicial process. Throughout my testimony, one officer spends the whole time doodling with a pencil, never once looking in my direction.

Settimo Gualandi is introduced as a defense witness and testifies on my behalf, saying that I never gave any indication of being afraid and that I had carried out my military duties well. Gualandi closes, saying that he could not remember whether Charlie Company had been the subject of artillery barrages on the 16th and 28th of October. His testimony tended to bolster the prosecution's case.

While listening to Gualandi, I realize that all the men on the detail are commissioned officers, ranging from lieutenant to colonel; there is not an enlisted man among them. Many of the officers are from the division rear, a safe haven. I believed that if an officer had committed the same offense, shamefully abandoning his company to seek safety in the rear, his commanding officer would have sent him to a rest center instead and then reassign him to a non-combatant outfit, because the American Army protected its officers.

Since my enlistment, I had served the military system as one programmed to submit and obey orders; in my world, plea bargaining and negotiating did not exist. To make matters worse, almost everyone in the church was an amateur soldier; a West Pointer and other professional soldiers might have been more understanding of the charges filed. Did these former civilians know anything about the standards of leadership and morale with which to measure my past effort? Most of us present were the short-term results of a mass-produced military assembly line, and that included my defense counsel. Basic training centers and OCS replaced the factory.

I was not allowed to choose, but was assigned defense counsel from the same divisional legal pool that assigned the prosecuting attorney, an unthinkable situation in civilian life. Predator and victim collude in a pre-ordained outcome; numb and resigned, I bare my throat to greet the last assault and sacrifice myself to preserve the system.

Recently, reflecting on this episode as a man no longer young, my defense would have been better served if I had insisted on a qualified lawyer for my defense and that the following character witnesses be called:

the leader of the tank destroyer column who saw me leap onto the turret and fire the .50 caliber machine gun at the fleeing Germans; my comrades for whose benefit I stood guard below the hayloft; the four for whom I stood aside and waited for the police car to return, risking capture or death at the farm if it didn't. Earlier on, these men had abandoned me in the open field at night. Should they be court-martialed for running away? I might have requested Commandant Binoche, Gendarme-Lieutenant Mathey, Major Cox, and Lieutenant Rickerson of the 2671st to appear. Cox could have validated my willingness to jump into combat without any previous parachute training.

His and another OSS citation would have been read to the court; below the silver parachute wings, the latter read, 'to Stephen J. Weiss, In honor of the 3rd Section and Missions Accomplished in the Ardèche, July 17-Sept. 7 1944.' We could have called the division psychiatrist as an expert witness to discuss the meaning of my déjà-vu dreams in relation to future combat performance. And Simmons! In what way did he mean to help me? If as an adult I could have advised the young, callow soldier, together we might have mounted a much stronger defense. The last sentence falls into the category of, 'If I knew then what I know now,' but life isn't like that. Since there were no further questions by the prosecution, the defense, or the court, Gualandi was excused and withdrew. He was wounded soon after and disappeared from my life, seemingly forever.

My court-martial ground on. The Defense requested that it wished to offer in evidence as defense Exhibit A the psychiatric report made by Major Walter L. Ford, the Division psychiatrist on Nov. 2, 1944.

Pros.: The United States has no objection.

Law Member: It will be received.

Defense: The Defense rests.

Pros.: If it pleases the court, the United States would like permission to recall the accused to the stand.

President: Permission is granted.

I was recalled to the stand, reminded that I was still under oath, and questioned.

Pros.: Weiss, are you willing to go back and fight?

Acc.: In another capacity, sir.

Pros.: Are you willing to go back to Co. C., 143rd Inf., and fight?

Acc.: I don't feel fit, sir.

Pros.: Have you made up your mind that you are not going back, Weiss?

Acc.: I have not made up my mind, sir. I feel I'm losing my mind.

Pros.: Have you ever tried exercising your mind, Private Weiss? You have made up your mind, however, that you would fight in another capacity?

Pros.: Off the line, sir.

Pros.: Will you or will not you go back and fight?

Acc.: I don't understand the question, sir.

Pros.: I think you understand my question, Weiss. Will you go back to your line company and fight?

Acc.: I don't think I can, sir.

There being no further questions by the prosecution, defense, or the court, I was excused and resumed my seat next to my counsel. Ours was not a collaborative venture. I don't remember defining the substance of the *Seventy-Fifth Article of War (Misbehavior Before the Enemy)*, nor did the prosecution. Recently, I discovered that it is a catch-all article that 'relates to any conduct by an officer or soldier not conformable to the standard of behavior before the enemy set by American military historical precedent.' The tactical relationship between an American soldier and his enemy is more important than the distance separating them. Since I took off when an attack was going in, the Article did apply. After the prosecution and the defense made closing arguments, the court was closed and adjourned to vote in the manner prescribed in *Articles of War 31 and 43*. By a secret written ballot, I was found guilty of misbehavior before the enemy.

I was asked to rise and face the court. The President of the court looked at me and said, 'Private Stephen J. Weiss, Army serial number 12228033, you are to be dishonorably discharged from the service, to forfeit all pay and allowances due or to become due, and to be confined at hard labor, at such place as the reviewing authority may direct, for the term of your natural life.' Gone were my $70 Army pay and $32 family allotment per month. I stood there, impassive. They didn't kill me physically, but at 19, my life over, I was nothing more than a living dead man.

Under guard, along with some other soldiers who had been sentenced, I spent the time trying to keep warm by stamping my feet on the iron-hard ground and banging my hands against my shoulders, but even with two field-jackets and two sets of trousers, thick socks and combat boots, warmth sold itself at a high price in the damp, freezing air. It was senseless to think of the future because I wasn't a man who had any. I felt regret for my family, some of the surviving members of my squad, and the men I had known who were either wounded, dead, or had just disappeared. And so I waited near the bunker, feeling numb between meals, eating small amounts of an unidentifiable mush that was ladled onto frozen aluminum mess kits. There seemed no point in shaving in cold water, brushing my teeth, or combing my matted hair because, as far as I could tell, I was headed for oblivion.

One dark, wind-swept night, we prisoners were indentured as a work detail and trucked to the banks of the Moselle. Because of the incessant rain, the river had overflowed its banks and engulfed a group of low-lying M-1934 pyramidal tents. We were sent to retrieve them. Walking across the soggy ground and wading into the torrent up to our hips, we had to pull on the ropes holding the tent pegs, anchored to the ground in three feet of water, to shake them loose. Hypothermia meant nothing to us. Battered by the rampaging river in which we continually lost our footing while dragging the canvas's dead weight, we tired easily. After retrieving the four tents, soaked and exhausted, we set one up on high ground and built a fire. Some of the men were hillbillies who, as they dried out, sat close to the fire, singing country songs such as *I'm Walking the Floor over You* and *Blood on the Highway*. I would have preferred listening to Glenn Miller's big band arrangements of *Serenade in Blue* and *At Last* rather than this hillbilly lament. Dry, our work at an end, we shuffled back to the stockade in the morning for some mugs of hot coffee.

7
Prisoner

In what seemed to be on a moment's notice, about 10 of us prisoners climbed onto the back of a 6x6 truck and motored 20 miles to Epinal, a large town and the capital of the Vosges department, situated on the banks of the Moselle. There were several detours, the driver was cautious, and we were on the alert for mines during our two-hour journey. Entering a walled courtyard, we were subsequently confined within a French barrack that had been hastily evacuated by the Waffen SS. Their rubbish littered the main room and their primitive sexual scrawling, some painted in color, adorned the walls and parts of the ceiling. According to the graffiti, the SS didn't think much of French women. Assigned to a room with another GI prisoner while the others were taken elsewhere, I sat on the cement floor, indifferent to my surroundings, leaned against the wall, and shut my eyes; a driving rain pelted the windows. Two days later, we prisoners were gathered together at Epinal's central freight yards.

Although bombed and strafed consistently by the Army Air Corps until liberated in late September, Epinal, being a major railhead for the Army and the local population, swarmed with black soldiers of the Service of Supply who worked as laborers around the clock unloading cases of ammunition and boxed rations from freight cars onto waiting trucks or into adjacent warehouses. Military goods trains, drawn by steam locomotives, arrived and departed with clockwork regularity.

We were waved on and jumped aboard a train heading west. Rumor had it that our destination was Paris, 150 miles distant. The few escorting MPs commandeered a carriage in front of our own; without a guard present, escape was nothing more than leaving the train at one's convenience. Without ambition, marooned in a foreign country, what was the point of escaping? The casualness between prisoner and guard had its drawbacks, however, because no preparations had been made to feed us, either on or off the train. Some prisoners, entrepreneurs and scroungers by nature, pilfered food supplies (boxes of the Army's luxurious '10 in 1' rations) from supply cars standing at sidings beside us in an attempt to ward off starvation. One 'tall in the saddle' Texan leaped from the open window of our car onto the top of an open railcar and stole three boxes of rations, tossing each one to us in turn. Whenever the train stopped, delayed for one reason or another in towns like Luneville or Bar-le-Duc, we'd jump off and build a fire beside the tracks. We'd fry bacon or ham to go with the powdered eggs, bread, and coffee. Although grimy from continuously living in our clothes, we ate very well during our four-day journey. Like 'knights of the road,' those tramps who rode the rails during the Great Depression, we were doing no more than just staying alive in the wet and cold.

I don't remember entering Paris, leaving the train, or becoming separated from the rest of the prisoners, but a jeep and driver were waiting for me at the side entrance of the Gare de l'Est, one of the city's principal train stations. It was late at night. The Paris that I reached in early December for the first time was not the Paris I had learned about from either the French Line color brochures or my high school French teachers. Both praised a life of Gallic culture and charm, an excellent cuisine, and great wine. Outside the station, I saw a city steeped in darkness, in which ghost-like figures walked quickly by. It was a 'city of silence.' Those few automobiles that sallied forth were of indeterminate vintage and charcoal powered. They put-putted along the remaining glistening cobbles, large fuel converters mounted on their backs like giant turtle shells. The rare café, open to the lonely passer-by, was an oasis of subdued light whose steamed windows blurred the interior into a romantic vision.

We drove in the open jeep with the wind whipping at our faces, past the closed department stores along the rue Lafayette to where it joined Boulevard Haussmann. From avenue de Friedland, it was a short distance to the Arc de Triomphe, standing in the middle of a star-shaped square surrounded by its wheel of cobbles. We skidded around its magnificent structure and headed down avenue Kleber, past the Hotel Majestic, a former German headquarters and the last enemy stronghold to fall during the Libération, to the Place du Trocadero by the river. Between the two curved buildings of the Palais de Chaillot, I looked across the Seine, overpowered by the imposing ironmongery of the Eiffel Tower, an upright slab of corrugated black steel against the dark winter sky. We followed the avenue de Versailles that ran along the river west to the Porte de Saint Cloud, where I discovered a reduced copy of Bartholdi's Statue of Liberty standing on the far side of the Grenelle Bridge. For a moment, I thought I'd come home. Joining Route National 10 on the outskirts of Paris, we headed for Le Mans, a large cathedral town in Normandy, about 140 miles distant.

All the MP could tell me was, 'You're going to be locked up for a long time.' I shrugged my shoulders in response and remained silent.

'How come I'm not handcuffed?' I asked moments later.

'You've got some place to go? Go ahead, take off. You've tried that before and where'd it gets you?' He was right. What would be the point? We stopped at a roadside truck stop between Versailles and Chartres to grab something to eat and to break the journey. Administered by the Army, the propriétaire and the waitresses were French. There were about 20 military vehicles in the parking lot, while inside, truck drivers and GIs sat in the warm smoke-filled room devouring their midnight breakfasts. Condensation gathered on the windows and rivulets of water scarred the panes. I was tempted to finger-paint my initials on one next to our table, but I thought better of it. Considering the impermanence, both my initials and I would disappear within the hour.

Back in the saddle, we raced across the flat farmland and approached Chartres. Where once summer wheat flourished, there was nothing but miles of empty fields. We reached the summit of a hill, expecting to see a continuation of the same monotonous landscape but instead, thrusting upward, as if shaking off its earthly restraints, the Gothic cathedral of Notre Dame de Chartres was boldly silhouetted against the skyline, not five miles away. This time the French Line and my French teachers were right.

The debris of combat, mute testimony of the Battle for Normandy, was strewn from the Channel beaches to the banks of the Seine. What we found west of Chartres were shattered villages and towns whose remaining inhabitants were digging themselves out of the ruins. Broken roads, busted bridges, and time-consuming detours made driving conditions hazardous. The twisted remnants of shops and cafés stood as temporary memorials to last summer's battles.

8
Living the Prison Sentence

The Loire Disciplinary Training Center (LDTC) was located near the city of Le Mans in Northern France, not in an existing city jail, but in an open field. Under the command of a Colonel Peck, there were three one-story red brick farm buildings of varying sizes on the premises. For administrative, cooking, and medical purposes, the Army had converted these buildings. No billets existed for the prisoners. We came to the end of a cow path, and I climbed out of the jeep and stood beside it in the mud while the driver and the stockade MP signed and exchanged forms and papers transferring me to the latter's jurisdiction. The driver's mission completed, he nodded, threw the jeep in reverse, turned and, I assume, drove to Le Mans for some rest and recreation before making the arduous return trip to Paris.

We, the prisoners, under the surveillance and guidance of a complement of MPs, who in civilian life were mostly 'big-city' policemen, and a section of an infantry battalion that never saw combat, ordered us to erect a stockade the size of a football field that eventually would house hundreds of men in outdoor cages.

Living conditions were elemental; two men shared a small crawl-in tent for sleeping. Blankets and straw were in short supply. There was a primitive inefficient communal toilet and washroom. Chow lines, one man behind the other, snaked into the kitchen through one door and exited another. In between, the usual Army fare was doled out onto each man's mess kit.

Work began at 4 a.m. the following morning, when three heavily laden trucks driven by black GIs arrived loaded with building materials. Under the supervision of rear echelon Army engineers, we began constructing our own prison from the ground up out of wood posts, rolls of barbed wire, and clinker-built watchtowers. We used iron bars to build individual underground punishment cells and worked in our combat boots that stiffened further with each drop in temperature. Dressed in our thin uniforms and lightweight overcoats, we were ill-suited to repel the freezing cold. Our clothing was not waterproof and the knitted olive drab gloves and knitted caps were worthless. Each work party ran into difficulties trying to crack the frozen earth with pick and shovel when power-driven pole-diggers and dynamite really were needed. All of us, stamping our feet on the 'tundra' and slapping our hands across our sleeves to keep warm, were prime candidates for trench foot, respiratory ailments, and frostbite.

Held hostage to the weather, we longed for something hot to eat and drink. The makeshift kitchen was ill-equipped to feed ravenous men who burned up calories at a rapid rate hacking away at the permafrost in sub-zero climatic conditions. And don't forget the wind-chill factor! After a week of struggling in these conditions, some of the men came down with pneumonia and were sent to the hospital. I struggled on, although the thought of running away crossed my mind. The penalty for such behavior, once caught, was a prison sentence carried out in a stateside Federal penitentiary. I concluded it was too high a price to pay.

Because we tired easily, I wondered if the camp authorities were deliberately keeping our daily caloric intake below the minimum needed for such exertion as part of our punishment. However, to be fair, we didn't get enough food on the front either. For the months that I spent as a prisoner, I dreamed of food every single night; juicy roast beef au jus or tender medium-rare charcoal broiled New York-cut steaks, roasted Idaho potatoes, and baby carrots. Sometimes, I'd dream of a full five-course meal that included wine with each course. For dessert, I chose an Italian or English trifle inundated with thick whipped cream, followed by a rare French Napoleon Cognac and steaming cups of Colombian coffee. As I wasn't much of a smoker, a Havana cigar was optional. Driven by hunger, I vowed that if I survived the miseries of incarceration, I would never starve again, regardless of the consequences.

Day after day construction continued, hemming us in more and more. The stockade was extended and divided into two interconnecting sections, finally reaching its prescribed shape about December 16. At the same time, rumor had it that a furious battle was raging in Belgium. Big Al, a former Chicago policeman and now one of the MP guards, said that the Germans had secretly attacked and had broken through a lightly held part of the American line in overwhelming strength and were causing havoc. Not only were there high casualties, but the enemy also seemed unstoppable. The Allied command had been taken by surprise.

A former infantry captain, recently recovered from wounds that included some facial disfigurement, arrived on an official sales mission.
Under the watchful eyes of the guards, all the prisoners were turned
out and ordered to form a single column in front of the captain's makeshift desk. He guaranteed freedom to any prisoner who volunteered
for combat during the crisis. All charges dropped! Coupled with its
usual stress and high casualties, a shattered American front line had
to be reformed and the enemy onslaught of 200,000 men blunted before the U.S. Army returned to the offensive. Volunteers were needed.
I thought, 'The manpower shortage, combined with the breakthrough
termed 'The Battle of the Bulge' had reached such dire proportions that
even we fuckups were asked to serve.'

When my turn came to respond, I turned him down cold. He, like
Simmons and the court, were not willing to compromise. It was either
front-line duty or nothing. He looked at me with loathing; turning, I
walked away in disgust, a feeling directed not only toward him, but toward myself. I no longer had the courage to do what he did, to take my
chances with death and wounding as outcomes. That time had come
and gone, and I returned to my tent. To the credit of some fellows I
knew, they volunteered and were assigned to bomb and mine disposal
engineer and air corps units — a common assignment, a dangerous
operation.

A bugle call broke my dream of food. Breakfast took place before day-
break. There was no need to get dressed, because my tent partner and
I slept in our clothes. To keep our combat boots pliable, we kept them
under the blankets. Walking to the end of our cage within the stockade, I stood in line waiting to brush my teeth in the wash house. Men
roamed about everywhere. I ran into two fellows I knew from another
company of the 36th. A GI from Detroit, of medium size with dark Polish features, looked more jazz-oriented than military, even in his fatigue uniform. His tent mate was much bigger, slower moving, and
from the Anglo-Saxon South. They performed a daily ritual between
them. The Southerner would ask his pal, 'What's a chicken, Willie?'
and his pal from Detroit would always answer, 'A chicken is a big-ass
bird.' For some reason, no matter how many times the question was
asked, I'd always burst out laughing after his pal answered.

The men of each cage spilled out onto the catwalk, singly and in groups, one after the other, according to the guards' timetable, to head for the mess hall. We would enter one door, mess kit in hand, hoping there would be enough to eat of the powdered eggs, porridge, bread, a dollop of marmalade, and coffee. Much of what hit the mess tins or emptied into our metal drinking cups was either spooned or ladled out of large dull aluminum pots and pans by four or five of the enlisted kitchen staff. There was another door beyond the last pot through which to exit.

One morning, on the way to the mess hall, I heard someone nearby shout, 'Get the lead out and hurry up.' I responded, 'Blow it out your ass.' I was grabbed by one of the guards shuffling beside me and marched up to the side of the mess hall. My nose was pushed into the rough red brick wall. I stood standing at attention, looking at the cracks and chips of the brick an inch away, for about an hour, worried and hungry, when 'Bow Legs,' the Staff Sergeant in charge of the guard detail, a small man with mean narrow eyes, a broken nose, and long arms approached. 'So this is the son of a bitch that won't follow orders,' he yelled in a New York accent. Whack! His right fist shot out and smashed into the upper left side of my face, forcing the right side of my forehead and cheek into the unforgiving brick. My eyes stung, blood rushed down my cheek, and dripped on the ground. Bow Legs, cussing aloud, pushed and shoved me up the steps and into the administration building where I expected further punishment, but in front of an officer and some of the MPs, I was at last allowed to tell my side of the story.

I said that when I heard the command in the dark, I thought it was one of the other prisoners. The MPs present were skeptical of my explanation; Bow Legs offered to put the gloves on with me and fight it out in the shower room, but I declined and stuck to my story. He taunted me some more, but by this time, he and the others became bored. Sensing they had drained all the drama out of the experience, their entertainment at an end, I was warned to stay out of trouble and keep my mouth shut...or else. Bow Legs had my name now and used it to his advantage. Soon after, I was visiting a friend in the other cage and overstayed my time. Bow Legs, on an inspection tour, caught me out of bounds. He carried a reinforced metal-clipped tent pole as if it were a British officer's riding crop and hit me across the back without warning, whipping the pole back and forth in quick succession; disregarding the pain he inflicted, I turned, looked at him, and laughed in his face. Bow Legs would have to kill me before I'd submit to his cruelty.

We were all amateurs: guards, MPs, prisoners alike. Even the colonel in charge of the LDTC was not an experienced prison administrator, but a building contractor in civilian life, specializing in street paving. Sometimes I'd see him walking from his office, a dour, inaccessible, crisp-looking officer, and wondered how he reconciled his position as a prison administrator, trapped in a backwater, riding herd on a bunch of misfits, when fighting colonels were leading men at the sharp end. Missing from his agenda was a plan to retrain the prisoners and return them to duty! There was no attempt to salvage our minds or restore civic pride. Instead, we did lots of calisthenics. I joined a 30-man choir that entertained wounded soldiers convalescing in hospitals near us. The sound of black spirituals reverberated through the wards a few evenings a month. Nevertheless, those satisfying moments aside, we simply were warehoused; time was wasted.

Many inmates believed that as soon as the war was won, we'd be released, honorably discharged, and shipped home to resume our lives. However, there was no official confirmation and, as far as I knew, whether I served my sentence in Europe or in the States, it was to be served to its fullness of time.

When the weather improved, we'd route march out of the compound, but in the vicinity of the camp, overlooked not only by the watch tower guards manning their heavy M-1917 .30 caliber water-cooled machine guns, but others, at ground level, carrying their M-1911 .45 caliber pistols. On a bright sunny afternoon, a prisoner in this loosely grouped formation walked a little further to the left than one of the guards thought acceptable and was warned, 'Hey you, get back in line.' I don't know whether the prisoner heard the warning, but when he repeated the move, the guard drew his .45, aimed, and fired. The guard struck the man at close range; the prisoner went down, as if kicked by a mule. The prisoner laid clutching his leg and writhing on the pavement. We stood there in disbelief. Others ran to the wounded man, shouting, 'Medic, get a medic up here.' A watchtower guard immediately phoned for medical assistance. Impotent rage rippled through the group, leveled at the armed guard's indiscriminate, abrupt, and unwarranted behavior. An ambulance arrived, moving slowly through the crowd standing in and on either side of the road. As soon as the medics completed their first aid, the wounded man was carted away.

Sometimes I yearned for the privacy of a life outside the wire in simple terms: a hot bath, a comfortable bed, and a girl. These thoughts were based more on fantasy than memory. If I were a prisoner of war (POW), escaping to reach the safety of my own lines or those of a neutral country was the purpose of the exercise, but I was simply a prisoner of my own government. To escape would incur the wrath of the French police and the American Army. Some of the inmates thought otherwise and gambled. Two prisoners, former 82nd Airborne Division paratroopers, evidently feeling they had had enough of life within the cage, cut through the wire one night and fled. They were found missing on roll call early the next morning. The military authorities began the search for them, which quickly spread to the rest of Normandy.

I was not only pleased with their accomplishment, but also delighted that they had lulled Bow Legs and the staff into thinking that, as prisoner athletic instructors, considered a soft billet, they would stay behind the wire. But these paratroopers by definition were nonconformists who lived by their own rules. The excitement and drama rippled through the cages. Prisoners repaired the gap in the wire, the infantry battalion increased its mobile guard detail, and jeeps with a three-man crew circled the camp, training their mounted M-1919 .30 caliber light machine guns upon us. Even the spruce, remote, and taciturn commanding officer, Colonel Peck, seemed visibly disturbed. Most of the inmates with whom I talked figured the paras would make a clean get away and placed bets, with cigarettes the common currency, to support their claim.

After three days without word, I figured that the paratroopers had passed into history and were well hidden and cared for in Paris, living off the black market and prepared to outlast the war. On the fourth day, I was shocked to learn that they had been captured. Trapped in nearby Le Mans, two disheveled and handcuffed paras were shuffled in and paraded down the catwalk. An exultant Bow Legs, walking beside them, berated us for our wishful thinking. At the same time, he shouted words of condemnation at his two captives. Undoing the latch of a small barbed wire and wood gate, Bow Legs led them into the small compound beyond. He squeezed, shoved, and pounded the weary paras, as if kneading dough, into the 'hole,' a subterranean one-man cell. They spent the next seven days submerged in these 'rat warrens,' existing on a diet of bread and water. Upon release, no attempt at reclamation followed. Instead, weakened by their ordeal, wearing handcuffs and leg irons, they were shipped to a permanent stateside Federal penitentiary.

Seventy-five percent of the inmates were black rear echelon soldiers who were confined for committing civilian crimes in uniform, such as theft, armed robbery, assault with a deadly weapon, and misappropriation of funds. Murder and rape were punishable by hanging. Usually, a day before a scheduled execution, Master Sergeant John C. Woods, the Army's official hangman, a small-framed Texan from San Antonio, the bottom front edge of his overseas cap resting at eye level, wearing a .45 automatic on each hip, arrived at the DTC, driving a large articulated truck and trailer on which rested a portable gallows. When I met Woods, as part of an unloading detail, he claimed that had hanged more than 300 men over a 14-year period. He never told me how he qualified for the job.

Woods traveled to the town or village with his portable scaffold whenever his services were required. French justice demanded, and the Army concurred, that any soldier found guilty of the murder or rape of a French national would face execution in the town square closest to the scene of the crime whenever possible. In rape cases, according to Woods, it was sometimes difficult for the victim to identify the offender.

Whatever the young woman's original intentions, the combined pressure of the situation and the demands of familial retribution conspired against accurate identification. Added to this coupling, the soldiers under suspicion were lined up on parade, displaying only minor variations in height and build and wearing identical uniforms. The harassed girl, walking between the ranks, followed by her irate mother and escorted by the company commander, was asked to identify the suspect. Considering that most assignations take place at night, the difficulty of choosing one man out of a hundred a few days later decreased the likelihood of accuracy. Pressed for time, wishing to defend her honor, the young woman may have sought to assuage her own conspiratorial guilt by quickly choosing a man at random. Considering the quality of Army juridical proceedings, the accused faced dire consequences.

Two of the victims I saw hanged were black; one had been found guilty of murder, the other of rape. On the day of one particular hanging, a few hours before the scheduled time, I was assigned as one of a detail to set up the gallows on a grassy knoll just outside the camp boundary. With the structure in place, Woods tested his equipment, particularly the trap door. Satisfied with his dress rehearsal, he notified the presiding officer that all was ready. The condemned man, having spent two weeks on the camp's 'death row,' a cage within a cage, was led from his cell. Walking past inmates also condemned to die, their bodies pressed against the bars of their make-shift cells, shouting obscenities and rattling their mess tins, he was escorted under guard to the execution site. His hands were manacled behind him.

I waited at the base of the scaffold. Mounting the steps, the guilty man faced the presiding officer, a chaplain, and an Army doctor. Words were exchanged and the order read aloud. The condemned man remained impassive. All the inmates stood at attention in front of their tents. Woods placed a black hood over the man's head, tied a rope around his neck, and sprung the trap door. The prisoner hurtled down and disappeared from view, because a green canvas material encircled the base of the gallows to ground level. The doctor descended the steps, opened the flap in the tent material, and entered. He was partially hidden from view, but I could see him stop the man from swinging and raise a stethoscope to his heart. In consternation, the doctor shook his head. The man was still alive. It would take another 15 minutes of his slowly twisting about, the weight of his body keeping the rope taut, before the doctor, having checked again, finally pronounced him dead. I felt nauseated.

Up to that time, I considered hanging to be an expeditious way of killing someone. Whether it was Woods's failure to kill quickly or the fault of hanging as a method, which allowed the condemned to linger inhumanely, may never be known.

Once the accused was cut down, his remains were shipped to and interred behind a row of trees in a remote section of the World War I American military cemetery near the Champagne market town of Fère-en Tardenois. His identity was kept secret and his family was never told the actual reason for his demise. The cemetery's custodian denied his existence.

9
Reprieve

I rather doubt if every inmate got to see the Army psychologist who visited the camp every few weeks, but my turn came a few months after the Battle of the Bulge was terminated successfully in late January 1945; by then, the Allied armies were fighting in Germany. I reported to a medium sized, dark-haired, scholarly man wearing glasses, in a small office in one of the camp's administration buildings. I noticed that nothing on his M-1941 olive drab field jacket revealed any unit insignia or rank. He nodded, shook my hand, and invited me to sit down. My file, lying on the desk between us was open and looked full, worn, and used. He asked me about my reasons for enlisting, my stateside training, and my experiences overseas. 'How do you feel,' he asked. 'I don't know. I don't feel anything. Burned out.'

We talked further, and he probed in a non-intrusive way, discovering that I was conflicted over a desire to serve my country and an urge to stay alive. He sensed that I was still angry with Simmons and the Army for letting me down, but that was carefully disguised. What wasn't is that I turned my anger inward against myself, and was left holding a bag full of anxious and depressive symptoms. He interpreted my actions as passive-aggressive; rather than 'taking off,' I should have confronted Simmons directly. Speaking softly, he continued, 'Enduring prolonged combat left you with very little choice — hang tough another day or withdraw. You chose the latter because it was no longer possible to tolerate that amount of anxiety. Let's say I don't believe your leaving implied failure or defeat, although it may do so. Rather, it seems that you simply tried to reduce the threat of being overwhelmed emotionally without having accumulated the required coping tools. Your youth was a factor.'

Pausing, he stared at me, shaking his head in disbelief, fingering some of my file papers, speaking softly, and said, 'Someone has made a horrible mistake.'

'What's that, sir?' I jumped inwardly and leaned forward.

'You don't belong here; you belong in a hospital.' My eyes filled with tears, my shoulders slumped. 'I'm going to recommend all charges be dropped and that you be returned to duty.'

A wave of relief surged through me. After all these months, someone had finally listened. I felt like exploding and trembled with an anger that had lain dormant for almost a year. I wanted to pound my fist on the table, to slam the door, rip off the roof! Having endured an unnecessary and protracted ordeal before the Army got it right, I was unapproachable for days afterward. To make matters worse, I was still a prisoner when President Roosevelt, a man I greatly admired, died in April. I was elated beyond words when Germany was defeated and surrendered in May.

Whatever wheels the psychologist set in motion, they didn't begin to gather speed until two or three weeks later. I was eager to escape from the constraints of prison life, the boredom, the personal degradation, but I was also frightened about leaving. However, one more hurdle remained — an interview with a visiting colonel from the judiciary branch with the power to keep me behind bars. I was warned by a few inmates awaiting release that if I valued my freedom, the response to his question, 'Will you fight in the Pacific?' had to be an unqualified, 'Yes, Sir!' To refuse would eliminate any possibility of rehabilitation and freedom.

I stood at attention in front of the old colonel, disliking him for his age, safe assignment, and plenipotentiary powers. Without looking up from the papers on his desk, he asked, 'Will you fight in the Pacific?' I responded in my best military manner, doing everything but clicking my heels, and exclaimed, 'Yes, Sir!' Even though that answer was my exit visa from the LDTC, I knew something he didn't know, or chose to ignore. General Eisenhower had issued an order stating that any soldier who had served in two theaters of operations would not be required to serve in a third. Having fought in both the Mediterranean and the European Theaters, I qualified!

Unfortunately, I wasn't sent to a hospital for treatment nor was my sentence expunged. For whatever the reasons, I failed to register a complaint or seek redress within the military bureaucratic labyrinth. Instead, I was assigned to one of a number of tented replacement depots in the vicinity of Reims. Here thousands of men either were being reassigned or shipped to the States or the Pacific from camps named after

American cities. After arriving at Camp San Antonio on a warm summer day in August 1945, lounging near the recreational area with some other former prisoners, I listened to an appeal for patience by General Eisenhower broadcast over the camp's public address system. He said that, although a shipping shortage existed, he was doing everything in his power to get the men back home. Until then, I never recalled any officer behaving in such a conciliatory manner. Orders were a driving force in the Army, issued from above and carried out by men of lesser rank below. No questions asked! An army does not operate like a democracy. It didn't take much political experience on my part to recognize a man building consensus and preparing for the Presidency.

I approached being free slowly, as if I were a Red Indian stalking a prey. I wasn't sure if I owned my freedom now, a freedom to fulfill myself, having had it seemingly snatched away forever at my court-martial. I felt satisfaction in being unshackled, feeling a sense of relief as the chains of the previous months' confinement fell from my wrists and ankles. Even so, I was overtaken by a profound sense of inner emptiness, manifested by an image of a burned-out tank. Enveloped by this mood and image, much like a thick fog blanketing a landscape, I refused to admit to the pain of the previous year's experiences. Crouching behind the fortress of my smiles, my face a mask disguising what lurked behind, I resolved never to get ambushed by a feeling again.

In late August, I was assigned to the 166th Signal Service Photo Company, commanded by Captain Dudley Hunter, its compliment consisting of former Hollywood photographers. The 166th was in process of being disbanded but was temporarily bivouacked near the cathedral city of Troyes on the banks of the Seine, southeast of Paris. Hunter greeted my return to duty with a scathing attack upon my lack of moral fiber. Although he had before him my 201 Army personnel file, he disregarded my full campaign record, three battle stars, an Indian arrowhead for an assault landing on D-Day, the OSS citation, and the Combat Infantry Badge. I stared straight ahead, impassive. He warned, shaking his finger in my face, 'I don't like fuckups in my outfit. If you don't tow the line, I'll make sure you end up in permanent captivity.' Forgiveness was not part of his character. I didn't quite believe him because his behavior was too measured, a performance. Before he was transferred out of the outfit, I had discounted half of what he said.

With the European war over, leave was easy to get. Jack, a still photographer friend formerly assigned to General Patton, and I would often hitchhike into Troyes. An ancient town on the Seine, it was particularly enjoyable on Sundays, when we could dance at one of the open riverside cabarets. Usually, its band consisted of a drummer, saxophonist, and piano player. I was glad to have a girl in my arms again, with whom dancing came easily to the simple orchestrations of French and American popular music. Our steps, however, didn't go beyond the dance floor, much to my regret. If the cabaret got too warm, it was easy to walk outside, cross the road, lean against the nearest wood railing, take a long swig of bottled beer, and admire the sun-drenched Gothic cathedral, like a ship riding at anchor, across the river.

With a two-day pass in my back pocket, I joined the whole American Army of four million men eager to get a glimpse of Paris before returning home. Truck convoys converged on the French capital from every direction, overflowing with cargos of soldiers on leave. The trucks arrived two or three hours later and parked on the huge tree-lined esplanade situated between the river and the Hotel des Invalides. The railroad-iron Eiffel Tower, positioned within walking distance, a landmark for the last 123 years, dominated the landscape and hovered above us. Leaping over tailgates and slatted sides, hundreds of enlisted men, loaded with cash, rushed off in search of entertainment. Unlike my first visit last December, Paris was beginning to shake off the years of German repression and occupation, albeit slowly. It was livelier and less sad. Somehow, within this vibrant city, I hoped to find Ronnie and Olga. In Lyon, Ronnie had given me the address and phone number of a cousin. I found her living near Blvd. St. Denis. Over drinks at a local café, she called another relative, who said that Ronnie and Olga were living in an apartment in the Montmartre district of Paris, near the Métro station Jules Joffrin. Within three hours, I had accomplished most of my mission.

At their Paris apartment, we rejoiced over glasses of champagne, humbled by the odds of surviving. Through our excitement and relief, we talked of our first meeting in Lyon and what had happened since our separation nine months ago. My search was not unlike that of eight million displaced persons, who, disrupted by war, tramped across Europe's pulverized roads and wrecked towns in search of family and friends without knowing if they were alive. I was successful, untold thousands weren't.

I had no intention of shocking the Haas family, but when I paid them a visit at their flat one evening on rue Rennequin, the same one they left to escape the Germans, they were aghast. Jean-Claude answered the door and shouted, 'It's Stephen!' The rest of his family came running. Startled, they waved me in, while I remained utterly confused. Jean-Claude explained. That afternoon, at an Army personnel office, he was told that I had been killed in early 1945. Thus, they were thunderstruck by my arrival. We celebrated my and their good fortune but wondered who that other soldier was.

A week later, I was sitting on the terrace of the Café de la Paix, sipping an aperitif, when a convoy of automobiles turned the corner, crammed with people inside and out, shouting and waving miniature British, American, and French flags. The tooting of their horns in short and long blasts mixed with people shouting, 'Japan has surrendered. Japan has surrendered unconditionally. The war's over.' We on the terrace leaped to our feet; passers-by stopped, overcome by the unexpected and momentous news. The messengers of good fellowship were contagious. I bought the latest edition of the *Stars and Stripes*, whose banner headline read, 'It's Over.' As the cars drove out of sight, most of us on the terrace continued our celebration. It was August 14, 1945, and beneath the glow, my feelings of depression corrupted and diminished my ability to truly participate.

10

A Free Man

Because the 166th left for the States, I was assigned to the 239th Signal Service Company in Reims. Billeted in the Caserne Jean d'Arc, near the town center, I was placed on temporary duty (TDY) as a photographer. Taking mechanical 'mug shots' of soldiers in a cramped office overlooking the town square, positioning the photos on newly issued identity cards, and then immortalizing both in plastic, was not my idea of creative photography. Away from this drudgery, I found living in Reims most pleasant and succumbed to its beauty. It was a large town filled with history and a memorable Gothic cathedral, surrounded by famous champagne vineyards. Sometimes a friend and I would picnic between the grass-covered trenches of an old World War I battlefield waiting to be explored. Accepting invitations from the local Champagne houses, such as Peiper-Heidseick and Mumm's, was a frequent occurrence. A newly discovered Red Cross girl and I mingled with and were surrounded by the *haute bourgeoisie* and French and American serving officers, eating canapés and sipping vintage champagne on the lawns of the *vignerons'* spacious estates.

The following is a cautionary tale, one in which the law of cause and effect applied. The consequences were bad enough; they could have been dire. Although the war was won, my inner battles remained. I first met Guy (Guido) Santandrea, an Italian-American from Hartford, Connecticut, at the Red Cross Club's coffee bar in Reims. He was a good looking, sturdily built, street-smart fellow in his early 20s. His mind overflowed with ideas, one of which was to travel to Paris together for a long weekend and sell our cigarette rations on the black market. Cartons of American cigarettes were selling from $10 to $20 a carton, and we could easily afford to sell two cartons each from our small private inventory. Guy had a strong desire to make as much money as quickly as possible and was prepared to play for high stakes to do so.

For example, I met Guy in his room at the caserne Jean d'Arc early one Friday morning before taking the train to Paris. He was sitting at his desk tinkering with an open carton of Chesterfield cigarettes. Packs of these, wrapped in clear cellophane, had a red pull-tab that allowed for easy access near their top edge. Using a razor blade, he carefully unfolded the cellophane and paper flap at the bottom of the pack, exposing the 20 cigarettes within. Two-inch mounds of sawdust were piled next to his left arm. Removing the cigarettes, he replaced each pack with an equivalent amount of sawdust, sealed the bottom flap and cellophane, and replaced the pack in the carton. The red pull-tab remained intact. Without opening the pack, you could not know that the cigarettes had been replaced. When we left for the station, Guy carried two cartons of ten packs each, filled with sawdust.

Arriving in Paris around noon, Guy and I took the Métro to the Café de la Paix situated near the Opéra, where he knew one of its waiters. We pushed through the crowded terrace, crossed the art deco interior, and bumped into Guy's waiter, who nodded in recognition. Not only was he interested in purchasing Guy's cartons, he was eager to buy mine. We accepted his offer of $10 per carton, exchanged our goods for bank notes, and disappeared into the crowd. Feeling that we had put enough distance between an incensed waiter and us, we paused. Guy chortled, pleased that his gamble paid off and not in the least concerned about his unethical behavior. According to him, he made the rules of the game.

While I visited the Dahans, who had left Montmartre to live on the rue d'Estrees in the more fashionable seventh quartier of Paris near the Invalides, Guy sought the charms of his newly discovered Françoise, a young woman who lived in the same arrondissement. I was intrigued. It wasn't that I was off women, not by a long shot, but my top priority was in playing the role of a caring and dutiful son to my surrogate parents, Ronnie and Olga, with whom I could achieve a semblance of emotional stability. Guy took my peccadilloes and dramas in stride.

Buoyed by our success at the Café de la Paix, he proposed another plan, not only more daring, but with a greater cash payoff. There was a small American Army office at the caserne, more like a hotel reception desk, located on the ground floor. It was most active during the day and, although manned at night by one enlisted man, little happened. From 1800 hours to 0600 the next morning, with the addition of a portable wood framed canvas cot, the office was converted into the enlisted man's sleeping quarters. During the previous week, Guy discovered that new Post Exchange (PX) ration cards were kept in a desk drawer adjacent to the cot. If he could steal those cards and add a forged signature to each, we could purchase large amounts of cigarettes and other scarce items and later sell them at a substantial profit on the black market in Paris.

Guy urged. 'If you come in with me, I'll find a way of getting those cards,' he insisted.

'Sure! Why not,' I replied. 'Count me in.'

That evening, when the new Charge of Quarters (CQ), a corporal, prepared to bed down in the office, we asked him for a temporary place to sleep. He pointed to a wooden swivel chair and a small couch, implying that was the best he could do. Guy and I nodded. We waited for hours, and finally the corporal fell into a deep sleep. Guy moved quickly, silently thrusting forward, his hand reaching across and inches above the sleeping soldier. Guy slid the drawer open, and deftly grabbed a handful of PX cards. Gently closing the drawer, he hid the cards in his musette bag. .

Elated with our good fortune, we met in Guy's room the next night and signed the 11 PX cards, using a variety of phony names. We predicted our profit from our potential purchases to be somewhere in the neighborhood of $500 to $1,000, depending upon the strength of the market. Considering that our monthly Army salary was about $75 per month, we greedily rubbed our hands in anticipation. The good life was just around the corner.

Feeling smug, we entered the caserne's PX. We assured the local French salesgirls that the extra cards belonged to friends of ours who were too busy to shop on their own. Our arms filled to the gunwales with cartons of cigarettes, silk stockings, and a variety of assorted items, we ended our shopping spree. We paid the bill and, with the approval of a mess sergeant friend of Guy's, temporarily stored our loot among his crates of number-10 cans of tomato puree and sacks of rice and potatoes in his kitchen's supply room.

While I was preparing to meet my Red Cross girlfriend for a 1:00 luncheon appointment, I was surprised to see an armed officer and two armed enlisted men approach my doorway. 'Are you Steve Weiss?' I nodded in the affirmative. 'Come with us, please.' I recognized the crossed pistols insignia on the lapels of his tunic and deduced that he and the others were from the caserne's MP detachment. On the way to the office, they picked up Guy, who was lounging in his room. He loudly protested being intruded upon.

In no uncertain terms, the MP captain demanded to know where we had hidden the 'goods.' Standing in front of the desk that Guy had rifled the night before, we feigned ignorance. Guy's responses reminded me of those Hollywood gangster films in which Jimmy Cagney says in a similar situation, 'You got nuthin' on me, copper; 'I'm clean as the driven snow.' The captain realized he was wasting his time and booked us. I had cause for concern. If the Army concluded that I were incorrigible and beyond redemption, it might leave me to languish in one of those grim stateside Federal prisons like Leavenworth.

We were taken downtown under guard and booked at the local French jail, located on the second floor of a commercial building. I think it must have been used as a storage loft that had been quickly partitioned into a makeshift jail when Reims was liberated. Barbed wire covered the windows and there were a few lockups, but security was lax for those who seriously considered escape. Guy and I were consigned to different parts of the jail.

Jail life was monotonous; there was nothing to do but to hang around between meals. We waited, we inquired, but nothing about our case was forthcoming. An exasperated sergeant of the guard shouted, 'For Christ's sake, when I have news, you'll be first to hear, so shut up.' I worried. Two inmates who tried to escape that night were easily caught on the roof and shipped out under armed guard the following morning. For three days there was no word, but on the afternoon of the fourth day, I received a visitor, an agent from the Army's Criminal Investigation Division (CID). A big burly man, devoid of rank, he offered me a cigarette, waved me to a chair, and said in a calm, engaging manner, 'Look, we found the stuff you left in the cook's storeroom.'

His revelation was like a bombshell! In quasi-legalese, he said, 'I recommend that you admit culpability, and admit that you purchased and then concealed the rations. If you don't,' he continued, his voice sharpening to a fine edge, 'if you deny your involvement, we'll throw the book at you, and you won't see the light of day for a long time. I'm not trying to frighten you, just giving you the facts. Don't be a fool; you're a young guy. Steve, all the power of the Government is behind me. What do you say?' I sat there in silence and stared at him. I took a long drag on my cigarette and exhaled, wondering what the hell to do next. How could I fight the whole U.S. Army when I knew it had me 'dead to rights'?

'OK,' I replied, 'we hid the goods after we left the PX.'

He turned to the MP at the door of the cell and said, 'Get Guy.'

Guy was as brazen as ever and denied everything, even when the whole caper was laid bare. 'It's a trap; there's nothing to find, because there aren't any hidden goods,' he insisted.

'Damn it, Guy,' I shouted, 'they know everything; they have witnesses, all the girls we tried to bamboozle. Let's get this thing over with.'

Although persistent and intractable, he finally realized that with the goods, witnesses, and my testimony, there was no longer any need to prolong the agony. Guy didn't cave in; he weighed his chances, defiant as always, played the only hand he had, and admitted to our conspiracy. 'You made a wise move,' the CID agent said.

We signed some papers admitting our guilt, which he put in his briefcase. 'What happens next?' I pleaded. He remained silent and, with a compassionate shrug of his shoulders, left.

Worry weighed upon me heavily. I didn't sleep, but tossed and turned that night. My mind raced. How could I have tempted fate with a character like Guy? Was my judgment impaired? My life seemed to swing from one extreme to the other, from narcissism's high to humiliation's low. Could I have contributed to my own imprisonment in a Federal prison? How could I face my family and my friends if I were sentenced again after such ignominious behavior? My life was unraveling! The next morning, our names were called. The Army decided to drop its case against us. To my great relief, we were released into the custody of the MPs. I vowed not to tempt fate again. They drove us back to the caserne, where I reported to the CO of the 239th Signal Service Company, a small, paunchy man who, sitting on a swivel chair behind his desk, twiddled with a big cigar.

I stood at attention all through his harangue. He would not allow me to stand at 'At Ease.' 'You are a very lucky young man,' he began. 'Since all of the booty was recovered right down to the last pair of silk stockings, the MP captain decided not to press charges. Nothing of this episode will be placed on your record, but you behaved like a damned fool. Did you really think you could get away with this? Every day carloads of champagne disappear. Bottled water and truckloads of pâté de foie gras go missing as commonly as do pork and beans, involving illegal black market transactions worth hundreds of thousands of dollars. You overreached, soldier! And stay away from that pal of yours! Dismissed.'

'Not so fast,' a disembodied voice spoke from the shadows.

'Oh, no,' I thought, 'Here comes Count Dracula, ready to puncture my carotid artery.' The vampire as first sergeant closed in, eyeball to eyeball, and continued, digging his index finger repeatedly into my chest, 'I'm placing you on seven days restriction to quarters, at which time you will work in the caserne's Signal Corps warehouse.' He looked at the captain, who nodded. 'You will line up with the German prisoners each morning at 0700 wearing fatigues. Those guys are the ones who have a large P printed on the backs of their fatigues, in case you've forgotten,' he said derisively. 'You will be under my direct supervision at all times. You see, soldier, your body might belong to God, but your ass belongs to me. Get the hell out of here.'

The following morning at 0700 hours, I lined up on the hard ground of the barrack square, last behind 12 German prisoners, all wearing Army green fatigue uniforms. The only difference between us was the large identifying white P painted on the backs of their fatigue jackets. I wondered what war stories they were hiding. An American NCO arrived, shouted 'Forward March,' counting aloud at each step. The prisoners peeled off at various work locations in ones and twos until I was alone with the NCO. The first sergeant was waiting. I followed him to the warehouse, where he spent about five minutes describing what I was required to do and then left.

I surveyed the scene; Signal Corps radio transmitters, receivers, and generators, in a multitude of combinations, ranging from fixed desktops to portables, were strewn all over the place. My mission was to make order out of chaos in the allotted seven days. Even though I worked right up to my lunch break, there was so much to rearrange that it was impossible to make a dent in this electronic traffic jam. I attacked the mountain of equipment again after lunch. Tiring, not having learned how to pace myself, I found a seat on the pile in an attempt to rekindle my fading resources. As soon as I sat down, the first sergeant stalked in. Spying me, he shouted, 'What the hell are you doing sitting on your ass?' I was at a loss for words.

My mind in a muddle, lips moving shaping silent words, knowing that any response was foolhardy, I jumped up, trembling like a frightened rabbit cornered by a fox and waited. 'I want this place looking as good as our company supply room, so get with it or I'll rack your ass,' he yelled, and stomped out. I toiled, lifted, shoved, pushed, and carried these dead-weight tubular, knobbed electronic monsters from one end of the warehouse to the other. They resisted, as if I were evicting them from a cherished neighborhood, only moving grudgingly when I exerted maximum force.

At the end of the day, I shuffled to my quarters, stood at the foot of my cot, and fell forward. I hurtled into oblivion and was asleep in mid-air. Suddenly, someone was shaking me and shouting close to my ear, 'Get up, get up.'

'Why am I being bothered?' Surely, I hadn't slept for more than a minute, feeling that closing and opening my eyes were part of the same movement. It was 0600 hours, as I sat at the edge of the cot, confused and weary. For six more days, I lined up with Fritz, Heinrich, and the others, worked in the warehouse, and fell into my cot at night. Whenever I took a break from shifting the equipment, the first sergeant stormed in to chew me out like a roaring lion. His timing was flawless, because he regulated my every move, disallowed a 'breather,' and propelled me into further activity. A man hunter, his stalking ability was exceptional.

At the end of the seventh day, I stood before him in the company orderly room, a shadow of my former youthful self. Believing I'd failed, I awaited an extension of the sentence.

The first sergeant looked at me and faced the captain and said, 'I've never seen anyone work as hard as this GI, sir. He turned to me and added, 'Weiss, you've done an excellent job.' I appreciated his unsolicited appraisal, hoping that my trousers wouldn't fall around my knees from lack of support. He smiled, said, 'Keep your nose clean,' then shouted, 'Dismissed.' The captain nodded approvingly. I was no longer restricted to quarters. On the seventh day I rested. Feeling chastised, humbled, despite the gallows humor, I sensed that an ethical outcome couldn't be a result of unethical behavior. Every once in a while, I saw Guy walking on the street, but I avoided him like the plague and refused to get within 50 feet of him. Call it a phobic reaction!

The Little Red School House stood businesslike near the Hotel de Ville. Here, in May 1945, General Eisenhower took the German surrender. Although I had never met the illustrious general, I was to meet another prominent officer of exalted rank. On one particular morning, with the sun streaming through the curtains, I walked over to my bedroom window, yawned, and noticed a paper tied to the steering column of my jeep parked on the street below. I raced downstairs and lifted the note. 'Steve,' it read, 'Photo Mission: Report immediately to the railroad station and await General Lee's arrival.'

General John C. H. Lee, also known as 'Jesus Christ Himself,' Eisenhower's Assistant Theater Commander and European Chief of the Service of Supply, loathed by front-line troops for failing to deliver the necessities of war in timely fashion, had set out earlier that morning from Paris in his own private train. I made it to the station just as it hove into view. On the platform, local military and civilian dignitaries waited for Lee to emerge from his private railway carriage as the steam locomotive hissed, rumbled, and ground to a stop. Coupled to it was a flatbed freight car, on which were anchored an olive drab four-door Buick sedan and two olive drab Harley Davidson WLA motorcycles.

The uniformed august visitor, a medium-sized, rotund figure, was superbly dressed, wearing an excellently tailored olive drab 'Eisenhower' jacket, similar in cut to the British battle dress blouse, and immaculate soft black leather boots. Three silver stars, glistening in the morning sunshine, were pinned to both shirt collars and the epaulets of his tunic, reminding those near him of his rank and status. As he, followed by his attending staff, stepped from the train onto the platform to be greeted by the local committee in attendance, their words were lost to the combined explosive sound of one automobile and two motorcycle engines bursting into life. A team of two large, powerful looking military policemen and one chauffeur drove their vehicles off the flatbed and down a steep wooden ramp onto the platform, the blare of their police sirens reverberating against the station's walls. General Lee was not at all disturbed by the fanfare; in fact, as he shook hands and exchanged pleasantries, he smiled in enjoyment. His sense and use of power oozed from every pore. What was this general officer, whose reputation as a martinet was well known throughout the ETO, planning next?

Between Reims and Chalons s/Marne, near the town of Mourmelon le Grand, on a 30,000-acre site, a series of U.S. Army tented transit camps, such as San Antonio, had replaced those buildings established by Napoleon III in 1857. Inspecting them was the object of Lee's visit; these camps were administrated locally by a two-star general under

Lee's jurisdiction. I followed in my jeep, last in a motorcade of 20 olive drab Ford and Buick sedans, whose large white stars were stenciled on the two front doors of each vehicle. In the lead, setting the pace, the two heavily armed, goggled policemen on their powerful Harleys served as escort. A red pennant with three white stars was attached to each front fender of Lee's Buick. Our destination was Mourmelon, 20 miles to the southeast. When we stopped for our first 'piss call,' one of the officers suggested that I leave my jeep by the side of the road and ride with him. Agreeing, I grabbed my full 4x5 Speed Graphic camera case and paused to chuckle as Lee, stars and all, took advantage of the stop to pee. Fifteen minutes later, the two motorcycle military policemen roared into the first camp and announced their arrival with sirens blasting and red lights flashing.

The camp's commandant, a full 'chicken' colonel, snapped to attention before his 'Eminence' gave him a crisp, energetic salute that Lee returned. He then ordered the colonel to act as his chauffeur on his inspection trip by jeep around the camp, a task usually assigned to a sergeant. The colonel blanched, surprised at the general's unusual demand and, lost for words, climbed in behind the wheel. There was a momentary hush as groups of men under the colonel's command fell silent, sensing his humiliation and shocked by the general's use of raw power. Lee repeated this maneuver at all of the five camps we visited that day; the response to his insensitive behavior was the same. Most of those present were citizen-soldiers, the majority waiting to return home, who believed in fair play. Lee's demeaning treatment of the colonels broke with accepted custom and practice. If he had ordered an enlisted man to chauffeur him and each colonel around, Lee's visit would have been remembered for other reasons and then soon forgotten.

After the visit to the camps, Lee dined with a French countess at her chateau near Reims while we ate lunch in the kitchen beneath the stairs until it was time to leave. We drove to the Little Red Schoolhouse and I followed Lee into the offices of the major general in command of the camps. While Lee and the general talked in the general's inner office, I waited outside. Ten minutes later, Lee called, 'Photographer, come here.' I entered to see Lee preparing to pin the Legion of Merit on the general's tunic. He paused and said, 'Take this picture,' which I did. Who was the general being decorated? None other than General Thrasher, Lee's brother in-law! There is a copy of the photo in Washington's National Archives.

The fort, Jean d' Arc in Reims, where the author lived for a few months in 1945

11
Life in Postwar Paris

I traveled to Paris on leave. On its journey through the Marne Valley, the train roared past slightly war-damaged towns and villages situated along the river. A year earlier, in August 1944, the Germans had retreated in headlong fashion toward the Franco-German frontier, but 26 years earlier, in August 1918, they attacked elements of the American Army, in which my father served. Many of these same towns and villages were destroyed and then rebuilt in the intervening years.

The American Red Cross Club in Paris was full of GIs, some of whom I knew. We decided to have dinner and then go on to a night club called the *Bal Tabarin* in Montmartre, whose floor show rivaled that of the *Folies-Bergère* and the *Lido*, two other famous theater night clubs. Supposedly its semi-nude displays included wild circus animals and trapeze artists. Life in Paris was expensive, but with the right connections and a willingness to pay the going price, an excellent dinner could be had, along with anything else. Prices were driven higher than need be by the American GI, who, although well paid, rarely sought value for money in most transactions.

Our Auvergnat patron was most helpful when I asked for the address of and directions to the nightclub. Feeling well cared for after our four-course dinner, we walked toward the *Bal Tabarin*. Unfortunately, when reaching our destination, what should have been the entrance to the nightclub was a padlocked door protecting an empty run-down shop. Perplexed, we walked further along the street toward the sound of an orchestra playing. Increasing our pace, moving closer, the orchestra sounded rich and full, much like those 17-piece bands I enjoyed at Manhattan's Paramount Theater. To our mounting displeasure, no ribald, multicolored neon signs flashed from above and pointed to the actual location we searched for. We turned a corner, rushed along another street, and entered a broad alley, exposing a series of three-story buildings whose backs formed a continuous blank wall.

As soon as we stepped into the alley, an unexplained electric-blue light clearly defined every angle, every shape and shadow. This urban landscape expressed the same strange, disconnected mood of a Picabia surrealistic painting. We roamed down the alley like a band of errant troubadours, individually affecting a stance, straining to listen, or collectively improvising a pantomime. I ran my hands along a portion of the wall, feeling its rippled stucco, as the music increased in volume, but the tips of my fingers were not sensitive enough to discover its source. That required the sensitivity of a safecracker or a locksmith! Caressing the wall with my cheek, using it as a primitive scanner, I sought the origin of the musical vibrations. The others did the same. Phantom-like, the orchestral sounds slowly drifted away. We looked at each other, defeated.

Then, as if cued by the wave of a baton, the silence was shattered by a shaft of musical energy that burst through the walls. Emerging were the first plaintive sounds of a lone wind instrument wailing in the night. From the clarinet's opening solo glissando, followed by the voices of the full orchestra, George Gershwin's *Rhapsody in Blue cascaded* upon us. My eyes filled with tears as I leaned against the wall, absorbed. So far from and so near to home! We never found the *Bal Tabarin* or even the orchestra's location, but we found something else, a rare sensate moment filled with magic.

I realized that most of the Army in Europe was being transferred to Japan via the U.S., so if I wanted to become a photographer, I'd have to do something quickly. The 3908th Signal Service Photo Battalion had its headquarters and billets on rue Octave Feuillet in the fashionable 16th Arrondissement of Paris and it was rumored that with so many men being deployed, there were openings for photographers. Ten days later, rather than joining the 3908th, which was inactivated, I was reassigned to the 3264th Signal Service Photo Battalion in Wiesbaden, Germany as a still photographer. I accepted the assignment with mixed feelings, because I preferred France to Germany and the French to the Germans.

Fortunately, for some unexplained reason, after reporting to Wiesbaden a week later, nine men and I were ordered to Paris on temporary duty. Prior to leaving, two of us drove to Frankfurt am Main by jeep to see what the massive Allied bombing had done to the city. On the way in, near Hochst, an irate German farmer hurled a pitchfork at our speeding jeep. My driving companion moved swiftly. Swerving, the jeep straddled the pitchfork's sharp spikes, and eliminated our chances of crashing with shredded tires. We cussed the hell out of him and, without losing speed, kept going.

Frankfurt was one massive crumble; the only important structure standing was the I. G. Farben building, used as Eisenhower's headquarters. This devastated city, its multi-storied buildings tilted, gutted, and wrecked, its inhabitants moving trance-like, overwhelmed by the bombing, was like a ghost town, exuding a stench of decomposing, hidden, and unrecovered corpses. By contrast, Wiesbaden, the Army Air Force's European Headquarters, about 18 miles away, was relatively undamaged.

The Frankfurt Red Cross Club was located across the way from the central train station, whose roof was a cobweb of shattered glass and twisted girders. Lounging near the club's entrance was a number of well-fed GIs mingling with some poorly clad, emaciated German civilians. As we approached, they were playing some sort of a game, because the soldiers intermittently exchanged fists full of dollars. I knew that GIs were known for their gambling instincts, but I was not prepared for what followed. They were betting on how quickly a German civilian could retrieve a discarded cigarette butt tossed away by one of the GIs. The payoff was based upon the fastest elapsed time, from GI toss to German pickup. I reckoned that the game was not without its destructive undertones, because it demeaned the participating Germans, forcing them to grovel for something as basic as a smoke. I thought of those cruise ships plying between the Pacific islands during the interwar period, when young natives dove for pennies thrown into the air above the blue sea by the arriving tourists. Viewing the destruction surrounding these Germans, still wearing their forage caps and diving for cigarettes, life was neither tropical nor carefree.

The Frankfurt-Paris Express, pulled by a powerful steam locomotive, left the battered city in the early evening, beginning an overnight twelve-hour journey of more than 400 miles. A lieutenant and we enlisted men shared two compartments on the same coach. None slept, some dozed, but I cornered the lieutenant and, like some obsessive character in a Somerset Maugham short story, made him promise again and again that when we arrived, I would be issued a Speed Graphic 4x5 press camera, auxiliary flash equipment, and camera case. As the locomotive slowly steamed and hissed into the Gare de l'Est early the next morning, under its canopied art nouveau roof, he said wearily, 'Yes, you'll get your camera.'

For living arrangements, there seemed to be a tacit agreement between the advancing Americans and retreating Germans concerning billeting; for example, when the enemy vacated the premises of the Majestic, Kléber, and Iéna hotels, we moved in. Fortunately, unlike the central post office in Naples that was booby trapped by the Germans in the autumn of '43 and demolished, none of these establishments was. We were assigned to the Hotel d'Iéna.

Before dinner in the large hotel dining room, we gathered around as one of our officers explained the structure and purpose of the WBS (Western Base Section) photographic detachment, consisting of still and motion picture cameramen and lab technicians. He explained that the detachment covered news stories in Paris and throughout France. Our work was defined as photojournalism, and that included subjects ranging from GI human interest stories to international Allied conferences. News outlets for our coverage included the Army's *Stars and Stripes* and the *New York Times*. In addition, assignments included photo essays for the historical record and photo layouts for technical military manuals. He depended on our creative talent to produce stories of our own for possible circulation. 'Film is cheap,' he concluded, 'so our headquarters in Wiesbaden would rather have an unpublished story in the can than miss it completely.'

It was only a 15-minute journey by truck from the hotel to the park-like atmosphere of Boulevard Suchet, a fashionable avenue that ran parallel to the Bois de Boulogne and the race course at Auteuil. Michèle Morgan and Jean Gabin, two prominent French movie stars with international reputations, lived within walking distance of our requisitioned three-story Mediterranean-style villa. It was once the residence of an Argentine Fascist and supporter of Nazi causes who fled just before the Allies arrived. The villa itself had been converted into a well-organized portrait studio, lab, screening room, photo archive and film library. A number of generals, such as Eisenhower and Bradley, had sat for their portraits here. Many 11x14 framed prints of these and other high-ranking officers adorned the walls.

I mentioned the lieutenant's promise of new photo equipment and was told that I would be fitted out immediately. The supply clerk began to fill the counter with camera, flash, film holders, batteries, and cut and pack film. The camera and flash equipment looked as if it had come out of a junkyard. I felt cheated and thought, 'I could do better with a Kodak Box Brownie,' when the supply clerk said, 'Don't worry, Steve, as soon as some of the older guys leave, we'll update your stuff. It won't be long.'

I mumbled, 'Thanks,' and signed the receipt forms.

Months went by, darkness arrived in early afternoon, and snow began to fall. Cameramen filled or unloaded their duffel bags, made themselves at home, or shipped out, including the lieutenant and the supply clerk. Not a witness remained who could verify the promise made on the Frankfurt-Paris Express. I was very busy fulfilling assignments with an unreliable camera and flashgun, much like driving a car downhill with faulty brakes. If my equipment were a defective artillery piece, I wouldn't be here to tell the tale. There seemed to be a diabolical arrangement between the flashgun and the camera shutter as to which of the two would fire first; they were rarely in synch, a condition required for optimum results. Rarely would I hear the bang and the click at the same time.

The day came when I was the only Signal Corps still cameraman remaining in Paris, operating out of a small, centrally located photographic office across the street from the Hotel Majestic on the avenue Kléber, number 26, with three other men, Toby, Jack, and an Officer in Charge (OIC) Lieutenant, Walton T. La Fleur. Bobby Hines joined us a little later as a motion picture cameraman.

I answered the phone one particular morning and was told to report to the top floor of the Majestic. Following orders, I emerged from the elevator, crossed the luxurious carpet and identified myself to the French secretary sitting at her desk beside two large mahogany doors. She said, 'Major-General White, commanding the WBS, would like his photo taken.' Entering his spacious office, I noticed a well-proportioned, handsome man with chiseled features and white hair sitting behind a large mahogany desk at the far side of the room. He wore a pair of silver pilot's wings and two large silver stars on his tunic and, unlike General Lee, imparted a worldly and friendly personality. Hanging on the wall behind him was a magnificent, richly colored Aubusson tapestry depicting a forest hunt. But the prize, and very much alive, was a beautiful, slender brunette he introduced as "the countess," sitting cross-legged in a Louis XIV chair beside the desk. Wearing what looked to be a black Chanel suit and a string of pearls, her long well-proportioned legs were shown to their best advantage as she looked up and smiled, offering her hand. I thought, 'How gracious! How civilized!'

The general was a dashing man and a cooperative subject who easily fell into the poses in which either the countess or I, a 19-year-old
amateur photographer, suggested. Together, the general and his lady
shared a relaxed intimacy. Stepping back, I took aim and fired, alert
to the required synchronous sound that signaled success. Predictably,
although they fired and tripped, flash and shutter failed to couple, but
I pretended with an air of certitude that all was well. My two inanimate
conspirators had again thwarted any attempt at gaining photojournal-
istic immortality.

While piling my camera equipment into its case, I assured the general
that he would have his 8x10 glossy prints in his hands within eight
days, even though the photo lab was now based in Wiesbaden. The
session over, I paid my respects to the general, flashed a smile toward
the countess, whom I much admired, and left. When the due date came
and went, fearing the worst, I called the lab and was told, 'Sorry, Steve,
we tried everything under the sun, but your negatives are unprintable
because of improper exposure.' The lab technician added, 'Hey, ever
consider having your camera shutter and flash unit tested and, if need
be, repaired? We can do that here.' I shuddered, swallowed hard, grit-
ted my teeth, and feeling like Vesuvius on the verge of erupting, all
smoke, ash, and molten lava, just groaned. Although the general's office was both patient and persistent, after more than two months of
trying, his secretary stopped calling. The general deserved better treatment and should have been told the actual state of affairs. He was a top
man with power and I was a private devoid of clout. I needed to avoid
my experience of being 'odd man out' again, but I failed him as much
as my camera did.

Back in the office, only La Fleur knew the combination of a large floor
safe situated in one of two small cubicles at number 26. A fairly constant
stream of Frenchmen arrived to see him; they talked in conspiratorial
low tones, lingered over a smoke, and then departed. Since La Fleur's
surname was French, I assumed that he and his visitors were, if not
related, certainly close friends. Between them, lots of money changed
hands, which he quickly assigned to the safe, the combination knob
whirling contentedly after each transaction. I wondered. Doing a picture story on an abandoned warehouse filled with hundreds of Signal
Corps 16mm and 35mm film sound projectors, I learned from Jack that
the Army issued La Fleur orders to sell them as surplus at a predeter-
mined price. Jack insisted that whatever La Fleur charged over that was

his to keep. He made the market and negotiated with interested French cinema exhibitors. Since a carton of cigarettes ranged between $10 and $20, it was easy to imagine what a projector would fetch. Whether it was by accident or design, money from an inheritance or from hard work, I never knew the true story. La Fleur and Madeleine, his French girlfriend whom he later married, lived comfortably for years on the proceeds. I might add that the business acuity of many Americans soldiers like La Fleur never ceased to amaze me.

A persistent question at the photo lab, one that remained unanswered for over a month, related to the processing of thousands of 4x5 prints of German soldiers. The men were nude except for the boots they were standing in. The operation was in charge of a colonel sent from the Pentagon whose purpose was to make sure we met his deadline. The problem revolved around German soldiers captured by the Americans and caged in their prisoner of war camps. Beginning with the pullout of Europe, and with an eye on the Japanese war, we turned them over to the French, although our funding continued. The French prison authorities allegedly cut the prisoners' daily rations. In short, if true, the Germans were being slowly starved to death — some died. Although the Americans didn't think the French were out for personal financial gain, they acted like Robin Hood by taking food from the prisoners and redistributing it among their own people. These photos were to be placed in evidence if the case came to trial. We completed the operation on time, but I have no idea what arrangements finally were reached with the French.

Before the lab on Boulevard Suchet closed forever, I screened every piece of unedited 16 mm motion picture footage shot by our combat cameramen in the ETO. Chronologically, I followed the war on film from the 1942 arrival of American troops in Northern Ireland to the German surrender three years later. I realized that very few cameramen took the risks needed to bring the war home to the viewer. The bravery of the cameramen was not an issue for two reasons: for the most part, camera equipment was technically inappropriate and ground combat was difficult to depict on film.

Although there were millions of American soldiers roaming around Western Europe and many thousands visiting Paris, I never ran into any of my school friends from Brooklyn until walking home one night from Montmartre. I turned right at a street corner and bumped into a GI coming from the opposite direction. 'Steve,' he exclaimed!

'Sid,' I shouted.

At a nearby café, we reminisced about working as waiters at a country club in the Berkshires the summer before we graduated from Lafayette, our Brooklyn high school, in 1942. Although Sid and I lost track of each other after graduation, both of us worked in Manhattan until our age guaranteed a wartime Army career.

Sid was studying at the Cordon Bleu Culinary Arts School at government expense. Taught by learned and highly skilled French chefs, the few attending students shared the daily training menu with their invited guests. I sat in the gallery, which could have been seconded to a medical school as an operating theater, and watched the chefs, Sid, and his trainee pals deeply involved in the preparation of a young pig, recently suckled, for roasting. Sid and his pack of 'vivisectionists' were perfecting their culinary art while I sat in the tenth row. Hearing Dr. Frankenstein summoned over the loud speaker would have been no surprise! However, to be fair, with money only a remote object, five-course luncheons accompanied by intelligently chosen vintage wines by the resident sommelier were daily fare for Sid's group. I participated in this once. Taking a line from one of the 18th-century Prussian Fredericks, I was '*Happy as a God in France.*'

Women found Sid's athleticism, spirit, and good humor attractive, so his hands were never far from an inviting waist. One evening, with my agreement, he invited two French girls out for dinner. They were attractive and playful; both spoke English. The restaurant he chose was small, full of drifting cigarette smoke, noisy, and crowded. Luckily, after squeezing our way in, we found a table. The girls ordered baked fish and Sid and I ordered steak and fries. Carafes of house red and white followed each other in a gentle blur. During dinner, Monique, my date, casually mentioned how difficult it was to get soap and toilet articles. Since my Army ration was more than enough for me, however rare and expensive for the French consumer, I offered to give her my surplus if she would accompany me to my hotel. I assured her that it wasn't a ploy because the Hotel d'Iéna was off-limits to unauthorized personnel. 'All right then,' she replied. A little later we parted company from Sid and his girl outside the restaurant.

We found two seats together on the Metro. As we proceeded down the line, Monique said, 'I feel dizzy and sick to my stomach,' and looked as if she were going to faint.

I put my arm around her and replied, 'There must have been something wrong with the fish.'

The color went out of her cheeks, as she leaned against me. Yet rather than feeling solicitous, I thought, 'What a bother!' Arriving at our destination, Monique felt too wretched to leave the coach. Between stations Pompe and Muette, she stood up, pitched toward one of the vertical stanchions and vomited all over herself and an innocent bystander. Her heaving was torrential. I, un-heroic as ever, beat a retreat to the far side of the carriage in a failed attempt to disassociate myself from her and her mess. We left, no, staggered from the train at Muette, where she poised before and then collapsed onto one of the station's benches. Bent over, holding her head in her hands, her eyes closed, she swayed and moaned.

I withdrew, beat a hasty retreat, escaped up the stairs, crossed over to the opposite platform and waited for the next train. Standing there, I looked directly across the tracks where Monique sat hunched over.

I could hear my train approaching; suddenly, I was filled with remorse and guilt. The train stopped, its doors opened, and I hopped in. A loud inner voice shouted, 'You bastard!' I jumped out before the doors slammed shut, ran up the steps, raced along the first platform, and sat down beside Monique, gasping for air

She turned, looked at me with watery eyes, her face a chalk white, and said adoringly, 'How nice of you to stay with me!'

'Jesus,' I thought, 'She thinks I've been with her all the time!' I tried to reassure her in my best tough-guy accent, took her hand, and said, 'Everything is gonna be OK.' Her first steps were tentative, but she felt well enough to wobble back to my hotel, where I filled a sack with the toilet articles she needed.

With them safely in her hands, I said, 'Look, Monique, go on home, wash up, get some rest, and I'll call you in the morning.'

'No,' she insisted, 'Come with me; you were so thoughtful and attentive.' She insisted, took my hand, and led me back to the Metro.

Her apartment was located on the rue Gabrielle, within walking distance of Sacre Coeur. Located on the ground floor, the apartment overlooked a courtyard. We stepped into it and surprised an old white-haired female concierge, wearing a black dress and frayed slippers, dozing in an overstuffed chair. Shocked at Monique's appearance, the old lady rose, embraced her, stood back, and inquired, 'Mon Dieu, what in God's name happened to you?' She reacted in dismay to Monique's story, saying, 'Ma pauvre enfant, ma pauvre enfant.' Toward the end of Monique's narrative, the old lady looked approvingly at me, nodding her head in affirmation. I was standing in a combination living room and kitchen and noticed a separate bedroom with an impressive late 19th-century brass bed. An old and heavy black stove dominated the other kitchen fixtures and utensils; I was certain it offered warmth on cold days. Bits and pieces of furniture of a bygone era stood like sentinels, partly covering an oriental rug of indeterminate vintage. Without a word, both women pushed and dragged a huge black copper bathtub, shaped like a baby carriage, into place between the table and the stove without asking for my assistance. They hoisted metal pots of water onto the stove, whose four gas rings were set aflame. As soon as the water boiled, they poured it into the tub. How ancient, how French Revolutionary!

Monique undressed with her back towards me, revealing a shapely torso and long straight legs. For a moment, she stood beside the bath, her brown hair falling to her shoulders. The old lady stood beside her, holding one of the bars of soap, as her young friend stepped gingerly into the steaming bath. Gleefully she shouted, 'C'est tres chaud!' Her face was flushed; her upper body was covered with suds as steam rose from the water and formed beads of condensation on the copper. She responded to the old lady's scrubbing and shouted in mock pain. Her soiled clothes, Exhibit A of our encounter, lay piled in a heap, to be dealt with soon enough. I was ushered into the bedroom by the old lady and undressed, knowing that part of Monique's return to pristine splendor was in tribute to me. I dug deeper into the mattress, gazed at the ceiling, and waited for Monique. Soon she came to bed and snuggled against me. Her transformation from the afflicted 'Muette foundling' to the gleaming, sensuous, and expectant woman was touching and impressive, even if she had incorrectly interpreted my behavior as an act of gallantry.

The author as photographer on Armistice Day, November 11, 1945 in Paris, at the Arc de Triomphe

12

The Consequences of Meeting Colonel Binoche

It was an 'April in Paris' morning; the weather was mild and the trees in blossom. After sitting in the canteen at the Hotel Majestic, chatting and drinking coffee with some off-duty U.S. Marines who served as guards at Admiral Harold 'Betty' Stark's U.S. Naval Headquarters at the nearby Hotel Raphael, I left to return to my office. I crossed the hotel's imposing lobby and entered the revolving doors. Once inside its glass cubicle, as I pushed forward I saw Colonel François Binoche standing on the sidewalk waiting to enter. We stared at each other through the glass partition, momentarily transfixed, as the door slowly turned, then stopped. I pushed harder, he moved closer.

Seconds later, I rushed headlong onto the sidewalk. Blurred by the excitement, all was in motion as we grabbed at each other and embraced. 'I've looked all over for you,' he shouted with delight, 'and now we meet by chance.'

'How great to see you again,' I replied, still hugging him, my eyes moist.

In unison, adding our voices to the sounds of the spring day, we declared, 'After all, it's great to be alive!'

I stepped back and said, my voice dropping an octave, 'I am truly glad to see you.'

'And where are Scruby, Gualandi, and the others?' he inquired.

'I don't really know — maybe back in the States.'

As if thinking aloud, he said, 'I would like to decorate all of you, but that might not be possible. Now I must attend a meeting.' I asked what he was doing in Paris. He couldn't be specific but, in general terms, it was something to do with Allied military intelligence. We exchanged phone numbers before we parted.

Two weeks later, my phone rang. 'Monsieur Stephen Weiss?' a French woman at the other end inquired.

'Yes,' I answered.

Speaking slowly in English, the woman said, 'This is the Ministry of War. The French Government has awarded you the Croix de Guerre (Military Cross) étoile d'argent (silver star). The presentation ceremony will be presided over by Colonel Binoche next Tuesday at 11:00, at the Ministry of War. Can you make it?'

'Of course, I will be there,' I replied, and hung up, overwhelmed by the news.

I stood at attention in uniform in front of Col. Binoche feeling proud to be decorated by an officer under whom I served in combat and admired so much. He read the following, '*Le Ministre des Armées Edmond Michelet cité à l'Ordre de la Division à Stephen Weiss, soldat de l'Armée Américaine, Pour services exceptionnels de guerre rendus au cours de la Libération de la France. Cette citation comporte l'attribution de la Croix de Guerre 1939–1945 avec étoile d'argent.*' Binoche stepped forward and pinned the Croix de Guerre on my tunic with his left hand. A copy of the photo taken during the event is available at the National Archives in Washington, DC.

Binoche shook my hand and said that it was customary to wear the medal all day. At the Allied Officers' Club at 33 rue Faubourg St. Honoré, those preceding us witnessed our arrival. The presentation of the award was reason enough for those officers to join in our festivities. Throughout the afternoon, champagne flowed and accomplished its intended purpose.

Soon after, Col. Binoche called again one August afternoon and dropped another bombshell, saying that I had been awarded the Médaille de la Résistance Française for the services rendered in the Ardèche. Created by General de Gaulle in February 1943, the award was a singular honor granted sparingly even to Frenchmen and practically never to foreigners. I was honored to be decorated by Colonel Binoche because he himself was a gallant officer who had received, among his many decorations, the Croix de la Libération from General de Gaulle. His name is printed in gold, with those of only 1,800 others, including Gen. Dwight Eisenhower and Prime Minister Winston Churchill, on a marble plaque at the Chancellery of the Liberation in the Invalides, Napoleon's resting place in Paris. In part, the plaque's citation reads (from the French), '*By the Ordinance of the French National Committee of the Liberation of 7 January, 1944, General de Gaulle, Grand Master of the Order, has recognized his Companions of the Liberation of France in the Honor and by the Victory.'*

Paris offered a variety of entertainments. 'Madame Bluebell,' the *Folies-Bergère* stage director and choreographer, an English showgirl friend of Olga's, asked if I'd photograph a theater performance of her troupe. Of course I readily agreed. When the train arrived at my Metro stop, Iéna, the carriage was crowded. I carried an Army canvas musette bag filled with camera equipment slung over one shoulder. A young woman wearing, among other things, a nondescript orange fur jacket that looked as if it had been in a fight with an alley cat, stood close to me. Although the style of her clothes was typical of Paris fashion impoverished by war, her bearing and elegance defied their poor quality and design. All on board was drawn to her — she resembled two famous contemporary actresses, Maureen O'Hara and Danielle Darrieux. She exuded a similar star quality and I wondered who she was. Her beauty impressed me. My destination was Cadet in Montmartre, the closest station to the theater.

I wanted to meet her. At Cadet, we both got off. I walked on ahead, excited and unsure of myself. I was about to forget it all when she came abreast of me and brushed against the side of my musette bag with her right hand. As she continued to walk on past, I called after her: 'Mademoiselle.'

She stopped and turned. 'Oui?' Feeling overwhelmed, I groped for the right word and, using an obvious ploy, asked for directions to the *Folies-Bergère*. She spoke in halting English, 'I am going part way, but come with me.'

We walked up the stairs and onto the street, talking as we went. 'Je m'appelle Stephen Weiss et j'ai habité ici comme un photographe américain à Paris sur avenue d'Iéna.'

'My name is Anne Marie Boucher and I live on rue de la Pompe, not far from you.'

'Why, that's one of the streets I drive by every morning on my way to Boulevard Suchet.' I laughed and said, 'We're neighbors.'

Approaching a darkened theater from the opposite side of the street, we stopped directly across from it. 'This is where I work,' she said, pointing to the theater. Displayed on the marquee were the words *La*

Célestine. 'We are in rehearsals now, and I have the ingénue lead.' So she was an actress after all!

'Let's meet after you're finished. I need to see you again.'

She paused and then replied, 'All right, but don't wait for me in front of the theater. Wait for me here and I'll come to you.' After kissing her on the cheek, I followed her directions and walked toward the *Folies*, my heart lighter than it had been in years. I was the guy who got the girl, against all odds and against the competition. She was a knockout, and I was in love.

I found the stage door of the *Folies*, introduced myself to the porter, and asked for 'Madame Bluebell.' Given the OK, I passed through a corridor that wove between dressing rooms, laden with stacks of props and cluttered with costumes. Stagehands were moving sets for the evening's performance, show girls were trying on huge colorful head pieces, others — including the principals — were limbering up, a pir-ouette here, a pas de chat there. Above the stage, gaffers were replacing a faulty spot light. The floor was made of big planks of pine grooved together, worn with years of use; ropes extending from the ceiling were tied to wooden pins in slots on either side of the stage. The unfolding scene brought to mind gangs of stevedores loading cargo onto a sailing ship. Bluebell and a small group of dancers stood center stage talking over ways of improving the existing dance numbers. Gesticulating, re-citing in English, counting slowly, Bluebell demonstrated the steps she wanted. Many of the girl dancers were English, chosen because of their long legs. Pinpoints of light shone at the lighting director's console and in the walkways. The showgirls, some with their breasts bare, some still in street clothes, others partially made up, looked magical and athletic. The pit orchestra was tuning up beyond the curtain. Bluebell broke away to greet me. She was an Englishwoman in her mid to late 30s, blonde, blue-eyed, with a dancer's body. I liked her at once. 'I've re-served a seat for you out front, but see the show from the wings first. You'll like the contrast.' The orchestra finished tuning up; silence, then the audience began filing in. I stood in the wings anticipating a stirring performance, but my mind kept bumping into visions of Anne-Marie at every turn.

The house lights dimmed as the orchestra played and the curtain opened, revealing a bevy of statuesque showgirls. Descending from ris-ers placed down stage, their lithe bodies swaying to the music, the girls wore their large decorative headpieces with an imperturbable air. The tempo increased and the show's top male and female dancers threw themselves passionately at each other in a portrayal of unrequited love and sexual fantasy. With heaving chests and perspiration beading on their brows, dancers rushed past me for a quick change off stage before returning. A volcano erupted, natives paddled their war canoes, and braziers gushed flame between the potted palms. The chorus line of dancers, clad in nothing more than hula skirts, were ravished by marauding tribal warriors. The curtain came down with the lovers lying entwined together at center stage, surrounded by a dancing, singing chorus. The audience, a mixture of Parisians and visiting military personnel, was ecstatic.

I sat out front for the next two scenes, enjoying the long legs, curved bodies, and bare breasts of the women, but at intermission I left the theater and returned earlier than planned to our arranged meeting place and waited in the shadows. There were few passers-by. Anne-Marie and some other people emerged from the theater lobby and stood chatting in the dark for another five minutes on the sidewalk. I was filled with anticipation and self-doubt. At last, they embraced, said good night, and dispersed, leaving Anne-Marie alone. She crossed over to me.

I held out my hand and greeted her in a way more formal than intended. She smiled. I felt somewhat abashed and tried to disguise my excitement. We walked along to the Métro. It began to drizzle and the street lamps reflected shimmering pools of light on the dark pavement. 'Might we find a café somewhere near and have a coffee?' She replied, 'Another time, if you don't mind; my father is old and alone.' The train was noisy and crowded, our conversation banal and perfunctory, which ran contrary to my intention. If love finds a way, we hadn't found it so far. When she left the train and walked toward the exit, I felt awkward and dispirited, without any sense of accomplishment.

I covered my disappointment by pretending that the last thing I needed was a close relationship. Traveling outside Paris did take up much of my time, but when we talked on the phone and could have met, my boastful and defensive manner denied us the opportunity. I never discovered what Anne-Marie's intentions were, but we did meet at a rehearsal, where she introduced me to others in the cast and those theatrical friends of hers in the audience. I can't recall their names, but this was the era of writers like Camus, de Beauvoir, and Sartre, of entertainers like Piaf, Aznavour, and Barbara, many of whom became favorites of mine later on. They met at the Café Flore and the Aux Deux Magots, cafés within reach of each other on the Blvd. St. Germain.

Though we had much going for us — youth, good looks, interest, and intelligence — our affair never took off, much like the plane whose design insisted it could fly but in actuality could never get off the ground. All we did was taxi down the runway.

After I returned from a photo assignment in Belgium, we met in Montmartre. I was tense with anticipation. We walked along the crowded street at night on the way to the theater. I've no idea what the subject of our conversation was, but she stopped and turned to me, measuring her words carefully, and said, 'You are not serious with me, you are not serious with yourself or, for that matter, with life.' I was taken by surprise, but I could not argue or plead. In some way, although her statement lacked a frame of reference, she was right. I didn't want this to happen but, intuitively, some part of me knew it would. For some reason, I contributed to this ending, as if a hidden and destructive part of me had been in control from the start. She admitted to no aberrant contributions of her own. I looked at her and glumly said, 'It's the war. I can't get cranked up about anything.' Upon reaching the theater entrance, she dismissed me with a wave of her hand and walked through the empty lobby.

Even if my intentions were disguised or dimmed, some part of me desired a relationship with her. Although I was just able to perform on an occupational level, underneath it all, particularly in romantic relationships, I agonized, defended my fragile self by blustering, and believed living well was the best revenge on my recent imprisonment. My words could not match my feelings, their presentations unclear at the best of times.

To lessen the pain of loss, I drowned myself in photo assignments across Europe. Roaming around Paris stirred up memories. Taken by surprise, I felt the searing pain of loss and rejection but didn't know what action, if any, to take. We never met again. However brief our encounter, regardless of the elapsed years, she was unforgettable. I tried to find her years later, but never did.

On one assignment to Normandy, before motoring through the 'Swisse Normande' countryside to Omaha Beach, I stopped for lunch at a restaurant overlooking Lake Rabondages. Fortunately, it didn't rain, although dark clouds threatened. Normandy had a reputation for erratic weather, consisting of nine-tenths rain. I dubbed it 'The Pisspot of France.' I had arranged to stay at a chateau not far from the American military cemetery at La Cambe, a hamlet situated about three miles inland from Omaha Beach. My assignment was straightforward: to photograph Omaha Beach, its surrounding area, and the Memorial Day ceremonies at La Cambe, the first since the end of the war.

The next morning, I drove the short distance to St. Laurent and parked the jeep on a bluff 150 feet above Omaha and the Channel. Nearby, much to my surprise, a work gang was constructing a cemetery on waterlogged ground, its many pools reflecting the lowering sky. Little flags strung on wire outlined an area of unexploded mines. I followed the path down a ravine to the beach below and then looked back, wondering why this landing site was chosen, because the location was a defender's dream, providing excellent observation and protection. To take the bluff, offloading from landing craft, American infantry had to cross a quarter mile of exposed beach and mount an attack up numerous ravines filled with scrub and long grass, in which, as elsewhere, the enemy was dug in. The invasion plan needed to work right from the water's edge to the bluff; it didn't, and was a near disaster. The enemy was obstinate, its use of small arms excellent, and many of the assault companies that landed in this sector suffered 50 percent casualties, a disproportionate amount. Death here was not a continuum of life, but a rupture.

Searching for a human interest story amidst the litter on the beach, I befriended an elderly couple that lived nearby, fishing at the water's edge. Wearing tattered clothing and rubber boots, scant protection against the wind and drizzle, they posed beside rusting landing craft, abandoned sections of the Mulberry harbor, ruined during the violent storm of June 19, 1944, dismantled beach obstacles, and reinforced concrete bunkers, their muted guns still pointing out to sea. Six of the photos were published later as part of a D-Day retrospective in the centerfold of the *Stars and Stripes*.

It rained intermittently on Memorial Day morning as I drove the short distance to La Cambe, a hamlet of a few abandoned stone cottages on either side of the cemetery's temporary entrance. Except for the gravel parking area, large patches of water glistened between the wooden crosses, each with its identification dog tag nailed to the center crosspiece. I found walking on the wet grass and waterlogged earth difficult; each step was followed by a squelching sound, resulting in another batch of mud gripping my boots. Norman fields, much like the Yorkshire moors, lend themselves to a funereal mood. Nature added to the effect with low-lying clouds and rain driving across the landscape. There were few visitors. I walked toward a woman standing alone, small, pinned against the sky, ensnared by crosses, and observed from above by an American flag angrily snapping in the wind. I spoke in French, but she quickly assured me that she too was American, an admission that I found startling, because State Department approval was required for those citizens desiring to travel abroad.

Introducing myself while shaking hands, I asked, 'What brings you to Normandy.'

'My son is buried here,' she answered calmly.

Taken aback, I said, 'I don't mean to intrude; wouldn't your son have been my age?'

She looked at me, as if absorbing every detail, then said quietly, 'Nineteen.'

'Yes, I thought so.' At the same time, I wanted to reach out and hold her hand. 'When was the last time you saw him?'

'He came to London on a weekend pass in May 1944; I was living there.'

'Was he overseas long?'

'No, not really.' Two or three months. And then, two weeks after we met in London, I received a telegram notifying me he had been killed.'

'Do you know where?'

'Yes,' she answered, her voice flat. Pointing, she said, 'Just outside the gates, near one of those stone cottages.' I glanced down and read her son's name on the cross next to us. Memory stirred. I joined the 36th on Anzio with 93 other replacements. When the war ended, only four remained. Bitterly, covering up feelings of impotence and rage, I concluded that he was killed after one day in combat!

A handful of us gathered around the wooden bandstand, painted in the same white as the surrounding crosses, and waited for the ceremony to begin. Climbing the wet steps to the platform, the principal speaker, a highly decorated infantry major, assured us that the dead had not died in vain. As he spoke, I stood close to the American lady and thought of her son and thousands of the others buried in their wooden pine boxes, encased in earth that never seemed to dry out.

My thoughts were interrupted by a succession of orations, spoken by visiting French and American politicians, who in turn expressed words of grief and hope in varying proportions. An Army chaplain assured us of God's infinite wisdom. Kneeling to pray at a Catholic mass in Anzio's mud the year before, I appealed to God for salvation and instead witnessed the horror that followed. No God, no father, I concluded, would allow his teenage sons to die such untimely and horrific deaths. I finished taking my photos, sensing that God and I were quits, and returned to her side. She stood composed, indifferent to the elements, although the wind whipped the edge of her dress and the rain dampened her face and hair. The firing squad lined up, took aim, and fired twice. The bugler stepped forward and played the first plaintive notes of 'Taps.' It was too much for her; it was too much for me. Side by side, heads bent, we wept.

Commander François Binoche of the French Army decorates the author
with the Croix de Guerre, Paris, July 1946

13

I Miss My Rendezvous with General Patton

I spent the Armistice Day of 1945 standing on the lead roof of an apartment building between avenue Pressbourg and the Place de l'Etoile, having received permission from the owner of the top-floor flat. In my eagle's lair, overlooking the Arc de Triomphe, a triumphal arch dedicated to Napoleon's greatest victory at Austerlitz in 1805, I had a commanding view of every major avenue entering the Etoile, Kléber, Hoche, Marceau, and the others. Camera in hand, I waited for the parade to begin, a tribute to the men who died in both World Wars. France not only had an army in 1945, it also had an empire. From Indo-China, the Caribbean, the South Pacific, Africa, and the Middle East, natives and tribesmen on their horses and camels, in their colorful uniforms and tribal dress, with their flashing swords and antique rifles, came to ride and march. A huge *tricolore*, suspended from the center of the arch, rippled in the breeze above the 'flame of remembrance' and the tomb of the Unknown Soldier.

Of course, to put a fine point on things, there is an arch at Thiepval, a village on the Somme, that commemorates the death of 79,000 French unknown soldiers who died, 'mort pour la France,' in the First World War. Moreover, the British have an unknown soldier of their own in Westminster Abbey, but they add another twist to the final leave taking. In one of their small, park-like cemeteries at La Boiselle, close to Thiepval, I found a gravestone, exactly like the others, on which was carved, besides his name, unit, and rank, the words, 'buried somewhere in this cemetery.' While trying to regain my mental balance, I wondered, 'What happened just before he was killed that removed any chance of lying under his own gravestone like so many of his comrades? Blown to smithereens?' According to regulations, he does not rate as an 'unknown.'

Almost one month later, on December 9, an Armed Forces Radio Network (AFN) announcer interrupted the music program to report that four-star General George S. Patton had been gravely injured in an automobile accident near Mannheim, Germany. Twelve days later, he died of complications at age 60 in an Army hospital near Frankfurt. His wife Beatrice was at his side.

Within an hour of his death, La Fleur called me. 'Steve, prepare to leave for Luxembourg right away and cover Patton's burial at Hamm Military Cemetery. Funeral arrangements are pending.' For Patton, the site was most notable because, during the Battle of the Bulge, he shifted his army in another direction, from east to north, within 24 hours, in a monumental feat of arms and logistics. He began an attack against the southern shoulder of the salient produced by the German Ardennes offensive during the winter of 1944. Much to Generals Eisenhower and Bradley's relief, and to his own satisfaction, he had accomplished what some of his detractors considered highly improbable.

When the funeral arrangements were made public, I stowed my photographic gear and a val pack stuffed with clothes in the back of my jeep and headed east out of Paris for Luxembourg City, 180 miles distant. Unfortunately, the winter weather was appalling, and I had no experience driving in blizzard conditions, which decreased the odds of getting there. As I took the route running parallel to the Marne River, the only real markers were the line of poplar trees on either side of the road; all other identification had disappeared under the full weight of the storm. Unsure of gauging the proper width between my jeep and oncoming vehicles, I drove toward their headlights like a moth to a flame when they emerged from the whiteout 40 feet away. It kept snowing, temperature and visibility dropped to zero, and without defrosters and variable speed windshield wipers, my jeep, with only a canvas top and no side covers, was ill equipped to function properly in the atrocious weather. After avoiding a head-on collision by the narrowest of margins for the third time, preoccupied with the freezing cold, I admitted defeat. There was little chance of getting to Luxembourg for Patton's burial on schedule. Mumbling to myself, I protested that driving such a distance in worsening Arctic weather, over poorly maintained and unmarked roads, was beyond the call of duty.

Near Epernay, a town world renowned for its champagne, I found an American unit that could stow my jeep and put me up for the night. Walking to the rear of a chow line, I ran into one of my former Blanding Basic Training sergeant-instructors, a small guy with big ears that we as recruits had playfully called 'Rabbit' because he looked like Bugs

Bunny, the animated cartoon character. 'Rabbit,' I shouted merrily, 'well, you finally got overseas after the shooting stopped, you dirty dog.' I joined him for dinner in a large converted garage, in which we talked about some of men we trained with at Blanding and his recent overseas posting, a cushy administrative job in an ordnance outfit. After my polar journey, I was glad to see a familiar face. Disappointed that my mission was delayed, well fed but exhausted, I bedded down for the night and slept deeply.

The next morning, garaging the jeep, I hitched a ride on a command car heading for Reims, thinking that if I could get an eastbound train to Thionville, a steel town near the Franco-Luxembourg frontier, I still might make the funeral. We followed the road north for 15 miles across a frozen landscape, deserted except for the long rows of twisted grape vines. Yesterday's wind had moderated as we ploughed slowly on. The cracking sound of the command car's tires moving over the dry snow, mixed with the click-whoosh, click-whoosh of the windshield wipers, underscored my apprehension. I reached the station and found that the earliest train for Thionville was scheduled three hours later. Time and weather conspired, and although an Army driver and command car were standing by at Thionville, ready to speed me to the cemetery, I had arrived too late. Patton was buried at midmorning on December 24 next to a GI killed in action during the Battle of the Bulge.

Eisenhower and his Chief of Staff (COS), General Walter Bedell Smith, were not invited to his funeral on specific orders from Patton to his wife before he died because the three men had fallen out. Failing to arrive on time not only cost me the story, but a meeting with the Patton family and Assistant Secretary of War Robert Patterson, who had been my father's company commander when he served with the 77th 'Statue of Liberty' Infantry Division in 1918. With a driving rain at my back, I photographed Patton's grave, piled high with flowers and wreaths atop the black earth, against a backdrop of the dark and sinister forest.

Patton considered Luxembourg and its climate as a region whose wealth was measured in heaps of manure, 'damned poor tank country and damned bad weather' but he would remain here forever, near the Duchy's capital city. Ill equipped to cope with peace, I'd say he got his wish. Rather than return without any story at all, I decided to shoot one about soldiering in an Army ordnance unit stationed in Thionville. It was a simple premise, a group of men fulfilling their assigned tasks on a daily basis. What I hadn't expected was the arrogant, self-centered attitude of the young GIs new to the ETO as part of the Army of Occupation. Those with whom I talked told me that overseas duty meant nothing more than a chance to make 'big' money. The guys I knew in Italy and Southern France simply tried to stay alive!

Before I left Paris, my mother had written that a very close boyhood friend of mine, Joseph (Yossi) Schildkraut, had been killed near Metz during an attack on Ft. Driant six months before the German surrender. According to her, he had gone overseas in late 1944 and joined the 5th 'Diamond' Infantry Division as a replacement. Like Patton, he was buried at Hamm.

I went in search of his grave with the ordnance company's driver. We left Thionville, crossed the Moselle, and drove 18 miles through the unrelenting rain. We found his grave, one of 5,000, in a wooded section tangled with undergrowth. The area reminded me of a crude building site and had an air of disruption and impermanence.

Late on this winter's afternoon, it was dark and eerie in the woods. I stood on the soft wet earth on top of his grave, facing the marker with its Star of David, took a few photos, and said in a voice mixed with bravado, denial, and self-protection, 'You goddamn son of a bitch; you ought to have known better than to get killed just before the war ended. You should have played it safe, kept your head down...' Suddenly, the thick, Ardennes earth collapsed, undermined by the rain. I yelled and fell halfway into the grave, exposing the top of the pine casket. The driver grabbed my arm and pulled me across the reddish clay onto the wet grass, where I regained my footing.

Emotionally shaken, we tried to repair the damage. On our way out, we reported the problem to the soldier on duty. Saddened and troubled by the event, I kept repeating, 'He' — meaning Yossi — 'set me up.' Clearly, I had no proper way of dealing with terminal loss, and Yossi was a stark reminder of my inability to cope. I felt glad and guilty that I had survived but, driving through the downpour, there was nothing to celebrate. I remembered that the war correspondent Ernie Pyle had written 'You feel small in the presence of dead men, and ashamed at being alive.' He didn't have to wait long. Soon after he wrote this, Pyle was killed by a Japanese sniper on a small Pacific island west of Okinawa on April 18, 1945.

I sent the photos to Yossi's mother, who I'd known since childhood, with a short cover letter, but never received a reply. Returning to the

U.S., I called and spoke with her, but she refused to talk about him. She closed by saying, 'Your photos were too painful a reminder and I have destroyed them.' I felt like an insensitive, bungling intruder. Although he had an older brother and a younger sister, he was the apple of his mother's eye. I thought bitterly: he waited to be inducted, I enlisted; I entered combat months earlier than he, and I lived, he died. Figure that out! A roll of the dice!

Still reverberating from the war's aftershocks, I was in no great rush to face my family or life in the States, so when I was offered a civilian position as a still photographer with the War Department in Paris, I accepted. My job description and responsibilities as a cameraman would remain the same, but there would be a substantial increase in status, pay, and benefits. I left the following day for Frankfurt, where the Separation Center was located.

I was humming *From This Moment On*, a popular romantic ballad written by Cole Porter, as I drove alone in the converted ambulance we used as a sound truck, following the Marne River to Chalons and beyond to Verdun. Reaching the crest of a hill, enjoying the warmth of a glorious spring morning, I suddenly realized that the land was blighted, exposing a vast area of white chalk. Without realizing it, I was in the middle of the Verdun battlefield, a district empty of vegetation, drummed out of existence by the massive artillery bombardments of the First World War. The Germans used flamethrowers here for the first time in 1916 and 600,000 soldiers were killed and wounded during the same year. The French called it *L'Enfer*, 'the Inferno.'

On the other side of Metz, once the most fortified city in Europe, finally subdued by Patton in three months of battle, I felt anxious and vulnerable, experiencing a sense of foreboding even though the war was history. I entered Germany as if it were enemy territory and stopped at Saarbrucken for coffee and doughnuts at a makeshift Army canteen. A German 88 mm high-velocity artillery piece stood poised near the entrance, aimed toward France. I continued my journey through a land mixed with forests, a few inhabitants, and vineyards, with the road sloping gently toward the Rhine, which I crossed near Mainz.

I stayed with two photographer friends, Stan and Jim, stationed in Bad Nauheim, a picturesque spa with three restorative springs and various medical institutions, 20 miles from Frankfurt. I planned to begin separation proceedings from there.

Lounging over coffee most days on the terrace of one of the local hotels, I learned that most GIs of the Army of Occupation completely ignored its attempt to prevent fraternization with German women. The edict was unenforceable and soon discarded, because GIs, viewing German women as spoils of war and theirs for the taking, refused to let attractive, accessible frauleins roam about alone. Whatever the conditions, young people have a natural desire to connect. Love required fulfillment. Besides, for a small investment in cigarettes or silk stockings, pegged to the going rate, there were many young women from whom to choose, and you had to be morally masochistic to go wanting. In Berlin, for example, women outnumbered men by two and a half million. German women were practical if nothing else, and some found a temporary safe haven in the world's oldest profession. If love deepened, marriage followed, and relocation in the States ensued.

About a week later, I received the phone call I was waiting for. It was from a Lieutenant Harvey L. Jones at the Frankfurt Army Separation Center, who was overseeing my separation. We met the next day. He leafed through my records, checked off some items, and grunted over others. It seemed that I was moments away from becoming a civilian. He paused momentarily, looked at one of the papers, turned to me, and said, 'Right! You've earned three battle stars and the combat infantry badge, but I'm under no obligation to award the Indian arrowhead clasp for an assault landing. There's nothing in the regulations that says I must.'

'That may be,' I replied, 'but if you check the dates against my combat record, you'll see that the arrowhead is deserved.'

'Well, you know as well as I that I've got to follow regulations,' he answered, retreating behind bureaucratic safety. I looked closer at Jones, certain that he had never been in harm's way or heard a shot fired in anger. I figured that he had just arrived by boat, re-enacting his fussy stateside office behavior and perpetuating his civilian job in uniform. For him, there would never be bugles, banners, or battle stars, and I, feeling righteously indignant, chose not to leave until I got the arrowhead. We argued. Could the regulations be out of date, a vital page missing? Wasn't that the usual case with bureaucracies? 'No,' he insisted, 'all is in order.'

An idea of mine emerged that might end the stalemate, and I put it to him. 'The records read that I landed with the 36th at Le Dramont near St

Raphaël on August 15, 1944. OK. Thousands of GIs and officers are be-ing discharged daily, here and in the U.S.; the officers remaining aren't sufficient to see if every 't' and every 'i' on every discharge paper is crossed and dotted, so by the time my discharge is checked, if it ever is, both of us will be long gone from the Army. Let's say some file clerk at the records center in St. Louis considers my arrowhead undeserved and reports it; so what — the worst that can happen is that the award is canceled, and I subtract it from my campaign ribbon. By that time, we'll be involved in more important things like raising a family and making a living. What do you say?'

Nearby, typewriter keys clicked and, in the background, file cabinet doors opened and closed. Without admitting anything, he picked up his pen and wrote 'Yes' in the box beside the printed arrowhead, shuf-fled the papers together, signed them, and shoved them across the desk for my signature. Our work completed, we shook hands, and I left with $400 in separation pay and an honorable discharge. After serving my country for 31 months, I was a free man! It was April 26, 1946. The words of a song that I had learned as a raw recruit came to mind: '*The coffee that they serve us, they say is mighty fine, it's good for cuts and bruises and tastes like iodine; I don't want no more of Army life; Gee, Ma, I wanna go home.*' I jumped in the air and clicked my heels.

14

My Return to Civilian Life Begins in Paris

I celebrated my return to civilian life in the main ballroom of the Kaiserhof Hotel in Bad Homburg, plied with numerous rounds of rum and Coca-Cola by Stan and Jim. I danced to the sound of a big band, holding Frankie, one of a number of good-looking American Army secretaries and court stenographers assigned to the Nuremberg War Trials, a newly established Allied court in which the top Nazis were to be tried as war criminals and charged with crimes against humanity. I had left town for Paris in the converted ambulance.

Paris never looked better, nor did the girls in their spring frocks. Much to my satisfaction, they were quick to show off their tanned legs and thighs as they spun by on their bicycles. I found a restaurant overlooking the Seine on the Quai Voltaire. Sitting at a table beside a first-floor window, I looked across the Pont du Carrousel and the Jardin des Tuileries, its perimeter outlined by streetlights standing like sentries along the river road. Chugging canal barges laden with ballast or coal, depending upon their direction, plowed and pushed the dark waters of the river against the stone banks hemming it in. Street and automobile lights reflected from the river, but only those created by the passing barges displayed a splash of colors, because of their navigation lamps.

Although a civilian, I was fitted with two officer uniforms and purchased an Army trench coat and a val pack for traveling. As a CAF-6 Civil Service employee, I had the use of a number of officers' clubs located in central Paris, but I soon settled for the one at St. Augustin near Boulevard Haussmann. It was spacious, the fare good, the portions generous, and the Allied clientele animated.

The personnel and housing officer at the Hotel Majestic said he had a furnished two-bedroom hotel suite for rent on the rue des Acacias for $25 per month. It was only a 10-minute walk from our office on avenue Kléber, and by following rue de Pressbourg to avenue de la Grande

223

Armée, a continuation of the Champs Elysées intersected by the Arc de Triomphe, I would find rue des Acacias off to the right. Following his directions, I found the hotel easily and fell for the suite's space, location, and convenience, which included a balcony. I sat in the lobby for a few minutes before I returned to the Majestic and signed the lease.

The distance I'd traveled overcame me. Not the distance from the Majestic, but from my change in circumstances. I started my Army career as a lowly 'dogface' and nearly ruined my life. Now, as a photographer, I had the equivalent Army rank of Major, with all of its benefits. I had status and a respected position. My tumultuous past was history, and the Simmonses and the 'Bow Legs' of this world no longer existed. Moreover, I fell in love with the Arc de Triomphe. Walking to work many times from rue des Acacias over the next six months, I watched the Arc become a living entity. Moving along Pressbourg to or from Kléber, with every change of angle my field of vision changed, revealing the Arc as a sequence of different visual images. With each click of an imaginary camera shutter, I advanced to the next frame. Both the Arc and I reveled in our vivacity, and I truly loved the journey.

15
Photo Missions Accomplished

I received orders to prepare a photo story about automobile tires manufactured at an Army depot in Courcelles, Belgium, about 150 miles northeast of Paris. I was to accompany two officers and a driver in a 1939 Ford sedan that lacked interior heating. The five-hour journey in freezing weather over battered, icy roads, during which it was impossible to keep warm, was an ordeal. Entering the Ardennes, a forested region in the eastern part of Belgium, the scene of the tremendous 1944 winter battle, more than remnants of the battlefield remained. The opposite of a winter wonderland, the woods and fields stood in mute testimony to the ferocity of the German onslaught and the Allied reaction. With the weather and the roads hazardous, driving verged on the impossible. I saw a plethora of downed telephone wires trailing in every direction, shattered tracked vehicles and spiked guns, twisted road signs, broken buildings, and smashed bridges waiting for either repair or clearance. The chaos seemed alive as we skidded along, zigzagging across a snow-covered landscape scarred by a battle known as the Battle of the Bulge.

We reached Courcelles, a small village six miles from Charleroi, where the Army was operating a small factory manufacturing synthetic rubber automobile tires. For the next two days, I photographed an operation that turned 'rubber' granules into tires but what really focused my interest was the history of our billet — the local chateau. It was more wood than brick, more somber than bright in mood. The interior absorbed the available light and cast itself in shadow, but during the Waterloo campaign, regardless of its gloom, the Duke of Wellington had claimed the chateau as his own. One hundred and thirty years later, I, like the 'Iron Duke,' used it as a temporary residence and slept in his bed. When I asked the countess who lived in the other wing of the house about the connection between the many battle flags hanging in the main hall, she replied, 'Oh, the flags are related to the battle that was fought just up the road at Waterloo in 1815.'

Upon my return to Paris, I entered the 239th General Hospital at Ville

Juif, close to Orly Airfield, for a check-up. While I was waiting for my results, an Army ambulance, with sirens blaring and red lights flashing, rushed through the gates with three German prisoners; they had been burned severely when their hot tar container exploded. Repaving a road, they were engulfed and set alight by its deadly contents. Lying on stretchers in the hospital courtyard, in desperate need of treatment, their burns grievous, the dermatologist could do little. The three were as black as the jacket potatoes we roasted on the sandlots of Brooklyn. They died as they lay there, spittle forming on the mouth of one. 'How ironic,' I thought, 'that these three men, after being taken prisoner and surviving the war, were killed in a road accident!' In an instant, I was a rifleman, knowing I couldn't make a deal with life or sell my soul to the devil for one more second of survival. My anger and the irony of what just happened mixed together. Aggrieved, I shook my head in disbelief.

16

The Most Satisfying Dinner I Ever Had!

I don't remember if I had just returned to Paris from Normandy, where I had the abbey, the village, and the rock of Mont St. Michel much to myself. The rock included Mme. Pollard's restaurant and inn, found halfway to the summit, whose omelets were world renowned. Or had I recently returned from an entirely different journey, where I enjoyed omelets of comparable quality prepared by a simply dressed mother and daughter, their legs red from cold, at half the price? The two operated a one-room restaurant, part of a single-story provincial house sitting beside the man road west of Chalons s/Marne. It contained four rough-hewn tables and sixteen wooden chairs, whose legs stood like sentries on the earthen floor.

Excluding some delicious and hearty meals devoured in Rome and Lyon during the war, and not counting the five or six milkshakes and sandwiches I consumed biweekly at the Army's 'Punch Bowl' soda fountain near Gare St. Lazare in Paris, an unforgettable dinner was about to begin.

Early one May evening, I circled the Etoile in Lieutenant Walton T. La Fleur's open jeep with Toby, Bob, and Jack, my photographic colleagues. Traffic was heavy and chaotic, as usual. It was an automobile obstacle course, a life or death event. We swayed from side to side as La Fleur tried avoiding cars entering or leaving the circle on one of Baron Haussmann's grand boulevards. I fantasized that if a vehicle slammed into us, the whole of the Paris photo detachment might disappear in an all-consuming ball of flame. La Fleur, as executive in charge, was a mild-mannered, easygoing, Signal Corps photo officer with a good sense of humor. He approved most photo assignments I proposed, lending his signature to printed orders in which were detailed the purpose, destination, financial expenses, and a car and driver, if required. Off I'd go in a cloud of dust for a week or two, eager to waltz through Europe at government expense.

But as we weaved across the cobbles, the issue was about food, not travel. La Fleur spoke in glowing terms of Madeleine, his live-in French partner, and her cooking, every time all of us were together. He raved but never invited. We hungered. When all seemed lost, while careening around the Arc, we finally struck a deal that appealed to him: the four of us would pay for the entire raw product, and Madeleine would perform her culinary magic. Since everyone was coupled but me, we totaled nine: four women, five men. Having decided on the date of the dinner, Madeleine, backed by La Fleur, prepared for the great event.

I've no idea why La Fleur had stonewalled us for so long. As a symbol of thanks for the excellent way we had fulfilled our assignments, an invitation to dinner would have been a morale-raising event. Surely, it couldn't be the expense because any one of us, with the extra revenue accruing from our individual cigarette sales, could easily afford to host a dinner of this magnitude. Did he want us to believe that money was in short supply and that he was just squeaking by on a lieutenant's salary? Nonsense! The black market flourished!

On the designated evening, I was the first to arrive at their apartment. Bob Hines, the cine cameraman, whom I called the 'poor man's John Barrymore' because of his resemblance to the great actor, arrived with Michele, his French partner. Toby, a still cameraman like me, was as small and round as the great Winston. His woman friend was as round and jolly as he. Jack, preoccupied behind his glasses, seemed more like an accountant than the team's projectionist. Taller than the accountants of the small sample I knew, he conformed nevertheless, having an eye for numbers and a demand for accuracy. The woman by his side belied her quick intelligence in deference to him. Madeleine was about five feet two inches, with dark fizzy hair and thick eyebrows. There were hundreds of women in Paris who fitted her description — those who queued and shopped for staples off pushcarts in almost every quarter — but whether they could cook at Madeleine's level remained unanswered.

All of us had arrived within five minutes of each other. The atmosphere was filled with the kind of team spirit found at a big sporting event, the World Cup, a Brooklyn Dodger-New York Giants baseball game, Christians versus Lions. Our taste buds — at least I'll vouch for mine — were taut with anticipation. Madeleine and La Fleur suggested a choice of aperitifs, ranging from Pernod to St. Raphaël Quinquina. Upholding the American side of things, he supplied a bucket of ice cubes. We sipped our drinks slowly before moving towards the table, festooned with a centerpiece filled with flowers, surrounded by the accoutrements of serious dining — without a paper napkin in sight. Beneath our playful and engaging badinage, we were primed for the 'dinner of the post-war era.' I chanted and beat time on the table with a fork. 'Rah, rah, bah, sis, boom, bah.'

With the war behind us, we had exchanged our uniforms for civilian clothes, retrieved recently from their stateside covering of mothballs. Our attire, including the striped knit tie and pegged trousers I wore, reminded me of day-old bread sold at a discount bakery, or a poor vinyl recording of a second-rate ballad sung by a discordant chanteuse. Noticeably, the French women at table looked comfortable, attired in their simple but tasteful clothes.

From the kitchen, Madeleine first served a *bouchee a la reine*, an individual pastry shell filled with sweetbreads on a rich, green and white Limoges dinner service. As we dined on this delightful mixture of flake pastry and meat medallions, slightly drenched in a light brown sauce, Madeleine said, 'Fine French restaurants offer a menu of six courses and I propose to do the same. To enhance our gastronomic adventure, I shall offer a different wine with each course.' Playfully, she admonished, 'Please don't rush, we've got all night.' Accompanying *the reine* were three bottles of Chateau des Labourons, a silky, fruity red Fleurie from the Beaujolais, its Gamay grapes grown on the hilly slopes south of Macon.

I peered into the kitchen after the first course and noticed that it was lavishly supplied with vital kitchen utensils of all shapes and sizes, each created for a different purpose. Most were kept at arm's length from the uninitiated. Small pots and pans, large mixing spoons, a cluster of knives, colanders, and whisks hung on large iron hooks above the chopping block, but the total space used to produce the end result seemed no larger than a postage stamp. Leaving the clutter and the clatter behind, Madeleine followed the first course with bay shrimp and a *vinaigrette de poireaux.* The Fleurie gave way to chilled bottles of Pouilly-Fume, its light golden grapes grown along the Loire between the towns of Cosne and La Charite. The Pouilly-Fume, refined and exquisite, is not to be confused with a Burgundian Pouilly-Fuisse, a white produced further east. It was as if the table was a stage before which a curtain rose and fell, revealing a new scene transformed by additional culinary magic.

Madeleine and La Fleur placed on the table two steaming platters of filets of sole, drenched in their natural juices, surrounded by chunks of lobster and mussels. After being served an ample portion, accompanied by such words from Madeleine as, 'There's more in the kitchen,' we added green beans and carrots, served from two serving bowls. As if by sleight of hand, bottles of Montrachet and Corton-Carlemagne from the region between Dijon and Beaune were placed strategically within striking distance. The contents of each were poured immediately, to everyone's approval. Drifting above the ambient noise, we offered gurgled praise after tasting the new arrivals. Trying to be poetic, I rhymed ungrammatically:

The two wines were a perfect pair

for the delicious sole and the fruit de mer.

Sensing that we were nearing the summit of our dinner, I paused longer between mouthfuls, finished what was left on my plate, pushed slightly away from the table, rolled my shirt sleeves above my wrists, undid my tie, and unbuttoned my collar. Taking three or four deep breaths, downing the remainder of my wine, I readied my leap into the void, much like a cat preparing to pounce.

All of La Fleur's manly strength was employed in carrying a huge, heroic, 12-pound thigh of roasted Charolais beef. It sizzled and crackled on the silver platter as he triumphantly paraded toward us. Bob yelled, 'Hail Caesar!' and Toby shouted, 'Mort pour la France.' All raised our glasses in tribute. There was spontaneous applause amidst the shouts and laughter. The beef's aroma was all embracing, and I saluted, French style, open palm. Madeleine lowered her head and glowed.

La Fleur carved. The cut was excellent, the fat being lightly and evenly distributed between the muscle fibers. Each slice was crisp on the outside and rare to medium within, the result of a roasting philosophy that included variations in oven temperatures until done. Roasting this way sealed in the natural juices, eliminating any need for a meat sauce later. Roast potatoes and sprouts replaced the peas.

Madeleine and La Fleur served two big red wines to 'sign post' our gastronomic journey, one a Chateauneuf du Pape, composed of 12 grape varieties grown near Avignon on the Rhône, and the other, a Chateau Lynch-Bages from Paillac near Bordeaux, combining the Cabernet and Merlot grapes. Both were scented and complex, with a glorious aftertaste. We had reached our previously unclimbed summit with flags flying and our napkins tucked under our chins. Henceforth, beef roasts were measured against Madeleine's creation. How could it be otherwise?

Unlike the firemen of a small Provençal village who, halfway through their annual dinner at the local inn, retreated from the table in search of a comfortable sofa on which to snooze before continuing, we sallied forth, fearless and without respite. A simple salad with an oil and vinegar followed. I associated the word plateau with the Wild West, but Madeleine, after the remains of that glorious roast disappeared into the kitchen, arrived with a plateau de fromages, followed in train by La Fleur with a panier of French bread.

I counted six varieties of cheese: Maroilles, a strong-flavored square-shaped cheese in a russet rind, from Lille; Pelardon des Cevennes, a small goat cheese with a rustic flavor; a wedge of blue-veined Roquefort, made near Millau from ewe's milk, mild yet piquant; Munster from Alsace, round in shape with a creamy interior and strong-flavored; Emmental, mild with holes the size of walnuts, from Franche Comte, a region close to Switzerland; and a wedge of Brie, creamy with a yellow interior and white rind, prepared from cow's milk in the Ile de-France, near Paris.

Regarding our choice in cheese, some of us were experimental, while others remained loyal to the familiar. I helped myself to two chunks of bread and chose a small wedge of Roquefort and a segment of Maroilles. The smell of it took my breath away; I thought of sweaty socks and stale sports locker rooms. My eyes verged on tears, not those of nostalgia but of repulsion. Was I a courageous man, a risk-taker? What was it to be? Should I consider a retreat to the safety of the Roquefort or a wrestle with the Maroilles? I don't know if my dining companions recognized my dilemma but throwing caution to the winds, leaping into the sea without a life jacket, I placed a clump of Maroilles on a chunk of bread and tentatively began chewing. Suddenly the stench evaporated with my former prejudicial thoughts; surprised, I discovered the combination to be delicious and, with a sip of the remaining red, an ode to my palate. I began singing the words of a song made popular by Vicki Autier. She was a popular French chanteuse I had known who accompanied herself at the piano. The song seemed appropriate for the moment — *Sans Toi, Je n'ai Plus Rien.*

We had been eating for five hours at a pace determined by Madeleine's preparation and service, which allowed our digestive systems every opportunity to embrace and savor the distinctive ingredients of each course. True, we were all slightly drunk by now — how could it be otherwise? — but appreciation and awareness of this experience never faltered or dimmed. The decorous Hines had exchanged his Homburg for a cushion sitting on top of his head and gazed upward as Michele, with arms around him, cooed in appreciation of his angular profile and sense of humor. He might have been a character in one of the classic films he enjoyed talking about. Toby and his woman sat so close together that it was difficult to see where one began and the other ended. Jack hummed a current swing signature ballad, *Polka Dots and Moonbeams,* to his woman, who smiled in appreciation.

Temptation arrived in the guise of bilberry tarts, a specialty of the Vosges, and an assortment of pastries acquired from the same local boulangerie/patisserie that supplied the baguettes. Madeleine asked La Fleur to offer Blanc de Blancs brut reserve champagne from Cremant, a small village south of Epernay. Unlike most champagne, only the Chardonnay grape is used in its preparation. Once the sound of the popping corks faded away, I enjoyed the sparkling wine's freshness and clarity. After coffee was served, La Fleur followed with an armful of after-dinner drinks — Calvados, Cognac, Armagnac, and Cointreau. Hines zeroed in on the Cointreau, defending his consumption by saying it lessened the pain of a questionable tooth. As for me, I poured an ample amount of Bisquit Cognac into a snifter, slowly whirled the amber liquid, inhaled, and took a swig. Alas, it was two in the morning and time to go. Reveling in our camaraderie, thanking Madeleine and La Fleur for an extraordinary evening, promising in tribute that we would never eat again, we lingered momentarily at the door. Toby said to Madeleine, 'I'm going to recommend you for the *Legion d'Honneur,*' and we shouted our approval.

Early the next morning, I drove to Bob and Michele's apartment on rue Lauriston, parked the car, and honked the horn. He and I had an assignment in Brussels beginning that afternoon. Michelle waved from an upstairs window as Hines silently entered on the passenger side, looking somewhat disheveled, his right cheek slightly puffy. 'I didn't get much sleep,' he said. 'The tooth kept bothering me, so I kept soaking it in Cointreau. We drove out of Paris, talking about the previous evening. La Fleur had been right all along. Madeleine was a kitchen virtuoso, and so impressed were we that the vow never to eat again quickly came to mind. We were two knights-errant and defenders of the faith, but with increasing appetites.

Two and a half hours into our journey, having stopped at a roadside restaurant, we were starving and in dire need of sustenance. Our resolution in tatters, the vow forgotten, we both ordered biftek and frites and a carafe of red wine. Hines went to the toilet. When he returned, some young kid was playing a clarinet, walking between the tables, and appealing for tips. Bob tipped him and asked to borrow the instrument. The kid handed it over. Hines was playing *Star Dust* when the food arrived.

A few days later, I sent Madeleine a short poem called *Feast Your Eyes on This*.

Is this the path our friendship takes?

Now and in the future

Honor bound by food that binds,

A metabolic suture?

The Man proclaims we voyage once

Across the fields of Life

Tis best to proceed armed to the teeth

With spoon and fork and knife.

La Fleur mentioned that some well-known movie stars had arrived in Paris to raise the morale of the troops stationed in the region, one of whom would tour the Post Exchange (PX) at St. Germain. It was a rare photo opportunity that would combine 'hometown news' with U.S. national coverage. At mid-morning the following day, I waited at the main entrance with my camera ready. Accompanied by an Air Force officer, Marlene Dietrich, an international and Hollywood actress, walked through the door. I took my first shot. She was beautifully dressed in a grey Chanel suit, wearing a feminine version of a derby hat, with a short black veil atop her shoulder-length blonde hair. The movie critic who wrote, 'See Dietrich and succumb,' was right. Her eyes were full of sultry daring, and there was a slight curve of merriment on her wide, lovely mouth.

But she wasn't simply a beautiful and talented woman. She defied

Hitler and left Germany, vowing never to return until he was over-thrown. She, a woman of character, entertained the Allied troops in Italy and France just behind the front. People gathered about as I in-troduced myself to her, saying, 'I saw you in Italy last year when you entertained the 36th Texas Infantry Division.' 'That's right,' she replied, 'Danny Thomas and Lin Mayhenny were touring with me, and we stopped for chow after the show, eating in the field with GIs from K Company.'

While we were reminiscing, three servicemen, a soldier, sailor, and a Marine, arrived to join with Marlene in a *Hometown News* picture story. I introduced all of them to my managerial friend, who was delight-ed and honored to have Marlene as a guest on his premises. She was warm, friendly, and full of grace to those who gathered around her. Her command of English and the ease with which she spoke it was a pleasant surprise.

I photographed her from every angle. Turning toward me, she asked playfully, pouting slightly, 'Don't you want to photograph my legs?'

I shrugged my shoulders, thinking, 'What's another pair of legs to me?' Fortunately, before she could respond further, I was jolted into action, remembering that she had the most gorgeous legs in Hollywood.

'Yes, of course,' I answered.

Seductively, she sat on a shoeshine chair and crossed her legs. The sail-or and the Marine sat beside her, while the soldier pretended to shine her shoes. For some reason, as I tripped the camera shutter, I thought of her singing, mildly off-key, as she did in the film *The Blue Angel*, '*Men hang around me like moths around a flame; if they get their wings burned, I'm sure I'm not to blame.*' She left as gracefully as she came.

I received orders to fly to England. The subject was the imminent de-parture of British war brides from the UK to the U.S., women who had married American servicemen who served overseas. Departing from Orly airfield, the twin-engine C-47 Dakota streaked into the darkness, leveled off at 10,000 feet, and droned along for two hours before land-ing at Bovington, an 8th Air Force bomber base in Buckinghamshire and an hour away from London.

We arrived at 'Little America,' not Admiral Byrd's Antarctic base, but the area around Grosvenor Square, the American Embassy, Claridge's, and the Connaught, near Davies, Mount, and Brook Streets. I roomed at Claridge's Hotel for the night. Rising early, I made arrangements to travel by car with a driver to Tidworth, originally called Tedworth, on the Hampshire-Wiltshire borders. Once an early 19th-century village on Salisbury Plain, about 80 miles west-southwest of London, it had become a camp, training ground, and an administrative area headquarters for the British Army by 1901.

Molly, my female driver, told me that about four years previously, the American Army's 12th Replacement Depot was located at Tidworth. It had a bad reputation for the average GI because it was run by a despotic commander; the place was well known for its inefficiency, bull, filth, and bad food — and was to be avoided whenever possible. Conditions were so bad that replacements and men recovering from wounds preferred combat to the time spent awaiting assignment there; whether the Army planned it that way or not, I don't know.

'Has it changed since the GIs moved out and the British War Brides moved in?' I inquired.

'Sort of,' Molly answered. 'Tidworth and Bournemouth were two staging areas established by the U.S. Army. Soldiers, eager to return to the States, resented being assigned as staff there, feeling that it slowed down their separation. It followed that many of the brides, some with children, were made to feel unwelcome when the program began last winter. At Tidworth, the women and their GI husbands, many waiting in America, protested, so that conditions slowly improved, including facilities for babies, discreet medical examinations, nightly movies, all that. It's better now, more routine, reliable.'

'Thanks for the info; I'll add it to my story, but it sounds like the same old Army to me.'

Somewhere on the windswept Salisbury plain, under lowering grey clouds, where units of the British armed forces trained and maneuvered, we found the group of olive drab huts and members of the staff, directed by an Army medical officer. With his cooperation, I would take a series of photographs documenting the arrival, stay, and departure of a group of war brides and their children. Simple health problems were corrected on the spot, eliminating any delays. If the patient required further treatment, travel arrangements were postponed. If all went well, the time spent at Tidworth amounted to a total of four or five days, in which paperwork was completed, tickets issued, currency exchanged, and British ration cards discarded before the intended departure from Southampton.

The following morning, I staged the arrival of a busload of war brides, taking a variety of shots from different angles. I followed that with close-ups of a few of the transients receiving medical and dental treatment and the mothers supervising their children at play in the unit's nursery. Life had improved!

Many of the women seemed apprehensive and plied me with questions about the States. I told them that life in New York differed from the surrounding countryside, that metropolitan areas like Chicago and Los Angeles not only represented different lifestyles, but these varied with those in rural America, depending upon the region. The automobile was king. America was so vast that a country the size of Britain would fit into the State of Florida, leaving 47 others to cope with. That stunned the women. More than one had married after a brief wartime romance. Would these men accept the babies born while they were away, fighting on the Continent? I tried to calm their fears, but we knew there were no guarantees, and I was too young to grasp and interpret in the first place their need to marry, and to whom.

When it came time for the 120-odd war brides and their children to leave, I traveled with them by bus to Southampton harbor, their port of embarkation. They were to sail on the *S.S. Beresford*. Moored beside the quay, its hull a dull black, streaked with rust, its superstructure a dirty off-white, it was much like the tramp steamer portrayed in Eugene O'Neill's play *The Long Voyage Home*. Stevedores and sailors prepared the ship for its transatlantic voyage to New York. The women followed each other up the gangplank, some cradling an infant, others carrying a small suitcase. Gathering in twos and threes after gaining the deck, they paused for a moment to catch their breath, looked at the land, and then gazed out to sea. Moving among them, I tried to capture on film their sense of adventure, anxiety, and determination.

Soon, the *Beresford's* engines throbbed. No band played on the dock to mark the brides' leave-taking, no steamers and confetti were tossed as gestures of farewell. Deep-throated boat whistles maintained their silence. Fireboat water guns tilted downward, inactive. No relatives or friends, their eyes filled with tears, came to wave and shout words of love, caution, and bon voyage as the *Beresford* edged away from her berth and headed for the open sea. Only a few of us clustered on the dock, port officials and military personnel, waving, standing next to the odd weapons carrier or jeep. The women waved in response. Good-bye to what? Five years of austerity and hardship? One's native country fades away slowly, gets smaller, becomes a smudge on the horizon, and finally disappears; to leave it behind, possibly forever, evokes an anxiety that potentiates with that of a life abroad not yet lived. A death? A new beginning? From my own war experiences, I had an idea of their feelings. I loaded up and drove off.

Southampton's central Victorian train station was not at all crowded when I boarded the London express. I delivered the 'war bride' negatives to Signal Corps Headquarters in Grosvenor Square for processing. London looked drab. Rationing continued, and women lined up outside one of the local fish shops in North London looked impoverished in their worn coats and shoes. St. Paul's Cathedral stood majestically above the surrounding fields of rubble, the aftermath of the Luftwaffe's eight-month firebombing of the city. Before leaving on the return flight to Paris, I picked up a copy of the *Stars and Stripes*. Somewhere above the Channel, browsing through its pages, I found a centerfold spread of my war bride photos.

17
Normandy Revisited

Paris was lovely; I don't know how many ways there are to describe its appeal, but Hemingway, Jefferson, Renoir, Gershwin, and Eluard certainly did and succeeded in words, music, and art. A sense of ennui had come over me, and I felt like one of the characters in that late 19th-century classic *Three Men In A Boat: And Don't Forget The Dog.* I even had a dog, a three-year-old German Shepherd, if the hair color around its muzzle was any indication. If I were correct, it must have been born when the Germans first occupied Paris. The shepherd probably had a Wehrmacht owner who skipped town with his buddies and abandoned the dog during the Allied advance on the city in August of '44. The Germans liked to give their dogs powerful names, like Wolf and Thor, so to mock them in absentia, I called mine Ziggy, after the great Jewish jazz trumpeter, Ziggy Elman. My musings ended when I fulfilled an assignment in Le Havre. Some soldiers' wives were arriving from the States by ship to be with their husbands within the next few days.

I drove up the hill to report to the Army's harbor master, a captain, at Camp Lucky Strike, a temporary staging area for soldiers returning to the States. All were named after popular American cigarette brands. From the road overlooking the Channel, I got a better view of the wrecked harbor and some of the half-sunken ships. Two years before, the British 49th and 51st Infantry Divisions had penetrated the enemy's harbor defenses and reached the same vantage point as mine. Le Havre constituted one of the strongest fortresses of Hitler's Atlantic Wall; provided with elaborate concrete defenses, extensive mine fields, and other obstacles, it had been badly damaged. Nevertheless, 12,000 Germans surrendered after two days of heavy fighting.

After I introduced myself to the captain, a friendly sort from the Midwest with a twinkle in his eye and the look of a rogue, he said, 'My wife and seven-year-old daughter are arriving from the States today.' Behind his office desk were the names of ships and their arrival and departure dates listed on a large blackboard; many of them were Victory or Liberty ships, but some were passenger ships like the *S. S. Saturnia,* a former Italian Line steamer seized by the Allies during the war. The first batch of American dependents, including the captain's wife and daughter, were passengers aboard that ship.

He was glad his wife and young daughter were arriving but felt it necessary to have a serious talk with his French girlfriend beforehand to straightened things out. I gulped. 'How'd you do that?' I inquired. 'Simple, really. I sat her on my lap, stroked her hair, and said, 'So long Suzette, my wife's coming tomorrow.'

'That's it?'

'Yeah, no fuss, no muss, and we've been living together for six months, almost from the time I got here.' I tried to act like a 'man of the world,' pretending to know something about man/woman relationships, so I sat there nodding my head in agreement and then said something inane like, 'Easy come, easy go.' Inwardly, I was shocked and surprised.

The captain and I drove to the harbor in his open jeep to await the arrival of the *Saturnia*. Many of the docks and sheds were crumpled and out of plumb — that added to the corrugated and twisted shape of the landscape, cut through by floating sea-level Bailey bridges, over which we traveled noisily, the jeep's tires humming against the iron matting. As we arrived at the debarkation point, the *Saturnia*, shepherded by two tugboats that toiled under the weight of the ship towering above them, entered port, a cue for my coverage to begin.

Once the ship was secured, we were the first to climb aboard, racing up the gangplank in search of the captain's wife and daughter. He spotted them standing together on the fantail, pressed against the railing, surrounded by their fellow passengers, who were as eager as they to make contact with their husbands and fathers. I recorded his wife and daughter pushing toward him, followed by a long embrace and repeated hugs. It seemed as if there were not enough arms to go around. They gathered together and posed, a reunited family, represented by a woman in her mid-30s wearing a black sheared lamb coat and matching hat, an officer in uniform, and a spirited prepubescent girl. If the captain were apprehensive about the meeting, he didn't show it, having seamlessly shifted gears from lover to dutiful husband, heralding the coming of the automatic automobile transmission. After being introduced to his wife and daughter, I promised to send them copies of the shipboard photos, wished them well, and departed.

I picked up my Buick and drove to my next billet in Le Havre, where I would spend the next few nights before returning to Paris. The reception clerk at Lucky Strike, a corporal, visibly impressed by my orders, placed at my disposal a small house within the compound listed as 'Generals' Quarters.' They offered the level of privacy, comfort, and convenience befitting the Army's highest-ranking officers while seaborne travel arrangements were made for them to return to the States in style. I walked onto the porch and, glancing to my left, I spied a one-star general sitting on a porch, an exact replica of my own, not 15 feet away. We nodded as I relaxed in a canvas-wood camp chair. His look turned into a stare. Out of the corner of my eye, I noticed that he peered through his glasses and leaned toward me, resting his weight on the arm of his chair, as if that would help in identifying me. I wore an Official U.S. Army Photographer patch on the left sleeve of my Eisenhower jacket, nothing more. He seemed perplexed, and for the fun of it, I avoided his gaze and made sure my body language discouraged conversation. The difference between us was apparent; I knew his identity!

He was the colonel who had commanded the infantry battalion that patrolled and secured the area surrounding the Loire Disciplinary Training Center in Normandy. Assigned to duty in a backwater, hundreds of miles from the enemy, the colonel never qualified for the CIF (Combat Infantry Badge). He may have dreamed of being another pistol-toting George Patton riding into battle on a tank, but opportunity never beckoned. Guarding dysfunctional American soldiers lacked romance. I, a lowly former NCO, avoided his inquisitive and intrusive demeanor, using silence as my revenge. Tiring of the game, I rose from my chair and walked inside without giving him a second glance, leaving him to stew. I gloated, my turnabout exceptional, but I think he would have died if he knew I never rose above the rank of sergeant.

With my mission in Le Havre completed, there wasn't any point in hanging around. At the local motor pool, I exchanged the Buick for a Ford sedan, accompanied by a French driver, for the 90-mile return journey to Paris. On the outskirts of Le Havre, the road seemed to run into a house blocking its path. Then without warning, the road unpredictably turned sharply left and continued on. The road and the old shell guessing game played at carnivals had something in common, expressed as, 'Now you see it, now you don't.' During the war, the road had been used extensively for military truck traffic, and the weary or unsuspecting driver often realized, much too late, that it was L-shaped.

Time after time, heavily laden 6x6 trucks crashed into the stone wall protecting the house, injuring the driver and strewing much-needed supplies all over the road. It's one of the war's mysteries that the road was never straightened. Maybe eminent domain didn't exist in France, but what was a little curative demolition and repair compared to the war's wanton destruction? I warned my driver of this problem. Assuring me he knew the way, observing the rules of the road, and following directions, he was a well-trained driver, but I was jumpy for reasons beyond my comprehension and criticized him unduly as we drove. Finally, he jammed on the brakes, pulled over, stormed out of the car, opened my door and shouted, 'I will not go one kilometer further putting up with your criticism. If you are displeased, then you drive, but if I'm to drive, shut up.' I did as I was told but continued to feel anxious. My stomach churned and I remained silent until the Eiffel Tower sprang into view. Later, sitting on the edge of my bed, I felt my behavior on the trip was disproportionate. As good as my life was, something was amiss.

18
Combat Fatigue Intrudes

I awakened slowly, wriggling my toes, feeling a faint Mediterranean breeze wafting across my face. It was morning; the hotel room in Cannes was cool and bright. I opened my eyes. The room was steeped in fog! Something was wrong! I was terrified and gripped the bed sheets. A blanket of fog half hid the window drapes and the edge of the bed. My clothes were draped across a nearby wicker chair. Frightened and unsure, I closed my eyes again and counted to 20 before opening them again. There was no change. My heart pounded and my forehead was damp. Was I going blind? I tried to rationalize and searched for excuses, such as hard travel and riotous living over the last month. I tried to allay my fears and turned my mind to more practical matters, such as the three-day drive back to Paris. As if relying on a proverbial wind, the fog slowly lifted. I blinked once or twice. I could see.

During the preceding month, I had been assigned to Major Daniel E. Day of War Department Public Relations. He was black and on temporary duty from the Pentagon in Washington. The Army was segregated. With Germany defeated, the major wanted to meet and talk to as many black officers and soldiers stationed in Europe as possible regarding their morale and living conditions. His orders covered every contingency and demanded travel arrangements by any means necessary, including submarine and flying boat. Although I had never dreamed travel orders of such magnitude existed, the major, being a practical man, settled for a 1939 Ford sedan and driver. At Western Base Section (WBS) headquarters, I found a small selection of maps indicating the location and types of black units situated throughout France, Belgium, and Luxembourg.

After four days of hard driving beyond Paris, during which time we had visited a number of quartermaster trucking, engineering, and railhead companies, whose black soldiers resented the way they continued to be treated by the Army, I realized that racial oppression remained a major problem. The soldiers' complaints defined the Army as a microcosm of American segregation and racial prejudice.

The complaints expressed by the officers and the men of another black ordnance company we visited were variations on the theme we had heard before, but lamentable, nevertheless. They felt they were nothing more than laborers in uniform and that combat had been denied them. Even with the European war at an end, most American troops continued to serve in segregated units because the policy of the War Department was not to intermingle black and white enlisted personnel in the same regimental organizations. The military called it 'Equal but Separate.' It was neither. Although the Selective Training and Service Act of September 1940 stated that 'there shall be no segregation against any person on account of race or color,' the implication was that the basic pattern of segregation was to remain. White officers at the higher levels of command had argued that the Army was unable to change its own policy on racial matters because of the prevailing ethos that segregation was part of the social mores of the country; having been established by the American people through custom and practice more than a hundred years ago, it was now institutionalized. The Red Cross, whose blood banks at first refused blood from blacks, then accepted it but kept the blood segregated, added insult to injury. One of the officers said, 'Segregation really hurt the war effort because it wasted black manpower, lowered unit effectiveness, and created unnecessary racial tension.'

When Major Day realized that the Army considered the black soldier inferior because of his low scores on the General Classification Test, which claimed simply to assess 'usable intelligence,' or that blacks were only adequate soldiers, nothing more, when led by white officers, he fumed and mumbled expletives under his breath. His vehemence surprised me because he was usually courteous and mild-mannered, but he was a man pushed to the edge by Army racial discrimination within the Pentagon and without.

As rear echelon Ordnance Company truck drivers, many blacks drove their 6x6 trucks, loaded with gasoline and ammunition, along the Red Ball Express, a special truck delivery route to the combat units during the campaign in Western Europe. Using two parallel highways that led from the Normandy beaches east to the furthest part of the Allied advance, trucks provided 100 tons of shipping space per day. Marked with red ball signs for drivers who wore out tires and trucks at an unprecedented rate, the route was in constant operation and off limits to unauthorized vehicles. 'A number of deliveries were never made,' the major said, 'because fully laden trucks disappeared before they ever reached the front, being reported missing in Paris, as a result of a collaborative venture between the drivers and members of the French black market.' He grunted in satisfaction. Although he didn't condone such thievery, he felt there was some justification in the drivers' behavior for all the years of slavery. It was a simple scam; the driver claimed that his truck was stolen when he stopped for coffee and doughnuts and left his vehicle unattended. With the truck hidden in a Paris garage, the driver reported his loss to the Paris-based MPs but, in reality, he was richer by many thousands of dollars for his part in the transaction.

'Sure,' Major Day continued, 'there were a few all-black combat units like the 99th Pursuit Squadron and the 332nd Fighter Group in Italy that flew cover for our 15th Air Force bombers; on the ground, the 92nd and 93rd Infantry Divisions were black, but most of the officers were white. The black pilots performed well, but the men of the 92nd suffered a breakdown of morale in Italy, complaining that their officers, black or white, were not fit to lead them in combat. The 93rd just drifted from one Pacific island to another without ever being in action.'

Ironically, while serving overseas, they found Western Europeans accepting of the black GI, according him a dignity and respect that he had never known in the States. I suggested that we go further afield and head toward Brussels for a mixture of business, rest, and recreation. We drove into eastern Belgium, another of my recommendations, so that the Major could see for himself where 4,500 black rear echelon soldiers, with little or no infantry training, were fed piecemeal into the Ardennes battle (Battle of the Bulge). The German surprise attack, which began in mid-December 1944 and ended a month later, claimed the following: 20,000 Americans killed, 20,000 surrendered, and 40,000 wounded. The German attack destroyed two U.S. infantry divisions and overwhelmed isolated U.S. units, many falling back in headlong retreat. For the uninitiated, it was a tough introduction to combat. The major softened somewhat, recounting a meeting General Patton had with the first group of Negro tankers preparing for combat in October 1944. Because of the lack of combat replacements, segregation in the Army was under pressure. The major, paraphrasing Patton, said, 'I would never have asked for you if you weren't good. I have nothing but the best in my army. I don't care what color you are, so long as you go up there and kill those Kraut sonsabitches.'

Brussels had been liberated on September 3, 1944 by the British Guards

Armored Division, which experienced only sporadic enemy resistance, the city suffering little physical damage. I recommended the Metropole Hotel in the center of the city because of its quiet old-world atmosphere, excellent service, and fine food. I had stayed here some months before when filming the sale of surplus U.S. military equipment at the Army's La Louvière Supply Depot.

Josephine Baker, the American chanteuse, was starring in a musical revue at one of the city's theatres. The major wanted to meet this black entertainer from St. Louis who had made her continental debut in Paris in 1925, at the age of 19, fresh from the slums of Harlem. From the moment she set foot on the stage of the Théâtre des Champs-Elysées, Josephine Baker became the toast of Paris.

The major and I met Josephine Baker backstage. She was dressed in a full 'showgirl' costume that included a highly decorative headdress. She smiled and held out her hands in greeting to both of us. Her American Midwest accent predominated, although she had been in and out of France for 20 years. The major was delighted to meet her, saying that he too came from St. Louis, affording both of them an opportunity to reminisce and compare notes. She was not surprised to hear that they both came from poverty, but each had solved the problem in a different way, he through education, she through entertaining. She was dismayed at hearing that a sense of alienation was endemic in the black units we had recently visited.

Before we departed, I took a few shots of Josephine Baker, alone and with the major. I added, 'We have something else in common besides being American.'

'What's that?' she inquired.

'We both served in the French Resistance.'

'Those were difficult times,' was all she said. The major and I thanked her for spending a few minutes with us; we said goodbye, brushed our lips against her cheeks, and made our way out through the stage door.

The phone line to Paris wasn't particularly clear, but La Fleur understood that our original four-day tour needed revision and more time. The major wanted to widen the scope of his trip and Ronnie Rozier, our French driver, was willing to continue the journey. La Fleur agreed to our extension, simply requesting that I stay in touch with him from time to time.

At one point during our journey, we stopped at a country inn near Villefranche, north of Lyon and had drinks with some of the locals. I did my best to converse in French, unsure of my grammar, but the men seemed to understand. The wine was fruity, light, and young.

'What kind is it?' I inquired.

One of the men laughed, responding with, 'Well, it isn't a premier cru, but it's a Beaujolais all the same, from around Belleville, 20 minutes north of here.'

'Ronnie,' said the major, 'tell them that I'm glad to drink with them.' Ronnie translated and, in addition, described our official mission.

As if on cue, we raised our glasses and Ronnie proposed a toast. I caught his last three words, 'à *la votre,*' before we drank. Major Day turned to me and, somewhat startled, said, 'Steve, there's no way that I could have a drink and 'shoot the breeze' with white farmhands in the South the way I'm doing now. The least they'd do is run me out of town.' The men verified what Josephine Baker had said in Brussels, 'Color wasn't a problem in France.'

We sallied forth early the next morning after a traditional continental breakfast. The road was relatively flat for the first 20 of the 30 miles but later, on the outskirts of Lyon, it rose and wove between rolling hills. Within the city itself, all of Lyon's bridges had been rebuilt according to their architects' original designs. Many of the city center's public buildings, damaged during Lyon's liberation, had been restored, their tricolors flying at full staff.

With Lyon at its back, the Rhône broke away from the city's southern suburbs and began its majestic sweep toward Marseilles, 180 miles distant. We followed the twists and turns of the mighty river and rubbed shoulders with it, driving along a wine road dotted with villages. We entered St. Péray an hour later and slowed to traverse the dusty town square on whose western end sat the Hotel du Nord. Near its simple entrance, one arrow-shaped road sign pointed to Alboussière, another to Soyons. My heart jumped. Memories of the night of August 24th came flooding back. All seemed normal now. Mortal danger had passed. Women, hurrying home for lunch, crossing the square bathed in dazzling peacetime sunlight, and carrying loaves of French bread, behaved as if the Germans had never intruded.

Ten minutes later, the bridge at Valence came into view, set against the oldest part of the town and the 11th-century Romanesque cathedral, situated almost at the river's edge. As we spun over the bridge's macadam surface, I was impressed with the breadth and swiftness of the Rhône, flint-blue and shimmering with spectral highlights at noon. Did I really escape across it in a wooden boat? Defenseless? My thoughts drifted back to the late afternoon of August 25th and an unanswerable question. 'Why didn't the Germans blast us out of the water?' A reaction to survivor's guilt? From the town's location in the Rhône Valley, I could feel the hint of a climate change, a warmer breath on the wind, supporting a lifestyle that discarded doors for hanging strands of colored beads and shoes for sandals.

It was another 15 miles to the highway bridge at Livron where the Drôme River trickles across sandy mounds into the Rhône River. On the night of August 16, 1944, a squad of 32 French Résistants, armed with 400 pounds of plastic explosive, shattered the bridge's southern arch, leaving a gap of 100 feet. When the German 19th Army, including the 11th Panzer Division, was retreating northward, it fought with typical ferocity to avoid being annihilated by elements of the American 3rd, 36th, and 45th Infantry Divisions and the local Resistance. The bridge was one of the bottlenecks in its path. Army Group G and its subsidiary formation, the 19th, was too powerful to be contained by the American forces at hand. One hundred-thirty thousand men escaped through the Loriol-Livron passage, but 2,000 enemy vehicles and 300 pieces of artillery were destroyed in the attempt. Having fought at the battle's northeastern edge, I wanted to inspect the bridge and the damage to the surrounding area. Parking the car on the east side of N. 7, the three of us approached the bridge. It reminded me of a grey whale, its sides damaged by innumerable shells; pieces of masonry were scattered everywhere.

As I climbed down onto the exposed river sand at the base of the bridge, beside which rivulets proceeded toward the Rhône, I saw the rusting remains of German trucks and other vehicles dotting the landscape like burnt offerings. What an excellent place to trap the enemy but, as I discovered years later, with the beachhead 255 miles away and transportation at a premium, we could not concentrate enough force and fire power needed to destroy an entire army. Escaping to the frontier, participating in the German Army's reorganization, known as the 'September Miracle,' it would defend the Fatherland for another nine months and cause further suffering and damage. Charlie Company had done what it could, but the German tide was too strong to stop.

That evening, I called La Fleur from Marseilles, having located a telephone kiosk just inside the gate of a caserne. Setting a pile of franc coins next to the telephone, dropping them one by one into the slot, I dialed his number in Paris. Coincidentally, when he came on the line, I looked through the paned glass window and realized that, according to the wrought iron sign above the entrance, the caserne belonged to the French Foreign Legion. Recruitment posters on the walls astride the entrance depicted heroic legionnaires in action. I told him we were in Marseille, that we need more time, say, another three weeks, because the major wanted to continue on all the way to Naples. He agreed because the war was over, and photo coverage had slowed. I heard him chuckle before the last coin jingled in the box and the line went dead.

My mind wandered to Gary Cooper as a brave, selfless legionnaire in the film *Beau Geste*. I toyed and then wrestled with the idea of enlisting in the Foreign Legion. As adventurous as it seemed, marching across the Sahara's hot sands lacked excitement. Enough of *la vie militaire*, although my step down the rue Cannebière toward the Old Port belied the fact. More adventure? There's a tablet in the cathedral here that commemorates the 1 million men of the British Empire who died in the First World War. It reads: *Dulce et decorum est pro patria mori.* (There's no greater honor than to die for one's country.)Early the next morning, the three of us prepared to journey along the Riviera from west to east by taking the smaller but more scenic Provençal coastal road, N-559. The villages along the way had suffered battle damage during our August 1944 landings, but it was now possible to order a bottle of a full-bodied and lively local white wine from Cassis or a memorable, long-lived red from Bandol during lunch at most seaside cafés. My promise never to go hungry again was coming true, in style.

Toulon, our next port of call, a city and naval base of 100,000 inhabitants, was in the process of being rebuilt after suffering serious battle damage during a week-long siege in late August 1944 by three of General de Lattre's French infantry divisions, supported by sea and air power. When the American 6th Corps, of which the 36th was a part, headed north, the French 1st Army moved west. French Admiral André Lemonnier, de Gaulle's naval chief of staff, wrote on the eve of battle, 'The siege has begun.' Twenty-five thousand Germans were walled up in the fortifications that protected the city against attack by land, sea, or air. Concrete bunkers flanked the valleys and crowned the heights.

Two hundred coastal guns aimed out to sea, 38 of them of wide bore. The anti-aircraft defenses were as powerful as those trained on the sea. Street fighting was fierce before the Germans surrendered.

St. Tropez, a pre-war international beach resort and yacht harbor 30 miles northeast of Toulon, had been badly knocked around by the preliminary American naval bombardment and the firepower of the 3rd Infantry Division during the landings that followed. The small port area, including the bars, bistros, and restaurants, had been demolished. Symmetrical Mediterranean-style four- or five-storied ochre and saffron-colored houses stood in the bright sunshine beside the beach with their roofs missing and rooms exposed. The church tower, a few streets from the port, standing relatively undamaged and overlooking the remaining rubble, reminded me of an injured party that had survived a mugging. Just outside of St. Raphaël, I left the car to stand silently on a small bridge next to the remains of a reinforced concrete enemy pillbox to recall that afternoon when Truman Ropos had lost his leg.

My French wartime adventure had begun on the other side of St. Raphaël at the seaside hamlet of Le Dramont, and I felt my heart pound as the D-Day landing site came into view. Only a few cars passed in either direction along the *Corniche d'Or*, a coast road constructed by the Touring Club de France in 1901–03 and the gateway to the Côte d'Azur. Gone were the sounds of battle and the shouts of men, burdened with equipment, wearing olive drab uniforms, and bathed in sweat. Except for the lapping of the waves and rustling of pine leaves, it was quiet. No marine engines coughed, sputtered, and whined. No ship's bottoms grated on the rocky shore and opened their bow ramps: men in motion, noise in action. The sky was no longer torn asunder by incoming naval gunfire, although the broken shape of a beached LST 282, blown sky-high on D-Day by a bomb-laden German drone aircraft, was still visible through the pine trees.

I felt anxious and alone, even though Ronnie and the Major waited nearby. Climbing down the cliff, I passed bathers sunning themselves on the shingled beach. Children jumped and splashed in the water, some wearing decorative, colored rubber life jackets; others took a turn at swimming a few yards. By our wartime arrival, I had played an infinitesimal part in giving this strip of beach back to its rightful owners. Those cavorting in the surf seemed oblivious to the price freedom demanded. I picked up a small flat stone and put it in my pocket as a souvenir. Some military historians have labeled Operation Anvil-

Dragoon, the landing, and the fight for Provence, the *'Champagne Campaign,'* which, to me is an over-simplification. Inscribed on the monument overlooking the Mediterranean that marked our passing, in both French and English, was the following testimonial: *Over this defended beach the men of the 36th US Infantry Division stormed ashore on 15 August 1944, together with their French allies. They began here the drive that took them across France, through Germany and into Austria to the final destruction of the German Armies and the Nazi regime.*

Gliding down from the Esterel Hills, circling Agay, then turning the corner at La Napoule, a sand beach stretched all the way to Cannes and Juan-les-Pins. We rolled toward Cannes in an anticipatory and frolicking mood. Abashed, I learned that its casino had been transformed into a fortress by the Germans and during the landings was practically destroyed. The municipal theater, the terrace, and the public swimming pool were a heap of ruins. And yet, other prominent landmarks remained undamaged: the Carlton Hotel, the promenade de Croisette, and a statue of Edward VII, all representative of fashionable good living in a life-embracing Mediterranean climate.

Forty-five miles to the east, I played roulette in the casino at Monte Carlo and lost, even though it was off limits to American personnel. With so few of us around, the police showed little interest in enforcing the rule. Overlooking the sea, it was housed in a Belle-Époque edifice designed by Charles Garnier, the architect of the Paris Opera. Invariably, a woman would brush against the sleeve of my tunic, having looked me over from a distance beforehand while I gambled in one of the public gaming rooms; a smile followed, then a word, ending in a rendezvous later. Her acceptance of my dinner invitation confirmed her willingness to spend the night. If there were a concert on the terrace, we'd attend, sipping our after-dinner drinks, before turning in. I wasn't kidding myself. Conditions in 1946 were difficult for many civilians, more so for women. Governments were in crisis, cities required rebuilding, and there was little employment. A woman like the one sitting across from me now was trading her good looks and wit for a pleasurable evening as a way of blurring a difficult present and an uncertain future.

I wasn't interested in their change of circumstances as much as I was in having a good time, to prove that living was what counted. Millions of people had suffered, and I, as a matter of survival, however brittle, had turned off all feeling as a defense against the shock of embedded wartime experiences. There was hardly any way to avoid bumping into some description of their lives. Every courtesan had a story to tell, but it was a litany that usually included a separation from a loving partner, a fall from grace, and a change in political circumstances, resulting in economic calamity. If collaboration with the enemy was hinted at, I could understand their temptation to back Hitler, who seemed invincible in 1940, albeit at a great moral loss. I didn't know what to believe; either way, it had nothing to do with me.

19

Adventures Across the Italian Landscape

My two traveling companions — the major and Ronnie — and I departed early one morning in January 1946 from the Hotel Excelsior, our base in Rome, and ventured south along Highway 6, one of two major roads connecting the capital with Naples, 112 miles away. Fifty miles before Naples stood the abbey of Monte Cassino and, at its base, the town of Cassino itself.

The road south led through mountains that were tilted and jagged, forming an almost impenetrable mass of rock whose major peaks rose to 6,000 feet. Separate from my assigned mission, I was determined to visit the abbey, a prominent feature of the 1943–1944 Italian campaign. Unlike the Allied armies that had pushed up from Salerno, we approached the town of Cassino and its abbey, *O veneranda sede di studi e di preghiera* (O venerable seat of learning and of prayer), from the opposite direction on Highway 6, formerly known as the via Casilina. On the steep slopes of a 1,700-foot mountain, St. Benedict founded and built a house of worship and center for Christian monasticism in 529 AD. Through the centuries, from the time Hannibal occupied the fortified town during the Second Punic War, Casinum, as it was called, remained an important road junction. In early 1944, the town of Cassino and its abbey became key defensive positions in the German *Gustav* Line that extended all across the mountainous peninsula from Gaeta on the Tyrrhenian coast to Ortona on the Adriatic.

Hitler's decision to defend the territory south of Rome included the demand that every foot of ground be contested. This edict thrust the four Cassino battles, and the attempt to cross the Rapido River, into a bitter and unrelenting struggle that ground on from January 20 to May 18, 1944. I was right behind the front when the final battle began.

During the first battle, two regiments of my division suffered 2,900 casualties in three attacks from January 20 to January 23, when 5th Army commander Lieutenant-General Mark Clark's ill-conceived plan to cross the Rapido River failed. As its name indicates, in winter the Rapido becomes a swollen 60-foot-wide torrent flowing at eight miles per hour, at a depth of nine feet, toward its junction with the Liri River. The approach to the river was under ongoing German observation from the Cassino massif. The terrain was open to heavy enemy artillery and mortar fire. Men and equipment were swept away in the torrent and frail rafts capsized. The marauding enemy easily snuffed the few who reached the vertical bank opposite.

Some of the American survivors of the first battle, with whom I served, spoke of under-strength infantry attacks mounted in mud, snow, and rain. Cassino was like a First World War battle fought with weapons of the Second World War, at altitude. They insisted that anyone who described Italy as 'sunny' was seriously ill informed, because in one winter month alone, U.S. non-battle casualties resulting from respiratory diseases, trench foot, and battle fatigue totaled nearly 50,000 in the 5th Army alone. Churchill feared that the struggle could easily turn into a miniature Stalingrad or another Verdun.

When attacks by the Americans, French, and New Zealanders failed, General Bernard Freyberg, commander of the New Zealand Corps, believing that the enemy was using the abbey as an observation post, demanded that it be bombed before his troops attacked in a third battle. On February 15, 148 B-17s and 82 B-25s dropped 564 tons of high explosive and incendiary bombs on both the town and the abbey, causing great destruction. Many years after the battle, I met a monk who had been a young boy at the time of the bombing. He insisted that the Germans never occupied the abbey before the aerial attack. The bombing was one of the most controversial Allied decisions of the Italian campaign because it was never proven that the Germans used the abbey for military purposes. Digging even deeper into their line, the enemy thwarted further Allied attacks until May, when French General Alphonse Juin, having devised an audacious tactical plan in the fourth battle, cracked it wide open during Operation *Diadem*. The Germans quietly abandoned their positions to the attacking Polish Corps. For Hitler, Cassino represented an opportunity to show the world that the German Army was invincible. He tried for nine months. Twenty thousand Germans died and are buried nearby. The Allies suffered over 300,000 casualties.

Ronnie turned the car around, its hood facing north, and parked the

Ford alongside the road about a mile from the town — or what remained of it — nestling against the mountains. All three of us climbed out of the car near some new single- and double-storied white stucco buildings amidst the ruins of the old and trudged toward the town, getting a feel of the Liri Valley beneath our boots. Small trees, to replace those the Germans had cut down to improve their observation and fields of fire, dotted the landscape. The dusty white road ran straight up against the mountain that forced it to turn left on the way to Rome. Dominating the landscape, hovering above the valley's grassland and the Rapido, stood the remains of the abbey, a child's broken sand castle. The basilica, open to the sky, the altar a flattened ruin, and the perimeter's jagged walls all stood in silence on that winter's day. The side of the mountain was torn away, as if from the aftereffects of a volcanic eruption. Below, a few small trucks moved along the road, but most of the other vehicles were hay wagons, drawn by undernourished horses and carrying building supplies. For whatever reasons, activity on the building sites had ground to a halt.

Against the dark background of the three adjoining mountains, two wagons remained stationary on the crudely paved road. One man stood beside each of the parked wagons, and the driver of each stood upright on the wagon itself, talking to his buddy below. I wondered how long it would take to rebuild the town, blasted into the lower parts of the mountain, and the ruined abbey, silhouetted against the threatening sky, at this imperceptible pace. I thought, 'The longer the countryside waits to be reclaimed, the longer it remains a war memorial. Is that what the inhabitants want? Tourists?' I walked to where Highway 6 crosses the Rapido, at present a placid stream, and found small rusty strands of barbed wire and a few used cartridge casings.

I found a crude sign surrounded by cypresses situated near the abbey, where 1,000 Poles who fought the Germans on the rocky slopes had died; it read, *Cimitero Polacco*. Further down the mountain, British, Canadians, New Zealanders, Cypriots, and Gurkhas are buried. The Americans who died after the first battle were gathered up and reinterred in a large communal military cemetery at Anzio, the site of another attritional battle. I stood at attention and self-consciously saluted my comrades in arms resting beneath the crosses: *Per la causa della giustizia e della libertà* another sign read. Returning to the road, we climbed aboard, and our driver turned the car around and drove toward Naples, relieved that Cassino's haunting scene was at our backs.

A few days later, we lunched al fresco beside the blue Mediterranean at Paestum. Major Day, in conversion between courses, decided to end his journey in Rome and return to Washington. I was saddened, not only by his decision, but by the memories of my earlier wartime visit. It was here that I bivouacked with the 36th and took amphibious training in July of '44. Soldiers I knew had come and gone. Lunch over, we visited the remains of the two Greek temples nearby and then drove to the mountain village of Altavilla that overlooked the landing beach. At Altavilla, Charles 'Commando' Kelly of the 36th won the Medal of Honor on September 13, 1943. Out of ammunition, he used mortar shells as hand grenades and tossed them at the enemy.

With our Ford sedan parked alongside the four-engine DC-4 at Rome's Ciampino airport, Ronnie and I shook the major's hand and wished him farewell. What had begun as a photo assignment for me had surprisingly resulted in a memorable life experience. The major had been a pleasure to work with, and I had learned much about the black soldier. When Major Day said that he would write a 'letter of commendation' to Lieutenant La Fleur on my behalf, I knew that by the time we circled the Eiffel Tower after our long journey, the letter would be waiting.

It took us two and a half days and 300 miles of hard driving along a tortuous coast road, ruined by war, to get out of Italy and re-enter France. We rolled into Cannes late at night and on the following morning, upon awakening, I viewed my world, as mentioned, through a layer of gauze. Frightened, I stumbled out of bed to meet Ronnie and two women friends. I felt anxious and weak walking toward the Croisette. I described my symptoms, but Ronnie smiled, blaming my condition on nothing more than riotous living. I moved cautiously and, in my mind, I questioned my grasp of sanity. Assurance was not forthcoming, either from within or without! During the day, the fog came and went. For no apparent reason, it lifted in the early evening, the way fog lifts from the sea. I felt ready to face life with gusto, relegating the experience to a one-off accidental episode. I had no idea that my sight impairment was a sinister warning, symptomatic of and a reaction to my war experiences. And there was no one to turn to for guidance, even if I sought it!

For most of the return journey along the French Mediterranean coast and up the Rhône Valley, Ronnie refused to speak English, which made matters worse, and I was forced to dredge and troll for the appropriate French word or phrase, placed grammatically within the sentence. The fog drifted in and out. It was donkey work; I suffered from headaches, a rare but new condition, but he remained steadfast, regardless of my supplications. The 'bastard' would correct me, demanding that I repeat the sentence properly. As a result, one night, I dreamed in French, the content having something to do with mailing a letter. When I awoke the next morning, not only did I have a sense of lasting accomplishment but felt fearless and ready for Ronnie's teaching onslaught.

Entering the Ardèche, we drove up the winding road from St. Péray, past the newly constructed bridge, to Alboussière to surprise my French friends. I had not been back since we left to join the OSS near Devesset in early September 1944. We entered the village at twilight, our arrival observed by Elise, one of the young women still working at the Hotel Serre. She began shouting, '*L'américain arrive, l'américain arrive.*' Guests rushed from the garden to the adjacent road, others gathered on the hotel patio to get a better view. Madame and Monsieur Serre hurried over from the main entrance. Greetings of welcome followed, affectionate words were shared, hands squeezed, shoulders pressed in embrace. We were friends who had survived the tidal wave. No matter if we twisted and turned through life, we were linked by our shared experiences forever. Dinner followed. M. Serre served the wine, a Chateauneuf, bringing a smile to my face, and a memory of Binoche and onions, followed by a vintage Hermitage from the neighboring slopes along the Rhône. In my honor, Mme. Serre created one of my favorite dishes, sautéed *marcassin*, young wild boar, dark brown in an almost black gravy, with roast potatoes and vegetables.

Monsieur Serre, in response to one of my questions, gave me directions to the Gendarmerie in Tournon, a well-established wine market town 15 miles away astride the Rhône, where Mathey currently was serving as OIC. Not only did the Serres refuse to accept payment for our overnight stay, but also I was presented with a most important gift, a recently published book entitled *Heures d'Angoisse*, which described the events leading to the region's liberation. One of its photos pictured Mathey, the Mayor, Scruby, Gualandi, Reigle, and me standing in the mayor's garden, holding our British Lee Enfield rifles at port arms. The caption below read, '*Quelques Americains à St. Péray.*'

For some unknown reason, I didn't pursue any line of inquiry or seek information regarding the farmer who saved my life and the farm house that offered us refuge east of Valence. If I were motivated and had succeeded, the discovery of the farm and the reunion with the others involved in the escape might have been too much for me to bear, the personal focus too intense, and the emotional experience overwhelming without the support of my seven comrades in arms. Each symbol, the tree-lined road, the irrigation ditch, the peach orchard, and the hayloft were reminders of life and death and how closely they were connected. Even my beloved Rhône evoked mixed feelings of sadness and exultation. I remembered the farmer and wondered why he risked, and possibly sacrificed, his life so that eight strangers might live. I cut myself short, too much thinking, stomach muscles strained. It was as if my surprise visit to Alboussière was all that I could handle. All this, a triggered reaction to an experience to be avoided!

Mathey's office was at the end of a long corridor. After being directed to it by the gendarme duty officer on the front desk, I walked toward his office, the door of which was open. Mathey was sitting behind a desk, looking directly at me as I advanced toward him, but he made no sign or gesture acknowledging my presence. Closing with every step, I thought that my dear comrade disapproved of my unannounced arrival. He sat there transfixed, Buddha-like, seemingly oblivious to my determined pace down the corridor. Just as I crossed the threshold, he stirred, and in one movement, stood up, whirled, drew two bottles of Champagne from the cupboard behind him, whirled again, and slammed them down on the desk between us, saying, 'My Dear Stéphane,' offered his hand, and laughed.

This was the Mathey I remembered, a driving force on his motorcycle, stalwart, and a man of action. My comrade! I was glad to see him. 'How's the shoulder?' I asked, referring to his wounding at Soyons.

'After the doctor removed the metal bits, it was sore for a short time but now it's as good as new. And you, dear friend?' he inquired.

'I'm OK. Unsure, apprehensive. Anxious feelings stir and hit me when I least expect them. My surroundings get fuzzy.'

'Probably just nerves,' he replied. While we were talking, he wiped the dust off the wine glasses. We drank and talked about Binoche, Rick, Wohlwerth, and the others. I invited Ronnie to join our celebration and, when the two bottles were emptied, we said goodbye. 'Come back, Dear Stéphane.' I embraced Mathey and left, cloaked in nostalgia. We arrived in Paris the following day.

Even after I unpacked, showered, and changed clothes, there was still time to walk over to the office before it closed to chat with La Fleur and whoever else was around. Strolling along Pressbourg to Kléber, the Arc changing its angle in cadence with my relaxed stride, I fell in love with Paris all over again. Even though I had rarely dealt with the 'shadow' side of my personality, unknowingly repressed, the combination of living in such an exciting and beautiful city and traveling throughout Europe struck me as an acceptable balance between business and pleasure, even if something unknown lurked within me, ready to pounce.

In my absence, La Fleur had lined up three assignments. The first was a Big Four international diplomatic conference at the Palais du Luxembourg, followed by a journey to Norway to film the disinterment of American soldiers and finally, a non-photo performance, leading a convoy of trucks driven by Polish nationals and carrying Signal Corps equipment to Mannheim, Germany. He apologized for the last assignment; I shrugged my shoulders and took it in stride.

A few days later, I reported for my first assignment. Taking La Fleur's security recommendations seriously, I unobtrusively walked into a four-star hotel off the rue de Rivoli, took the elevator to the fourth floor, and then walked down to the third. Dressed in civilian clothes, waiting until the corridor was clear, I checked the time and went to the number of the hotel suite and, as advised by La Fleur, knocked on the door three times — two short, one long. A captain with pale blue eyes and armed with a .45 in a shoulder holster opened the door part way and looked at me inquiringly, 'Yes?'

'Swordfish,' I submitted.

'We've been expecting you; come in.'

Seated near the window in easy chairs separated by a round imitation Louis XIV occasional table were two Air Force brigadiers, their immaculate and well-tailored uniforms serving as a background for the pilot's wings and stars they wore. Because of the sun's transit, their faces were in shadow while mine was front lit. I sat down facing them and leaned forward in expectation. 'I'll be brief,' the general to my left, who looked like a graying Clark Gable, said. 'You've been chosen to cover a very important international meeting composed of foreign secretaries of state and their staffs.

The American Ambassador to France, Jefferson Caffrey, likes your camera work and recommended you for the conference.' The general to my right, who chomped on an unlit black cheroot and reminded me of an overweight Humphrey Bogart, regarded me sternly and, in a low rasping voice, said, 'At the end of each day, you're to hand over all of your exposed film to the captain. We will keep count of your unused film. Right?' My answer leaped out of my mouth, like a steeplechaser jumping a barricade; sitting upright, I shouted without hesitation, 'Yes, Sir!'

What followed was a description of the ministers and the prominent members of their staffs, the timetable and purpose of the conference, and the kind of photos they demanded. I sensed that they didn't trust and were suspicious of Russian intentions, as if their army was going to break through the Fulda Gap and overrun Western Europe, driving all the way to Brest on the Atlantic. On no account was I to move from the one designated area to another within the palace without official escort. Both general officers nodded to the captain, who nodded in turn. Their final request demanded that I remain silent about the assignment, to say as little as possible on site, and to respond in the broadest possible terms if spoken to. What would they say next, 'Burn before reading'? My debriefing would follow at the close of the conference. To me, they were making much ado about nothing, but I knew little of how high-ranking intelligence officers functioned in their clandestine world.

Situated near the rue de Vaugirard, the longest street in Paris, the Palais du Luxembourg was originally designed for Marie de' Médici in 1615 and overlooks a succession of attractive and extensive gardens. Usually flocks of children, accompanied by their mothers or nannies, come to sail their toy boats in the large octagonal pool. But on the day of the conference, police cordoned off the area for reasons of security. Special passes were required and I had to show mine before my car was waved on. The palace's parking area ran out of gravel against a series of broad semicircular steps leading to the main entrance. The scene was formal and civilized, an appropriate setting for a gathering of premier ministers. I carried my camera case and its contents up the steps, rotated through the large revolving door, and positioned myself to the left side of the entrance.

I loaded my camera with a film pack containing 12 pieces of film, connected my battery-driven flash unit to the camera, licked the bottom of the flash bulb to improve the electrical connection, and inserted it, ready for my first shot. I prayed to the patron saint of artists, Martin of Tours, for his divine intervention concerning my questionable equipment. The Foreign Secretary of Great Britain, the Rt. Honorable Ernest

Bevin, and his entourage were the first to arrive on that late April afternoon, in two very large black Rolls-Royce sedans, displaying a Union
Jack pennant on each of the two front fenders. As he came through
the door, a portly man with glasses set on a round pudgy face, followed by his aides, I began firing. Secretary of State James Byrnes followed, a slender man with angular features, accompanied by a delega-
tion from Washington that included Senators Tom Connally of Texas
and Arthur Vandenberg of Michigan. I continued to fire, framing the
Senators and the Secretary together. Clicking away, shutter and flash in
sync, I caught Georges Bidault, formerly of the Resistance and now the
Foreign Minister of France, with offices on the Quai d'Orsay, looking
dapper in his double-breasted blue pinstripe suit; he rushed the steps
and spun through the entrance. Sauntering over to greet the previous
arrivals, he expressed himself with diplomatic friendliness and Gallic
volubility. In the '60s, he would break with de Gaulle over Algeria and
go into exile in Austria, a fugitive.

On came the Russians, the tires of their two automobiles grinding to a
stop on the gravel, spreading some stones, flattening others. Car doors
were flung open before the sedans came to a full stop and two body-
guards jumped out. Vyacheslav Molotov, the Soviet Union's Foreign
Minister, infamous for signing the Nazi-Soviet pact of August 1939,
looking neat and scrubbed like a country doctor, strode through the revolving door. He fumbled with his pince-nez and his face looked grey
below the brim of his grey Homburg.

And then it dawned on me! If I were a political terrorist or simply a
psychopath seeking notoriety, nothing stood in the way of murder-
ing any of these diplomats, except my own sanity. God knows what
the political fallout would have been! Except for the police cordon and
the identification requirements, no further security was in force: I was
never searched and, more to the point, nor was my camera case, large
enough to hold six hand grenades, two .45s, and plenty of ammo. I
shuddered and forced the thought from my head. Between the two
brigadiers and me, sanity had been taken on trust. My debriefing seems
unimportant now, but who knows what the steely-eyed captain made
of it. Soon after the two-day conference ended, I heard from La Fleur,
who said, 'The generals are pleased.' I reacted abruptly, 'they sound
like that Navy pilot who said with remarkable alliterative brevity early
in the war, 'Sighted sub, sank same.'

Telegrams rarely brought good news. Terse words from home stated that Joe, my paternal grandfather, whom I affectionately called 'Gramps,' had died. Stunned, I reread the telegram a number of times before staring into space, feeling mindless in the privacy of my apartment. I loved and felt close to him. Gramps was a good friend with whom I shared the same bedroom during my early teenage years. He was supportive in many ways. When all seemed lost, Gramps was the one who miraculously found $5 with which to buy the traditional white flannel slacks, part of the required uniform, for my junior high school graduation in June 1939, one of the Depression years.

Reasonably enough, my parents asked that I return home for the funeral. But I didn't want to go, however irrational the idea; yet my grandfather deserved my presence. My fuzzy eye symptoms were spontaneously reoccurring at the most inopportune times. Decidedly anxious, hyper-vigilant, and easily irritated, I found it increasingly difficult to mask my anger and disillusionment. Feeling worthless, standing on my small balcony early one evening, I considered leaping into the street below. Struggling to identify the sources of the trouble, I failed. Thus far, my job performance remained relatively unaffected, but there was no guarantee. Most nights I lay awake, afraid to sleep. When I did, the war continued in the manifest content of my nightmares. Murder and death always threatened. I awoke in a cold sweat.

I admitted my circumstances to a friend, who countered with, 'You're too young and successful to be so unhappy.'

I responded, spitting out the words, 'You're saying I should be happy? Happy? Christ, I don't even know what the word means, or if it even exists.'

'Steve, at your age, you've everything to live for,' he countered.

Feeling fragile and selfish, seeking maternal tenderness, I invited Olga to lunch at a restaurant on the Left Bank. From the first time we met in Lyon, I felt secure talking to her. We found a table overlooking the square. Once comfortable, waving the waiter away for the moment, I lit a cigarette and said, 'I'm safe, the war's over, but I feel desperate. To make matters worse, I've just had an argument with my parents over the death of my grandfather.' Regardless of my explanations for not going, future photo assignments or an upcoming auction of Army surplus watches and camera equipment, I was being economical with the truth, because there was something impeding my return and acceding to my parents' request. Suzanne!

The author in Rome in 1946, standing before the Ford sedan in which he traveled 3,000 miles through 5 countries

20
Suzanne

One spring afternoon in 1945, crossing the Seine by the Pont de la Concorde, I strolled east along the Boulevard de St. Germain, its trees in blossom. Stopping before the visually pleasing crowded veranda of the Café Flore, a gathering place for artists, photographers, politicians, and students, I found a table. Writers and philosophers like Sartre, de Beauvoir, Camus, and Duras enjoyed the Flore's art deco interior and the sanctuary of its upstairs meeting rooms. So did Barbara, chanteuse extraordinaire. Black was the fashionable color for women, who dressed in tight-fitting tops and sweaters, short skirts, and ballet shoes, while many of the men wore felt jackets and woolen tartans designed for lumberjacks. They all lived on coffee and sandwiches, cigarettes and cheap wine.

I was indifferent to the rumors suggesting that the Flore was a gay hangout and cared even less when I squeezed in between a group of aficionados who were passionately discussing politics at one table and a young woman sitting quietly reading at another. I caught the eye of a tireless middle-aged waiter wearing his *rondeau*, the traditional white apron that wraps around the waist and reaches to the floor. I ordered a double espresso, molded into a colorful wicker chair, and fumbled in one of my trench coat pockets for a packet of Camels and my chrome Zippo lighter. I placed them next to the empty art deco ashtray on the green, brass-rimmed table.

After gazing across the boulevard toward Lipp's, frequented by Hemingway, a brasserie known for its Alsatian food, I turned to the woman sitting alone, and asked in English, 'Are you enjoying your book?' Waiting for her response, I looked at her closely for the first time. I dallied. She was casually dressed but with that special flair associated with women who have an extraordinary sense of bringing out the best in their appearance. Her long black lashes protected her intriguing dark eyes. Her nose, straight and slender, was properly balanced between each high cheekbone. Individually curvaceous and well proportioned, her lips were rich and slender. No blemish, no wrinkle dwelled between her well-shaped chin and forehead. Completing the image, her hair was a rich dark brown that fell almost to her shoulders, luminous in the mild sunshine. I reckoned her to be 25. Dante would have found her breathtaking because, at first glance, I felt out of breath, my visual standards in tatters. If I were being superficial, I was also enjoying myself!

Before she answered, I offered her a cigarette, hoping that she hadn't noticed the slight trembling of my hand. She accepted. I found her smile encouraging and introduced myself.

'I'm Stephen, but my friends call me Steve.'

'Call me Suzanne,' she replied, offering a slender hand. Speaking in a well-shaped English accent, in response to my question, she said, 'I have mixed feelings concerning my book because, although assigned reading, it's also complicated.'

'The subject?' I inquired.

'I don't want to give you the impression that I'm terribly serious, but it does deal with life and death, ethics and morality.'

'Does it relate to your wartime experiences?' I asked.

'Not necessarily, although I lived in Paris through the German Occupation; it has more to do with being a medical student,' Suzanne said.

'Here in Paris?' I countered.

'Oh, yes, at the Faculté de Médecine — and what about you?' she asked, changing the subject. 'In fact, what brings you to Paris?'

'I live here, working as a photographer for the American Army, but during the war I had the dubious pleasure of being a combat soldier,' I responded with a tinge of sarcasm.

'Were you in Paris during the Uprising and the Liberation?' she asked.

'No,' I replied, 'I was involved in fighting further south.'

Her voice dropped slightly when she said, 'You look so young!'

'All combat soldiers are young, dead or alive!' I quickly answered.

I caught the waiter's eye and ordered two more espressos.' ''I will have to leave soon,' she said, looking somewhat saddened. 'I have a seminar in 20 minutes.'

'Surely, we must meet again!' I insisted, feeling nervous awaiting her reply.

She hesitated, and then said, 'We can, but only as friends because, you see, I'm married!'

I inwardly collapsed. Trapped between reality and fantasy, searching for the right response, *le mot juste*, overcome by a sense of devastation, hoping that my disappointment wasn't written all over my face, accepting the inevitable, I stammered in agreement. We exchanged telephone numbers, using the table as a desk, while our waiter hovered nearby, a bird of prey, impatient to land his coffee-laden china cups as soon as space became available and our transaction was done.

Business-like, Suzanne said, without looking up, 'You can always leave a message at the school office on the rue de l'Ecole de Médecine.' After kissing her on both cheeks, I followed her movements as she moved gracefully through the crowd — a lissome five-foot-three — receding east along the boulevard and disappearing.

Grudgingly, I admitted with a modicum of irony that women who are simply seeking friendship need not apply. However, I concluded that if I restricted my emotional investment from erupting into unrequited romance, there was much to enjoy by seeing her again. Acting as if I were responsible for this set of circumstances, I fumed, 'Damn! Why in hell did she have to be married?' Thus, I remained conflicted and distracted by our brief encounter throughout the following week and, in a fit of pique, I tossed away the paper scrap with her telephone number on it.

Early one afternoon, two weeks later, on my way to meet a friend, I passed the Flore and heard a female voice call my name. Sitting at one of the tables on the veranda, a smiling Suzanne waved for me to join her. I squeezed in beside her. 'Coffee?' she offered.

'Yes, please,' I said. Her eyes sparkled in anticipation.

'There's something I need to tell you.' Slowly, looking directly into my eyes, she said,

'My husband and I have had another falling out, and we've decided to separate. I thought you'd be interested to know!'

In response, moving closer, feeling her leg through my trousers, I placed my arm across the back of her chair, and said, amidst a cluster of joyous feelings, 'I'm over the moon, overwhelmed, speechless." She smiled in approval. I continued, forever the problem-solver, 'What will you do next? How will this affect your studies?'

'I will move in with my parents who, having been told, are most unhappy, but what other choice do I have? Much to my regret, my husband is a childish and selfish person whom I married to please them. They now blame me for failing as a wife.'

I probed, 'Where do they live?' she countered, 'in the 20th arrondissement, on the outskirts of Paris.'

We met that evening for dinner at Polydor's, an inexpensive restaurant frequented by American ex-pats in the '20s, on the rue Monsieur le Prince in the 6th. Its rustic wooden chairs and long, rough-hewn tables were unforgiving, its fare simple; simple, that is, if you liked Boeuf Bourguignon. Hemingway did. During the meal, the subject of families came up and she spoke about hers. She lit a cigarette, inhaled, and in a quiet voice began.

'My father, Louis, a farmhand of 17 and son of Italian peasants from Calabria in Southern Italy, left an impoverished home in search of work and took to the open road for Paris, 1,200 kilometers distant. It took two months to make the journey, interrupted by laboring in the fields and sleeping rough.

'When he arrived, he discovered that extreme poverty, ruthless exploitation, and pollution existed in a life without hope in the working-class suburbs of Paris. He settled in Menilmontant, *un quartier pauvre, le plus defavorise* (the most underprivileged) and *ilot insalubre* (a small island of ill-health), set in sunless narrow streets and squalid little apartments. He shared a room with four others, originally built for one.

'Being unskilled, he intermittently labored on building sites for wages so low that he doubted his ability to survive; after three years filled with loneliness, and disheartened by grinding poverty, he decided to marry. His Calabrian relatives complied and sent Rosina, a 16-year-old girl from his village. She hated leaving her native province for a man she had never met. Resenting her future husband even before their first meeting, she felt betrayed by her relatives.

'Although uneducated and illiterate in French, Rosa, soon to be my mother, possessed a natural intelligence. Weighted down by their impoverishment, the newlyweds viewed each other with hostility and contempt; he started beating her and she remained frightened of him throughout their marriage, although she did protest.

'I was the first-born, followed by my brother Pietro. I was bright and attractive; Pietro, sickly and problematical. Embittered, Rosina hated me and idolized Pietro. Even if Louis, insensitive and pompous, hadn't seduced me physically, he did so emotionally, because the solace he offered was conditional and on his terms.

'With Rosina's help, Louis converted an empty shop into a local café that specialized in basic Southern Italian cooking. The workers of Menilmotant liked the pasta dishes and rough red wine enough to support the café financially; the owners toiled late into the night, all through the year — without pause. Nevertheless, within the framework of poverty, the café thrived.

'As a health professional,' Suzanne continued, 'I learned that all through interwar period, 30 percent of the inhabitants in the poor suburbs like Menilmotant suffered from tuberculosis, the death rate reaching as high as 43 percent. Social benefits and medical care were nonexistent. No social safety net existed. There was a chronic shortage of food, and the young suffered from malnutrition. In winter, the old virtually starved to death or were swept away by flu.

'Before the Germans invaded France in June 1940, my parents had saved enough money to buy a dilapidated two-bedroom late 19th-century apartment above the café and moved in. Although intellectual inquisitiveness was nonexistent in my family, my innate intelligence and curiosity contributed to continuing success at school. Ever since I was a little girl, medicine appealed to me.'

'Where did you learn English,' I asked?

'While in my mid-teens, working for three years as an au pair for a well-off English family living in the 16th. I left because the girls' father tried to seduce me.'

'And your husband,' I inquired further?

'We met in the café. He was a frequent caller, a smallish man of Corsican/Moroccan stock, unskilled and poorly educated, boastful and of a violent temper. I never called him anything other than *Le Croc* (Fang).'

'My God, why him?' I implored.

'My parents, and particularly my mother, 'the ice maiden,' wanted to me to leave, and I was desperate to escape, but I had no one to turn to.'

I looked into her eyes and tried to reassure her. 'Surely, there's something I can do!'

'And your brother?' I questioned.

'Pietro was killed by a German sniper during the Liberation. My parents would have preferred that he lived and I died.' She fell silent then said quietly, 'He was such a nice boy!'

We left the comfort of the restaurant and paused outside the entrance to gauge the chill night air. Staying close to each other without impeding our forward movement, we walked down the hill to the Metro. The mist diffused the multi-colored neon signs on the distant boulevard, whose soft blackness shimmered in the invisible drizzle. Before reaching the Place de l'Odeon, I turned her toward me in one sweeping dance movement, took her in my arms, and kissed her. Releasing my hold, I looked at her and said, 'I love you!' She looked at me and then pressed her head against my shoulder. Suzanne stepped away, her hands in mine, and said, 'I don't want to leave, but I must.'

We walked across the Metro's concourse, through the barrier, and down to the platform. The approaching train roared out of the tunnel, creating a wind that pushed and rippled against us. As the train slowed, the moving interplay of light and shadow that paralleled and reflected its passage on the station's tiled walls slowed simultaneously and fell beside the tracks. We promised, in protest to our immediate separation, to meet again soon. She entered the carriage, and watched me through the door's window. I remained standing on the platform until the last carriage rocketed out of sight. While feeling the afterglow of the evening, I left the *bouche de metro*, hailed a taxi, and returned to my hotel.

Suzanne called on the following Friday. 'Let's meet tomorrow and spend the weekend together,' I suggested.

'Never on Saturday,' she replied. 'That's when I help my parents at the café, but we can always meet on Sundays.'

'I'm disappointed.' 'Don't be,' she said, 'I'll make it up to you. I'm free right now,' she offered.

Using an assigned converted ambulance as my personal transportation, I picked her up. We drove beyond Boulogne-Billancourt to Versailles, 14 miles west of Paris. Versailles is a lovely town with wide boulevards, shady side streets, some 17th-century houses jumbled together, and an imposing 17th-century chateau of universal proportions. General Eisenhower had used the palace as his headquarters after the German retreat from Normandy in August 1944, and Maurice Chevalier, the great French music hall performer, lived in an adjacent village with the most joyous-sounding place name I've ever known: Marnes La Coquette. It's as attractive as it sounds.

As we slowly motored down the Avenue de Trianon to the Allée des Matelots, between ripening wheat fields — once the domain of Louis the XIV, the Sun King — and grazing sheep, we could go no further. Café Flotille's latticework surrounding the terrace offered privacy. The large windows allowing shafts of sunlight to reach across the floor offered an appealing view of the formal gardens and stands of trees. With its dark wooden tables and bentwood chairs comfortably spaced upon the Italianate-tiled floor of the café's interior, La Flotille became an enchanted refuge. An old copper-bright espresso machine, whose giant boiler gurgled a rhythmic accompaniment at the slightest turn of the tap, stood next to the bar. It was in this *fin de siècle* setting that I wished to propose to Suzanne.

We ordered a cappuccino sprayed with chocolate and a tarte aux pommes with crème fraiche for two. The waiter walked away as I lit a cigarette and offered it to her. Sensing I was eager to know how her week went, she began by saying, 'Class lectures are no problem; studying at home is. One of my parents is there all the time. It's difficult to concentrate, and they think I'm crazy for choosing a career in medicine, particularly when they need my help in the café. *Le Croc* comes over frequently now that he knows where to find me and pleads that I return to his cold-water flat. My parents take his side, believing I'm a damned woman.' She inhaled and said, 'I'll wager they give him money to live on!'

'I lit another cigarette and said, 'I've an idea. Through my connections at Army Headquarters, arrangements can be made for the two of us to live together.' Feeling unsure,' I continued, 'It's been done before!'

She leaned closer saying, 'I know you care for me, but I'll sort it out. The French government pays for my medical studies, an outcome of the 1944 *Resistance Manifesto*, and even some research projects pay well for students.' She avoided the housing issue, so I held my hand up. 'Might we leave it at that for the time being?' I asked.

'May I order a short walk in the park, then dinner in Versailles at the Brasserie du Theatre? The food is good, simple fare, and so is the wine. Sound OK?'

She was pleased. The dinner was all that I hoped: a six-ounce steak, fries, salad, and wine. Suzanne expressed her enthusiasm with every approaching course. Over coffee and cognac she said, putting on a brave face, 'During the Occupation, there was a shortage of food; rations fell below the subsistence level: 350 grams of bread a day, 350 grams of meat, and 40 grams of cheese weekly per family; milk, eggs, and fish were virtually unobtainable. Like the others, I lost weight, felt close to exhaustion, and easily fell ill. The lack of food produced a continual lightheaded feeling, as if a slight breeze could easily tip me over. After dining like this, those memories seem shrouded in the mists of time, yet my feelings of humility and sadness tell me that it was not so very long ago.'

Looking at Suzanne now, I wouldn't have believed that she and most of the population of *Grosse Paris*, as the Germans called it, were being slowly and deliberately starved to death in systematic fashion. Both of us knew something about deprivation. I said quietly but forcefully, 'We will never go hungry again!'

Returning to Paris and dancing at Mimi Pinson's Club on the Champs Elysees, we discarded the unexpectedly somber thoughts evoked over dinner. The band played swing as well as Latin music, and we jitterbugged or tangoed with equal panache. We danced well together because we naturally listened to the music and moved a fraction before the beat. When I repeatedly spun her away from me, holding her hand as she turned, dancing to Glenn Miller's arrangement of *In the Mood*, Suzanne returned, weaving rhythmically from side to side. Our movements expressed closeness, separation, and return that added to the drama of becoming known to each other. We were most serious when dancing the tango, a dance that was born more than a century ago in the brothels of Argentina, portraying the relationship between a prostitute and her pimp; there was no way of avoiding each other — not that we wanted to — but with my hand around her waist, her body pressing into mine, I felt the inside of her thighs as we pivoted, dipped, and glided across the floor, sustained by music that was both seductive and haunting.

Welcoming this intimacy with quiet discretion, we hastened the end of any remaining inhibitions. After doing another deep bend, she whispered quivering words of endearment in my ear. I nodded in recognition. We walked off the dance floor side by side, left Mimi's before the band finished playing *La Cumparsita*, the last tango of the evening, whose lyrics spoke of love and intoxication, and drove the short distance to my hotel.

Without speaking, both of knew our time had come. The intensity of a merged and controlled eagerness that we expressed dancing the tango cascaded over our lovemaking. We wanted each other out of youthful exuberance and thus were gladiatorial. We shoved, pushed, and pressed against each other, fighting for the same space; our bodies were arches, crescents, and flying buttresses, supporting deep thrusts in either direction. With her back on the mattress, she thrust her body into mine, attacking my position from below.

I grabbed her calves and drew her toward me, her back skimming across the sheets. Twisting away, she gained the upper hand, and sat on top of me. Somehow we recognized the nature of the struggle, the diversity and differences, which existed between us as primordial man and woman. Love making? It was combat, a fandango, a dance of mutual interaction and satisfaction. This was a cosmic act, not so much a case of did the earth move but the universe. Our kisses were as deep as the ocean. We wanted to and succeeded in pleasing each other with the utmost athleticism, as if it were the most natural thing in the world. Ours was not a struggle of dominance or supremacy but an admission of equality. I grabbed a clump of dank hair and pulled her head closer to me, forcing her down. She winced when I slapped her bottom. After reaching orgasm, she opened her eyes, catlike in the shadows, and growled.

Breathing deeply, I laughed and experienced a mental and physical completeness. We said little, conscious of and overwhelmed by the night's events and the shock of recognition they provoked. We regarded each other differently, a deepening respect added to the equation; our relationship became a serious matter to us both, a millennium away from anything resembling a frivolous and fleeting 'roll in the hay.' From now on, one plus one made three, and I stood before the relationship as life itself, with the utmost humility. At least that's how I felt! When she kissed me goodbye and left soon after, the door lock clicking behind her, I fell asleep.

We met later that day and I proposed to her again. Agreed upon by my Army friends in charge of food and accommodation, it was OK for her to live with me.

She wasn't overjoyed. I was surprised at her response 'Have you ever lived with a woman before?' she asked.

'No, but I've got to start some time, and I'm willing to try, particularly when you're the woman.'

Suzanne, responded, 'I've no idea if we're compatible. We hardly know each other, and I don't know if your problems are more or less complicated than mine, and easier to solve.'

'Suzanne, I've no need to compare my problems with yours. I think mine are in a different category and war related.'

'And I'm not like you, apparently free from family responsibilities. I have to help my parents and deal with *Croc.* We're separated not divorced,' she said. I felt nervous and lit cigarettes for both of us. We fell silent. Finally she said, 'I've never been offered such a gift before. No one ever felt I was worthy of consideration.' Her eyes glistened with tears. She seemed deep in thought. 'All right, I accept.'

Relieved and satisfied, I felt an added responsibility and speculated how her family and her husband would receive the change in living arrangements. The removal of her books and clothes had to be solved. With the two of us working together, little time would be spent loading the converted ambulance, which would serve our purpose admirably.

With the help of the hotel staff, my large suite was converted for double occupancy. To say the least, with Suzanne at my side, I was even sure that my French would improve.

Having had a late breakfast at the Officers' Club on Place St. Agustin, after our second cup of coffee, we descended the marble staircase, crossed the lobby, and drove away. 'Let's take the 'scenic' route to your parents' apartment, 'I suggested, 'but when we get into the 20th, you'll have to guide me.

OK?'

'Oui, mon cher,' she said, her eyes full of merriment.

Paris was almost empty of automobiles. Traffic was occasional and gasoline at a premium. Skirting the Eglise de Ste. Marie de Madeleine, its full name, designed in the style of a Greek church, we entered the 17th-century Place Vendome from the north, with the Ritz Hotel situated on our right. During last year's uprising of late August 1944, Ernest Hemingway, posing as a swashbuckling war correspondent, liberated the hotel's wine cellar with his band of 30 irregulars. Amidst the excitement, he asked the manager for 73 dry martinis — and got them!

In the center of the square, Napoleon's column loomed. A stone core 133 feet high entwined in a spiral containing more than a thousand captured Austrian cannons, on top of which stands a statue of the emperor that was built to celebrate his victory at Austerlitz in 1805. We exited from the rue Castiglione and as we turned left into the rue de Rivoli, I pointed to the Hotel Meurice. Prior to Hemingway's arrival, German General Dietrich von Choltitz, a destroyer of Russian cities, using the hotel as his headquarters, refused to carry out Hitler's coded order, 'Is Paris burning?' Rather than destroy the city, he surrendered to the Paris Resistance.

Across the wide thoroughfare, on the outer wall of the Tuileries Garden, a long line of small square crypts was filled with flowers. Plaques embedded into the stone wall above commemorated those French soldiers and Resistance fighters who had died liberating the city. Driving by the Place des Pyramides, with its flaking gold equestrian statue of Jeanne d'Arc in need of paint and repair, as if she had lost, not won, her battles against the English, we continued on. Between the Palais Royal and the Louvre, to the Hotel de Ville, each building displayed a shopworn regality.

On its way to the Place de la Bastille, the rue de Rivoli becomes the rue St. Antoine in the 4th arrondissement and the superficial well-being of the middle class 'beaux' quartiers of Paris — the 1st, 7th, 8th, 16th, and 17th — are replaced by the shoddiness of a convoluted working-class district.

The street is honeycombed with courts and passages and interlaced with used furniture stores, where once small cabinet-maker workshops stood. We had to slow down, although the streets hadn't narrowed, because people and pushcarts, their corrugated roofs offering little shelter against the rain, were in evidence. The invasive smells of wood, varnish, produce, and decay provided a backdrop for a pathetic human comedy, where *clochards* (tramps) searched for scraps on the damp pavement between the carts of used goods and produce.

We bounced over the *paves* (wooden cobble stones) because many were missing, having been ripped up, stolen, or used for firewood the previous winter. Others were used to attack the Germans. Adding to the noise of commerce was the sound of wooden-soled shoes knocking against the pavement, like terrestrial woodpeckers. Young women cycled beside us, their short patchwork dresses accentuating the shape of their thighs, while others walked the crowded sidewalks, like a fractured line of chorus girls, wearing high fantastic-looking hats of their own making.

I thought of Carmen Miranda and the large basket of tropical fruit she wore as a headpiece when dancing and singing to a Latin beat in Hollywood musicals. A young woman tripped, stubbing her toes on the uneven sidewalk. 'Merde,' she cursed under her breath, while trying to regain her balance and dignity. Serving as a backdrop to this street scene were houses with grey shutters, abandoned shops, grimy buildings with peeling paint, and walls devoid of plaster, exposing their construction of mesh wire and broken wooden slats.

 We crawled straight down rue de la Roquette until we approached one side of Pere La Chaise Cemetery, in which are buried some of the great luminaries of France, such as Napoleon's marshals, Moliere, and Edith Piaf, all resting among hundreds of highly chiseled decorative memorial stones and park-like trails, enclosed by a high outer stone wall. Turning left on Boulevard Menilmontant, then entering the Place Metvier, Suzanne pointed to an art nouveau Metro entrance whose floral design was repeated on the façade of the Rond Point Café nearby.

'Take the rue des Amandiers,' she ordered, pointing to a broad tree-lined avenue tilting in front of us. 'It will run into rue de Menilmontant.'

Moments later, we parked at the end of a side street, empty except for two black children playing with a small wagon. Although beyond the age of toilet training, the child pushing it wore a worn makeshift paper diaper, while the older of the two steered. Above, tattered washing hung without hope of drying in the damp air. Walking past a series of single-story stucco dwellings separated by a narrow cobblestoned alley, Suzanne stopped, pointed, and said, 'These one-room shacks were once stables built for the *Relais de la Poste* (Postal Service) during the late 19th-century. Now, instead of horses, people are quartered here, usually three to four to a room three by three meters square. There is no electricity. Washing and lavatory facilities are communal. An out-door pump serves the current occupants with a limited supply of water that often freezes in winter. Cooking is done over outdoor wood fires. Blood sausage and sardines are the daily fare for the hollow-eyed diners, nauseated by their own stale sweat.' We walked away in disgust!

After 50 yards, we reached the top of the street and paused. Suzanne nodded without pride to a café on the other side of the street. On the edge of its green awning *Café Gambetta* was printed in faded white letters. 'That's the family business,' she said.

I followed Suzanne into the café to tuneful greetings; a gaggle of old laborers and habitués, swarthy and small in stature, seemingly all from countries bordering the Mediterranean, sat side by side, leaning against the stained green walls. Some drank; others drank and played cards in the dimly lit interior that softened the outline of the imitation-wood Formica bar and the bentwood chairs. The Mafioso type behind the bar eyed me suspiciously and looked as if he could throw a knife with the same ease he could wash a soiled cognac snifter. Shaking off his gaze, I followed Suzanne through the drifting tobacco smoke to a flight of dark narrow stairs leading to the apartment above.

Rosina and Louis were sitting at the green baize-colored dining room table when we entered, surrounded by a jumble of nondescript furniture. A hanging brass crucifix, bright against the drab walls, caught the sunlight. Neither parent rose to greet us, but Suzanne, Rosina, and Louis began talking immediately in harsh-sounding and unfriendly tones in a language unknown to me. Moments later, her mother rose abruptly and walked behind her seated husband, presenting an opportunity for me to observe her more closely. Wearing an ordinary black dress that hung limply on a thin narrow frame, Rosina wore her thinning black hair short and parted in the middle. More like an unkempt dark hedge in need of trimming than hair! Her even features were distorted by anger and cynicism, and her gaunt body looked exhausted from years of toil, although there was a faint residue of youthful attractiveness. Vituperative, she hissed and spat her words at Suzanne, who tossed them back like hot coals, if I correctly judged the quality of her feelings. Suzanne stood there, arms akimbo, legs apart, a street fighter, slashing her words against Rosina's flank, driving them deep into her chest. Between them, it was bruising, a crude shouting match, its only purpose to inflict the maximum pain.

Louis slammed his right fist down on the table, rattling the glasses. He rose to stand beside his wife. They stood with nothing between them but air, two alienated and decoupled hostile people. He was fat, watery-eyed, and heavy handed, an angry man who wore a thin pencil-line moustache, more grey than black. He shouted at me, Rosina nodded, and I understood nothing. I was excluded from actively participating and considered an outcast because I was not one of them by nationality, class, or background; thus, I was less than dust.

'Suzanne, what's he shouting about?' I implored.

'They insist I stay with them, among my own people. You are a bad influence,' she translated.

'Even if my proposal is in your best interest?'

'To them, you're a menace, an enemy alien!'

'Don't they know I love you? Tell them, Suzanne, for Christ's sake!' I demanded.

Suzanne repeated my words in Italian. Rosina and Louis were implacable, tribal, pagan, and scornful of my love. To them, love was an insubstantial commodity; family and money everything! I thought, 'They suffer from and are stuck in a peasant mentality forever.' Suzanne was defiant and tearful. As she moved to collect her possessions, her mother moaned, swaying, and her father, fists clenched, yelled, 'Get out! Get out!'

In less time than I expected, we were carrying down our last load of books when *Le Croq* entered. I put my box down and waited. *Le Croq* looked every inch a dandy, full of himself, a bantam cock. He yelled; spittle formed on one side of his mouth. 'Do not think you have stolen her from me,' pointing a finger in my direction. 'She'll come crawling back when I snap my fingers!'

He joined Suzanne's parents and stood beside them. Rosina, 'The spider woman' injected venom into every word; Suzanne's father added to the chaos, shouting repeatedly, 'You ungrateful bitch.' This was opera, a musical in its own way, but deadly reptilian. Amid a tidal wave of curses rustling the clothes on our backs, we made our getaway. Circling the Etoile, Suzanne, summed up our adventure by concluding, 'They will never forgive you. Your good will means nothing to them. My parents and *Le Croq* hate you.'

With their curses ringing in my ears, I, as a novice in close relationships, found our commitment totally new. I was content to be near Suzanne, sharing a quality of repose and quietude even when we were immersed in our own thoughts or individual projects. Some Sunday nights we'd cross the Seine to the Left Bank and dance to the music of Django Reinhardt and Stephane Grappelli, creators of their own style, a blend of swing, jazz, and Gypsy harmonies. *Melancholie*, an Italian-inspired waltz, was a song we awaited eagerly. Whether it was a paso doble or a lindy hop, we were our favorite dance partners, even if the dance floor was crowded and postage stamp-sized. Dancing increased our pulse, perspiration, and passion.

One night, four months later, having dinner with Suzanne at a local brasserie near the Place de Ternes, I felt anxious. We were separating for the first time because I was leaving the following morning on a photo mission to Norway. I voiced my concern and spoke with a sense of foreboding about separation and trust, seeking assurance from her where none was required.

'Stop it,' she interrupted. 'You're behaving like a child. I have no intention of doing anything foolish while you're gone. Remember, I have my medical studies to occupy my time. Your doubt has more to do with you than me, and I prefer not to join with you in so foolish an enterprise.' She lowered her eyes, took a deep breath, reached across the table, took my hand in hers, and spoke softly. 'Come, darling, in two weeks' time you will come back to me.' I felt relieved and called the waiter for the bill. Early the next morning, Hines and I flew from Orly Airfield to Oslo in an Army C-47.

On the evening of the 13th day of our separation, having accomplished my mission, I returned home eager to see Suzanne. She rushed toward me with outstretched arms, her face aglow in greeting. All my doubts vanished. I showered while she put my soiled clothes in the hamper; we chatted and I fixed drinks. We saved the details of my trip for dinner at the Officers' Club. After we were seated, Suzanne wanted to learn more about my recent assignment.

'It was rather straightforward, but filled with emotion for the participants, who were Norwegian inhabitants and American next of kin. It featured OSS operational group which were on a sabotage mission by air from England to Norway in 1944. Over Norway, they crashed into a mountain in the north of the country. No one survived. Local residents who henceforth tended their graves buried the bodies at the foot of the mountain. After the war, identification of the dead was established, and their relatives in the U.S. were notified. They then were given a choice of a final resting place, either in a U.S. cemetery or one in Norway. Before the relatives decided, the bodies were disinterred and reburied in an Oslo civilian cemetery with full military honors.

'I began my photo essay from that point, which included another disinterment. I included the practical methods and procedures employed between the U.S. and Norwegian authorities to conclude successfully the whole process of reclamation, return, and reburial as requested by the next of kin. The sequence of photos begins with Norwegian workmen digging and uncovering the remains and establishing the identity of each casualty. Fifteen photos later, the story ended with a coffin being placed aboard a C-47 U.S. Army Air Corps cargo plane, the first leg of a journey bound for America.'

Nodding in appreciation, Suzanne, her face taking on a serious expression, leaned towards me, and said, 'Stephen, while you were gone, I have given much thought to our relationship. I would feel more comfortable if we changed it from a love relationship to one of friendship. It would be a better arrangement for me.'

I'm not certain if my right hand, lifting a dessert spoon to my mouth, stopped in mid-air or continued to rise in response to a sudden shock. I looked at her, unsure of what I had just heard. I replied, 'Excuse me, would you mind repeating what you just said?' my voice trembling. As she began to speak, I interrupted her and said, 'I've had a difficult two weeks and a tiring flight, so maybe my ear and brain are malfunctioning. Probably, there's no time like the present, but why the hell couldn't you have waited until after I had a decent night's sleep.'

Frightened, she reached for a cigarette, lit it, and repeated what she just said.

In protest, I replied, 'I've no idea what's going on, but it's my worst nightmare come true. You assured me when I left that all would be well, that any concerns of mine were unrealistic. Now this!' She sat there forlorn and alone, tearful, the table a mile-wide gulf of separation. Attempting to speak in a normal voice, I suggested, 'Why don't we let the idea rest for a while and leave.' Tearfully, she nodded as I thrust my handkerchief across the crumbs between us.

We sat in the living room looking at each other in silence. 'Do you want me to leave?' she asked.

'I'm not sure. If we can't remain lovers, then I think we ought to end it. I couldn't be simply friends now, not after what we've been through, not for a long time.'

'I'll go into the other room,' she said, 'so you can think it over and get some rest.'

'There's a sweater for you in my bag; you might as well take it, I've no intention of fobbing it off to another woman.' She took the package, walked into the other room, and closed the door. I, in turn, full of regret and sadness, was left to deal with her receding footsteps.

The door opened after I lit my 10th cigarette. Silhouetted in the doorway, she stood wearing the sweater and high heels, nothing more. Suzanne came over to my chair and sat on the floor beside me, put her head on my lap, and sobbed. I gently caressed her hair, offering words of comfort. Contrite, she apologized, saying, 'How could I have been so cruel?' but no explanation followed. Suddenly, in some primordial way, I knew!

I lifted her chin and said angrily, 'You went to bed with another man! How could you?' Without hesitating, she replied, 'I missed you.' Her response was a confession, 'The days were long and your side of the bed was cold, empty. I tried to resist; at first, it was simply a flirtation. It became serious later.'

There was an angry edge to my next question, 'Did you know him?' She replied, 'No. I met him on the Boulevard St. Michel.'

'In a shop?'

'On the sidewalk, he was selling cosmetics.'

'A street hustler?'

'He was friendly, sympathetic, available.'

I turned practical, repressing my feelings, denying a desire to hit her, 'Did you catch anything?'

'No, the doctor at the medical school told me the test was negative.'

Angrily, accusingly, I turned on her. 'How could you be so damned foolish to put both of us at risk for nothing more than a momentary fling? Hell, there's temptation galore in this world, and you had to fall for a winning smile from a con man. How tasteless can you be! Can't you distinguish between excitement and danger?' I prodded. It was as if, I, at 19, was proclaiming a new psychology, when I myself was green behind my ears. 'Look, I'm not sure if 'forgive' is the right word or if even 'salvation' fits, but I'm not about to cast the first stone and condemn you to hell. I'm not one to talk, having screwed up my own life. My Army personnel file is full of errors of judgment. The thing we don't want to do is to keep making the same mistakes.' Before I continued, I decided to opt out of this drama, a combination of inquisition, trial by jury, and religious confession. I rose and paced the room, then stopped.

'Maybe, I was gone too long from your point of view. Even with your rotten family and the shocks of war lining up against me, it would seem that for most couples, a two-week separation wasn't anything to get nervous about.' When I stopped talking, feeling emotionally exhausted, she seemed penitent and relieved to be understood. We went to bed, desperately clinging to each other, but three days later, as we walked to our favorite restaurant on the Place de Ternes, she said offhandedly, and much to my astonishment, 'Don't be surprised if I do the same thing again!'

This was one experience I was not prepared to repeat. I asked her to leave, and a few days later she walked out of my life and was gone.

21
Norway and Dead Bodies

Before I left the city for the assignment in Norway, I photographed the Catacombs near the Place Denfert Rochereau. Climbing through a manhole at street level and descending by ladder to a subterranean labyrinth, I followed my guide, whose flashlight illuminated an eerie scene. How much easier it would have been, I thought, if I were armed with a small 35 mm Leica rather than the ponderous 4x5 Speed Graphic that seemed to sway and clank into the bones of previous Paris inhabitants. Arriving at the bottom of the cavern, I walked slowly through a maze of Gallo-Roman tunnels, stopping to photograph macabre displays of skulls and crossed tibias. Almost 200 years ago, millions of skeletons had been gathered from local cemeteries and stacked here. In the present, our voices sounded distorted, reverberating and echoing off the damp walls, but no sounds penetrated from the Paris streets above.

Never knowing when my sight might turn to fuzz, I felt a wave of anxiety wash over me. It seemed that after each episode, I needed more time to recover. However, I put on a brave face while the guide, whose flashlight barely penetrated the surrounding gloom, told me that after the Liberation of Paris, the Resistance revealed its best-kept secret. It had used the catacombs for its headquarters while the German occupier patrolled the streets above. Finished shooting, perspiring in the cold damp of the main gallery, I climbed the ladder following my guide to the surface, realizing there was still time to break a leg. We emerged from a grotesque world through the manhole, like sailors exiting from a submarine's hatch. Sucking great draughts of air, I returned to a world full of taxi horns and human sounds.

Norway beckoned and dawn came much too soon. As I emerged from the lobby, the driver got in behind the wheel and started the engine. Hines was waiting in front of his apartment block, his baggage stacked beside him. When he got into the car, I said whimsically, 'Ah, the poor man's John Barrymore; how nice to see you again. Are you and your repertory theater company ready to tour Norway?' He rose to the occasion. 'Steve, m'boy, only if you play the female lead.' Driving to Orly, Hines reminded me that we were to fly to Bremen to meet a Grave Registration (GR) unit based in that north German city.

We were tasked to film the exhumation of 10 American servicemen who had been killed in April 1945 while on a covert OSS special operations mission to Norway, code-named Westfield. It was designed to tie down German forces in Norway from reinforcing the final defense of Germany. Two planes, flying from a base in England as part of the operation, ran into bad weather and crashed into a mountain over Norway, killing all those on board. Local inhabitants had tended the graves near the foot of the mountain for two years, but later the remains were transferred to a cemetery in Oslo for reburial. William Colby, later to become President Nixon's CIA director in 1973, was part of that mission. However, he and his NORSO Group successfully parachuted into Norway from Sweden.

For the third time, the dead men were to be meddled with, this time in preparation for their final burial in the U.S. as requested by their next of kin. I wondered what ever happened to the notion of 'rest in peace.' Not only would Hines and I film the transfer but we would create a generic picture story that revealed the methods concerning the discovery and identification of U.S. servicemen killed in Norway and their shipment back home. Part of the story would stress the cooperation between the local inhabitants, the regional Norwegian authorities, and the U.S. Army. Originally we were to travel from Oslo to Trondheim by sea on a Norwegian destroyer, but for some unexplained reason, that part was canceled at the last minute.

The twin-engine C-47 Dakota aircraft that waited for us at Orly was manned by a pilot, co-pilot, and a flight sergeant from the U.S. 8th Eighth Air Force, an organization that, at its height, during the later stages of the Allied bombing campaign of 1944, consisted of 250,000 men and 8,000 fighters and bombers. Hines and I were the only passengers within the stark, bucket-seated metal interior, but the two pilots and the flight sergeant were playful and relaxed. Two hours into our trip, crossing from eastern France into Germany, I viewed a landscape dotted with ruined cities, battered towns, and destroyed villages on a scale beyond my imagination. Through the industrial haze and scattered clouds, under which Bremen lay, we made the best of landings — uneventful.

During the war and after, GR was assigned to clean up the battlefield and identify and bury the dead, a grisly job done by enlisted men at the lower end of the cultural and intellectual scale. We in the infantry fought the battle and moved on, leaving others to cope with the practical effects of its aftermath. Hines and I were introduced by the unit's commanding officer to the two men who were to accompany us from Bremen to Oslo.

That evening, the GR unit's first sergeant invited us to a party in one of its billets, a requisitioned German house. Hines and I willingly accepted. We walked the short distance to the house, from which no light emerged, and entered through the front door, accompanied by three or four of the staff. Before the house lights were turned on, one of the men, carrying a flashlight, illuminated a grotesque scene composed of hanging skeleton cardboard cutouts and stuffed and dressed straw cadavers. Colored lights flashed on and off, punctuated by screams that broke the funereal silence, a mad 'son et lumiere.' Taken by surprise, we piled into each other and sought refuge in our collective presence. We had entered a charnel house, in which death and violence stalked us from room to room. Staff in make-up and dressed up as the living dead and accident victims attacked us without warning, their hands dripping blood. From Dr. Frankenstein's laboratory, a hospital morgue, or a coroner's autopsy chamber, they brandished knives and thin steel ropes. By creating a bizarre theme park, *une dance macabre*, the unit expressed its own brand of humor, and shocked and frightened innocent wayward travelers like me. I feared and trembled unto death. Escaping onto the street to the sounds of laughter and the slamming and squeaking of doors, I registered my dissatisfaction to some of the staff, who felt hurt and unjustly criticized, lamenting in one collective voice to Hines and me, 'Aw, c'mon it was all in good fun. Can't you take a joke?' Hines admitted that his reaction was much less severe than mine. I wondered if the party wasn't a defense against being ordered to do a job few people would choose to do.

When we were taxiing down the runway the next morning, I described our adventures of the night before to one of the pilots, who regretted having missed all the fun and excitement. Ten thousand feet over Copenhagen, at a speed of 180 miles an hour, we cruised toward Oslo. Pilot and co-pilot emerged from their cabin and sat down across from Hines. 'Thought we'd catch forty winks,' they remarked, and both stretched out on some of the bucket seats to sleep. Anxious, I entered the pilot's cabin to find the flight sergeant flying the plane.

'Hey, Sarge,' I asked in a trembling voice, 'you know what you're doing?'

'Hell, yes,' he answered, 'It's an easy plane to keep in the air. All you have to do is keep it steady, that is, as long as no one's shooting at you.' He looked at me quizzically, over his shoulder, and asked, 'Wanna try?' When he took his hands off the wheel, I jumped with fright and he laughed, enjoying my apparent discomfort.

We crossed over into Swedish air space at Malmo and headed up the coast toward Oslo, 310 miles away. I found the landscape forbidding, made up of half-sunken islands, great tracts of woodland, scores of lakes bumping into each other, and meandering rivers drifting nowhere. With few roads and villages, there was little to be seen of man's hand on this glacial, primeval, and brooding land, much like eastern Canada and Maine. Two hours later, the C-47 flew above the entrance of the 50-mile long Oslo Fjord, with the pilot at the controls. He nosed the plane downward until we were skimming over the water at an altitude of about 400 feet, and Hines and I commented on the sense of exhilaration we felt as people waved from small boats or waterside homes, marking our passing.

How much different it was when, on April 9, 1940, a German fleet, led by the pocket battleship *Leutzow* and the brand new heavy cruiser *Blucher* attacked Norway without warning and entered the fjord. Some 20 miles below Oslo, because the channel is only 600 yards wide, it is known as the Drobak Narrows. At this critical point, land batteries consisting of heavy caliber Krupp guns, installed at the turn of the 20th century, and manned by units of the Norwegian Army, attacked the German ships. Firing at point blank range, the shore batteries' 11- and 8-inch shells smashed into the *Blucher*. Added to this concentrated firepower, torpedoes launched from the shore exploded under the hull and wrecked the main engines. The *Luetzow* was damaged but not disabled and retreated out of range; however, the 10,000-ton *Blucher*, ablaze and torn by its exploding ammunition, sat dead in the water. Although the order to abandon ship was given, the ship sank with the loss of 1,600 men. Those who survived were taken prisoner as soon as they reached the shore. A day later, Oslo, the nation's capital, surrendered to German paratroopers.

We flew right over the *Blucher* at mast height on our way up the fjord.

The pilot headed right for a forested hill blocking our path. He pulled up hard over it and, in the same breath, pushed down on the steering column, and quickly leveled out just as our wheels touched the grass runway. It was a tight, precise, and well-executed maneuver, responsive to the airfield's hilly surroundings and small size. A Norwegian army captain greeted us on the tarmac, standing beside his jeep and trailer. He was to serve as our liaison officer and looked and acted more British than Norwegian, with his military brush moustache, beret, and battle dress. Captain Anderson, the Norwegian officer, drove us to American GR headquarters in Oslo. Just as we were about to enter the building, I remembered that all our gear and photographic equipment was stowed on the trailer and left unguarded. I asked Anderson if it were wise to do so. 'Oh that's all right,' he replied with a smile, 'your equipment will be safe — no one steals in Norway!'

At mid-morning on the following day, we were met at the entrance to Oslo Cemetery by two junior-ranking American officers on detached service from the GR unit in Bremen. The American dead were buried within a portion of the cemetery that was cordoned off and turned into a building site. Two Norwegian gravediggers began digging; a mound of damp earth mixed with tufts of grass gave way to earth alone; the excavation increased in size beside the graves with every spade full. An hour later, their shovel reached the first of the caskets, dapple-grey against the dark earth. The workmen stood silently within the first grave's four walls, wiping the sweat from their foreheads with large handkerchiefs. Digging a trench around the casket, they shifted it from its resting place. The workmen heaved and groaned, cursing in Norwegian as they lifted the box, thrusting it upward at an angle. Fine dark earth showered off it and fell into the hole before the workmen placed the casket across the top of the open grave. One of the two GR men straddled the grave and pulled open some of the top slats and, as if peering through a broken fence, partially exposed the remains within. The body was in the later stages of decomposition. Full of gas, it had pressed and wedged itself against the remaining slats. The face was a swollen pulpy grey with two holes for eyes, a curved line for a mouth. I didn't see a nose. Only the uniform indicated that once someone alive had lived within.

The gravedigger's scene in Shakespeare's 'Hamlet' was a theatrical performance, an entertainment. It was without a decomposing body and its invasive odor, the shiny skull nothing more than the actor's stage prop. What followed was not playacting. Reaching down, the GR man searched, found, and tugged at the forty inch partially embedded beaded metal chain, clinging to what had been a neck. Shifting it, he found the attached two-inch by one-inch metal dog tag on which was stamped the soldier's name, serial number, blood type, and religion. He compared it to its twin, nailed to the wooden cross which moments ago had stood at the head of the unopened grave. The soldier called out the dead soldier's name and serial number. In turn, the officer repeated the name and serial number aloud, checked them against the records on his clipboard, nodded, and called, 'OK.' It was late afternoon before all four graves were opened and the bodies verified. Each casket was repaired, cleaned on site, and then loaded on the back of an Army two and a-half ton truck for the drive to the local morgue. Our C-47 crew would fly the four caskets to Bremen for eventual shipment to the States. Patiently waiting were the next of kin!

The GR conspired to add to my 'entertainment' without consulting me beforehand. As part of my continuing coverage, I arrived at the morgue one morning and spoke through the door to the GR personnel within. 'Fellows, I know you're in there,' I called. 'Before you open up, put all the dead bodies away, please.' A disembodied voice answered, 'Right, Steve, the last body is back in its bin, so enter whenever you like.'

Entering, I was shocked to find three GR GIs trying to force a 6'2" drowned seaman into a 6'-pine box. Of course he wouldn't fit! Even as an amateur, I knew it couldn't be done. As professionals, they knew better, but tried nevertheless. All three men, surrounding the box, squeezed and bent the poor departed fellow one way and another, as if he were a party balloon. If they pressed one way, he bulged in another; with his knees higher than the box, it was impossible to close the lid and seal his fate. Although none of their attempts succeeded, they thought it good fun, laughing all the more, sensing my mounting irritation.

'C'mon, Steve, just don't stand there, give us a hand. Or better yet, grab one. The more the merrier. Be a sport.'

'You're all mad!' I shouted.

That made them laugh even more. I left them to their bizarre task and stormed out, but the joke was really on me. As an afterthought, I never became used to the severe and pervasive odor that went with this work and I don't know how those guys did, either.

My picture story was almost complete. To finish, I needed to record the process by which the bodies scattered through some of Norway's remotest regions were found and exhumed. The cooperation between the local villages and the GR in Oslo was vital. Much depended upon newspaper advertisements requesting information and assistance. Combined Norwegian-American teams, including locally recruited gravediggers, would make their way to a recently discovered burial mound. All that followed was the same as I described previously. We completed our assignment soon after. When the CO invited us into his office, he offered us another assignment in Spain. Some Special Forces personnel had crashed there, too. For light relief, I switched my mind to castanets, guitars, and wailing for singing. 'Sounds good,' I replied.

On the terrace of a restaurant, on a beautifully clear and crisp sunny day, with a magnificent view of Oslo fjord and the harbor, our lunch conversation turned to film and Hines asked, 'Have you ever seen Marlene Dietrich in *The Blue Angel* ? or Conrad Veidt in *The Cabinet of Doctor Caligari* ?' I shook my head. 'These films, except for *La Grande Illusion*, which was produced in France, were produced in Berlin between the wars.' They're classics; try to see them. All three will add to your appreciation of film as an art form.' Four years later, enrolled in art school and studying photography, I saw all the classic art films he recommended; not only was he right, but I never forgot them. The return flight to Paris was uneventful.

22

I Lead A Group of Poles Across France

At the close of the Nuremberg War Crimes Trials in late 1946, the Allied court sentenced 11 Nazi war criminals to death by hanging. Only Hermann Goering, former Commander of the Luftwaffe and Reichsmarschall, the 11th to be executed, escaped the hangman by swallowing a vial of potassium cyanide hidden on his person a few hours before he was scheduled to be executed. Some of those who didn't escape were former Foreign Minister Ribbentrop, the former head of the Central Security Service, Ernst Kaltenbrunner, and the former Chief of Staff, Field Marshal Wilhelm Keitel.

In his book *Nuremberg*, Airey Neave wrote that, 'photographs taken after the Nazi war criminals were hanged in mid-October at Nuremberg showed that many had blood on their faces caused by striking the trap door as they dropped. Woods assured the Allied officer in charge that the injuries occurred after their necks were broken and they were dead. Reports by journalists who witnessed the executions claimed that the executions were bungled, and that the men died slowly. One said that they choked to death and Ribbentrop struggled for air for twenty minutes.' This account corroborates my own experience with Woods as hangman.

I had no further news of Woods until, by accident, I found a short two-column article in a European edition of the *Stars and Stripes*, the Army newspaper, that a master sergeant, identified as one John Woods, hangman, was found dead, washed up on the shore of an island in the South Pacific months after Japan surrendered. No reason for his death was given.

Soon after, my opportunity to shoot a picture story in Spain fell through because General Francisco Franco, the Fascist dictator, refused to open his country to foreign fact-finding cameramen and journalists. In place of Spain, I was assigned to lead a convoy of five 6x6 trucks containing Signal Corps radio equipment to an Army supply depot in Mannheim, Germany. All of the truck drivers were Polish, whose command of

English was rudimentary.

When I arrived at the office, La Fleur had all of the necessary documents ready in a large manila envelope sitting on his desk. He handed the envelope over and walked me to the door. I stood there talking for a few more minutes, 'I'll pick up a jeep from the motor pool and rendezvous with the drivers at the Invalides.'

'Don't forget, after you've delivered the trucks to the Supply Depot Officer in Charge at Mannheim, make sure the Polish drivers are safely on board the Paris train. After that, dream up a picture story for me and shoot it on your return. Take your time. OK?'

Walking down the steps, I turned, waved, and said, 'See ya.'

In the artificial twilight of the underground garage, the motor pool mechanic, an Italian kid from Brooklyn, assured me that my assigned jeep was in top shape. He added gasoline to the tank and Jerri can, filling both to the brim, while I signed off the trip ticket and tossed my val pack and camera gear on the rear seat. 'Take it easy, and don't put any money on the Dodgers!' I shouted as I gunned the engine and drove up the ramp into the sunlight. After racing over the Pont Alexandre III, I entered the esplanade, skidded to a halt in front of the lead truck, and parked like the others.

The drivers, dressed in dark green Army fatigues, stopped what they were doing. A young, well-disciplined Polish lieutenant came forward, stood at attention on the sidewalk, clicked his heels and saluted. Representing the others, he introduced himself and offered his hand. I climbed out of and leaned against the jeep. Having opened the manila envelope, I shuffled through the papers and found the personnel list. I gave it to him and requested he call the roll. After each name, the man in question shouted, 'Here' until all the names were called. He turned to me, saluted again, and said, 'Sir, all 11 men are present and accounted for.'

I nearly returned the salute but stopped my arm from going higher than my waist. With the equivalent rank of major, I was still a civilian in uniform. Grudgingly admitting I was enjoying my new role of convoy commander, reveling in the twin feelings of power and importance. I sensed why General George S. Patton, leading an army of a quarter of a million men into battle, wore a lacquered helmet with four silver stars emblazoned across its front, a holstered ivory-handled revolver clinging to each hip, strapped and highly polished leather field boots, and a beribboned tailor-made tunic. My God! This was Take One. This was theater!

I addressed them in my most serious parade ground voice. 'As you know, each truck will have a team of two men; however, the lieutenant, acting as my chief of staff and liaison officer, will be my driver. I suggest that we leave now, drive to Metz, and spend the night there. We ought to cover the 200 miles in about six hours. We'll take a meal break at Chalons s/Marne, which is little more than half way. I've traveled this route a number of times, so if the weather holds and the route isn't too torn up, we shouldn't have any trouble. OK?' Running to their trucks as if they were a squadron of Battle of Britain Spitfire pilots at some forward fighter airfield in Kent, they climbed aboard. I said to myself, 'Christ, Steve, lighten up, this isn't a suicide mission.' I walked over to the grass verge in sight of my troops and shouted, 'Start engines,' which was followed immediately by a burst of noise and a cloud of blue exhaust as they coughed into life.

While the lieutenant sat behind the wheel awaiting my orders to move out, I stood erect in the open jeep, holding on to the edge of the windshield, and motioned with the double up-and-down clasped fist movement of my right arm the signal for 'Let's get the show on the road.' We crossed the Seine and drove toward Meaux, an ancient town in the Marne Valley, 30 miles distant. 'If you can maintain an average speed of 40 miles per hour,' I told the lieutenant, 'we can make our estimated time of arrival to Metz, give or take an hour.' He nodded.

At Chalons, we stopped to eat at a converted house/restaurant where I had eaten before. It was owned and operated by a mother and daughter. Not only were they glad to see me but also pleased that I had a tribe of very hungry customers in tow. 'Men,' I said, 'you are about to be served the best damn omelets in the world.' One of the drivers returned from his truck carrying a concertina, on which he began playing a Polish love song. Some of the others began dancing to the plaintive melody they knew so well. Between mouthfuls, we sang to a musical accompaniment. Before we left, two men jumped on to a table and did an acrobatic Polish country dance to the strains of one of their homeland's most popular folk songs. At the finale, they waved their caps in the air, shouted, and leapt from the table. There was much applause and cheering. As we mounted our trucks for the drive to Verdun, 25 miles away, the two women, our Crusade's Hospitallers, stood in the doorway, dressed in their simple cotton frocks and aprons, and waved goodbye, wishing us God's speed.

One hour later, we crossed the Meuse River and drove through the fortress town of Verdun. At Metz, food and shelter beckoned for the night before we went on to Mannheim the next day. We were passing through a region of Lorraine familiar to General Patton's combat divisions, a region of rolling hills, countless rivers and streams, deep green forests, and tangled woods, where towns and villages were once fortified. Because the ground rose gently from west to east, his troops had to attack uphill. In September 1944, he and his army became bogged down in a ghastly war of attrition. It took us a little over an hour to drive from Verdun to Metz. It took Patton three months to cover the same distance. To thwart his attacks, Metz was protected by a series of 35 forts anchored to Fort Driant, which from the air appeared to be one large concrete slab covering 355 acres. Ringed by concrete walls seven feet thick and moats, and defended by four batteries — two each of three 100 mm guns and two each of three 150 mm howitzers, as well as two 100 mm turret guns, and heavy and automatics weapons — it was a daunting and formidable enemy obstacle.

American infantry attacks mounted against Driant in severe cold and freezing rain, through mud and across flooding rivers, were repulsed by the German defenders. In 10 days of fighting, 50 percent of the assaulting infantry were killed or wounded, forcing the Americans to withdraw. Finally, Metz fell to the 20th Corps, the first military force to capture the city by storm since 451 AD; the Germans capitulated on November 22 after heavy house-to-house fighting, but the defenders of Driant held out for another three weeks. A victorious Patton entered the city's gates with sirens screaming. Our arrival was punctuated by the honk of our jeep's horn cautioning pedestrians to stand clear. The siege of Metz was remembered as one of the longest and bloodiest battles of an ugly attritional campaign.

We billeted in Ft. Driant. The trucks, parked in a courtyard, were protected by armed guards. Covered in dust, a consequence of the poor roads en route, we showered in bathrooms deep underground and after dinner, before turning in, I was shown the fort's subterranean layout and impregnable defenses. When I showered and shaved the following morning, my bath towel was missing. One of the drivers kindly offered his, which I gladly accepted. I rubbed my face and body down vigorously in the brisk morning air, not realizing that I would pay a high price for his kind gesture and my ready acceptance.

Driving east through the broken countryside, dotted with aging camouflaged Maginot Line forts dug into the hills, we followed the road through a large tract of tangled woods. The dense vegetation, large hardwood trees, and coniferous evergreens prevented the sun from reaching the forest floor. Beyond the third rank of trees, regardless of direction, a still blackness took over, concealing everything. I'd felt the same unease and anxiety on patrol in similar surroundings during the war. The winding road rose in height to a thousand feet and exposed the convoy to lashing rain and the full force of the prevailing northwest winds.

Provoked by the gloom of the encroaching and sinister forest, I recalled that during the fall of 1944, in the Vosges mountains of eastern France, my depleted outfit and others like it were in short supply of everything — clothing, ammunition, and even food. A stale bar of concentrated chocolate per day failed to maintain health and vigor. Sometimes in the early evening, a jeep and trailer laded with aluminum containers of hot food arrived over unmarked trails. It was difficult to survive in such a deprived environment, high in lethality. We were more a rabble than an army, clinging to these forested slopes. Without proper food and rest, the induced physical stress was many times greater than fighting on the relatively flat terrain found elsewhere in Europe. Italy, the forgotten campaign, was the exception.

I shuddered and turned to the lieutenant. He told me that some of his drivers had fought at Cassino, having served in the 2nd Polish Corps under General Wladyslaw Anders. The lieutenant and his men were in the 2nd Polish Armored Brigade, in support of the 3rd Carpathian and 5th Kresowa Divisions, which fought a life-and-death struggle against the best unit in the German Army, General Heidrich's 1st Parachute Division. Many of his friends were killed while taking the monastery of Cassino. The battle raged from May 11–14, but when it was over, half the paratroopers were dead.

'I was within 10 miles of your lines,' I replied. 'Your gun flashes were lighting up the night sky above the mountains.'

'We are comrades,' he said solemnly. Forbach near the Franco-German border and the once fortified Siegfried Line were three miles distant.

An American survivor of the battle for Forbach described it as 'A grey and miserable dawn, with drizzle falling through a blanket of thick fog. In the murk, the battle went on, house by house, street by street, throughout the day.' My jeep and trucks bypassed the town, rolled through battered Saarbrücken, and stopped for free coffee and dough-nuts at the roadside commissary at Kaiserslautern, still sporting the same spiked German .88 mm artillery piece out front. Just like the pre-vious GIs who had penetrated the primary German defenses in front of the Siegfried Line in 1944, we had entered Germany east of Saar-brücken in the region of the Saar-Palatinate.

By following the corridor for another 35 gentle sloping miles, we'd jump the Rhine at Ludwigshafen and hit Mannheim on the other side. 'Jump' was part of British Field Marshal Bernard Montgomery's unoffi-cial terminology. He rarely used the word 'cross' when planning a river operation, possibly thinking that by substituting 'jump' for 'cross,' he increased the possibility of reaching the far bank successfully, possibly believing that words are magical and the thought the deed. By early afternoon, we stopped on the western edge of the Rhine to get a better look at the river and the city on the opposite bank, more than 300 yards away. Allied bombing and ground fighting had flattened large parts of both cities. One steel bridge, courtesy of an American Army engi-neer battalion, allowed for river 'jumping.' All the previously existing bridges had been destroyed, but their collapsed central spans had been removed, allowing for river traffic. Under the direction of an MP sign-aling us to move on, we drove across, our tires whirring over the steel mesh matting. On the Mannheim side, the damage to its port facilities and town center by Allied air raids were clearly visible and made for slow going.

Toward the end of the war, the 44th Infantry Division took Mannheim on March 29, 1945 without a fight. A Baedeker guidebook described Mannheim in 1911 as an attractive city located at the confluence of the Rhine and Neckar rivers, with a town center forming a chessboard of 144 residential blocks known only by letter and number, according to their position. Somewhere within the remaining chessboard was the Signal Corps depot I was searching for.

The city's inhabitants were still digging themselves out from the war. The Signal Corps depot was located in a large factory warehouse situ-ated on the Mannheim chessboard's perimeter, whose buildings and brick walls were separated by a high main gate. I reported to the officer in charge and signed and exchanged the required documents. The men and I would be billeted at a hotel the officer's unit had requisitioned. Returning to his office, he ordered a three-quarter ton truck and a driver from the motor pool to carry the Polish drivers. Taking our leave, the lieutenant and I followed in our jeep while the men sat in the rear of the truck.

German POWs waited on us at dinner in the hotel dining room, fussing over our every move. 'God,' I thought, 'All we need now are violins, canaries, and Franz Lehar's music to recreate Wilhelmine Berlin.' Although the hired German chefs were inventive and combined local produce with American supplies, the fare — solid Army chow — failed to surprise. White bread, almost impossible to find in post-war Germany and rationed in France and England, was readily available in the Army mess and much sought after by the indigenous population emerging from the rubble. White bread, like clean white bed sheets, was a symbol of a nation's economic health and recovery.

We moved from the dining table into the lounge nearby and ordered cognac from another obsequious waiter, who quickly scurried away to fill our order. I wondered what he did in the war and felt uncomfortable. Maybe the drinks were getting to me, because I remembered the GI in Charlie Company who received a 'Dear John' letter from his girl, after being wounded in Italy. He read it aloud to Reigle, Gualandi, and me at mail call one afternoon, just before we moved from Salerno. In a style befitting a telegram, she told him that their relationship was ended, stop, because she met and fell in love with a civilian, stop. The jilted soldier believed he was fighting in defense of virtuous women everywhere. He, like Christ, displayed his scarred shoulder and wounded chest as proof.

Wanting to leave Mannheim earlier than planned, I prevailed upon the officer to provide for the Polish contingent's rail journey to Paris. On the following morning, taking my leave right after breakfast, I walked out of the hotel to find the Polish lieutenant and his 'band of brothers' gathered around my jeep. Now I knew how Washington, Napoleon, and Patton felt when they took leave of their troops for the last time, experiencing the ineffable, the hint of a tear, the gravel throat in need of clearing. I mumbled something incomprehensible under my breath while the lieutenant walked me to the driver's side of the jeep. Before I climbed on board, he clicked his heels and saluted. I put my free hand on his shoulder and squeezed gently, as we shook hands. Deeply touched, trying to make a fast get away, I mistakenly shifted into second gear rather than first. The jeep howled against such abuse and bucked along like a pinto pony until I found the proper combination.

I followed the river road south to Hockenheim and reached Speyer on the west bank of the Rhine. The fighting here, as in the rest of the 'Saar-Palatinate triangle,' was part of *Operation Undertone*, the third stage of the Allied advance to the Rhine in early 1945.

Rather than stop at Strasbourg, the capital of Alsace, which had been absorbed into Hitler's Third Reich and suffered until liberated in late 1944, I carried on another hour before reaching St. Hippolyte — St. Pilt in German — a picturesque village of half-timbered houses nestling against the Vosges on the western edge of the Rhine plain. Baskets of red flowers hung from every window, in contrast to the background of the crossed black timbers and white plastered walls of the houses. Chipped, gouged, and scarred by artillery and tank fire, they were stark reminders of the disruptive signs of battle.

Impressed, I strolled along one of the narrow streets leading to the surrounding vineyards, in search of a local négociant from whom I could purchase a variety of bottles. Two aging women, dressed in black and with thin white hair, one sporting a slight moustache below her arched nose, the other with an eye that drifted off on its own, ignoring the movement of the other, observed and greeted me from a window seat. 'What are you doing here?' they asked in affectionate and motherly tones.

Playfully, I said, 'I'm on my way to purchase some of your wine and then visit Haut-Köenigsburg.'

Assuming I was an American in uniform, they cackled like magpies, 'Did you know that an American infantry division, the 36th from Texas, arrived in St. Hippolyte on the December 2, 1944?'

I nodded, 'That was my division,' but they waved my words away and eagerly continued.

'We saw the soldiers emerging from the nearby hills. There were many explosions, and bullets and shells flew in every direction. Look.' they pointed their gnarled fingers at the ragged bullet holes carved into the plaster on both sides of the window, and where shell fragments had left creases on the walls of the house. 'We were extremely frightened and trembled on the floor before seeking shelter in a wine cellar.' Both of them nodded, recalling their bittersweet ordeal and emotional anguish. Before closing their shutters, they said in unison, 'Thank you for coming.' Walking away, I didn't know if they meant now or then.

I found a wine merchant; the ground floor of his house was used as a commercial enterprise and tasting room. Attached to his living quarters was a large warehouse piled high with crates and barrels of local wine. Within, the air was cool and smelled of fermented grape. He was a big man, with large hands and a leonine head, dressed in dungarees and a blue denim shirt open at the collar, looking more like a field hand than a businessman. Like the prominent veins on the back of his hands, he seemed full of life. What seemed to be a millimeter away from his lower lip and almost merging with it was the dangling stub of a live cigarette. How Frenchmen avoid burning themselves when smoking remains an unsolved mystery to me. He let the cigarette stub drop to the floor and lit another, inhaling deeply. 'If you are looking for exceptional wines, you have come to the right place,' he said proudly. 'We are fortunate here, and you will benefit, because the high Vosges above us protect these vineyards.'

I sampled. He paused, 'Well? What do you think?'

'Each wine is delicious and distinctive, much as you've described, but I have decided on a half case each of the Pinot Blanc and Gewurztraminer.' As I paid the bill, he mentioned something of his experiences in the local Resistance and the coming of the 36th. Learning that I too had served, he looked directly at me, shook my hand, which became lost in his, and insisted that I accept a bottle of Crémant d'Alsace, a dry sparkling white wine, as a gift. There was something to be said about wartime comradeship in a country that prides itself on its food and drink. I would imagine that gifts of comradeship vary from country to country; an elephant tusk, a standing stone, some more portable and potable than others.

The jeep was in its element. I traveled a winding, increasingly steep road west of the village for eight miles to the Chateau of Haut-Köenigsburg, taken undamaged by the 36th before attacking St. Hippolyte. Standing 1,500 feet above sea level, it has served as a mountain bastion for nobles, clergy, and robber barons since 1147. Ordered by Hitler to flee from Vichy, Marshal Pétain and his entourage stopped here on their way to Sigmaringen, Germany in August 1944. From the ramparts, through the slight haze and smoke, I could see the outline of the Black

Forest, 27 miles to the east across the Rhine plain.

Although interested in the chateau's history, I had come for a differ-ent purpose. According to Hines, Jean Renoir, the director and son of the Impressionist painter, filmed much of *La Grande Illusion* on location here in 1937. I walked around, visually recording the fortress's stone galleries and outer walls, my boots scraping against the precipitous wooden steps whose path followed the contour of the hill. Penetrating the stark interior, I found it empty of furniture and the walls damp and unadorned. Entering the chapel alone, there seemed to be few visi-tors. I felt that Haut-Köenigsburg knew little of human habitation. Like Dracula's castle on the Borgo Pass, remote in its wooded surroundings, a medieval stronghold whose time had come and gone, it offered little consolation and joy to the innocent, unassuming passer-by. Much like our own world, shattered by war, it was seeking to regain a lost confi-dence.

Consulting my map, I entered Ste. Marie aux Mines 15 minutes later, where 12,000 inhabitants clung to their steep Vosges surroundings like pronghorn antelope, at an altitude of 1,200 feet. I sipped schnapps for warmth and ordered lunch at a restaurant overlooking the town square. While awaiting my first course, the small guide book on the table iden-tified Ste. Marie in text and pictures as a holiday village surrounded by flowers in summer and snow in winter, proposing that its silver mines, forests of firs, and ski runs were well worth a visitor's time. As carefree as the guidebook sounded, by contrast, the men of the 36th spent two weeks during the winter of 1944 trying to wrest Ste. Marie and a series of Vosges passes from the Germans. I remembered that the sky was perpetually overcast, darkness came early, and shelter from an endless mixture of rain, sleet, and snow was unobtainable. In this miserable winter wonderland, its quietude interrupted by the crunch of explod-ing shells on the frozen earth and the rattle of machine-gun fire, no attacking army had ever forced a crossing of the Vosges from west to east until the 36th arrived.

The young waitress, after placing the soup tureen and bowl on the ta-ble, caught my eye and smiled, pleased that I was an American and the proud owner of a jeep, lamenting that few soldiers passed through the town now. 'After the excitement in late January 1945, the whole town slumbered.'

'What do you mean?' I asked.

'Well, I was serving lunch that day when the square filled with GIs. While my customers were eating, I noticed that the number 28 was stenciled on all the trucks' bumpers, and the GIs wore a red shoulder patch shaped like a keystone.'

'Easy enough' I said, showing off my grasp of military knowledge. "That's the 'Bloody Bucket' shoulder patch worn by the men of the 28th Infantry Division, originally a National Guard outfit from Pennsylvania.' Thinking out loud, I mused, 'I thought it fought the war with the American 1st Army up north, first in Normandy and then through the horrors of the Huertgen Forest near Aachen — but here? Maybe they were part of a convoy, traveling from point A to point B, and stopped for a break,' I asked.

'No, not at all.' she interposed. 'They were here for an execution!'

'What?' I nearly shouted and added, 'How would you know?'

'Well,' she replied, unaffected by my questionable behavior, 'I could show you the house and the courtyard where the prisoner was shot.'

'Is the house close by?'

'Yes, on the rue du General Bourgeois, number 86. That's where it happened.'

'Wait a minute,' trying to regain my composure, 'suppose the victim was a German spy impersonating an American? The Germans did use SS men masquerading as American soldiers, who were trained to infiltrate behind the lines to cause as much chaos as possible.'

'No,' she insisted. 'He was an American. I'm certain.'

'I'd like to see where the man was executed,' I said, and waited for her answer.

She nodded. 'I'll take you there when I finish working.'

We walked off the square through the drizzle; it was only a short uphill walk to number 86, a private dwelling overlooking a large courtyard enclosed by a high stone wall. I calculated from the wall's perimeter that the courtyard was large enough to contain a firing squad, the victim, and visiting dignitaries. There was nothing more to be seen. 'What did the townspeople make of it all?' I questioned.

'They wondered why Ste. Marie had been chosen. When we heard the rifle fire and saw puffs of smoke drift over the wall, we were as startled as farm animals.'

'More than you bargained for?'

Her voice dropped. 'Yes,' she replied. I concluded that the man executed on the other side of the wall in this wet and dreary village, threatening at every corner, or so it seemed, to slide into the valley below, had deserted before the enemy. Rape and murder, civilian crimes committed by a serving soldier, are punishable by hanging. Thinking of my own brush with the military, I wondered what the stranger had done to deserve such a fate.

I thanked the waitress and followed the road up and over the Ste. Marie Pass to Epinal. As I rolled through eastern France, thoughts of the executed GI eventually disappeared from my memory without a trace, or so I thought. Another eight years would elapse before I discovered who this soldier was.

23
Barber's Itch

Early the next morning, the phone rang in my Paris apartment. 'Steve?' It was Helen, a Red Cross friend from Reims, asking if I would be interested in a seven-day assignment to Holland two days from now. I was interested, but I wanted to clear it with La Fleur. We agreed that I'd call her in two hours with my answer. I staggered into the bathroom, bent over the sink, and ran cold water over my face and head. Looking in the mirror, I saw that my face was red and swollen. Sun poisoning? Small sores had formed on my cheeks. Before I did anything else, I'd better make an emergency visit to the medics.

The doctor at the clinic put on a pair of rubber gloves, took my face in his hands, and turned it slowly from side to side. A light-colored liquid slowly oozed and dribbled down my cheeks from the sores he pressed. He swabbed my face with cotton and told me to visit the Skin Ward of the 239th General Hospital because they were much better equipped than he. 'What you've got is a bad case of impetigo, commonly known as 'barbers itch.' In medical terms, it's a contagious pustular disease of the skin. You haven't used anybody else's bath towel lately, have you?'

'I don't think so.' My journey to Holland was out of the question. He must have sensed how flat I felt, because he restrained himself from trying to be funny.

The nurse on duty took one look at my face and swathed it in bandages so that I looked like the actor Claude Rains in the '30s film *The Invisible Man*. I didn't get any rest that night, 'gift-wrapped' in bandages, because the ooze penetrated through sections of the gauze and stuck to the pillow cases anyway. Trapped within the bandages, my face itched.

I lay vulnerable and isolated in the darkened ward. Only the nurse's station offered an oasis of light. My thoughts churned. How easily was I tossed aside by a bout of impetigo and a photo assignment ruined! I grudgingly admitted that life wasn't here for my convenience. On the contrary, it was filled with trouble. If I didn't leave room for the unexpected, any flexibility in living based on an acceptance of circumstances beyond my control would be lost. If I chose not to face reality, there was nothing left but fantasy's pain and disappointment. I could do something about reality; there was nothing I could do about fantasy, except dream on. My thoughts droned on and on until finally dawn came, but not before I thought: If only there were someone to talk to.'

When the doctor, accompanied by the nurse, made his rounds early the following morning, there was nothing for it but to have my headdress removed. Trembling from the ordeal that followed, sitting up in bed, looking out from my ravaged face, my eyes no more than pinholes of light, I felt dismantled. The doctor corroborated the first physician's cursory diagnosis of 'barber's itch.' 'Any idea where you might have picked it up?' he asked.

'Probably Metz — I borrowed a towel to dry my face after shaving. How was I to supposed to know how contagious impetigo was?' I said impatiently.

The doctor ordered, 'You will have to wash your face at least three times a day with a medicinal soap. No,' he corrected himself, 'You will have to scrub your face at least three times a day if you want to stop the rot and get out of here. A week's effort ought to do it. Scrubbing will keep any more scabs from forming and allow the air to get at the existing ones.' He walked away, saying, 'Next time you better be more careful.'

My face, alive and phobic, felt raw and jumped at the touch. I must have winced a thousand times while scrubbing across the open sores proliferating on my face. Primitive? Desensitized? Was there an alternative? I hated it! The soap looked like a composite of crushed paving stone and cement, abrasive as sandpaper. Even following orders, the battle seemed lost for the first three days. My eyes glistened. The daily route march across my face was an ordeal but, halfway through my scouring, the ooze and scab production seemed to lessen; both the nurse and the doctor agreed. On balance, I had gained little because my face was in tatters.

I became sensitized to the scrubbing and afraid to look in the mirror. When I did, I saw long irregular scars running down both cheeks to my lower jaw, and my eyebrows were missing! The nurse told me they were gone forever, never to return. Stunned by the news, I physically slumped. Somewhere in a lost trunk there is an identity photo taken soon after I left the hospital. It's supposed to look like me but looks more like a mangled Martian. I was *Scarface* doubling for the *Man in the*

Iron Mask or the *Phantom of the Opera*. Forced to choose between anonymity and visibility, admitting that no woman would ever come close to me again or stay for a while, I was finished!

Released from the hospital, I sat alone in the bus. I gazed through the window, avoiding eye contact with any of the passengers, and reminded myself for the thousandth time that life offered no guarantees, no free lunches or safe harbors. Later, I purchased a black fedora and wore it to keep my face bathed in shadow.

24

An Intercontinental Romance

World War II was considered to be the most destructive armed conflict in history. Much of Western Europe lay in ruins. Combat, artillery, and bombing destroyed roads, bridges, and railroads and scorched the countryside. I traveled along one of these roads during the early fall of 1946, and I remember the road mileage clearly between Brussels and Paris. It was 198 miles. Something happened along it that remains embedded in my memory!

This road, designated as 'main' or 'national' during the days before auto routes and freeways, had been poorly maintained during the war; truck convoys moved along it day and night, and it was badly damaged by shellfire. There were potholes from one end to the other. Here and there along its journey there were truck stops, where a driver, usually a black soldier from a Quartermaster trucking company, could get a questionable cup of coffee — usually tasteless, always tongue-scorching hot — and doughnuts.

Enter Eric Pilkington, a British minister, who was chosen by His Majesty's Government because of his experience and knowledge in the construction and building industry. He was to negotiate with the American Army's liquidation representatives at their La Louviere depot near Brussels. The Americans were selling the kind of surplus material he sought — engineering equipment and heavy-duty earth-moving machinery. In Britain and other European countries in need of reconstruction, machinery was in short supply.

A former British Army officer, Pilkington had fought in East Africa during the war and had a reputation as a big game hunter who considered the African buffalo to be the most formidable and dangerous of game. Assigned to him, I would create a photo essay of these proceedings and the equipment purchased. Eric was destined to be the essay's main character. He and I became good companions, particularly after time spent at the Metropole Hotel bar in Brussels. The road in question was on the city's outskirts. Once the surplus sale ended, Eric and I, at

307

his invitation, would head for Africa and hunt for the African buffalo.

The amount and size of earth-moving equipment on sale was awesome, rarely seen by most civilians in daily life. Consider that in an armored engineer battalion and comparable units, equipment consisted of armored bulldozers based on the Caterpillar D9 civilian design. Steam shovels, cranes, excavators, track loaders, and trucks also were used, as required, as part of winning the war, and were now for sale. Shipping was a vital factor for consideration.

After two days of preparation and shooting, I completed the photo essay and in the early evening made for the Metropole's bar for a last drink with Eric. I was leaving for Paris the following morning. Much to my surprise and satisfaction, I met, for the first time, the regal Gladys Holland in a U.S. Army officer's uniform, two bar stools away. Tall, curvaceous, and blonde, there was nothing unfeminine or disproportionate that could camouflage her ample charms. Eric knew something about Big Game and began his hunt. I had much to learn. She wore her overseas cap at a slight angle, the end of her tie folded in between the second and third buttons of her properly pressed shirt, in regulation. She smiled and slowly twirled the stem of her glass clockwise. 'What a knockout,' I thought. In her presence, the bar seemed to be one shade brighter. If I were 21, I figured she must be about 23. I knew where I had traveled from — I wondered about her. Although dressed in her American uniform, she spoke English with a sophisticated French accent. Not unusual, but distinct for one so attired. Eric's charm worked wonders and soon we were a threesome going off to dinner.

Her story was simple and direct, not unlike one written for a 'damsel in distress.' Her administrative position with an Army headquarters in Brussels was due to end in a few days. She was reassigned to serve as a general's private secretary in Berlin as soon as possible.

I glibly said, 'So what's the problem? Take a train to Berlin. Problem solved!'

She looked across at me, replying, 'There are no trains from Brussels to Berlin. The lines are down.'

'Come on,' I said impatiently, knowing how the Army operates. 'There's gotta be an alternative.'

'Yes,' Gladys, answered, 'Rail lines run to Berlin from Paris.'

'So,' I said, feeling in command. 'I can get you to Paris. I've got an Officer's WC-7 Command Car with a French driver at my disposal. That is, if you can leave early tomorrow morning. Then I can arrange to have you on a sleeper for Berlin in plenty of time once we arrive at Paris' Gare du Nord.' Eric looked across at me with a quizzical expression, the stalking of his 'prey' doomed by a sudden unimagined ending. Gladys was most thankful.

She seemed more relaxed with the Berlin situation sorted out, and with a few more glasses of wine smoothing her way, we learned that what was once a mystery vanished with the telling. Her mother was a French-Belge who married a First World War American soldier from Texas. They moved to Ft. Worth, where Gladys was born. The marriage ended in divorce, and Gladys and her mother returned to Belgium to live. Educated in Brussels, with dual citizenship and being bilingual, Gladys found important office work easily within the Allied command. The dinner at an end and facing a long drive the next morning, we separated to pack.

Vowing to meet again, Eric and the two of us said goodbye in front of the Metropole. Hunting African buffalo would have to wait. Off we went. Eric stood there and then faded from view. There was ample room in the command car's rear seat for Gladys and me as the French driver settled down on the road to Paris. It was not long, about 10 miles out of Brussels before we ran into what I called 'La Route Fracturée,' a beat-up road, because of its endless potholes, uneven surfaces, and cracks. Not only did the tires take a pounding, but also the shock absorbers compressed to the metal chassis with each unexpected jolt. We too took a pounding, but one result was as unpredictable as it was fortuitous. About 10:30 in the morning, Gladys and I were thrown together by two sharp jolts that sent the torsion bars quivering. Not only were we surprised by the violence of the toss, but also we ended up in each other's arms. After the shockwave diminished, there followed the discovery of an enjoyable embrace. Feminine and manly smells combined. We didn't let go, much to our own surprise and that of the French driver. We kissed, and with each passing pothole and surface crack, we became as intimate as we could be under the circumstances. Was it too good to last? It lasted 'forever,' remorseless, affectionate, and exploratory. Either one of us could have demanded the driver stop or he, being older and wiser, could have pulled off the highway for a 10-minute break. Why we didn't remains a mystery. A parking space, a military vehicle with the ignition turned off, the French driver gone off for a piss call and a cigarette as we satisfied our sexual thirst, would have put 'paid' to our myriad gyrations and acrobatics.

In tribute, for almost 200 miles of this spine-shattering journey, Gladys was a willing, generous, and creative partner. We entered Paris with flags flying. So much for youth! Kissed out, both in need of a dentist, with chafed lips, we hugged each other in farewell when she boarded the Berlin Express. Eagerly, we promised to meet soon, once normalcy was achieved.

We did try but for one reason or another, we never did, at least not in Europe. Even though we talked on the phone frequently and our interest in each other never waned, something always interfered at the last minute. Although I left Paris in November '46 for New York, before departing, I called her in Berlin to say 'Goodbye.' Rest assured, I never forgot her or our journey.

In late '47, I drove from New York by car to Los Angeles and lived there for 42 years before moving to London in '89. There I continued my graduate studies at King's College. One afternoon in '95, weary of research and writing, I turned on the television set as a diversion. Burt Lancaster was starring in a Western film I had never heard of, *Ulzana's Raid*, a 1972 production directed by Robert Aldrich. I would have preferred something else but before I turned it off, a woman portraying a cowboy's wife caught my eye. That face was familiar. I rose and walked closer to the screen for a better look. It was Gladys Holland! Stunned, I watched the remainder of the film to its conclusion. The closing credits verified my belief. She was the only woman in the film; her part was small but well done.

I was inundated with memories of her and our memorable journey. I had to find her! She was seemingly alive and well. Having connections in Hollywood, I was able to make contact through her theatrical agent, identifying myself and requesting a meeting the next time I came to Los Angeles. Her response was immediate, stating how delighted she was to be found again after 60 years! With everything set, we decided to meet at Dupar's Restaurant in the Farmer's Market on the city's West Side at a time and date specified. I arrived first. She arrived soon after. Sitting behind the wheel of a late-model Mercedes convertible was a most attractive blonde who could be no other than Gladys. She entered. Greeting her, we embraced, as if we were still on the road and not in the foyer of a restaurant. What an exciting 'homecoming' after all these years! She felt as good as ever.

As an actress, she had a reasonable but not an extraordinary career playing character parts, such as 'Mrs. Rukeyser' in Ulzana's Raid. Her most memorable achievement was acting alongside Cary Grant and Grace Kelly in the 1955 production of *To Catch a Thief*, one of Hitchcock's best. In one memorable scene, standing beside Gladys, who was playing a sophisticated French woman, Grant drops a gambling chip down her revealing décolleté evening gown. She responds in French. The scene was filmed in the casino at Monte Carlo. Gladys corroborated what I had already gathered from my Internet search, that is: she was an American character actress who played small roles in a number of 1950s films. She was born in Texas and got her start in theater. Later, having learned French from her Belgian mother, she became a French dialogue/voice specialist. What was not stated was that she had been married and had a child who is now a young woman living in New York. Gladys lives in the Hollywood Hills and is widowed. Most of her parts now come from TV commercials.

Gladys invited me to lunch, not at her home in the Hollywood Hills, which was being refurbished, but at her motor home, parked in a fenced cement lot in Burbank. It was on a delightful Southern California day that I drove out there. The lunch was as simple as it was appropriate, a Salade Niçoise, a crusty baguette, and chilled white wine. We still had much to catch up on, but my time in the Southland was running out, and I had other friends and relatives to see from my television days at CBS. Over coffee, I mentioned that I would have to leave soon and explained why. She was disappointed. As I got up to go, she looked at me and, after sharing farewells, said, 'Aren't you going to kiss me?'

I felt somewhat awkward about her request, and responded by saying, 'Well, Gladys, even though we met a long time ago, it's only been a few days since we've reconnected again, and I am a gentleman.'

Her eyes glinted, and she complained, saying, 'Well, they don't make men the way they used to!' Not to let my side down, honored and touched that she remembered too, I grabbed her in my arms and completed what I had failed to do on the road to Paris.

25

Farewell to an Ambulance in Paris

Enough of the pain, the chain-smoking and weight loss, the suicidal thoughts, and the sleepless nights. I grudgingly admitted that it was time to leave Paris. Filled with apprehension, in the fall of 1946 I decided to take a month's vacation and spend it with my family, admitting that it could be a bittersweet and trying episode. Whatever my feelings, my parents had waited long enough for my homecoming, and I couldn't stay away forever. Not that I would add to their enjoyment by my presence after all the hell and anxiety I'd put them through. Most of my worldly goods, cameras, watches — always watches, those that I had acquired while living in Paris — had been packed and shipped.

Prior to leaving, I tried to return the sound unit/ambulance to its rightful owner, the U.S. Army. However, the task wasn't that simple, because I had no idea to which unit of the Army it belonged. Historically, the converted ambulance had been passed from one cameraman to another when the previous owner, if I might use the term loosely, bid farewell before quitting Paris for the last time. When I had first seen the vehicle parked on avenue Kléber, its white unit bumper markings indicated it belonged to the 3264th Signal Photo Service Battalion, but when the 3264th was disbanded and the 3908th took over, the existing bumper numbers changed. Now, with the depleted 3908th on its way home, the ambulance was left behind. If there had been the usual complement of cameramen assigned to Paris in my time, I could have repeated the ritualistic process but, like a parson whose parishioners had evaporated, I had no heir apparent, no young Prince Hal to accept the crown.

The ambulance *cum* sound unit in my possession, having performed yeoman-like service from 1944 onward, was the worse for wear. The transmission growled when shifting into second gear, and the radiator leaked, overheating the engine. The olive drab paint was flecked and the big white star emblazoned on either side of the body, once the symbol of American military might, was fading. Gone were the days of splendor, from the time she had rolled off the assembly line at South Bend or Willow Run to carry the wounded from the beaches of Nor-

313

mandy or the mountains of Bavaria to a hospital. As long as I guided her from behind the steering wheel, I never called her 'Old Girl' or painted 'The Belle of Brooklyn' on the hood; she wasn't my ship, and I wasn't her captain. I didn't steer, I drove.

I talked to a Tech/Sgt. in charge of the motor pool, who told me that without paper work, vehicle registration, and unit designation, it was not his to take. Scanning a long list of vehicle numbers, he found none that matched mine. But it's Army property,' I protested. 'You're right, but not mine,' he said with finality.

The Army moved in strange ways, but my problem remained unsolved. Over the next few days, I called three different motor pools in the Paris area without effect. Out of desperation, I cornered La Fleur. Might one of your French business friends take it off my hands? He shook his head, claiming they were cinema specialists, not auto dealers. I walked out of the office, defeated by the system.

Then I hit upon an idea. I'd sell the damn thing on the black market. 'Why not?' I tried to convince myself. With France returning to normalcy, an owner of a small delivery company would find the vehicle a welcome addition to his business. Sure, he'd have to put it back in shape, but I'd deduct the cost of repairs from the selling price. Seduced by my own thoughts, I gravitated to the smell of a fast buck and was overcome by a sense of greed.

Some sense of sanity intervened. I wondered, 'What was the penalty for selling government property? How long a prison sentence, five, ten years? And just for money. 'Gee Mom and Dad, I was only kidding!' I'd have to be crazy to put myself at risk and toss my future into the garbage can. An inner voice said, 'Stevie boy, when are you going to learn?'

So I devised another scheme, much less fraught with exposure and penalty. The focus of my latest operation zeroed in on the parking lot at the 239th General hospital. I'd dump the ambulance there and walk away from it without even saying goodbye. I wasn't married to the damned thing. I was simply ridding myself of an internal combustion mobile device without attributing any human feeling to it. There were to be no tearful farewells, no community property settlement, no lawyer fees, or Bogart saying, 'We'll always have Paris.' I suppressed or denied any pathetic fallacy! I'd simply ask a friend to follow me in his jeep while I drove to Villejuif. Once within the confines of the hospital's lot, I'd park, turn off the ignition, close the door for the last time, lock the cab and push the key through the partially closed window, climb into the jeep, and evacuate the premises without a backward glance. What was once stuck was now unstuck, and *Operation Oil Change* succeeded without a hitch two days later. Sitting next to my friend in the jeep, waiting for a light to change at Port d'Italie, I said, thinking of Raymond Chandler, film noir screenwriter, 'Farewell My Lovely.' Oops!

'So she didn't mean much to you?' my friend inquired.

I stiffened, holding back the memories. 'Oh,' I responded as casually as I could, 'Just a bit of nostalgia. You know, Freud.'

Paris was in its autumnal glory as I walked across to the Majestic to have lunch with Dan Riley, a civilian colleague who worked in the office above mine. Our friendship was still in its early stages but we liked each other from the start. About 10 years older than me, of a tall, angular build, he seemed sane, sensible, and serene and, from what I gathered, an able administrator. After lunch, strolling down avenue Kléber together in the warm sunshine, Dan figured that a drive along the Seine to Normandy would be a most suitable excursion. 'Ah,' he mused, 'if we only had a car.'

'I guess timing is everything,' I replied, caught up in his enthusiasm, 'because until a few weeks ago, I had one.'

'What happened to it?' Riley asked. 'Somebody steal it?'

I laughed. 'No, just the opposite. The Army refused to take it off my hands, so I dumped it.'

Riley said, 'What do you mean, dumped it?' We had stopped walking and faced each other.

'There wasn't a motor pool sergeant in Paris who was interested in adding a beat-up ambulance to his inventory, so I abandoned the thing over at the 239th General's parking lot.'

It was as if the sun went into total eclipse, plunging the world into complete darkness. Mild man became wild man! He roared. 'So you're the guy!'

'Wait a minute,' I said, backing away, arms outstretched in self-defense.

'Steve, I'm the administrator of the 239th, and that ambulance wasn't part of *my* vehicle allotment either. There was hell to pay!' He looked menacing.

'Listen Riley,' I was desperate. 'The ambulance was 'persona non gra-
ta,' so the parking lot caper was the last resort.' I appealed to his sensi-
bility. 'What would you have done?' I implored, 'Drown it in the Seine?
Next time, you try getting rid of an ambulance.'

'I did, from the time we found it, while the investigating MPs failed to
find the elusive Weiss, address unknown.'

He paused. 'All the other Weiss's we picked up had clean alibis and
knew nothing of the 239th and a battered ambulance, while you slipped
through our net. In the end, we sold it through the recently instituted
Army Surplus Program to a French farmer who works a property east
of Paris. He probably uses it to haul everything, including manure.'

Riley and I remained friends, but each time we meet, he bows slightly
and inquires, 'Ah, the mysterious Mr. Weiss! Going for a drive?' It's a
small price to pay for the torment I had caused him.

26
To the States

La Fleur decided to host a farewell dinner party in my honor at the Officers' Club and reserved a corner table for our small photographic detachment. All of us had shared a number of experiences that were embellished once again in the telling over drinks and dinner. Warming to the gathering, I thanked the four of them for being such good friends. I told them of my plans, to fly to Bremen the day after tomorrow, stay with the photo detachment there, and notify Army transportation in Bremerhaven where I could be reached. That way, while waiting for a ship heading for New York, I would eliminate most of the inconvenience of sharing space with thousands of other GIs camped at the port of embarkation, eager to ship out. My return date was scheduled for December 14, but I'd check with Army headquarters in Manhattan about a week before. Staten Island was both my entry to and exit from the States. At the end of the evening, I was presented with a stainless steel black-dial Hamilton Army wristwatch with a phosphorescent dial and hands, to be sure I returned on time. I assured them we'd be together in a month.

I went to see François Binoche to say goodbye. The bond between us remained as strong as ever. It was 4:00 when we parted, and I changed direction, allowing 35 minutes to rendezvous with Olga at a salon du thé on the Place du Palais Bourbon, situated behind the Assemblée Nationale. Olga was waiting for me in front of the tearoom just as I entered the square from the rue Aristide Briand. She waved. Olga, the consummate Englishwoman on French soil, looked beautiful in a white blouse, a slender necklace of white pearls, a black Chanel suit, with handbag and shoes to match. 'So you're leaving?' she said, pouting, as I kissed her on both cheeks.

I followed her into the salon. Moments later, we were seated across from each other at a table overlooking the square and ordered drinks and dessert. 'Stephen, you're looking better than when I saw you last.'

'Let me guess. My face, swollen in the bright sunlight, a café on the

Champs Elysées just after my return from Mannheim. Right?'

'No, in the hospital after that.'

'I didn't know you came.'

'You were asleep, your face wrapped in bandages. I looked at you for a minute, fiddled with the sheets, asked the nurse how you were, and left. Didn't she tell you, a thin girl from Oklahoma?'

'That's Jesse, but she never mentioned it.'

'Well, you're easily recognizable now; your good looks have returned, but something is missing.'

She looked at me closely, as if dividing my face into squares for better observation. 'Stephen!' she exclaimed.

'Yes, I know; I've lost my eyebrows.' She must have seen how wretched I felt, because she reached across the table and took my hand. From my jacket, I placed a packet of cigarettes on the table.

'The scars are receding, although shaving is a trial, lots of bumps and grooves. There isn't a woman this side of Monte Carlo who'd be interested in me. 'To know me is to love me' won't work anymore.

I can imagine my mother saying at first glance: My God! What have they done to your face?'

She replied, 'Don't jump to conclusions. An ocean voyage will set things straight and by the time you walk down the gangplank, you'll be as good as new.' She looked at me and waited for my response.

'Easy for you to say! A year ago, I weighed 185 pounds. Right now, I'm down to 159 and feel as if I'm my own battlefield, minus a strategy! The war shattered whatever I was at frightening speed. It's as if I don't have the wherewithal to cope on a daily basis. Disturbing, but as yet, not absolute.' I paused and felt like a car firing on three cylinders, not four, with a breakdown a real threat and no rescue van in sight. 'I'm alive, insisting that every day is a bonus, but I don't feel that way.' I took a long drag on my cigarette and slowly exhaled.

'What you need is a change of pace — and time,' she replied. 'How long have I known you, Stephen?'

'Since September 1944,' I answered. 'We met a week before my 19th birthday.'

She took my hand again. 'You're still so young, like a diamond in the rough. Things happen when you're about. Go home, rest, and come back.'

I called for the check and then we stood on the sidewalk, taking a few more minutes before saying goodbye. It began to drizzle. Hugging her, I said lightly, 'See you in early December. In the meantime, thanks for everything, and give Ronnie my regards.'

I left Orly early the next morning with six other passengers on an olive drab C-47 that still had its black- and white-striped D-Day markings on both wings; flying east at 10,000 feet and cruising at 180 miles an hour, we inched toward Bremen over a variegated landscape through cotton candy-looking white clouds. Cities like Brussels and seaports like Antwerp were easily identifiable from the air, but I could only guess at the names of the landlocked towns and cities we crossed en route. Unless you closed your eyes, the *Neder Rijn* (the Lower Rhine) stood out in bold relief, even if it were hundreds of miles away from its Swiss glacial source. Its size and power were impressive, even from our great height.

A car and driver from the Bremen photo detachment were waiting for me on the tarmac near the control tower. I tossed my gear and case of American cigarettes into the back seat of the command car. As we left the airfield and drove toward the city across a flat landscape, I viewed the bomb damage from the 1,000-plane Allied raids. According to RAF estimates, the city was virtually destroyed by the fall of 1942, but I thought Frankfurt looked worse. On the ground, before Bremen surrendered, the level of fighting in April 1945 was intense. British General Brian Horrocks's 30th Corps threatened to cut Germany off from occupied Denmark, which he eventually succeeded in doing.

We parked before a three-story red-brick turn-of-the-20th century private dwelling on a street where some other houses remained intact, having survived the ravages of the bombing. Over drinks in the large ground floor lounge, I was introduced to two of the cameramen and then shown to my room above. I tossed my belongings on a large bed with big pillows casually resting against the curved mahogany headboard and looked around. It was a pleasant, high-ceilinged bedroom containing two neo-Gothic chairs, a carved table on which rested a Grundig radio, a tall armoire and, behind the door, a full-length mirror. Two large windows framed three or four fruit trees standing in a well-kept garden. The remains of a small air-raid shelter tilted toward the rear entrance. I wondered what had happened to the family who lived here before the photographic unit requisitioned the property.

That evening we drove into the medieval market square, watched over by a statue of Charlemagne, and were joined at dinner by Charlie Mazur, who was on the local staff of American Counter Intelligence (CIC). He didn't say much about his work but he turned out to be a rewarding dinner companion who, because of his assignments, knew Bremen and its surrounding area very well. The hotel dining room had seen better days, much like an actress no longer young enough to play the ingénue, but it had two redeeming features: a large rectangular picture window overlooking the market square and, within the room itself, a jazz quartet entertaining in the style of Stéphane Grappelli, Django Reinhardt, and Teddy Wilson; this unknown group of consummate musicians played ballads of the interwar period and slightly beyond. Their interpretation of *You Go to My Head*, performed in 2/4 time as a daring blend of jazz harmonies, was a haunting refrain that evoked thoughts of Suzanne and intensified the meaning of the song's words.

Our conversation turned to photography and those *Life* magazine, Army, and former Hollywood photographers who had documented the war. Some of them, like Robert Capa, Lee Miller, and George Rodger, became celebrities in their own right. The Army photographers from the 163rd and 166th Signal Service Photo Companies who were assigned to an Army headquarters like Patton's Third and covered events throughout his command were relatively unknown. Former Hollywood directors John Huston and George Stevens put the war on motion picture film, sometimes in color, even if part of their documentaries were staged. French photographers Henri Cartier-Bresson and Robert Doisneau used small lightweight cameras to capture aspects of French life under the German Occupation and during the liberation of Paris. By contrast, the authorized Army still camera, the 4x5 Speed Graphic, was the wrong camera for the job. The damn thing was too heavy, weighing about seven pounds, almost as much as the M-1 infantry rifle. Limited in purpose, its wide-angle lens placed the subject too far away. Lifting it out of a foxhole and aiming it at the enemy wasn't something to be recommended because both you and the camera became easy targets.

Before the evening ended, Charlie offered to drive me to Hamburg, where he knew a man who had a brand new Leica IIIC camera for sale. 'What's the going price?' I inquired.

'Forty cartons of cigarettes.'

I calculated, 'That means the camera is worth at least $400 at the going rate. OK, let's do it.'

The following morning, I spoke to an Army clerk in Bremerhaven who said that I would be shipping out at the end of the week. An hour later, Charlie and I drove out of town, armed with 40 cartons of Chesterfields tossed into the back of his 1942 Hudson sedan. Surprisingly, the car was in mint condition, and its chrome fixtures and new paint gleamed. 'How in hell did you find a car like this in war-torn Germany?' I asked, in awe. 'Break into a museum?'

'Hey,' he replied, 'This Hudson is the outcome of a lot of work and effort. When I found it on the outskirts of Bremen, resting on blocks in a bombed-out garage, I didn't think the car would ever run again. Let's say for now that the fellow we're going to see in Hamburg had everything to do with the result.'

It's 50 miles from Bremen to Hamburg via the Autobahn, across the bleak and undulating landscape of Luneberg Heath which separates the two cities. Most of the highway was in good repair, except for a few bridges that had been blown up by the retreating Germans during their headlong retreat from Montgomery's 21st Army Group in April 1945. Soon after, he placed his tactical headquarters and personal caravan somewhere on this inhospitable peat-bogged land that stretched to the horizon and demanded that all enemy forces still resisting in Holland and Denmark, and those parts of Germany west of the Elbe still in German possession, surrender unconditionally. Emissaries from the German High Command agreed and this Regional Instrument of Surrender, to be superseded by any General Instrument of Surrender, was signed at 18:20 hours on May 4, 1945.

Charlie suggested we make a detour of 36 miles to visit the Bergen-Belsen Concentration Camp and the makeshift memorial erected to its inmates. Although I had heard its name mentioned before, I never realized that the camp was constructed on the heath or that one of its inmates was the young Dutch Jewish girl and diarist, Anne Frank. She died from her ordeal a few months before the war ended and was buried somewhere nearby. For this and other incalculable sins, Joseph Kramer, the camp's commandant, known as 'The Beast of Belsen,' was seized, sentenced, and executed in November 1945. Without explaining in detail, I said, 'If you don't mind, Charlie, I'd rather not. I've had enough war to last a lifetime.'

When we entered Hamburg, Charlie downshifted because of the rubble. Obliterated architecture was submerged in a sea of stones, through which we drove cautiously. The stones were piled about four feet high. They reminded me of the stone walls I had climbed on farms in upstate New York. Dark entrances appeared at ground level about every 25 yards in this seemingly lunar landscape. Did people live underground, fearful of and allergic to the weak sunlight? Had Allied bombing polluted the atmosphere? Were they hedgehogs burrowed into the hedgerow? Even coal miners rose to the surface at the end of their shift. The remnants of a church stood like a bent crucifix in the middle distance.

Charlie pulled over to where the road widened slightly, shifted into neutral, and said, 'What you're looking at is the result of a series of night and daylight raids performed by the RAF Bomber Command and American 8th Air Force. Although Hamburg was the target of 187 air raids during the war, bomber attacks reached their height between late July and early August 1943. During this ongoing operation, codenamed *Gomorrah*, the two air forces dropped more than 9,000 tons of bombs, many of them incendiaries that created the first firestorm, an oxygen-laden hurricane-like thermal column, racing in from the outskirts toward the center to replenish the flames hungry for oxygen. Temperatures as high as 1,400 degrees Fahrenheit induced by this phenomenon vaporized thousands of civilians who took shelter. Eight square miles of the city suffered enormous devastation.'

We drove to the Aussenalster, the lake in the center of town where some people had survived the explosions, the metal fragments, and the collapsing streets converted into a raging furnace by jumping into the water. Watching the gentle movement of the lake, I remembered seeing a photograph of a baboon that sought safety from its enemies in an African water hole. Sitting in the center, alone and miserable, the baboon's face was indelibly lined with horror and disgust. I turned to Charlie, saying, 'Who would have thought something like this could happen?' Toward the end of the war, the Allied air forces deliberately bombed German towns and cities of no military consequence.

We paused at the lake for a few more minutes, gazing over a shattered jigsaw puzzle skyline, our eyes trying to fill in the missing pieces where nothing existed. As a young American naval officer on temporary duty with Hamburg's Blohm and Voss shipbuilding yard in 1913, Commander in Chief, Pacific Command (CinCPac) Fleet Admiral Chester Nimitz wrote, 'Hamburg is a wonderful city, and I believe it is more beautiful than any city I have ever seen. Certainly none of our cities can equal it. There are more gardens, parks, and such places, and believe me there are lots of beer kellers.'

Charlie spoke first. 'I think we ought to meet with my German friend.' We plunged back into the rubble, moving painstakingly in first gear, the Hudson bucking in protest over the reduced speed; 15 minutes later we stopped alongside one of those innumerable dark entrances. How Charlie ever found it, I'll never know, because there were no distinctive markings to distinguish it from the others. Charlie removed the distributor cap, put it in his pocket, and then lifted the case of cigarettes off the rear seat. I was right behind him when he bent down to gain entrance without hitting his head and found a flight of wooden stairs. He waited a few steps below ground before continuing until my eyes became used to the half-light. As we scraped from one step to another, I counted 20 steps in descending order before we ran out of them and stood upright in a dungeon-like clearing. Charlie placed the case of cigarettes on the ground beside him, glad to be relieved of its bulky shape, and called, 'Fritz?' The wick of an oil lantern burst into flame, defeating the half-light, forcing it to retreat against the earthen walls; at the same time a deep booming voice reverberated through the enclosure, 'Ach, meine grosse freunde, Charlie. Welcome. You've brought someone.'

Slouched in a tattered, overstuffed easy chair, the speaker was a man of immense proportions. The planes of his face and his lionesque-shaped head were accentuated by the chiaroscuro effect of the lantern. The 16th-century French painter Georges de la Tour effectively used backlighting from a single burning candle to illuminate his portraits in similar fashion. The interplay between the rich highlights and deep shadows achieved the desired mood and cloaked his characters in mystery.

Charlie greeted the big man as if they were old friends. 'Steve, meet Fritz Auber, former racing driver and automotive engineer. He's the fella who built the Hudson.'

I nodded in greeting, and said, 'Congratulations; I'm most impressed.'

He waved us to be seated on the two wood-and-canvas picnic chairs within reach. Glancing around this subterranean lair, I checked the German's inventory. There were three five-gallon Jerri cans of water. Strewn about were some misshapen aluminum mugs, a variety of plates, four chipped cut glass goblets, a few battered kitchen uten-sils, the bottom part of a Welsh dresser, an unmade camp bed, a rough wooden dining table, a few ammunition crates converted into shelves, the oil lantern, and a curved Meerschaum pipe that Fritz sucked on while he and Charlie conversed in German. More times than not, Fritz would reply to whatever Charlie said with an, 'Ach, Zo,' inhale on his pipe, and nod in agreement. The word 'Leica' came into their conversa-tion frequently. I felt the damp earth floor beginning to seep through my boots; pieces of iron water pipes had broken through the existing walls, dripping slightly, and bits of wood flooring stuck out of the ceil-ing. Primitive man and French soldiers serving on the Maginot Line would know such a place. Bottles of wine would mature and flourish here in the chilled air, but capacity was limited. Was this cellar the sole remnant of a house destroyed three years before?

The conversation had come to an end. Charlie said, 'OK,' and turned to me. 'Fritz has a Leica IIIC with a black and chrome body, including the standard Leitz .50 mm lens. According to Fritz, the serial number on the camera indicates it was made in late 1944 and is brand new, never having come out of its box.'

'What's he want for it?'

'He says it worth 40 cartons of cigarettes on today's market.' Charlie looked it over first and passed it on to me.

I checked the shutter speeds, the winding mechanism, and range find-er, concluding, 'Seems fine to me.'

Charlie said. 'Right! It's a done deal.' I shoved the cigarettes over to him. 'Here's the goods, all 40 cartons.'

Fritz grunted in satisfaction, including another, 'Ach, Zo,' and we shook hands. To conclude the deal, he extracted an unlabeled bottle of schnapps from the Welsh dresser and poured some of its caramel-looking contents into three of the dull cut-glass goblets. He raised his hand and pronounced, in an ancient Anglo-Saxon accent, 'Here's mud in your eye.' We laughed.

Using Charlie as my interpreter, I said, 'There's one more thing I'd like to settle before we leave.'

'Ach, zo?'

'Charlie says you can build a Hudson for me during my time in the

States and have it ready for delivery when I return. Thirty to forty days?'

'Yes. Hmm.' He deliberated for a few minutes. 'If I can get all the parts, and if Charlie can assist with some of the purchases...' He interrupted himself. 'I will need some sort of down payment.'

'How much?'

'Thirty percent of $800.' He did the calculation in his head. 'Say, $250? That's not too much?' he inquired.

Charlie interrupted, saying, 'Don't worry Fritz. Go ahead. 'Build it! 'If Steve changes his mind, I'll take it. Lots of guys would die for a car like that. In other words, I'll cover the costs as we proceed and when Steve returns, he can pay me the eight bills.' I liked Charlie and his shaggy lion friend, business-like, reasonable, and accommodating. We said goodbye, climbed to street level, crossed over to the Hudson, surrounded by a band of kids, and gently ground our way out of the area before picking up speed on the Hamburg to Bremen Autobahn. The Leica sat on the seat between us in its black leather case.

The call came through from the Port Authority on the morning of October 30. I was scheduled to sail with the tide on November 1 aboard the M.I.T. Victory. I called Charlie and asked him if he could drive me downstream the 35 miles to the Army base at Bremerhaven, Bremen's deep-water port, situated at the mouth of the Weser. We agreed that early afternoon would be a suitable time to meet.

At 1:00, Charlie arrived. Our drive along the river was an opportunity for taking care of unfinished business, such as my return travel arrangements, approximate arrival time in Bremerhaven, and disposition of the Hudson. 'Steve, once our final plans for payment and delivery are settled, we can meet Fritz in Hamburg and test drive the car. When it's ready, I'll take some leave so we can drive to Paris together.'

Approaching the port, we were overcome by a strong odor of fish. 'Whew!' I said, shaking my head in disbelief, 'Break out the gas masks.' Charlie explained. 'We're passing through the southern part of Bremerhaven's fishing port; the odor clings to everything and gets under your skin. There are 200 fishing trawlers based on Bremerhaven that catch about 1,400 tons a year. It's a big business and a big smell, but tough on the breathing,' Charlie complained.

The MP at the main gate, satisfied with our identification, waved us on. Charlie and I sat in the Hudson for a little while, going over our plans once again, and then he left. I stood on the sidewalk and watched the Hudson recede. There goes one hell of a guy. Harry Shanklin, my old squad leader, and Charlie had much in common. They were kind, reliable, and aware. Seeing Charlie go, I missed them both. Dear Shanklin!

So, as a civilian, I returned to Army life with its long lines, minimalist facilities, and crowded quarters. My papers were approved and stamped for shipment on the M.I.T. Victory. Included was a berth and cabin number, but it was all hurry up and wait. I was one 'sad sack' among many, and the human traffic was bumper to bumper. Still, I couldn't complain, my time here was limited compared to the average GI.

The transportation officer looked small standing in front of a large olive drab cargo ship moored behind him. As he waited for me at the gangplank that bridged the pier to the ship, one among many, it began to drizzle, and smoke curled upward into the leaden sky from the ship's only stack. Holding a clipboard filled with papers in one hand and a pen in the other, the officer ticked off my name after I called out, 'Weiss, Stephen J.' Soldiers, American civilians, and sailors already onboard observed the dockside procedure from various sections of the ship. As I climbed the gangplank and it creaked and swayed under my weight, I mumbled something about the dark, sullen water below and entered an environment in which insulated electric and communication cables, routed in every direction through junction boxes, were clamped to steel bulkheads. Amidst this tangle, I found a sailor who directed me to my cabin, where two two-tiered metal bunks, a few chairs, and a washbasin were jammed together. After carving out a space for myself, I slipped the lock on the porthole and looked out onto a wet, bleak landscape dotted with the somber roofs of commercial sheds and warehouses.

Climbing the gangway to the open deck above, I was curious about my new surroundings, a transport preparing to cross the North Atlantic with a cargo of soldiers and ex-GIs. One of the sailors, dressed in dungarees and a stained white cap, a member of the work party, was taking off a pair of soiled brown leather gloves and reaching for a cigarette when I arrived. Cargo nets loaded with stores swayed in concert with the movement of overhead booms and shouted orders before their contents were lowered into the hold below. The whirring sound of steel cables winding around capstans and the sound of donkey engines under load illustrated the seriousness of the enterprise. 'What's going on?' I asked the sailor.

'We're in a rush to meet the deadline and sail with the tide.'

We sailed on time; the ship's propellers beat a passage down the Weser in the fading light and we headed for the open sea. Past the Frisians and somewhere off Calais, with the North Sea behind us, we entered the Straits of Dover, steaming into a lashing wind. Small fishing boats, many with unfurled sails and fluttering tricolors, tilted at a 45-degree angle on a swiftly moving sea dappled with whitecaps and tossed spume. Salt spray and the odd wave splashed those of us on deck without warning. Soldiers, using the fresh air to fight sea sickness, gathered on the open deck below and leaned against the railings; a few, too ill to watch the French coast slip by, shuffled into the wind, trying to keep their balance. Sea gulls took up formation around the ship and kept us company for the long voyage home against a dark, threatening sky and scudding clouds. Looking out across the Channel, I was reminded that of all the wartime pilots who ditched, only 40 percent survived, rescued from the cold and unfriendly sea by boats suited for the purpose. A sailor on watch pointed in the direction of the June 6, 1944 Allied invasion beaches, extending from Ouistreham on the east to St. Marcouf on the west. Thousands of American and British soldiers had given their lives on and off the beaches and were buried on the high ground beyond, while I, as young as they, was shipping out across the North Atlantic.

EPILOGUE: Searching For Peace in the Post-War World

Three interwoven strands of my life demanded attention: my health — both mental and physical, the pursuit of a career, and the need to put my war experiences and those with whom I served in perspective. From the first, my health took pride of place and became the top priority, without which the other two strands would have remained incomplete and suffered.

After returning home on Armistice Day, November 11, 1946, Brooklyn became my personal ground zero. From the time I walked down the gangplank to my waiting family, I treated my mother, father, and sister Helen Ruth as adversaries. Arrogant, defensive, and frightened, I warned them I wouldn't be staying long. I was wrong. The physical and mental symptoms, experienced intermittently in Europe, reoccurred with added intensity and increased duration. Their son had left as a smiling teenager and had returned a total wreck. Not only was I a liability to myself but to my parents as well. They had no idea what to do, nor did anybody else. I certainly didn't. Photos of me, taken at the time, were inescapable examples of my depressed and irascible mood. Jeanie and I met once by accident. She was married with a young child. There was nothing to say, certainly not in my condition, and we never met again.

I remember walking down Flatbush Avenue in Brooklyn as if in an agitated dream, the gauze as thick as ever. Distracted, I was lucky not to have been killed by oncoming trolley cars. Having passed the Brooklyn College entrance exams — against all odds — once the term began, I sat in one classroom after another and failed to concentrate. Overwhelmed by anxiety, with my heart palpitating at a rate that seemingly would cause imminent death, I could not fulfill my academic obligations and dropped out.

Most nights, recurring bad dreams increased, and one in particular caused alarm. The dream revealed German panzer grenadiers tossing hand grenades and firing mortar shells from their side of our kitchen, as I laid down withering machine-gun fire and tossed my own grenades from behind a barricade of cabinets, utensils, and appliances. The noise was deafening and death approached in a tidal wave. Explo-

329

sion followed explosion.

The severity of my headaches increased. All I wanted to do was to stay in bed and sleep for untold hours. Hyper-vigilant, easily irritated, argumentative, I would jump at the sound of a car backfire or the whine of a siren. The fog before my eyes remained, an accompanying, personal, persistent fog. I was my own battlefield.

Those reflexive reactions still exist. For example, some years ago, a resident of London, I emerged from the Baker Street Underground and walked in the direction of my flat a few streets away. It was a sunny spring day and I had not a care in the world. As I strolled towards my destination, I suddenly realized I was no longer on the sidewalk but in the middle of the road, with its familiar apartment buildings towering on either side. Because I have an astute internal monitor, its voice asked, 'What are you doing walking in the middle of the road?' I immediately answered, without a moment's hesitation, 'I'm looking for snipers!' Enemy snipers in peaceful Britain? Didn't the war end 67 years ago? Evidently not for me! The trigger was a white window curtain fluttering against an opaque background.

My mother became so alarmed, she insisted I see a brain surgeon to eliminate any possibility of a brain tumor. The subsequent x-rays were negative. A visit to a psychiatrist followed as a last resort, and a meeting with my family GP, Dr. Saul Livingston, who had known me from birth, resulted in hollow statements of, 'Oh, you'll do just fine,' and 'Go away and work hard!' I didn't plead, but I did take his advice and worked like a slave as a bellhop one Easter vacation at a Catskill Mountain resort that lacked an elevator. Even working around the clock, my spirits didn't lift, nor did my feelings of doom subside, as manifested by the usual symptoms — tachycardia, increased muscle tension, dry mouth, loss of appetite, and reduced physical activity.

I moved to Los Angeles in 1947 and did odd jobs in darkroom photography. Desperate, more anxious than ever, my relationships were at an all-time low, a 'feared of living and scared of dying' syndrome. I concluded after one of many arguments, this time with a girlfriend, that if I were right and she wrong, I'd be feeling manifestly better. I didn't. I felt abysmally depressed and forlorn. Standing in front of her house after slamming the door and walking out, I admitted that something had to change. I had hit rock bottom. If I couldn't find a way out, I'd kill myself. Clarification came in two three-word phrases: 'Sink or swim! Do or die!' Searching, I accepted the recommendations of the Veterans Administration doctors and began my first exploratory psychotherapeutic session with a psychiatric social worker in 1949. It was the beginning of a long, arduous, and painful journey that included two other therapists. In today's terminology, I was probably suffering from Post-Traumatic Stress Disorder (PTSD). By definition, it may take months or years between the onset of traumatic events and the emergence of symptoms before the diagnosis of PTSD may be applied appropriately. In my case, the contributory events involved actual or threatened death or serious injury during the war. Subsumed under the broad heading of 'combat fatigue,' the only treatment in 1949 seemed to be Freudian psychoanalysis, a long drawn-out and expensive psychotherapy, not necessarily rewarding or appropriate, although effective in some other mental disorders. After one year of two sessions a week, my symptoms diminished. However, with my therapist's approval, I chose to face my symptoms head-on without the aid of psychotropic prescriptive drugs such as Seconal, Placidyl, or Valium. In the analysis, I exchanged old inappropriate coping tools for news ones appropriate to a post-war society. In so doing, and not without emotional struggle, I learned much about myself and others. Today, there are a variety of therapies specifically molded for problems related to bereavement and post-traumatic stress, such as Cognitive Behavior Therapy (CBT), a simpler, more direct process.

Striking up enough courage in 1949, I entered college, this time in Los Angeles. After three years, I graduated with a degree in Fine Arts Photography. During that three-year period, I supplemented my income from the GI Bill, an educational and financial government subsidy, by fulfilling customers' orders at a few local restaurants. Two careers spanned 35 years of working life as a music and videotape editor for the CBS television network and Consolidated Film Industries in Hollywood. Throughout my early television career, I continued in therapy, ultimately deciding that I wanted to become a therapist myself.

Dr. J. Victor Monke, an eminent Beverly Hills psychoanalyst and one-time President of the Southern California Psychoanalytic Institute, encouraged me to complete my studies. By acquiring an MA in Clinical Psychology from Goddard College, Vermont in 1976, accumulating more than 2,000 clinical and supervisory hours, and passing the California State Board exam, I qualified to practice. During the next 15 years, Dr. Monke and I worked together in an expanding practice that included individual, marital, family, and group psychotherapy. After my retirement from these two careers in 1989, I added a third and entered King's College London as an MA student in War Studies.

Working in network television was a dream come true. To illustrate: during the early afternoon of August 15, 1944, having just come ashore from a landing craft, I stood, taking a break, next to the open hatch of a Sherman tank. I was listening to a light radio program whose stars were Bob Hope and Bing Crosby. As a kid in Brooklyn, I remembered them in a film called *The Road to Morocco*. The scene changes, the war's over and 13 years later, I'm setting up a CBS television camera in the living room of Crosby's Bel Air mansion. Bing comes up the stairs, sees me, and says, 'Hey, you look kind of cold, how about some coffee and doughnuts?' Touched by his generosity, I accepted his offer and thanked him. He left, returning soon after, climbing the stairs with a pot of coffee and a plate of doughnuts.

It was at this level of intimacy, within their own homes and on the set, that I met many stars of stage, screen, and radio. Sophia Loren, Humphrey Bogart, Ginger Rogers, Frank Sinatra, and Fred Astaire come easily to mind. The '50s and '60s were truly the 'Golden Age of Television,' it being new, innovative, and experimental, attracting the best talent. I'm certain I should have paid CBS for such an opportunity, not the other way around. And we as former soldiers, loving every minute, worked as a team and got the job done. As an added personal benefit, I improved my sense of humor and timing during numerous rehearsals scanning a two-year period of 'The Jack Benny Show,' Jack being one of America's best-known comedians.

For a change of pace, during the early 60's I left broadcast television for a few years and became the owner/manager of an intimate French/Italian restaurant/coffee house called Cyrano's, on Hollywood's Sunset Strip. We catered to show business luminaries like Mel Brooks, Carl Reiner, and Barbara Eden. The motion picture director Sam Peckinpah and I were close friends, having begun our careers at KLAC-TV 10 years before. He directed 'The Wild Bunch,' one of his numerous classics. His life was stormy and he died early. In 1963, I returned to network television and post-production.

Through the 80's, I spent most summer holidays taking a variety of courses at Cambridge University in England. Later, in 1989, I moved to London and during the next five years acquired another MA and a PhD in War Studies from King's College. My career as a military historian, lecturer, and a Senior Visiting Research Fellow in War Studies at King's had begun. The association continues. Since then, I've lectured at colleges and attended conferences in Europe, America, and the Middle East. For example, I enjoyed a conference on 'Military Ethics & Civilian Terrorism' in Jerusalem and the annual 'Reality of Conflict' seminar at the Royal Defense Academy in Shrivenham.

It is not only a cohort of veterans from my generation who have shared their wartime experiences with the young middle-ranking officers of the three services immersed in a year's study at the Academy, but serving soldiers with stories of their own, recently returned from Iraq and Afghanistan. In a large measure, what has changed is the prior relationship between the WWII military generation and an inexperienced younger generation of officers. Now I learn as much as I impart from young serving officers. It is at this educational level that I chose to present my analysis of modern war and its psychological aspects.

I spent most of 1998 lecturing on 'Post Napoleonic European Military History' and administrating for the University of Maryland at its overseas campus in Hungary. At a United Nations-combined American and Hungarian military base south of Budapest, I experienced Army garrison life for the first time in 50 years. The American GIs on their way to Former Yugoslavia called me 'Doc.'

Rosemary Valaire, a former English ballet dancer, ballet teacher, and choreographer and I were married in Los Angeles in July 1957. We spent the next 23 years creating a family, traveling abroad, and improving our career skills. Three children followed: Claudia (1960), Alison (1962), and Andrew (1964), all of whom remain stimulating and fun to be with. When they were young, I regaled them with a variety of books and films and made-up songs, much in keeping with my father's vaudevillian style. Unlike him, I couldn't tap dance.

Our children now have children of their own, seven boys and one girl. As a family, we spent a portion of our summers traveling in Western Europe. Before the children were born, Rosemary and I journeyed for 1,700 miles through France during the summer of 1958 on a motor scooter, following the route of the troubadours that Eleanor of Aquitaine and her entourage had taken in the 12th century. I introduced her to the Dahan and Haas families in Paris.

Sad to say, due to career interests, Rosemary and I separated, and in

1982 divorced amicably but not without pain and loss. Growing careers took precedence. I moved to London in 1989 — her early home — and she remained in Los Angeles with the children. Our friendship was never in doubt. Rosemary died of brain cancer, much before her time, in 1999. Neither of us remarried. Beauty aside, she was the most artistic and practicable person I ever met. From the first and last, she was the woman with whom I desired to marry and have children.

In July 1972, I planned a family summer vacation in Europe that included meeting Mathey and his wife for lunch at the hotel in Alboussière. Sitting by myself on a bench in the hotel's garden the day before the Matheys were due to arrive, I felt a stirring of memories that evoked anxious and contradictory feelings that the familiar surroundings could not dispel. 'I never should have invited Mathey and his wife for lunch,' I thought.

'So what if we were comrades, I'm too old for this self-imposed added stress.' My discomfort persisted. 'To hell with the past' was a 30-year weight that translated into autonomic discomfort. 'A good war,' I reflected. 'You've got to be kidding!' Trying to regain a semblance of composure, I inhaled deeply a few times and, speaking silently once more, said, 'Be kind to yourself, Stephen,' stressing the 'ph' in mild derision, mocking the way my mother pronounced my name. 'You can't avoid life. It will break you if you try. Either meet the Matheys or get the hell out!' I insisted. 'This lunch isn't the end of the world, just a short-term social event!' I decided to hang in. 'But what the hell did I do to deserve this?' My emotional exercise ceased when Rosemary and the three children came walking down the terrace steps and shouted, 'Dad, let's go for a walk.'

On the following day, a few hours before our intended lunch, I drove to St. Péray alone to have a commemorative Pernod and soda at the Hotel du Nord. Standing at the bar in the cool morning, talking to the bartender while he cleared and washed the early morning breakfast dishes, I described my first meeting with the Resistance on that night in August. The room, just off the bar where the Resistance questioned me, was now filled with a pool table and a television set. The bartender, a teenager at the time, remembered French motorized units filled with truckloads of North African soldiers rolling into the town square. The local populace they came to liberate immediately engulfed them. Such was their joy!

'Did you know Ferdinand Mathey?' I asked. 'Wasn't he a Gendarme Lieutenant during the war?' he queried.

'That's right. He and I were on a patrol when he was wounded during the liberation of Soyons. We have a luncheon date later on at the Hotel Serre in Alboussière, the old headquarters of Captain Binoche. My family and I are staying there for a few days.'

'Sounds nice,' he said, drying another glass.

'There's a bridge on a mountain road and a river nearby that I hold sacred. If this were Ireland, leprechauns and goblins would be jumping about it. Drop zones, bridges, an L-shaped irrigation ditch, and the Rhône are splashed with memory and endowed with mystery. The land around Verdun evokes similar feelings of veneration by three generations of Frenchmen on a much grander scale,' repeating, 'Il ne passeront pas.'

Just as I finished talking, someone said, 'Oh, Mathey, I knew him. He played each side off against the other, a consummate juggler, and finally jumped to the winning side when victory seemed assured.'

I turned to see a man, looking more like a shepherd than a postman, a small sack hanging from his shoulder. Both were silhouetted against the light-filled wood entrance. Failing to stare him down because his eyes were deep in shadow, I could barely make out his features, although he was of medium height and build.

'What do you mean?' I asked. 'No offense. He was like millions of Frenchmen. Don't forget that after defeating the French Army in six weeks, the Third Reich was to last for a thousand years, not twelve, and like most of us, he had a family to feed.'

'Would you like a boisson, Pierre?' the bartender interrupted.

'Yeah, have one on me,' as I searched for some coins in my trouser pocket.

'Merci, but just something cold to quench my thirst.'

'Anything more about Mathey?' I asked.

'He made his decision under threat, but I'll say no more.'

The postman took a long swig, wiped his lips with the back of his hand, nodded in my direction, tossed some letters on the counter and left. I looked for solace from the bartender, but he remained impassive and said nothing. Shaken, I drove back to the hotel, thinking that it was pure bad luck to have met the postman and his disquieting news, which to many of the locals may have been common knowledge. Nevertheless, I knew Mathey as a stalwart and brave man!

I overcame my anxiety in the tumult of our meeting. Gone were my feelings of disappointment and doubt, resulting in our lunch becoming a warm and affectionate affair. Reminiscing, we shared our wartime exploits with our families. Extending our conviviality, we invited the owner/chef to join us for a drink, which he accepted willingly, realizing the importance of the occasion, during which his young teenage daughter played Schubert pieces on the piano from within the dining room. While the chef added his experiences of the war and its aftermath to ours, our lunch was interrupted by a phone call from a reporter on the *Daphine Libere*, a local newspaper, requesting an interview based on our meeting. I agreed to meet him later that day.

For Mathey and me, our meeting was bittersweet because we knew our goodbyes, interlaced with tears and manly hugs, were forever. Mathey retired as a Gendarme Major and became a successful regional insurance agent. He died a few years later in Tournon. When I became a Citoyen d'Honneur of St. Péray in 1989, his eldest son, who resembled him, attended the ceremony at the Hotel de Ville and stood beside me. I was honored by his presence.

The following day, after our lunch, I was called to the phone again. This time it was from a man who introduced himself as one Gaston Reynaud, a farmer from the other side of the Rhône. 'Monsieur Weiss, my friend Marcel Volle, a retired police officer, read the newspaper article about your reunion, exclaiming, 'You must be one of our Americans.' By reviewing some of the important details of the battle, we knew that I was his American and he my long-lost farmer.

Using the Hotel du Nord as a landmark, we decided to meet in St. Péray and then drive to his farm. I was apprehensive, thinking, 'What would a fruit farmer and I have in common?' Gaston, Madeleine, his wife, and Claudia, their daughter, were waiting beside their car when we arrived. They looked familiar to me, but the girl, now a woman, had changed the most. We introduced ourselves and shook hands, admitting that it was sheer luck meeting like this, a real long shot. We followed the Reynauds across the river, through Valence and its eastern suburbs, along a straight tree-lined road to the quarter of Les Martins.

The Mediterranean-style house, the barn, the surrounding fields — one in particular — and the peach orchards, all filled in what I truly had never forgotten. The unfolding scene jogged my memory into place.

I stood alone in the farmyard. The iron railing and stairs leading to the hayloft were at my back. Rosemary and children stood nearby, observers of the unfolding drama. People who had waited for our arrival broke from their clusters, one by one, and walked, not rushed, towards me. The first was Rene Crespy, Gaston's farmhand and helper, a simple soul who had brought us buckets of water as we lay hidden in the hayloft's August heat, 28 years before. We embraced. I was overcome. Marcel Volle and Richard Mathon, the two police drivers, followed. We shouted, embraced, tears rolling down our cheeks, roiled with emotion, and kissed each other. Of course we remembered. The Reynauds stood alongside my family and quietly expressed tears of relief, joy, and sadness. By sheer accident and good fortune, having found each other, our days of wondering and searching were ended. The citizens of Valence ought to know. The media was informed.

I climbed the stairs to the hayloft and entered, my heart pounding. Every step was sacred. The gloom was there waiting, full of secrets. Sensing it was too much emotion in one go, I retreated to the foot of the stairs. I walked alone through the peach orchard and partway across the field until I found the irrigation ditch, smaller than I remembered. I stood there, emotionally turned upside down, head bowed, paying silent homage to all of us who used both the hayloft and the ditch as sanctuaries. Scruby, Gualandi, Wohlwerth, Reigle, and the others, as always, were with me. For Rosemary and the children, our reunion was the making of family history, in which they were witnesses and active participants at the same time.

The dinner that followed was a gala event for 'this happy breed,' 'this band of brothers' that participated in the escape, and their families. Champagne flowed. Each table was decorated with small crossed French and American flags surrounded by flowers. Red, white, and blue bunting hung from the ceiling. Words of appreciation and deliverance were spoken in toasts that followed each other. I learned that Captain Ferdinand Levy, the man in civilian clothes who carried the brown package of police uniforms into the hayloft, was killed on September 30, the day that Valence was liberated. I was filled with sorrow.

Rosemary rose and, speaking in French, thanked the Reynauds and the gendarmes for saving my life. 'Without that, my children and I would not be here celebrating this evening.' While the applause faded away, most of us were inwardly glowing from a mixture of Lyonnaise cooking, enhanced by delectable local wines. Madeleine gave Rosemary her 'silent butler,' a device for gathering crumbs, simply because my wife liked it. In this heady atmosphere, regardless of value, it seemed that anything the Reynauds owned was ours for the taking.

Madeleine described the arrival of an SS officer at the farm soon after our escape. He placed a pistol at Gaston's head. He threatened to kill him, demanding to know where the Americans were hiding. Gaston refused. The officer insisted and cocked his Luger. Gaston lied, 'The Americans have escaped towards Chabeuil.' In disgust, the Germans left, only to return the next day. The SS officer questioned Gaston further, again threatening him at gunpoint, his finger curled around the trigger. Severely interrogated and slammed about, Gaston remained obdurate, even when confronted with some of our abandoned equipment they had found. Other Frenchmen had been killed on the spot for less! Finally, for reasons unknown, 'Les sales Boches' threw up their hands in desperation and left. They didn't return.

'Why did you put your life at risk and place your family in jeopardy for us?' I implored.

'Didn't you and the others, as strangers in a foreign land, do the same for us?' he asked. Soldiering and duty came to my mind, but his point was well taken.

Gaston wanted to know what happened to the other Americans. I knew that Reigle was alive, but I didn't know about the others. I promised to find out.

Back in Los Angeles, I wrote and called various members and agencies of the Federal government, supplying them with as much information as I had gleaned from the outdated 36th divisional roster. Reigle, in Philadelphia, knew no more than I.

While I was awaiting answers, I wrote a one-page tribute to those gallant Frenchmen involved in our escape, which was approved and read into the *Congressional Record* by the Honorable Tom Reese, my Congressman in the House of Representatives. I sent Gaston copies.

I could tell Gaston about Reigle because he and I remained in touch from the time I moved to Los Angeles. He lived in the Philadelphia suburbs, was married, the father of a young daughter, and worked as a supervisor for a large company making kitchen appliances. We met only twice during our long friendship, which was mostly conducted by mail. Under no circumstances would he leave the Philadelphia area, no matter how much I tried to entice him with trips to France, particularly to the Ardèche and Valence.

With my help, he was awarded the French Legion of Honor for the part he played in the Liberation of France. Although reluctant to attend the medal ceremony, conducted by the French ambassador in Washington, Reigle admitted that the event brought tears to his eyes. I, in turn, was touched by his simple and evocative letters regarding our combat experiences.

For example, quoting in part from a March 7, 1993 letter, he wrote 'Sometimes on TV, they have movies about the war in Europe. I have to laugh, because they always show the guys up front on the lines and they argue with one another and say some silly things. We were always scared. I hated to go on patrol, always waiting for a counter attack — and hated the mines and shells that were coming in. Besides being cold, dirty, and hungry and marching all night, and then attack. Well, we made it anyway.'

Another, Nov. 28, 1993. 'Do you remember how young we were, when we were in the service? How about overseas, when we slept on the ground, mud up to our knees, marched all night, soaking wet and eating them lousy rations. Also drinking wine or anything we could get or steal. We could not take it today. It was tough, scary, and hard on us, but what an experience it was.'

Oct. 12, 2004. 'I want to thank you for sending my service record (letter of recommendation) to the proper people. I forgot to send my address along with it. If I am lucky enough to receive the medal (*French Legion of Honor*), I know that you will see that I receive it again. "Thanks."… When it gets cold I must keep warm. Do you remember when we were in the big WWII war, how cold we were, with all of the mud, rain, and even snow? How we covered the fox holes with tree branches to try to keep warm. To me, they were not the good old days.'

I was impressed with his descriptions of conditions and the absence of descriptions about the battles themselves. That is, until I received the following letter, in which he talked about the grueling war in Italy. '… When you mentioned the Rapido (river) and Cassino, thoughts came back to me as if it were just yesterday. I crossed the river two times, only to be driven back. Went across in a rubber boat. A light haze on the river and it smelled of gunpowder. Dead GIs laying on the bank, in the water. My feet were frozen, cold, and wet. We lost a lot of good men there. We lost the battle…'

Retired and widowed, he enjoyed his daughter, Donna, with whom he lived. Being around his grandchildren and great-grandchildren brought him much satisfaction. Then, about a year ago, he lost his zest for living, became ill, and refused to seek medical attention. In his letters, Reigle never revealed the extent of his illness or how he felt about growing old to me. For the most part, they were light hearted. He died in the hospital on September 20, 2008. A foxhole buddy, I miss him and his simple, clear reality. With his passing, as far as I know, I'm the sole survivor of the night of August 24, 1944.

Discovery of the men's whereabouts was a slow and time-consuming process but, after three months, through the combined efforts of those government agencies I contacted, I had a portion of the service records of at least four of the six and a last known address, but not necessarily a current one. Garland and Fawcett could not be found, but according to the documents I had received, there was a William F. Scruby of Chillacothe, Missouri, and a Settimo Gualandi of Peoria, Illinois, an Emil T. Caesar of Indianapolis, Indiana, and a Sheldon Wohlwerth of Cleveland Heights, Ohio.

I called Caesar first, because I knew him least. The long distance operator had a listing in Indianapolis for a Caesar, Emil T. I dialed his number as soon as she switched off.

A man answered and I identified myself. 'Steve Weiss from the 36ᵗʰ?'

'Who?' he asked, with surprise in his voice.

'Look, I've just come back from France and by a stroke of luck met the French farmer who helped us escape. He'd like to know how you and the others are getting along.'

Caesar had married and was working in the printing business in Indianapolis. He sounded relaxed and engaging, much more so than in France. We both agreed that it was great to have survived the war, if the others had.

I called the Cleveland Heights operator only to find that there was no telephone listing under Sheldon Wohlwerth. Some months later, I entered a stationery and greeting card shop in Westwood Village, a suburb of Los Angeles, in search of a birthday card. The two middle-aged women owners of the shop, with whom I was on friendly terms, were first cousins. During the course of light-hearted conversation, I learned that they both came from the Cleveland area and that their maiden name was Wohlwerth. Surprised, I told them that I knew a Sheldon Wohlwerth during the war. Any relation? They looked at me with a blend of distress and relief, saying that Sheldon was their first cousin.

They told me that he died of a heart attack in 1968 at 52 and left a wife and three children. Now it was my turn to look aggrieved. Damn, I'm a few years too late. I mentioned some of the experiences we shared together in Italy and in France and asked if his wife and children would like to know more about his life in the Army. His family might feel relieved. The younger of the two didn't think so. Both agreed that Sheldon's wife was bitter about Wohlwerth's death, blaming the war for shortening his life. They reminded me he'd been badly wounded.

I asked them for Sheldon widow's phone number. 'There's nothing to lose! And all his wife can do is say no!'

'If we call on your behalf, your chances might be better.' They had a point, so I gave them my phone number and left.

A few days later, one of them called and said, 'Sheldon's wife isn't interested, but thanks you nevertheless…something about opening old wounds.' Stuck with fading memories, I imagined Wohlwerth striding in front of me, within arm's reach, his helmet streaked with mud, carrying a soiled combat pack and crossed bandoliers, his M-1 at port arms. Just like the rest of us, a beast of burden! You didn't seem rugged enough for the infantry, Wohlwerth, and now you're gone!

But in one sense, he wasn't! Time shifts to an afternoon in late 1999. I was working on this manuscript in my London apartment when the phone rang. The man on the other said, 'Congratulations on being awarded the French Legion of Honor. I read about it in on the front page of *The Los Angeles Times*. I think you knew my father, Sheldon Wohlwerth. I'm Russell, one of his sons.' I replied, haltingly, almost too overcome to speak. 'Sheldon and I were buddies; that is, we dug fox holes together in Europe.'

I met the Wohlwerths — his widow and their three grown children —

in Paris the following February. We were invited to an awards ceremony in Valence in Sheldon's honor, arranged by Claudia Brule-Reynaud and me. At the Hotel de Ville, on February 16, 2000, Mayor Patrick Labaune bestowed upon Sheldon a posthumous Citoyen d'Honneur for his participation in the liberation of Valence. He presented the medallion and diploma to Mrs. Wohlwerth. I spoke briefly of our wartime episode and thanked the townspeople present. *Le Dauphine Libere*, the regional newspaper, gave the story pride of place on its front page, topped by a banner headline.

The next day, we visited the Reynaud farm and, with Claudia's help, showed the Wohlwerths the farmyard and the hayloft, below which a Moroccan family of fruit growers lived. Although Valence has expanded further east, part of the field and the entire peach orchard remain. Being winter, the bare peach trees offer little cover. The worn cement steps and iron railing still lead up to the hayloft door, although both are more weather-beaten than before. Inside, it is too dangerous to walk on the disintegrating wood planks. Cobwebs and litter are everywhere, although the shutters where Scruby once signaled seem to have stood the test of time. I can see part of the orchard and the fields below. The neighboring farm buildings, torched by the SS after the battle, have been rebuilt.

Before the Wohlwerths returned to Los Angeles, we drove through Valence and south along the river road, a route affording an excellent view of the Rhône, older and less turbulent than before. I couldn't identify the small stone farmhouse, nor am I certain about the embarkation site, although from where we stood, the village of Soyons was clearly visible across the river, as it was in 1944. Nor could I identify the house on the other side that was to become our refuge until nightfall. That fortunate discovery would have to wait until 2007. The Rhône looked wider than I remembered, symbolizing for me a division between death and freedom, acceptance and indifference, stagnation and growth, and rejection and love.

The Wohlwerths and I parted in Paris. What we had accomplished in Valence was the filling of a gap in Wohlwerth's wartime record, unknown to his widow and grown children for years until now.

I looked over Scruby's record once more before calling. The Army document was a standard personnel form, but the details in the printed boxes set each man apart accordingly: William F. Scruby. Born, 1924-

from Chillicothe, Missouri; Graduated High School, 1942; Civilian Occupation, Farm hand; Hobbies, hunting and fishing. Enlisted, 1943. 745 Rifleman.

I placed the document next to the phone and dialed. After three rings, a man with a Midwestern drawl answered. 'Scruby?' I inquired.

'Yes,' he answered.

'Hi, this is Steve Weiss; remember — we were in the 36th together in France.' There was a pause. I waited while he cleared his throat.

Finally, he spoke, 'You've got the wrong Scruby. I'm the mayor, William E. The Scruby you're looking for is William F., my nephew. Was named after me.'

'I see. May I talk to him?'

He spoke slowly. 'I'm afraid that's not possible. You see, he died a long time ago, soon after he returned from Europe.' I felt sad and angry.

And I imagined his uncle shaking his head in disbelief in an attempt to defy reality. 'He lost a leg in France and was sent to an Army hospital in Texas to recover. That's when I saw him last, back in 1945. The medics did all they could. He never recovered and died of his wounds. Such a sturdy lad! He's buried at the Kosciuszko Military Cemetery in northern Alabama, named after some Polish general who fought in the American Revolution. Mean anything?' He paused and said, 'I was William's only living relative.'

My chest hurts. 'Sir, Scruby saved my life and the lives of six other GIs in France, August, 1944. The French farmer who helped us considered him brave, and so did a French officer named Binoche, who later became a general, and so did we. People ought to know that. You have every right to be proud, Your Honor.'

Gualandi came from Peoria, a grim and tough industrial town in Southern Illinois, part of the 'rust belt.' Gualandi and I hadn't talked to each other since November 1944. Somewhere I have a photo of him, taken near the Vosges farm house and dark woods, a medium-sized fellow with dark curly hair and a glorious smile, posing with Reigle, Dickson, and Ward, my Second Scout. Gualandi lost a foot stepping on a German schuh mine, specifically designed to severely wound the lower parts of the body.

The operator said that there were a number of Settimo Gualandis to choose from. 'All of them please, one by one, until I find the right one.' Reaching the second Gualandi on the list, I was told that the GI Gualandi was a postal clerk who supplemented his income as a bartender. Calling the number I was given, a familiar voice answered. I responded. 'Gualandi, it's me, Weiss from Charlie Company.'

'Who?' he questioned.

'Weiss, your friendly First Scout!'

He responded with a 'Hmmm.' I persevered to no avail, and after the third or fourth attempt to identify myself, I gave up.

Nevertheless, I explained the reason for phoning and then said, 'I'm not calling to stir up painful memories.' To relieve him of any anxiety, I changed the subject, saying that I was married, had three kids, worked in network television, and lived in Los Angeles.

His voice changed and, in a sing-song unearthly way, said, 'I've got three kids'; it reminded me of Lennie, a retarded character in John Steinbeck's theater production *Of Mice and Men.*' Sensing failure, I got off the phone soon after. Well, he's alive, I thought — just!

Three months later, I received a letter from Gualandi, written in a simple scrawl, postmarked, Peoria. It began, 'Dear Steve, Your phone call caught me by surprise, and I couldn't deal with it — all the hurt, until now. Yes, of course, I remember you and the others. Reigle and I exchange Christmas cards.' It took three months for his denial to lift, allowing our shared experience in France to reach consciousness.

I thought, 'Isn't there another way to live, without the past being so destructive in the present?'

Before I could connect with him again, he died within the year of diabetic complications, but something else may have contributed to his untimely death, a syndrome unheard of at the time called PTSD. To take a line from one of Cole Porter's songs of the period that seemed appropriate, '*Every time we say good bye, I die a little.*'

My son Andrew and I visited Madeleine Reynaud a year later, and Gaston's brother gave me Scruby's helmet and helmet liner, the one he wore during our encirclement, on which he had inscribed his last name. At first, Gaston kept them as souvenirs of those fateful days; after he died, his brother kept them. We visited Marcel Volle, who had driven the car on the second trip. Now retired from the police, he honored us at his home in Valence. We dined on his home-grown snails in garlic.

The battle at Les Martins and our encirclement remains part of the history of wartime Valence, even if the town itself has encroached onto the battlefield. The irrigation ditch has disappeared. The road from the Reynaud's farm to D68 is now called rue Gaston Reynaud. Elise, who married Paul Valette, still lives on the edge of St. Péray. Jean-Claude Haas is alive and well and living in Paris. He achieved prominence as an international investment banker. His mother, aunt, and uncle died many years ago. Odette Serre, Simone, and Paul Valette have died within the last 10 years.

Trips to Paris always included visits to Ronnie and Olga's. Throughout the post-war period, Ronnie did well as a women's dress manufacturer and an investor in Paris real estate until he retired and then died of a heart attack in 1976. When Andrew, then 13, and I first arrived in France in 1977 to spend a summer holiday, Gerri Dahan, their son, reached us by phone at an inn in Tours s/Marne, 60 miles east of Paris. Full of sadness, he said, 'Olga died. Please come to Paris now. I need you here.' We changed our itinerary, canceled our stay in the Champagne, and immediately drove to Paris.

We arrived at the apartment on the rue d'Estrees and learned that Olga chose not to go on living without Ronnie and, according to Gerri, may have inadvertently contributed to her own death by overmedicating herself. Gerri said, 'She tried to stay alive until you arrived, Steve, but had not the strength to do so.' As the three of us stood in the half-empty apartment, which years earlier had been a second home to me, Gerri, as if reading my thoughts, said, 'My mother loved you as a son. Whatever you see in the apartment is yours.' Words could not express my feelings of loss and gratitude, and as a 'memento mori,' I settled on an 18th century gilt-edged oval mirror that for years hung over the living room mantelpiece. When our first child was born, we named her Claudia Dahan. Gerri has been married for many years and is the father of two sons and four grandchildren. He and his wife Rosine live in Dreux, about 50 miles from Paris. We meet a few times each year.

François Binoche left the Army as a highly decorated general officer, receiving, among many decorations, the Croix de la Liberation from General de Gaulle, one of 1,800 so decorated. Two other prominent recipients were Prime Minister Winston Churchill and General Dwight D. Eisenhower. Binoche retired and lived in Nice from the mid-1970s.

Although he lost an arm in combat, he still reached the pinnacle of his profession. Binoche commanded the French Foreign Legion's 5th Regiment from 1948 to 1949. After a number of other assignments, he served as the leading French general in Berlin in 1973.

On special occasions, he would write to me thus: '*A Mon Camarade de Combat, Mon Ami, Stephen Weiss, en souvenir de sa presence dans la Résistance Française en Ardèche, Aout-Septembre 1944...*' Together, we attended the 40th anniversary of the Southern France landings at Le Dramont in 1984.

However, during the next 10 years, he increasingly retreated from life, which surprised me, he being so vital a personality. I sensed his unavailability and regretted that my limited, albeit improving, command of French, even at the best of times, failed to keep him fully engaged. In failing health, he may have found the sudden loss of his second son, Serge, a professor of history, insurmountable. Serge died of a heart attack at 42, leaving a wife and two young children behind. The general's wife, Madeleine, died in 1995. François followed her two years later. All three are buried in the small medieval village of Désaignes, on the road to St. Agreve, in his beloved Ardèche.

Seeking to learn more about the general's family and not wanting to lose touch, in 2008, doing research at the Chancellerie de la Liberation, I found the address and phone numbers of his nephew, Gerard Binoche, who was living in Paris. His father, the general's older brother, was still alive but not well enough to see me. Gerard mentioned that there were some Portuguese family connections in Portugal and South America, that the general's oldest son was a professor at a French overseas university, that the original family business was printing, and that Juliette Binoche, the French movie star, was a close relative. As I suspected, General Binoche stood up against the corrupt collaborationist Vichy government as a young officer, was tried for treason, but successfully defended himself in 1942. Post war, he was strongly anti-German and was against the reunification of Germany.

In 1984, at Désaignes, General Binoche introduced me to retired French colonel and historian Louis Ducros. Included in *Combats Pour La Liberation*, the third volume of his trilogy, *Montagnes Ardechoises Dans La Guerre*, is a detailed account, with accompanying photos, of the battle near Reynaud's farm and our escape. I asked Louis about Mathey. He replied that, like many men who joined the Resistance reluctantly at first, he served its cause very well from the spring of 1944 onwards.

In 1984, I was made a *Citoyen d'Honneur* of Valence at the invitation of the town's mayor. Attending the ceremony in the Hotel de Ville was my 22-year-old daughter, Alison, Madeleine and Claudia Reynaud, Louis Ducros and his family, and police officers Marcel Volle and Louis Mathon and their families. Louis Salomon stood beside me. At the end of the ceremony, Mayor Rodolphe Pesce took me aside and said, 'You realize, Monsieur Weiss, that you are the second person in the history of Valence to be so honored.' I replied, asking the obvious question, 'Tell me, who was the first?' Without batting an eye, and recorded by the media in attendance, he responded, 'Napoleon.'

While we stood in the salon sipping champagne, Louis Salomon recounted his visit to the farm on August 25, 1944. Before arriving, cycling from Valence, he was stopped at the edge of the battlefield by a German officer who demanded his papers.

Arrogant, the officer said, 'Those American swine, we really taught them a lesson last night. We knocked out three tank destroyers and killed and wounded about 70 men within 10 minutes.' I was waved on. Once in the farmyard, dismounting, Louis said, 'Gaston, I think there may be something you want to tell me.' And Gaston whispered, 'I've got a terrible problem that needs to be solved. 'What problem?' Gaston continued, 'I've got eight Americans hidden in the hayloft.'

Louis Salomon returned to Valence and filed his report with Chief of Police Gerard, who urgently called a meeting of the Resistance cell within his department. Five policemen, disguised in civilian clothes, gathered in a cellar beneath the Crystal Bar, a Resistance hideout in Valence, to launch an escape plan. We know now that they decided on the use of police uniforms as a disguise. 'You saved my life,' I said, when we finally met in 1984.

Louis pondered for a moment, then thought out loud, 'What would have happened if Chief of Police Gerard hadn't asked for a volunteer that August morning? What if I, who knew the area so well, had not volunteered? And what if I had not picked on my friend Reynaud to visit?' It is not difficult to imagine what would have happened. Thanks to Louis, 8 GIs survived the experience. After many years of public service, Louis Salomon, *the Guardian de la Paix*, the police officer I had held in the cross hairs of my rifle, had retired to a Cistercian monastery at Hautcombe, on the shores of Lake Bourget. There he would exchange a life of action for a life of contemplation.

As an expression of friendship, Louis Ducros surprised me with two bottles of Chateauneuf du Pape, vintage 1937, from his personal wine cellar. Leaving Valence by train, I looked out of the open window onto the two Louis's — Salomon and Ducros — who were standing on the station platform a few feet away, the three of us waiting for the train's imminent departure. As the train began to move, both Louis's entwined the fingers of each hand in front of them, waist high, moving them slowly up and down, symbolizing how inextricably entwined we were. I did the same until both men were lost from view. Louis Ducros died in 1993 of natural causes and Louis Salomon died in St. Etienne a year later.

Elise Valette and I had not met in 30 years; she was working as an administrator at St. Péray's Hotel de Ville. When we did, she walked down the marble staircase from her first-floor office to greet me. I waited at the bottom on the ground floor where the bannister curved and stopped above the last marble step. As she came into view from above, I said in French, 'Elise, it's me, Stephen,' and she replied, 'Oh, Stephen, that's not necessary. I'd know you anywhere!'

General Eisenhower awarded Louise — one of six OSS OGs, each designated by a female code name — a unit citation for outstanding performance of duty in action in support of the invasion and against the enemy in southern France. The unit would see action in China before Japan surrendered.

Rick and I found each other through the OSS Society's address directory. He and his second wife, Alice, were living in Alexandria, Louisiana. Early in the new century, Rick and I planned a trip to the Ardéche, but the two of us would never meet again. Before we could execute our plan, he died of a stroke in February 2001.

Hines was the only fellow from the photographic unit I met again, accidentally running into him at Grand Central Station in Manhattan in 1956. He and Michele married soon after I left Paris, were now parents of four children, and living on Long Island. He was out of work and desperate. There was little I could do. Soon after, he found a position with the nascent space program in Florida as a cinematographer, recording NASA's down-range sub-orbital flights. He and his family settled along the Banana River until his retirement.

In 1997, I interviewed a glamorous French woman in Bayonne, France who as a teenager worked as a Résistant for the Comet Escape Line during the war. She volunteered to help downed Allied airmen, disguised as civilians, who were shepherded through France and across the Pyrenees in an attempt to reach neutral Spain and possible safety. By pretending to be an airman's lover, she and her charge would pass safely, arm in arm, through the German police barrier at the town's central train station. She was caught in early 1944 in such an attempt and sent to a concentration camp. Luckily, she survived. In her scrapbook, I discovered two photos of Michele and Hines, taken during a reunion of the Comet survivors in Manhattan during the early '80s. Michele came from the St. Juan de Luz-Bayonne region, close to the Spanish border, but she never spoke of her involvement in the Resistance. Until a few years ago, Hines, Michele, and I kept in touch, but since then my last letters have remained unanswered and their phone has been disconnected.

Hal Sedloff was returned to civilian life. When I met him in Manhattan in 1956, he was working as a butcher. Depressed, divorced, and married for the second time, he never recovered.

Laurence Kuhn and I planned to meet at a divisional reunion in Dallas, Texas some time during the early '80s. When he didn't arrive at the appointed time in the hotel lobby, I called his home in Beaumont, Texas to no avail. Some veterans at the reunion, having heard of my concern, phoned the Beaumont sheriff's station and the local fire brigade office. A squad car and a fire truck were dispatched to Kuhn's home, only to find no one there. For some unknown reason, he never made it to Dallas. I was sorely disappointed, and when the 36th 'Newsletter reported a few years later that he had died of natural causes, I felt his loss and a conversation that went begging.

I had become a member of the Confrere des Chevaliers du Tastevin, a French wine and food society, in 2002, whose headquarters was situated in a 12th-century Burgundian chateau. Within striking distance of the U.S. Military Cemetery at Epical, I went to pay my respects to Harry Shanklin. When checking his plot location in the cemetery's office files, I accidentally discovered two other names listed as former Charlie Company soldiers. I was unnerved by the information. Since the war, I believed that these men, S/Sgt. Bocarsky from New York and S/Sgt. Jerstad from Wisconsin, the former street-smart and lucky, the latter well-trained and experienced, had survived the seven campaigns in which the 36th had fought, from Italy to France to Germany to Austria. In telling about them, I admired their luck and fortitude. For 60 years, their living affirmed my own. To discover that they were buried nearby destroyed my own immunity, however unrealistic; I too was now subject to the slings and arrows of outrageous fortune. It was as if I had been living under a fixed, false belief. As 'odd man out,' I was devastated. As my father used to say, 'It took the starch out of me!'

In February 1993, I received a letter from Ed Torres, formerly of Charlie Company, which read in part, 'It was really a pleasant surprise to hear from you after all these years. I remember very well our last conversation (during the heavy shelling in the Vosges), and have often wondered how you fared afterward. As for the rest of us, we went up that bare hill with no cover. Heavy fire on both sides; then there was cover, but not a shot was fired at us. At the top, we took eleven prisoners and two machine-guns. Another of those inexplicable bits of luck that I had during the war. Thanks for writing. Yours, Ed.'

Ed wrote again in 2007. The letter contained further information about the shelling that took place when Charlie Company was resting behind the lines and I had just returned from MIA and was camping in the Vosges farmhouse in early October.

'Yes we were in basic training together at Camp Blanding and went over to North Africa in the same ship. In Italy, they mixed us with a large group of odd classifications from cooks to truck drivers to typists and with one phony week of training as riflemen, we were sent up to the 36th.

'There were eleven of us from the basic training group and by the end of October, I was the only one left. Only one came back months later after being wounded at Eloyse, in the Vosges. That was Larry Zintel, who must have been in your squad at Blanding.

'You write about your military experience being different because of service with the FFI and the OSS. I know pretty much about your stay with the FFI group that rescued your lost group of eight men in the advance up France, as I was closely associated with one of the men in your group — Frank Skala. (Author's note: he wasn't.)

'Steve, you referred to a night shelling as the event of our last meeting, which actually took place about ten days later in the advance on Bruyeres. I think that I have pinpointed that occasion, which occurred in the evening of my return from a twenty-four hours rest camp back of the lines. That night is engraved in my memories because my life was spared by something that was contrary to all logic.

'The rest camp was simple but there was one happening that might be of interest to you — I met the man that was your trainee squad leader at Camp Blanding, who you may remember had all the qualities of leadership that the army was looking for. Not any more — he was a nervous wreck who told me that he had deserted a couple of weeks before and was keeping alive by mingling with chow lines whenever he could. I felt sorry for him but could not help.

'A Sgt. Gonthier and I returned to C. Co. only to find that in our absence, it had been taken off the line and was in reserve. I know that you were there as in my wartime photo album, I have a snapshot of four G.I.s sitting or lying on the ground. The caption underneath reads 'Denton, Connelly, ETB (me) and Weiss at chow.' At dusk, there was a good gabfest going on when Gonthier and me got up to set up a pup tent at the end of the line that ran along a fence. Back of the fence there was a strip of woods beyond which, unknown to us, was a battery of our 4.2 mortars. We were stopped from setting up our own tent by a chorus of invitations not to bother, just come in with the mortar men. Three men in a pup tent? It could only happen in the combat infantry where any bed that was above ground and dry was a luxury. Comfort was not a factor. We were both pleased and embarrassed because picking tents might offend somebody, so we just picked the two end tents and squeezed in.

'Gonthier was in the last tent, right next to the spot where we were going to set up our own tent, which was also the precise spot where the first shell landed. The first man in that tent, Dentino, died of wounds. The man in the middle, who was small, was not hit but suffered the worst shell shock I had ever seen, and he never came back. Gonthier was wounded in the head and feet and did not return for five or six months. The top of my tent looked like a sieve but we were not hit because we didn't budge. I know of four casualties we had that night, when we were not on the line and there were very likely many more. I have not forgotten, a big Texan whom I knew only as Ted, cried out as they carried him away with part of his right foot gone, saying, 'Don't feel sorry for me, Boys, I'm going home!'

'That's the way it was for month after month, and it is a miracle that we lived through it.

Sincerely, Ed'

The 36th Division *Newsletter* printed in its 'Taps' column that Truman Ropos had his leg amputated and worked for the State Department in Prague during the '80s before he died of diabetes. I finally found out how Shanklin got killed. Reigle wrote to me on 1 March, 2005 and put paid to my question.

'Now about Shanklin. This is what happened to him in September, in the Vosges, at the Moselle River. We advanced to a large wooded area and it was getting dark. When we got there, it was dark, and we got into holes that were already dug. At the time, we did not know that there were Germans already there. About an hour later, after we were asleep, they came and shot some of our guys in the holes. They killed Shanklin and a few more men. Me and a few other guys were on the edge of the woods, so we heard the shooting and hid on the outside. We then saw the Germans taking some of our guys prisoners. We could not shoot because they had every other guy in a line and it was hard to see who was who. We lay there until it got light and then checked the holes where our boys were shot. I forgot who was taken prisoner. It was about four or five guys.

'I remember Scruby. He always walked with a funny gait. I remember one time we just moved to a[n] advanced position. The Germans coun-terattacked and the guy next to me jumped out of his hole and started yelling while walking straight up and ran towards the Germans. They shot him; all day, he lay there screaming and eventually died. I didn't know his name, only he was a red head. He went out of his head, that is why he did what he did and ran toward the enemy. Also, there was a time, when it was dark and we were in our holes, the guy next to me gave the pass word and someone coming toward us gave the counter sign. It was a German and he shot our guy in the hole. We all shot and killed the German. One more time, I remember – Did you know a guy called Hutch. He was about six feet tall and was a Southerner. We were taking a break from marching and he sat next to me. A shell landed on his right side and took part of his arm and shoulder off. He took the brunt of the explosion and saved me.

O. K. Steve, that's enough of that stuff.

Love, Bob'

Were these letters descriptive of what constitutes a 'hard luck' division or were they simply typical experiences that any infantry division and its riflemen endured? For example, J.D. Salinger, the celebrated and reclusive American author who died in 2010, probably saw more combat than most authors. He hit Utah Beach on D-Day as a sergeant; at 26, he was assigned to the 12th infantry regiment, 4th division. Of the 3,080 members of Salinger's regiment who landed with him on June 6, 1944, only 1,130 were alive three weeks later. Of the replacements for the original 3,080 regimental soldiers who went into the September 1944 – February 1945 Huertgen Forest campaign, only 563 were left when the regiment was relieved. In December, Salinger fought in the Battle of the Bulge and in the liberation of Dachau concentration camp in April 1945. Margaret, his daughter, said that he could not get the smell of burning flesh out of his nose for the rest of his life. His postwar literary success increased his abnormal reclusiveness. I think it was a means of coping, however inappropriate, with combat fatigue or PSTD. Is it so different from Reigle's unwillingness to dig and share a foxhole with another soldier or Weidaw's decision not to speak? Shock and awe, loss and pain! The aforementioned is not a theme in Tom Brokaw's book, *The Greatest Generation*, but it is central in Thomas Childers' book, *Soldier from the War Returning*. In sum, I suggest every combat division is a 'hard luck' formation.

On October 15, 1946, Master Sergeant John Woods executed 10 Nazi officials and German military officers at the Allied War Crime Trials in Nuremberg, Germany. Hermann Goering, Former Commander of the Luftwaffe and Reichsmarschall, who had been captured by the 36th in Austria, was the 11th Nazi sentenced to death. He evaded the hangman by committing suicide in his cell a few hours before the sentence was to be carried out. He swallowed a hidden vial of potassium cyanide. There was no further news of Woods until I accidentally came across a short two-column article and small sketch in an issue of the European edition of the *Stars and Stripes*, the Army newspaper. It stated that a master sergeant, identified as one John Woods, hangman, was found dead, washed up on the shore of an island in the Pacific. No reason for his death was given.

I did not learn until 1996, after requesting a copy of my court-martial from the Army Judiciary, that Gen. Dahlquist, commanding the 36th, had reduced my sentence to 20 years, as of November 9, 1944. His decision was based on the recommendation of Lieutenant-Colonel Stephen

J. Brady, who as Staff Judge Advocate wrote,' It is my opinion that this man possesses a very strong will power and could stay at the front if he so desired. He strikes me as being a rather intelligent person who has definitely decided that he is not going back to the infantry. In view of the fact that the accused has had some combat experience and has a mild psycho neurotic condition, it is recommended that the sentence be reduced to a term of years in the hope that this man can be rehabilitated.'

At the same time, I discovered that an investigating officer reviewing the trial noted that the prosecution's case was weak, but I helped it considerably by admitting that I ran away. The same officer believed that corrective action was unnecessary: 'He's only nineteen, appears highly intelligent and probably will be rehabilitated and possibly restored to duty in approximately six months.'

My interest in the Slovik case was revived in 1974 with the broadcast of a TV drama based on William Bradford Huie's book, The Execution of Private Slovik. Sentenced to death for desertion in 1944 by an American military court, as were 48 others, Eddie Slovik was the only soldier in 88 years actually to face death by firing squad. I needed to discover if there were any similarities between my wartime experience and his. After viewing the TV drama, reading the book, and scrutinizing the text of his court-martial, I concluded that all we had in common was the lack of a fair military trial, that we were both replacements assigned to an infantry division, and that we had 'visited' St. Marie aux Mines for different reasons. At 10:05 on January 31, 1945, Eddie Slovik was shot and killed there by an American infantry rifle squad. Although struck by 11 bullets, none seemed fatal. There was a moment of panic, but while members of the firing squad were reloading, he died. I could have suffered the same fate; both he and I were vulnerable to outrageous fortune! The Army, in his case, had made a grievous error in judgment.

I met Colonel Vincent M. Lockhart (ret.) in the mid-'70s when I submitted to a series of interviews that he conducted in Los Angeles. The interviews related to a book he was writing called *T-Patch Victory to Victory*, emphasizing the soldiers' experiences while serving with the 36th. Lockhart served at divisional headquarters when I faced court-martial in the Vosges. On October 10, 1982, after verifying my escape story with after-action reports and corroborating statements of former battalion commander Lt. Colonel David M. Frazior (ret.), Vince wrote the following unsolicited letter from El Paso, Texas. Please note that Colonel Lockhart was a newspaperman in civilian life, not a lawyer.

'Dear Steve,

'Sometimes, as we ride the chariot of memory through the past and in the light of the present, we blend them into a reality of what has been.

'This morning I was recalling an autumn night in Bruyères, where my office was in a large red brick building, with plenty of space. I find it significant that I can recall where I worked but not where I slept.

It was late — perhaps 10:30 or so — and an MP brought in a young soldier from the stockade. The MP approached and said he had a prisoner who wanted to speak to Captain Lockhart. Permission was granted.

'Are you the one that gets them off?' the prisoner asked.

'If you want me to defend you,' I replied, 'I will do my best.'

'I did not get him off. He was flagrantly guilty of leaving his machine gun post in the face of the enemy. I did do my best, and, at least, he did not get a death sentence.

'This morning I was thinking: 'What if the MP had brought Steve Weiss to you that night?' Your approach would have been different, but my own dedication to getting at the truth would have been the same. Not because I am something great, or someone specially talented, but simply because I believe if the obvious facts had been brought to light, you would have been acquitted.

'I believe that had we met then — instead of thirty years later — you would have been acquitted immediately, instead of the six or eight months later after you had lived the life of one accused and found guilty.

All the best,

Vince'

We exchanged a number of letters over the years, but part of another one Vince wrote on April 20, 1991 is applicable to my story. '...Your kind words about the beginning of our friendship — my letter to you in 1982 — bring back some fond memories. When you sent your FFI (French Forces Interior) story, I frankly did not believe it. Are you aware, every story in *T-Patch to Victory* was checked with at least one other source? So I checked with Dave Frazior, who was the First Battalion Commander at the time you went 'missing' and he vouched for it, saying: 'I remember it distinctly, because we were so glad to get them back!' Too bad that stupid bastard who was your company commander didn't see it that way....' A fair man and a good investigative reporter, Vince Lockhart died peacefully on the morning of August 10, 2002 in Alamogordo, New Mexico.

During June 1994, the 50th anniversary of the D-Day landings, I met Major Dick Winters, formerly CO of Easy Company, 506th PIR, 101st Airborne. He had a reputation for sound leadership. Easy Company's wartime exploits were immortalized in Stephen Ambrose's book *Band of Brothers* and in the TV series that followed with great success. From our conversations and from what I read about him later, he demonstrated an appropriate level of self-control, emotional stability, and courage, what Ernest Hemingway called 'grace under fire.' I was sure Winters felt that officers should fight alongside their men and share all of their hazards. The best officers (like Winters) did not order or ask men to expose themselves needlessly or to attack in the face of overwhelming odds, unless necessary.

Although it didn't happen in Charlie Company, in others some incompetent line officers were 'fragged' (killed by their own troops) for incurring higher than necessary casualties. 'Dick,' I said, 'If you had been my CO in the old days, I'd have followed you anywhere.'

He wrote in *Overlord Coastline*, a book I was using on the trip, 'To Steve Weiss, June 5, 1994, Sharing memories of June 5th, 1944, Hang Tough, Dick Winters, Co. E., 506th, 101st Airborne.' In 2009, we missed each other by two weeks at Aldbourne, England, the village where he and Easy Co. were billeted before jumping into Normandy. He died at the age of 92 on January 19, 2011. He suffered from PTSD, among other ailments, although it was never mentioned.

Compare the above assessment with what Reigle wrote in February 2005. 'I remember Gualandi. I remember his smile. I know he came into the outfit after me. I was the oldest man in the outfit when I was transferred to the MPs. Did he not get his leg off? I still remember when Shanklin got killed. I also remember some guys and never got to know their names, when they came in as replacements and they would be either killed or wounded. And it would be their first time up on the line. At least one thing we'll never forget was the fun and bad times we had to be with the outfit. It was all free but we paid dearly for it. We marched all night, got cold and wet, ate cold rations, dug plenty of fox holes, and that was even before we reached the front lines. Could you do it now? No, no, no!'

'Then every few days 'Big Deal' Simmons would have a runner come up and ask for a count in the men left in your squad. I often wonder after I left if he ever got a promotion, what happened to him.'

With front-line conditions in the parlous state they were, in which teamwork rarely existed, I read something recently that underscored the differences in treatment ascribed to the Army. On page 192 of *The US Infantryman in World War II*, written by Robert S. Rush, I found the following passage that evoked suppressed feelings within me:

With the slowdown in casualties, he noted that marginal or burnt-out officers were being relieved of their assignments and sent to the rear for reclassification. They were replaced by officers wounded earlier during the campaign and now rested, new officers from the US or battlefield commissionees. The same situation applied to NCOs; however, they were normally demoted to private and kept in the line instead of being sent to the rear. Others made it back to the Service Company as privates. It didn't seem fair, especially for those who had been through it all and bordered on combat exhaustion.

At the same time, as a tourist on one of his tours, I met Stephen Ambrose, the American military historian and founder of Ambrose Historical Tours, deeply involved in the D-Day proceedings. Earlier, we exchanged letters, and herein is one pertinent to my academic career and Normandy itself:

January 1, 1993, University of New Orleans.

'Dear Mr. Weiss,

Thanks so much for your letter of Dec. 16, and of the book on the 101st at Bastogne, which I had not seen before, and am glad to add to our collection.

I was fascinated by your war career, which was as varied as it was distinguished. You should do a memoir. Who is directing your work on 'Anvil?' Good subject.

I will be in Normandy on June, 1994, so please stay in touch and perhaps we can get together. Sincerely S.E. Ambrose.'

We did meet; he was encouraging regarding my studies, and I began the first draft of my memoirs. Between the receipt of his letter and the

Normandy anniversary, during the spring of '94, I devised a one-page, two-sided, psychological questionnaire to determine if WWII veterans were suffering from PTSD 50 years later. I sent a copy to Ambrose for his consideration and approval. He, in turn, made copies which he sent to the 'Band of Brothers' of Easy Co. Ambrose requested they send the completed questionnaires back to me, which they did. From their responses, I concluded that most of Easy's men were not suffering from PTSD. I've never forgotten his gesture of good will.

How could I have known that, 10 years later, I would be leading tours for his company, Stephen Ambrose Historical Tours, under the direction of Yakir Katz, CEO, to Normandy and Paris, Normandy, The Battle of the Bulge to the Rhine, and the Italian Campaign? In 2003, I planned a tour with a Swiss friend, Hugo Banziger, for a family of four. As part of the tour, the family, Hugo, and I jumped into the Channel off Omaha Beach from a high-speed Zodiac rubber boat, dressed in wet suits, at 6:30 in the morning. This was the exact time that men of the 1st and 29th U.S. Infantry Divisions hit the beach on D-Day, June 6, 1944. In so doing on this and other tours, I made friends with some delightful and dedicated people, put my military knowledge to the test, relived and evaluated some of my war experiences, and learned more of France, which had become an integral part of my life.

Italy was no exception. I was profoundly impressed with two men, one, Massimo Rendina, an Italian former head of the Resistance, the other, Don Germanno Savelli, an Italian Catholic monk and academic. Professor Rendina was a strong personality and an important person in the war's resistance movement, and is now a top official in the Associazione Nazionale Partigiana d'Italia (ANPI). Having contributed to Rome's freedom, I accepted his and the mayor's June 2007 invitation to attend the ceremonies and reception in Rome commemorating the 63rd anniversary of its liberation from the Germans. It was the first time that I met Résistants other than the French. Many were forceful and dominant personalities.

Don Germanno was a medium-sized, strongly built man with short steel gray hair and penetrating brown eyes. He was five years younger than I. Although he spoke no English, I sensed and was attracted to his force of character, liking him from the start. Educated at the Abbey of Monte Cassino, he witnessed the four major battles there in late '43 and '44 and the controversial bombing of the abbey. He insists that the Germans did not use it as an artillery observation post, the reason for its destruction by the Allies. The controversy persists to this day.

The Italian curator of the local war museum at Cassino introduced me to Jupp Klein, a visiting former German paratrooper who served with Fallschirmjager-Pioniere der 1. Fschig. Div. I've never felt that comfortable meeting former German adversaries, however reasonable they seemed, because if they, with Hitler's blessings, had won, the result would have been cataclysmic for everyone. For Klein to have survived the battles was a miracle in itself. Having gone over the terrain at the Rapido River and the mountain massif from Cassino to the Mignano Gap, I thought that the Allied generals who planned the succession of attacks, executed in deplorable conditions, needed therapy more than I.

In 1957 in Los Angeles at CBS, I met Sophia Loren, Italy's leading film star. She told me that she had been born and raised in Pozzuoli and remembered our division's arrival and departure in August '44. At the same time, I was the subject of a nationally syndicated article written by newspaper columnist Vernon Scott, UPI's Hollywood correspondent at the time. Its focus was on one particular role I performed on the Ed Murrow show, *Person to Person*, for CBS TV. What follows is an excerpt:

'Ever wonder where the microphones are hidden when Ed Murrow invades a celebrity's home for his cozy 'person to person' interviews? Feminine guests slip the tiny mikes into their brassieres. Male participants tuck the gadget beneath their neckties. Actually Murrow's stars are walking radio stations…The man in charge of wiring Hollywood's guys and gals for the show is Steve Weiss — and he loves his work.'

'I've had to strap the mike and batteries on people like Rhonda Fleming, Dinah Shore, Ginger Rogers, and Julie London.'…Weiss says he concentrates on his work. He doesn't pay much attention to the girls he's working on. 'Not that it matters,' he adds, 'My wife, Rosemary, isn't the least bit jealous.'

Note: during a rehearsal, when Ed Murrow asked Julie London how she and I were getting along, she volunteered, from her bedroom, 'Oh, Steve, can charge my battery any time!'

Bill Colby of OSS and the CIA and I met at the British embassy in Paris in 1984 at a Jedburghs Special Forces ceremony and reception. We talked briefly about the 1945 Norwegian clandestine operation. He died in 1992 in Rockport, MD of a heart attack.

The French have always been generous of heart and dear to me. I was traveling on a Paris bus with my senior French Résistant friend, Bernard Gilles, one summer afternoon in 1993. While we were talking about our different experiences in the Resistance, a young fellow sitting close to us became interested, then involved in our conversation. I was getting off at an earlier stop than Bernard. As I walked to the exit, the bus stopped and opened its doors. At the same time, Bernard shouted to him and the other passengers, 'You see,' pointing his finger at me, 'That American was in the Resistance!' Just as I stepped off the bus, everyone inside applauded.

By 1993, the war had been over for 38 years and I was living in Los Angeles. Within the 36th Texas Infantry Division Association *Newsletter*, in a welcoming announcement under the heading 'New Members,' was a listing of the name and address of Russell Darkes, former executive officer of Charlie Company 143 Infantry. I wrote to Darkes, identifying myself and stating my feelings in the strongest possible terms regarding his failure as an officer and my antipathy towards Simmons. In closing, I said: Much time has passed since we were members of Charlie Company. We're grandfathers now, so let bygones be bygones.

I received a letter from Darkes soon after. He appreciated my comments and feelings, but then went on to say that since so many men passed through the outfit, he couldn't connect me with my name. And that was my whole point, rhetorically speaking; how the hell did both he and Simmons survive 19 months of combat, when hundreds, if not thousands, of men came and went? Rifle companies were known to suffer losses of 120 percent! What follows is an excerpt from a 1991 monograph Darkes wrote that might offer some explanation of leadership as defined by him and Simmons.

Before the battle for San Pietro, Captain Horton, C. Co. commander, in December 1943, called all platoon leaders to assemble at the very crest of the mountain to issue his attack order before darkness approached. It was to be a night attack. Suddenly, there was a sharp crack followed by a light 'thud.' After several seconds trying to determine what happened, Lt. Simmons from Belfast, Maine, and I, noticed that Capt. Horton and the other two lieutenants were lying very still and bleeding profusely from their heads. All three of them were killed instantly by one lone bullet fired by a German sniper from the A. Co. area.

Darkes received a Silver Star for action on the Rapido.

To be fair, instead of demonstrating a reasonable standard of leadership throughout, both Simmons and Darkes, having experienced the trauma on the crest of the mountain, rarely put themselves in harm's way. The Army ought to have reassigned them to less hazardous duties rather than having kept them in combat for such an inordinate amount of time. I wonder if the same sniper who killed Horton on December 9 killed Captain Henry T. Waskow, CO of Baker Company of the 143rd? Waskow died on December 14, 1943 on the slopes of Mt. Sammurcro (Hill 1205). Both Horton and Waskow are buried in the same U.S. Military Cemetery at Anzio, where I held a graveside ceremony for them in 2007.

In his Nov. 28, 1993 letter, Reigle wrote, saying, 'Yes, I remember Lt. Darkes from Lebanon, PA. When I lived about twelve miles from him, I invited him to my house. He only stayed about an hour and all he talked about was how he had 'had it' in the service and what a rough time he had. He was on the ship, when I came home and he did not even speak to me.'

1984 was a pivotal year. The 40th anniversary of the Liberation of France was celebrated throughout the country and, as a veteran and Resistance comrade, I attended most of the ceremonies and meetings, much to my appreciation and satisfaction. I visited Normandy, searching for the military cemeteries at La Cambe and St. Mère Eglise #1 and #2. I had photographed the cemeteries for the *Stars and Stripes in* '46 and failed to find them in '84. I checked my maps for cemetery icons to no avail and felt as if I were going mad, only to discover later that the remains from those cemeteries had been relocated to an all-encompassing military cemetery of 9,000 at St. Laurent. Now called Colleville, it overlooks Omaha Beach. A commemorative plaque marks the earlier cemeteries. La Cambe has been the official German military cemetery for 50-odd years.

During one of the breaks between Liberation anniversary ceremonies and meetings held in Paris, Mlle., Valerie Delescure and I decided to meet for lunch at the Brasserie Lipp, known for its Alsatian cuisine, on the Left Bank. She was a young aristocratic French woman and close friend, whose family were the proprietors of Chateau des Labourons in Fleurie.

Popular with writers and students dating back to Hemingway's day, Lipp was crowded. The maitre d' told Valerie there would be a 45-minute wait. Both of us were famished. I asked her to do something I'd never requested before. 'Would you mind telling him that your guest is an American who served in France during the war and holds the Médaille de la Résistance?' Reluctantly, she did, and returned reporting that we would be seated within 10 minutes. Moments later we were called. Valerie followed the waiter and I trailed behind. When I came abreast of the maitre, whose face and reputation had been well known since the early 30s, I introduced myself and thanked him. He responded with a slight shrug and said, 'That's all right, I know my priorities!' I was deeply impressed with his response.

A few years preceding the 40th anniversary of the Liberation, I wove a fantasy about myself. Fade up: an ambulance is parked at the Place de l'Etoile. Two uniformed paramedics wait by the curb. Framed within the full inner curve of the Arc de Triomphe, a lone figure is seen making his way up the Champs Elysees. It is the figure of an old man trying to look soldierly, dressed in an outdated World War II American Army uniform with a breast full of military decorations. Arriving at the Arc, he pauses to regain his breath, stands at attention, and salutes before the flame of the Unknown Soldier for a few minutes, then collapses. The paramedics rush to his side but they are too late. Death has overtaken him. Fade out. As I've said, it was only a fantasy.

In reality, after a wreath-laying ceremony in the Bois de Boulogne, Colonel Arnauld, then president of our Association de la Médaille de la Résistance Française, suggests I meet him at 2:00 where the rue de Berri joins the Champs Elysees. Arriving at the recommended hour, the colonel insists that I remain by his side amidst an ever-increasing throng, the gathering of a full military band, former combatants carrying flags, and a bevy of motorcycle policemen wearing white gloves and blue kepis. The hum of the crowd is interrupted by the blare of bugles. Colonel Arnauld takes my arm and leads me, surrounded by the band and the veterans forming up in increasing numbers, to the center of the avenue, where he and I stand in the first rank. With the flag snapping in the breeze and the gendarmes keeping the crowd from spilling off the sidewalk, the motorcyclists roam about freely.

It is a picture-postcard afternoon: blue sky, white clouds, and warm breeze. Suddenly the band begins to play and, on cue we begin our march up the hill to the Arc. While we advance, I use the camera hanging from my shoulder to shoot waist-high pictures of the scene unfolding before my eyes. Clear of vision, I disbelieve every step I take. The click of my camera shutter is lost in the sounds of the parade. Closer and closer, up the avenue's slight incline, we march to the blare of the bugles and the beating of the drums; the soles of our shoes bang on the cobbles in 4-4 time. Within the shadow of the Arc, we arrive at the flame burning above the Tomb of the Unknown Soldier and the veterans gather around. The colonel insists that I grasp the long metal rod he already holds, so that together we shall extinguish the flame. I feel the weight of the moment. With one concerted twist, the flame is momentarily extinguished. Turning the rod the other way, we quickly ignite the flame to the shouting of commands, the flash of cameras, the sound of martial music, and the crowd's applause.

Moments later, in the pleasant post-ceremonial atmosphere, I pinch myself, mindful of the fantasy, finally understanding that the journey was always a matter of life and death.

The whole experience that began with the night attack on one side of the Rhône is like a well to which I have returned at various times in my life for further understanding and interpretation of my relationships with myself, family, and friends. The outcome? Nothing much, except a small improvement in living with others and myself. Add a soupcon of compassion, forgiveness, and possibly wisdom thrown in.

2007 was another eventful year. Although an American citizen, I sought French citizenship and succeeded. When asked by the French Consul-General in London why I wanted to become a French citizen, I replied, 'For a number of reasons: my war experiences, an affinity to the French way of life, and its concern for the individual citizen, as explained in 'The Rights of Man.' Having said that, I realize France has as many economic and political problems as any other modern state. I find liberty appealing.'

Earlier in the year, I was elevated to the rank of *Officier* of the French Legion of Honor at a ceremony at the Invalides and a reception and luncheon that followed at the Cercle de l'Union Interaliee, a 17th-century former Rothschild mansion and 20th-century officers' club. Separate from this kind of accreditation, I receive a small yearly pension from the French government for my participation in its Liberation. When I think of being a French citizen, a light shines within and a smile crosses my face.

The honors and awards bestowed upon me by various French communities in recognition of my contribution to their liberation have been accepted on behalf of myself and others, never on me as the sole recipient. In combat, I was always part of a team, whether it was with my rifle squad, a member of the Resistance, or Rick's Operational Group. What we accomplished together could not have been accomplished alone. What I experienced and learned, having had three careers, I have attempted to give back to a society which made it all possible.

The Rhône is like life: dynamic, constant, and forever changing. When I die and am cremated, Andrew, my son, is to spread my ashes over the river at Valence. 'Toss them with the wind at your back,' I suggest. 'Otherwise, you'll get a face full of ash.' At my invitation, I've invited my family and friends to a celebration dinner at the three-star Restaurant Pic. Anne-Sophie Pic. The female owner-chef, is a direct descendant of Madame Serre. Chateauneuf du Pape and champagne will be served. But I have regrets, knowing it will be impossible to join in the proceedings because my ashes will be floating down river by the time they start their first course.

When I was First Scout in an infantry rifle squad 67 years ago, I sometimes thought that with every advancing step, I converted that bit of earth underfoot from German occupation to Allied liberation — a freedom movement on the march. Eleven men trailed behind. My movement toward an unseen enemy was fraught with danger. Hyper-vigilant, with adrenalin rushing through me, I would hear an inner voice shout, 'Achtung, minen; you are entering enemy territory.' Regardless of the terrain over which I fought, an intrusive and enervating level of uncertainty went with the territory. Out of all proportion and expectation I, like the others, was ordered to defend the realm, an extraordinary and expensive burden, supported by cooks and bakers, rear echelon service and supply soldiers, who rarely heard a shot fired in anger and slept warm in their beds. The apportionment of responsibility and the difference in expectations by those in charge haunts me to this day. I have no patience with those former rear echelon soldiers who talk of a 'good war.'

There were other demands placed upon us from that summer of 1944 until the end of the war almost a year later, and what is listed above was only one aspect of close armed conflict. Fire and maneuver were other key elements. Our apprenticeship began with a short three-month infantry course in the States, followed by overseas 'on-the-job' combat. We were lucky to last six weeks.

We defeated the Germans by overwhelming them with our ability to replenish combat losses quicker than they, in men, equipment, and supplies. According to General George Marshall, the U.S. Army Chief of Staff, American industrial output and the nation's skilled work force were the 'true organizers of victory.' Unfortunately, the two systems of training and production were based on quantity, not quality, and the results were dire. Infantry recruits lacked mental and physical hardness and professionalism, and our basic weapons were no match against comparable German ones. Losses mounted, battles lingered. The last days of the Bulge are a good example. Our basic machine gun dated from the First World War, and the best and the brightest had been hived off to the Army Air Corps.

For those of us on the ground and in 'harm's way,' we were anxious and depressed, our behavior erratic more times than not. Leadership and ingenuity suffered. Trying to stay sane in an insane world, we mounted unconscious psychic defenses and survival was the name of the game, instinctually.

An olive drab shirt offered scant protection to a human torso that hadn't changed in 50,000 years. By contrast, modern technology, machine guns, heavy-caliber cannon, and four-engine bombers killed and maimed at unimaginable levels. Combat soldiers were impaled on the horns of a psychic/cognitive dilemma: we were required, if necessary, to die without comment for our country, even though as youngsters we had everything to live for. Youth demands its time of fulfillment. But the venerable leader, a father figure, said, 'Don't you know there's a war on?'

If men are competitive and seek dominance, they are also logical. Therefore, doesn't it follow that when confronted with their own vulnerability and possible annihilation, under circumstances rarely experienced in civilian life, they might want to rewrite the script? 'Living is the best revenge,' Pascal trumpeted in the 17th century. Life couldn't have cared less if I lived or died. It demands payment for its disbursement of 'luck' in exchange for my survival. Gone forever were my relatively carefree days of pre-war adolescence or the traditional and peaceful 'rite of passage,' instead replaced by an unpredictable post-war flare-up of neurotic symptoms and frightening thoughts, insisting on treatment or early death. Being hobbled was normal functioning. Today, medical clinicians call it 'post-traumatic stress.' Labeling has little to do with 'shelf-life!'

Tony Bennett, the pop singer and a former combat infantryman who fought in Europe, said, 'Anyone who thinks war is romantic has never been in one.' Tramping into battle, the mid-20th century recruit, with tunes of glory ringing in his ears, discovered a world the French soldier of the 1914–1918 War already knew, exemplified by Verdun. He called it 'The Inferno.' The music fades, replaced by inrushing sounds of another tune and another war, that of 1939–1945. Rising to the war's demands and prevailing, honored us. Our fathers' generation had done the same. It too, was 'The greatest generation,' if one demands a soubriquet.

If Ernie Pyle, the American war reporter, writing on many fronts, from North Africa to Iwo Jima, was correct in stating 'that the American infantry were the underdogs, the mud-rain-frost and wind boys who had no comforts and learned to live without necessities — and in the end were the guys that wars can't be won without,' how as an underclass, in some ways a 'forgotten army,' were we expected to fight and win? Combat is a young man's game, one in which few survived? Longevity was measured in weeks. A sense of betrayal lingers!

And yet the men who fought with the 36th, allegedly considered a 'hard-luck' division, acquitted themselves with honor. After five years of Federal military service, two D-Day assault landings, seven campaigns — Naples-Foggia, Anzio, Rome-Arno, Southern France, Rhineland, Ardennes-Alsace, and Central Europe — 400 days in combat, 27,000 casualties, and 176,000 enemy soldiers captured, they had won 14 Medals of Honor, 80 Distinguished Services Crosses, 2 Distinguished Service Medals, 10 Presidential Unit Citations, 2,354 Silver Stars, 49 Legion of Merits, 77 Soldiers Medals, 5,407 Bronze Star Medals, and 88 Air Medals. They stood up to a storm of steel and were counted. The modern Army record for consecutive days of combat, which it set at 132 in France, still stands. The 143rd Infantry alone suffered 9,000 casualties of the divisional total and won 5 of the 14 Medals of Honor. Five Presidential Unit Citations were awarded to units of the Regiment.

Commanding General of the 36th John Dahlquist and 143rd regimental colonel Paul Adams, combat commanders during the period 1944–1945, achieved four-star general rank. Wartime regimental colonels George Lynch, John Harmony, and Charles Denholm reached two-star general rank, post-war. Two illustrious and infamous enemy officers were captured in Austria by the division during the closing hours of the war. They were Field Marshals Gerd von Rundstedt, German Commander on the Western Front and the Nazi Reichsmarschall Hermann Goering, designated by Hitler to be his successor.

Reality, sought after and ultimately revealed, is stronger than myth, and I have attempted to portray the former. In so doing, I have paid homage to the men of the combat arms, who, for the most part, didn't record their wartime experiences. Prior studies have merged them with the rest of the Army, but I have tried to give them the 'stand-alone' identity they deserve. They fought in olive drab, those in support wore khaki. I hope that my narrative will offer a clear reflection of their accomplishments through my own experiences, against all odds. Perhaps the hope for my redemption that Lt. Col. Stephen J. Brady, the Army Judge Advocate, expressed in 1944 has been fulfilled.

The sun streamed through the windows of the chancellery. De Gaulle's portraits stood in bold relief, the room stirred. The medal of the Legion d'Honneur was pinned to my left jacket pocket and General Simon kissed me on both cheeks. Jean-Jacques de Bresson, President of the Médaille de la Résistance Association, and American naval attaché, Captain Brian Fennessey, representing the United States and the American Embassy in Paris, hovered close by, waiting to express their congratulations. I was embraced by friends and relatives. Vice President Bernard Gilles read aloud a letter of felicitations from Monsieur Jacques Chirac, President de la République. I accepted the honor on behalf of my comrades in arms, both French and American, and myself. Photos were taken, wine served, toasts proclaimed. A luncheon I hosted followed at the Club Francais Libre, founded by General De Gaulle. Claudia, my eldest daughter, 39, married and mother of three, said, 'Unless my daughter wins an Oscar, none of us are going to top this.'

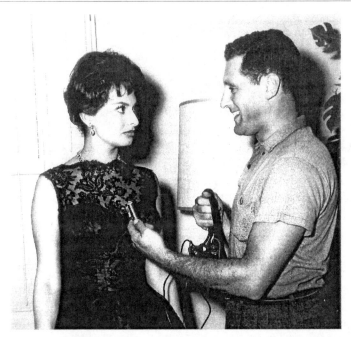

Sophia Loren and the author in Hollywood during a network televsion rehearsal, Summer 1957

The stairway leading to the hayloft on the Reynaud farm. From the left: farmhand Rene Crespy, the author, policeman Marcel Volle, Gaston Reynaud in the early 1970s

RÉPUBLIQUE FRANÇAISE

Guerre   1939 - 1945

CITATION

EXTRAIT DE LA DECISION N° 260

Le Ministre des Armées Edmond MICHELET

CITE A L'ORDRE DE LA DIVISION

S T E P H E N   J.   WEISS - *Soldat de l'Armée Américaine -*

« Pour services exceptionnels de guerre rendus au cours de la Libération de la France »

Ces citations comportent l'attribution de la Croix de Guerre 1939-1945 avec étoile d'argent

A Paris, le 05 juillet 1946
Signé : MICHELET

- *EXTRAIT CERTIFIE CONFORME*
A Pau, le 20 janvier 2003
Le lieutenant-colonel Ch. BRU
directeur du bureau central
d'archives administratives militaires

Croix de Guerre Citation 260, Paris, July 1946

D É C R E T

portant attribution de la

MÉDAILLE DE LA RÉSISTANCE FRANÇAISE

●

LE GOUVERNEMENT PROVISOIRE
DE LA RÉPUBLIQUE FRANÇAISE

Sur la proposition du MINISTRE DES ARMEES

Vu l'Ordonnance N° 42 du 9 Février 1943, instituant une Médaille de la Résistance Française ;
Vu l'Ordonnance du 7 Janvier 1944, relative à l'attribution de la Médaille de la Résistance Française ;
Vu l'avis de la Commission Nationale de la Médaille de la Résistance Française,

D É C R È T E :

Article 35 :

LA MÉDAILLE DE LA RÉSISTANCE FRANÇAISE
est décernée à

M   Stéphen J. WEISS

Article 115 :

Le MINISTRE DES ARMEES
est chargé de l'exécution du présent décret qui sera publié au Journal Officiel de la République Française.du 13 Octobre 1946.

Fait à PARIS, le 3 Août 1946

Par le Gouvernement Provisoire
de la République Française : G. BIDAULT

Le Ministre des Armées
E. MICHELET

— *POUR AMPLIATION* —

PARIS, le 27 Février 2001.

Le Général d'Armée Jean SIMON
Chancelier de l'Ordre de la Libération.

Médaille de la Résistance Citation, Paris, August 1946

ORGANISATION DU TRAITE DE L'ATLANTIQUE NORD
NORTH ATLANTIC TREATY ORGANIZATION

This is to Certify that
Le présent document atteste que

Steve J. Weiss
United States Army Europe
National Support Element

Has been awarded the NATO Medal
for Service with NATO on Operations
in Relation to the Former Yugoslavia
During the Period

A reçu la médaille de l'OTAN
en récompense des services rendus à l'OTAN
dans des opérations ayant trait à
l'ex-Yougoslavie
au cours de la période

01 January 1998 to 20 July 1998

The Secretary General
Le Secrétaire Général

United Nations citation for services to Former Yugoslavia in 1998

Citations, Decorations, Awards, and Diplomas

Officier de la Légion d'Honneur Française

Chevalier de la Légion d'Honneur Française

Croix de Guerre, two citations à l'Ordre de la Division

Médaille de la Résistance Française

Médaille Com. Française de la Guerre 1939/1945

American Bronze Star Medal

Combat Infantry Badge

OSS Plaque for missions accomplished in the Ardèche, September 1944

European and Mediterranean Campaign Medal

Three battle stars, one Indian arrowhead for Operation Anvil-Dragoon D-Day Landing, August 15, 1944

World War Two Victory Medal

Good Conduct Medal

Carte du Combattant

Le Titre de Reconnaissance de la Nation

Naturalized French citizen, October 2007

NATO Medal for service related to operations in Former Yugoslavia in 1998

Citoyen d'Honneur Tendon d'Ancy sur Moselle, Charmes sur Rhône, Digne, Grenoble, Nice, St. Péray, St. Raphaël, and Valence (8 municipal ceremonies and official medallions) Diplôme le Citoyen d'Utah Beach & Ste-Marie-du-Mont

Diplôme de Membre d'Honneur des Vosges et de France

Diplôme d'honneur de Cavalaire-Sur-Mer

Diplôme d'honneur engage dans les combats du débarquement en Provence et la Libération 1944–1945

Diploma — Honorary Citizen of the State of Texas, awarded by the governor

Honored guest of the Mayor of Rome and Chief of the Italian Resistance on the 63rd anniversary of the Liberation of Rome, June 3, 2007

Clubs and Associations — for the most part related to the war — of which I'm a member: In Britain — Special Forces Club, Victory Services Club, Army/Navy Club, King's College Alumni Association. The Confrérie des Chevaliers du Tastevin, the Association de la Médaille de la Résistance Française, and the Mémoire de la Bataille de Montélimar Association are located in France. The American Society of the French Legion of Honor, the 36th Division Association, and The OSS Society are found in the U.S.

Bibliography

Addison P. & Calder, A. (eds.), *Time to Kill, 1939-1945, The Soldier's Experience of War in the West 1939–1945*, (London, 1997)

Adelman, R. H. & Walton, G., *The Champagne Campaign*, (Boston, 1969)

Ambrose, S. E., *D-Day June 6, 1944*, (New York, 1994)

Beevor, A., & Cooper, A., *Paris After The Liberation: 1944–1949*, (London, 1994)

Bond, H. L., *Return to Cassino*, (London, 1964)

Bonn, K. E., *When the Odds Were Even, The Vosges Campaign*, (Novato, 1994)

Bowlby, A., *The Recollections of Rifleman Bowlby*, (London, 1989)

Brokaw, T., *The Greatest Generation*, (New York, 1998)

Clarke, J. J., & Smith, R. R., *From the Riviera to the Rhine*, (Washington, 1993)

Childers, T., *Soldier from the War Returning*, (New York, 2009)

Cowdrey, A., E., *Fighting for Life*, (New York, 1994)

Cox, A. T., *O. S.S. Secret Operational Report Company B 2671Special Recon Btln.*, (Grenoble, 1944)

Cray, E., *General of the Army*, George C. Marshall, (New York, 1990)

D'Este, C., *Patton, A Genius for War*, (New York, 1995)

Ducros, L-F., *Montagnes Ardechoises Dans La Guerre III*, (Valence, 1981)

Ellis, John, *The Sharp End, The Fighting Man in World War II*, (New York, 1980)

Esvelin, P., *Forgotten Wings, Planeurs en Normandie et dans le Sud de la France*, (Bayeux, 2006)

Fourcade, M-M, *Noah's Ark*, (London, 1973)

Freud, S., *On Murder, Mourning, and Melancholia*, (London, 2005)

Funk, A., *Hidden Ally*, (New York, 1992)

Gabriel, R. *No More Heroes*, (New York, 1987) *The Painful Field*, (New

York, 1988)

Gaujac, P., *August 15, 1944, Dragoon, The Other Invasion of France*, (Paris, 2004)

Glass, Charles, *Americans in Paris, Life and Death under Nazi Occupation 1940–44*, (London, 2009)

Gray, J. G., *Reflections on Men in Battle*, (New York, 1970)

Hue, A., *The Next Moon, A British Agent in Wartime France*, (London, 2004)

Huie, W. B., *The Execution of Private Slovik*, (New York, 1954)

Lockhart, V. M., *T-Patch to Victory*, (Canyon1981)

Maslowski, P., *Armed with Cameras*, (New York, 1993)

Masson, M., *Christine*, (London, 1975)

Moats, A.-L, *No Passport for Paris*, (New York, 1945)

Morehouse, M. M. *Fighting in the Jim Crow Army*, (London, 2000)

Overy, R., *Why the Allies Won*, (London, 1995)

Pyle, E., *Brave Men*, (New York, 1944)

Robichon, J., *The Second D-Day*, (New York, 1969)

Rush, R. S., *The US Infantryman in World War II*, (Oxford, 2003)

Sainclivier, J. & Bougeard, C., *La Resistance et Les Français*, (Rennes, 1995)

Shephard, B., *A War of Nerves*, (London, 2000)

Slawenski, K., *J. D. Salinger, A Life*, (New York, 2011)

Smith, B., *The Shadow Warriors, O.S.S. and the Origins of the C.I.A.*, (New York, 1983)

Speller, I., & Tuck, C., *Amphibious Warfare*, (Staplehurst, 2001)

Spilmont, J-P., *Pour l'amour de la France, Drome-Vercors 1940–44* (Valence, 1989)

Steidl, F., *Lost Battalions, Going for Broke in the Vosges, Autumn, 1944*, (Novato, 1997)

Sussna, S., *Defeat & Triumph*, (Indiana, 2008)

Wagner, R. I., *The Texas Army*, (Austin, 1991)

Walker, F. L., Major-General, *From Texas to Rome*, (Dallas, 1969)

Weiss, S., *Allies in Conflict*, (London, 1996)

Whiting, C., *Death on a Distant Frontier, A Lost Victory*, (London, 1996)

Wilt, A. F., *The French Riviera Campaign of August 1944*, (Carbondale, 1981)

Yeide, H., & Stout, M., *First to the Rhine, The 6ᵀʰ Army in World War II*, (St. Paul, 2007)

Glossary

Anvil	Code name for Southern France Landings of August 1944; later changed to Dragoon
Army Group	A military organization consisting of several field armies, self-sufficient for indefinite periods, i.e., U.S. 6th Army Group
B-17 Flying Fortress	U.S. heavy bomber used in supply drops to the Resistance
B-24 Liberator	U.S. heavy bomber used in supply drops to the Resistance and in support of clandestine operations
BAR	Browning .30 caliber Automatic Rifle
Battalion	A unit made up of three rifle companies, a weapons and headquarters company
Bazooka	WWII nickname for the 2.36-inch recoilless rocket launcher
C-47	American transport plane, also known by the British as a Dakota
Charcoal driven	Autos converting charcoal to gas as a substitute for scarce gasoline
Citroen Traction Avant	French automobile used both by the Gestapo and the Resistance
Combat Stress Reaction (CSR)	Known as 'shell shock' or 'combat fatigue' due to stress in battle
Comet Line	Best known escape line of the war. 100 line helpers perished
Commando Order	Order issued by Hitler in 1942 that stated all Allied commandos encountered by German forces in Europe and Africa should be killed immediately, even in uniform or trying to surrender
Company	A unit of three rifle platoons of 200 men led by a captain
CP	Command post, the headquarters of a unit
Déjà vu	Subjective falsification of experience, one hav-

	ing already occurred
Diadem	The Allied operation in Italy of May 1944
Division	Formation of three regiments of 3,000 men each, led by a Major-General — additional units can be attached
Dragoon	See Anvil
DZ	Drop Zone, a chosen landing site for men and materiel
DUKW	A half-ton amphibious wheeled vehicle
'88'	German high-velocity dual-purpose antiaircraft, anti-tank weapon
ETO	European Theater of Operations
40 & 8 Great War French term:	A box car capable of carrying 40 men or 8 horses
442nd Regimental Combat Team	Japanese-American unit accreted to the 36th, used primarily in the rescue of the 1st Battalion, 141 RCT, 'The Lost Battalion'
First Special Service Force	Well trained U.S.-Canadian Commando/Ranger unit
Foxhole	A protective hole in the earth, usually for one or two men
Free French	French men and women who followed de Gaulle and fought against the Germans
French Forces of the Interior	Resistance forces combined as of February 1944
Gestapo	German abbreviation for *Geheime Staatspolizei* (Nazi Secret Police)
Halftrack	A combined wheeled and tracked armored personnel carrier
Halifax	British heavy bomber assigned to cover clandestine operations
Jedburghs	An Allied three-man team dropped behind enemy lines to disrupt and harass German forces in France
L-2	Army designation for the Taylor Cub light aircraft used for Allied artillery spotting and observation

LCA	Landing Craft Assault, maximum load is an infantry platoon — to land infantry in a beach assault
LCI	Landing Craft Infantry, sea-going assault ship for carrying up to 200 men in amphibious combat operations
LCT	Landing Craft Tank, a craft capable of taking nine Sherman tanks and landing them over a bow ramp onto shallow beaches
Lee Enfield 4 MK 1	.303 caliber British standard rifle
Lost Battalion	Identified as a unit of the 36th Inf. Div. surrounded in late October 1944; rescued by the 442nd RCT, the most decorated unit in the U.S. Army; the unit was composed of Japanese-Americans
'Louise'	Name of OSS para unit operation in Southern France; the object was to strengthen resistance of Maquis and harass the Germans
LST	Landing Ship Tank, the most important ship in the Allied War effort, as used in amphibious landings
LZ	Landing Zone, chosen for glider landings
Jeep	The quarter-ton, four-wheel drive truck
Luftwaffe	The German Air Force
M-1 Garand	American semiautomatic .30 caliber rifle
M-4 Sherman	American medium 30-ton battle tank
Mark IV	German medium tank; it weighed 25 tons, had a 5-man crew
Maquis	Originally, thick underbrush; thus, where Résistants could hide — defines the fighters themselves, those defying German obligations
Messages Personnels	Codes messages transmitted by BBC Radio to agents in France
MTO	Mediterranean Theater of Operations
Mine	An explosive device triggered by pressure or trip wire

OG	Operational Group (OSS paratroopers, normally consisting of 28 men and 2 officers)
OSS	Office of Strategic Services, American intelligence gathering and secret operations department modeled after British Special Operations Executive (SOE)
Overlord	The Allied Normandy invasion of France, June 6, 1944
OWI	U.S. Government Office of War Information: censorship and propaganda
Panzer	A German armored vehicle or armored formation
P-47 Thunderbolt	Single-engine, single-seat U.S. fighter and fighter-bomber
P-51 Mustang	Single-engine, single-seat U.S. long-range escort fighter aircraft
Platoon	Unit of about 40 men commanded by a second lieutenant
RCT	Regimental Combat Team, consisting of infantry, tanks, and cannons
Resistance	A term referring to organizations and individuals who opposed and fought against the German and Italian occupation of France
Résistant	An individual fighting in secret against the Occupation
Route Napoleon	The route (N-85) from Cannes to Grenoble used by Napoleon after his escape from Elba and later by the 36th Texas Division in 1944
Secret Army	Gaullist military forces, Armée Secrete or AS
Schuh Mine	German anti-personnel mine, the explosive charge in a wooden box
Service Du Travail Obligatoire	All Frenchmen of a certain age could be inducted to work in Germany or German factories in France (STO)
Shingle	Code name for the January 1944 Allied landing at Anzio south of Rome

SOE	British independent secret service formed to conduct subversive warfare in Axis Occupied Europe
SOP	Standard Operating Procedure
SS	*Schutzstaffel*, the most dedicated Nazi soldiers
Sten Gun	British 9 mm submachine gun
TD	Tank Destroyer, similar to Sherman tank, but with open turret
Teller Mine	German anti-tank mine with 10 pounds of high explosive
Texas Division	The 36th Division, formerly a Texas National Guard division
Thousand Yard Stare	Coined to describe the glazed, vacant look of a stressed, combat- exhausted soldier
T-Patch	Sleeve insignia, a gray 'T' on an blue Indian arrowhead background
Tommy Gun	.45 caliber Thompson submachine gun
Tree burst	Explosion of shells against trees, designed to destroy troops below
ULTRA	Code name for German messages deciphered by the British
Walkie-talkie	Hand-held radio, also known as the SCR-536
60 mm Mortar	Close support infantry mortar firing a three-pound shell one mile

Index

AWOL. *See* desertion

B

Bad Homburg, Germany, 223

Baker, Josephine, 246–247

Band of Brothers, 356

Banziger, Hugo, 358

barber's itch. *See* impetigo

Barbie, Klaus, 126

Bastogne, Belgium, 357

Battle of Normandy, 167

Battle of the Bulge, 171, 177, 216–217, 225, 245, 353, 358, 365

Bay of Salerno. *See* Salerno: Bay of

Beaumont-Valence, 80

Bennett, Tony, 366

Bergen-Belsen concentration camp, 321

Beverly Hills, 331

Bevin, Ernest, Right Honorable (Foreign Secretary of Gr. Britain), 260–261

Bidault, George (Resistance and Foreign Minister of France), 261

Big Four International diplomatic conference, 258–261

Biledeau, Adrian, Sergeant, 111

Binoche, François, General, 92, 94, 96–97, 99–100, 109, 119, 162, 205–206, 214, 317, 335, 345–346

black market, 183–188, 245

black soldiers, 30–31, 54, 243–245, 247, 256

as prisoners, 175–176

Blucher (cruiser), 286

Bocarsky, Staff Sergeant, 27, 349–350

Bogart, Humphrey, 332

Boudreau, Paul, Lieutenant, 117–118

Brady, Stephen J., Lieutenant Colonel, 353–354, 367

Brechitosse, 144

Bremen, Germany, 284–285, 317, 319–321, 325

Bremerhaven, Germany, 321, 325

bridges

at Drôme and Rhône Rivers, 248

over Rhône River, 94, 111

Brigade, Polish Armored, 2nd, 295

British Battle Drill training, 54

Brooklyn, 15–16, 23

friends from, 199–200

home from war, 329–330

Brooks, Mel, 332

Brussels photography trip, 245, 247, 307–308

Bruyeres, France, 350, 355

Byrnes, James (Secretary of State), 261

C

Cabeuil-Valence D-68, 80

Caesar, Emile T., 79, 130, 340

Caffrey, Jefferson (American Ambassador to France), 259

Calabria, Italy (Suzanne's father), 268

Camel Force, 62

About the Author

Dr. Stephen J. Weiss holds two MA degrees, the first in Clinical Psychology from Goddard College, Vermont, the second in War Studies from Kings College London. He was awarded his Ph.D. in War Studies from Kings in 1995.

Dr. Weiss served as a first scout in an American infantry rifle squad in Italy, France, and Germany. He landed on D-Day in Southern France. Listed as 'Missing in Action' in France, he served with the French Resistance and an OSS Operational Group behind enemy lines. For these exploits, he was awarded the French Resistance Medal, the Croix de Guerre (2 citations), and the American Bronze Star. President Jacques Chirac bestowed upon him Chevalier of the Legion d' Honneur in 1999. On 22nd June 2007, in Paris, he was elevated in rank to Officier de la Leigon d' Honneur.

Dr. Weiss also worked as a licensed California clinical psychotherapist in Los Angeles. As a former photographer and music editor, he spent many years in American network broadcast television. In his lectures at Kings and elsewhere, he brings his war experiences directly into the classroom.

Dr. Weiss is conducting research on and assessment of Post-Traumatic Stress Disorder (PTSD) in a select group of World War Two Veterans. The Canadian landings in Normandy on D-Day is another project under investigation.

He lives in London.

CPSIA information can be obtained at www.ICGtesting.com
Printed in the USA
LVOW07s1733200813

348821LV00005B/210/P

9 781780 392325